What people ar

The Devil's Pupil is a dark and unthinkable story leading to the remarkable transformation of Cody Bates. After reading his book, I put it down and remained speechless. Crime and cocaine were no match for the cross of Jesus Christ... you owe it to yourself to read this book!

—Robert Melnichuk
Director, Western Canada YES TV

Cody Bates's powerful testimony of how he was pulled from the deepest, darkest pit into the transforming love of Christ will reveal something about Jesus's relentless love to every reader. Cody's story will draw you closer to Jesus.

—Martie Van Niekerk
President of Crossroads Prison Ministries of Canada

THE
DEVIL'S
PUPIL

Convicted Killer,

Notorious Gangster,

Diagnosed Sociopath,

Drug Addict

— Prodigal Son

CODY BATES

Printed in Canada

ISBN: 978-1-4866-1811-8

Word Alive Press
119 De Baets Street, Winnipeg, MB R2J 3R9
www.wordalivepress.ca

Cataloguing in Publication may be obtained through Library and Archives Canada

To my Father in heaven, whose gracious glory set me free,
to my dad, who never gave up on me,
and in loving memory of Avery Neufeld and Devon Newson.

CONTENTS

PART III

PART VI

A SPECIAL THANKS

To Stephanie Erdt
Your passion and flame for the lost is beyond any inferno capable of being set by man, and your encouragement has been a true blessing. God has given you some very special assignments. I can't wait to see where your ministry takes you.

To Jeff Smith
It's been an honour and a privilege to serve with you, my friend. Thank you for believing in me.

FOREWORD

The Devil's Pupil is unique in many ways, just like its author, Cody Bates. Just when you think his story can't get any worse, it can and does.

When Cody came to the Adult & Teen Challenge Okanagan Men's Centre in early 2018, he spoke in chapel and immediately won over the hearts of all the staff and students. What Cody didn't know, but which God had already ordained, was that while Cody was feeling the call to evangelism, we were praying as a leadership team for an evangelist to bring on staff.

That day, when Adult & Teen Challenge and Cody Bates came together, arrived after a season of praying for Cody. We hadn't even known it was him we were praying for.

When the regional director called me and told me about Cody, I couldn't help but be intrigued. I looked him up on social media and saw a picture of Cody, tattooed from his neck down, wearing earrings, and his hair had frosted tips. I soon found out that he was also a highly motivated man, with an infectious personality, who loved Jesus more than anything.

There isn't any particular mould or type of person you have to be to be used by God, since all He needs is a willing heart. Cody certainly fit into the willingness category. He was asking to be a part of Adult & Teen Challenge, and he wanted to start an evangelism ministry. We were, as Cody described it, "drinking in Jesus through a fire hose" and he wanted to be under our covering.

Cody came on as an intern at first. He wanted to immerse himself totally into the Adult & Teen Challenge culture and get a real sense of its DNA. He lived as a student for a month, then moved into a staff role.

We know that God has big things for Cody Bates to accomplish and we are honoured and privileged that God has asked us to go on this ride with him.

Since starting at Adult & Teen Challenge, Cody has taken on students from the Okanagan Men's Centre and groups of volunteers who just want to be a part of what God is doing. Together, they minister to people in downtown Kelowna who are affected by homelessness and drug use. They hand out snacks, pray with people, and distribute Bibles.

While obeying the Great Commission, Cody is always the first to encourage new believers to be baptized in the name of the Father, Son, and Holy Spirit. I have personally seen him get into zero-degree lake waters to baptize a fellow brother.

When I began reading Cody's book, *The Devil's Pupil*, I was captured by this story of a man who seemed to be at the end of his rope. Then, in a moment of clarity, he was completely and forever changed!

How does that happen? In the middle of hell on earth, can someone hear the voice of God so clearly? It's unmistakable.

Cody is able to write in such a way that he takes you on this journey with him. He has a way of making you feel like you are in every chapter, walking alongside him through every valley and over every mountaintop. You will feel the utter devastation of what it's like to live a life separated from one's Maker. You will also feel the over-the-top joy of being snatched from the pit of hell in a split second.

Cody has had a miraculous transformation, to say the least. Our very real and present enemy, the devil, would have liked nothing more than to carry Cody off to hell at any one of the points when he stood at death's door. But Cody often describes those brushes with death as failures, because death wouldn't take him. He knew without a doubt that there was a reason.

God is using Cody Bates, through his life and this book, to showcase how much power He has. The reason Cody lives, breathes, and writes is to lift Jesus high, and it's all for the glory of God.

—Janalyn Martin
Provincial Director
Adult & Teen Challenge Society of BC

INTRODUCTION

January 4, 2017

As I sit bleeding from the wrist on my grungy bedroom floor, I'm perplexed by a question: how does a man come to the point in his young life where he's ready to die? I watch, intrigued by my bright red blood as it washes away the ash that covers my hand. The ash represents the junkie I have become and the blood represents the end of my pain.

It's taking too long. My heart is crushing itself inside my chest and my eyes are blurry with tears. The cut wasn't deep enough; the next one will be better. The next one will find the vein that releases me from this unbearable anguish.

I take a second to gather my thoughts so I may bundle all my hurt feelings and visions and deliver one last fatal blow to my left wrist. In my right hand I hold the bloody instrument of my destruction—a large butcher knife. I put my head back against the wall and close my eyes.

How did it come to this?

I open my eyes and look back on the grisly scene. My feet rest atop the box spring mattress I sleep on and my butt is on the floor, my back against the wall. The bedroom window is right above my head, early morning sunshine engulfing my room. It's extremely bright. My TV plays the music from my Xbox 360 console; it's too jovial for my current situation, but it's quiet enough that it doesn't distract from the task at hand.

I need to kill myself.

My whole body is marked with battle scars: ash, blood, and tattoos from years in the Calgary underworld. My tattoos mostly have no meaning to me. They are all products of circumstance from my time in a maximum security penitentiary. I was in jail for six years for orchestrating a turf war homicide. Just as I had on the street, I made money in jail by capitalizing on addicts. I viewed them as hopeless and futile. I also made a profitable living as a bookie, running an opportunistic gambling line.

I lived as well as anyone could while subjected to a twenty-three-hour lockdown for six straight years. Looking at it now, the experience was comparable to gerbils fighting over the only wheel in a tiny cage. But I held my own. There was nothing but hustling and murder plots all day in the Max. Only the worst of the worst went there.

I, for one, was lucky, because I was a member of a notorious gang. As the front-runners in a vicious gang war, my crew was responsible for painting the streets of Calgary red with blood. The war claimed too many lives, including the lives of innocent people caught in the crossfire. For twenty months, I called the shots for all my gang's members in prison—while in solitary confinement. During that time, we went to war with the largest Native prison gang in Alberta.

As I ponder gang life and my time in the Max, my vision snaps into focus. I stare at my filthy carpet, marred with cigarette burns and ash stains, and want to puke. I come to the realization that I have never seen a room so disgusting, so junkie-ravaged. All I can see are crack pipes cut in half, empty bottles of alcohol, crumpled beer cans, empty cocaine bags, scales, bits of tinfoil, knives, spoons, empty lighters, and baking soda.

This would send anyone's nasal passages into complete revolt, but not mine. After all, I have a $1,500 per day cocaine habit; simple math says that I'd spent in the range of a million dollars in two years. The habit had long robbed me of my sense of smell. You could have literally crapped in my hand and I wouldn't have been able to smell it.

By the front door is a poster I really hate—the picture of a woman sitting on the ground, in trippy purples and pinks, her long legs showing and a joint in her mouth. This poster is a 24/7 reminder of my despair and hopelessness. When I moved into this house three months ago, I unrolled that poster after a box had been sitting right on top of it, so parts of it are still flattened and protruding from the wall. I hung it with a single tack, letting it hang crooked. I'm always so fixated on my next hit, so consumed with pain and disconnected from reality, that the poster has remained crooked all these months. I can't even spare a minute to fix it, because I have to take a hit instead, to make me forget all the torment of the world.

My attention returns to my slashed wrists.

Why is killing myself so hard? I feel like a coward that I haven't done it yet. Why is it that I can plan a homicide so easily, but suicide is so evasive? I've wanted to die for so long, have tried countless methods of suicide only to fall short. It's becoming another bad habit.

Know that I've never been a fan of hurting other people—or myself. Naturally, I'm a really nice guy. Very loyal, genuine, and kind.

However, I'm also a diagnosed sociopath.

I started earning a psychology degree in the Max because I wanted to learn more about my diagnosis. I always thought that if I could put a label to what was wrong with me, I would be able to either change it or embrace it.

So I'm a diagnosed sociopath, but belittling others and getting enjoyment from their torment doesn't tickle my pleasure centres. Mass manipulation and charismatic administration? That's my forte.

In my first year out of the Max, I got a job as a car salesman. That year, I sold thirty-nine cars in a single month. All the salesmen were seeing the same number of customers and the average sales were between three and ten cars per month. I consistently sold twenty. I knew nothing about cars and yet sold two hundred forty my first year. In fact, I was honoured by the City of Calgary at a banquet for being one of the top salesmen in the city.

The only explanation I could draw was that it was because of my sociopathy. A man with a normal brain would have been psychologically stunted after being locked up so long in a six-by-nine room. Yet for some reason I prospered.

During my reign at the top of the struggling car industry, I succeeded most when I gave thanks to the God of my own understanding. I was three years clean and sober and living in His love. It was a fantastic feeling. I began every single day with prayers and worship in the form of reading, singing, and fist pumping the Big Guy. This was followed by daily Alcoholics Anonymous meetings, volunteering at treatment centres, and sharing my experience, strength, and hope with others. I had the world in my calm, collected hands.

I also met a woman the likes of which I have yet to encounter since. Anna was gorgeous, genuine, loving, kind, and compassionate—the girl of my dreams, with a French accent to boot. She and I had built a life together and I'd dreamed of being with her forever.

After almost four years sober, though, I fell victim to my own self-pity. I walked away from God and began playing for the other team. My precious gifts from God—passion, gab, and the ability to evoke emotion in others—became tools of the devil. I quickly rose to the top of the underworld.

I built a massive dial-a-dope operation in south Calgary, controlling everything from my couch and watching it unfold through surveillance cameras. Paranoia became my only true companion. My ottoman held at least six phones, each with a specific counter-surveillance purpose. I had a CB radio, a bug detector, a frequency jammer, and my own personal cocaine book with lines of high-grade cocaine. I also had a machete and a fully loaded Ruger with an extended clip complete with twenty-four hollow-point bullets—always one in the chamber.

In front of the ottoman was a large TV equipped with surveillance monitor feeds. I stared at them for days at a time, only getting up for bathroom breaks, to pull more cocaine out of the safe, or to remove the barricade from my door so my runners could bring me money.

I did my best to keep as little cocaine in the house as possible, even hiring a guy at one point to keep it all in a safe at his house. I also paid him to do all the bagging for me. I would message him in codes, and he was under strict orders to never talk on the phone because then his voice could be recorded by a tap. I had a phone meant only for conversations with him. It was imperative that no one ever know who he was, and that only I deal with him.

The only problem was he couldn't keep up with the product, which eventually resulted in me needing to keep an abundance of cocaine at home.

The people who worked for me all had crotch-rocket motorcycles with out-of-country licence plates, CB radios strapped to their waists, and phones always busy with impatient customers. I understood the market and knew that the largest profits were produced in small sales, so I networked, marketed, and advertised my empire like a business. I sent mass shoutouts, raffled giveaways, and created referral programs.

And I had the best cocaine you could find, the stuff dreams were made of.

I would give out free blow and meet every one of our customers personally, nominally so I could break bread with them, but also so I could conduct a screening process to protect the unstoppable money train I had built. On the days I left the house, I strapped on a bulletproof vest and placed at least ten grams of high-grade cocaine in a vial around my neck, so I could snort it easily.

My life was nonstop criminality for three years straight.

My work ethic and unrivalled passion for cocaine led me to the top, but also to my own demise. After three years of snorting, then smoking, and eventually shooting cocaine, my health problems got out of control. I suffered multiple heart attacks, liver problems, and stomach ulcers. I only slept for a short few hours every six days. At the age of thirty-one, my heart was failing—the end result of the drug I had so passionately sermonized.

When I found out I was going to die, I felt a strange sense of freedom from knowing it was going to be over soon. I pushed everyone out of my life and secluded myself so I could stay high until the fateful day when I would be released from the prison I had created.

But that day never came.

A physician explained to me that the sheer amount of cocaine I was doing probably was the only thing keeping my heart beating. I had gotten the promise of death only to be told that the same thing that was killing me was also keeping me alive!

I reached a point of loneliness few could understand. I just wanted to disappear.

I need to get high, I think to myself. *Not for the rush of finding euphoric bliss, but for the agonizing pain of coming down. That's how I will kill myself. I'll scrape together what pitiful tease of drugs I have left and deliver one last, liberating slash to my arm.*

I can only describe the ferocious process of coming down by comparing it to the dying will of a man being drowned in a bathtub filled only halfway with water, his lips only inches away from the air he needs to survive. All the strength and tenacity in the world won't propel his mouth to the oh-so close salvation.

Only for an addict, it's even worse. An addict feels like he's holding himself underwater.

I can't take it anymore. I hold the end of the pipe to my mouth, my eyes filling with tears as I tap the lighter against the crack and watch it melt into the ash. I steady my lips while circling the lighter in a spiral toward the middle of the bowl. Then I suck back, as I've done a thousand times before. I pull the pipe away from my mouth, praying for even a small rush of bliss.

As expected, it doesn't come. These few scraps of blow aren't enough to get the monster high I crave.

Cody Bates, everybody. Take a good look.

A massive rush of pain sweeps over me as I drop the pipe. Ash and charcoal litter the carpet. I grab the knife and push the tip through the skin of my wrist. I remain still for a second, not moving the knife. A sense of calm sweeps over me. There are no more tears, only purpose.

It's time to die.

It's time to claim my place in hell.

Say goodbye to Cody Bates.

PART
I

Chapter One

PLAYFUL SPIRIT

I was born almost three weeks late on April 4, 1985, at 3:41 a.m. to my unprepared parents. Holding the little bundle of joy, they gave me the name Cody William Bates. Bates was my mother's maiden name; she wouldn't let me carry the last name of my father.

My parents had met at Smuggler's Inn in Calgary. My father had always been a very soft, gentle, kind man. He never lost his temper and was excellent at being the compassionate introvert. He turned out to be the most positive and influential role model in my life. My mother was a headstrong woman—hard-working, beautiful, and intelligent. At the age of nineteen, she decided to raise me herself.

My parents were ill prepared to have a baby, yet they made the best of a bad situation. Their relationship ended before I was even born.

I cannot recall much of my early childhood, but my earliest memory was also my first encounter with death. I was three years old. My mother and new stepfather, George, the second person I called Dad, had married and brought my baby sister into the world. One day, they took me to a public swimming pool. I don't really know how it happened, how my parents could forget their three-year-old at a large swimming pool while one went to change and the other went to return my water wings, but I was left alone. I don't remember anything up to the point when someone found me floating face down in the hot tub, lifeless for only God knows how long.

I try to imagine the horrific scene as lifeguards worked tirelessly to pump air back into my tiny lungs. I try to imagine how my mother must have felt as she rushed to see what the commotion was about, only to be met with the horror of seeing her own precious blond-haired boy on the tile floor.

While onlookers watched, my mother got down on her knees and screamed, reaching out for her unconscious child. No mother or father should have to watch their child die.

Luckily for them, this day was not one of sorrow but rather joyful reckoning. I don't know how long I floated in that hot tub, but God decided to spare me.

My first memory is actually the dreams I had while floating in the hot tub. In the dream, I stood at the edge of the wave pool, the water lapping against my toes. There was a rope in front of me, but it was too far to reach. In my steadfast determination, I wasn't about to be thwarted by this. I remember reaching for the rope, experiencing a rush of elation as I grasped it with my willful hands and used it to swing into the water.

It has occurred to me that this might not actually have been a dream, not entirely, and yet I know there were no ropes hanging over either the hot tub or the wave pool that day. Did this really happen? Maybe the rope represented something evil enticing my playful spirit while my unsuspecting parents were nowhere to be seen.

I woke up in a hospital bed just as George walked into the room with a big smile. I had unusual apparatuses all over me, and one was even plugged into my nostrils; I understood that it was helping me breathe even though my mind was still very young and immature. I recognized George though the plastic sheet draped around my bed, and I noticed that he carried something in his hand—a toy from the hospital gift shop.

This is a nice memory. I don't remember my mom being there, but I'm sure she was. For some reason, my mind has completely abolished her.

My baby sister was the centre of my attention during my three-year-old delinquency. I would wake up in the morning, before my parents got up, and wheel my sister's crib into the middle of her room. I would then proceed to spray her with my water gun, taking her poop-filled diaper off and making her wear her spoils, and even one day accidentally knocking out her front teeth by dropping her face-first against the stairs. My poor little sister.

She was such a sweetheart growing up. Despite my early tortures, we became inseparable for many years. We adored each other.

The third man I called Dad was named Gary, and he loved me as his own son. He was handsome, charming, and witty. He was everything a child could ask for in a father figure. I've referred to him as my dad for as long as I can remember, a label he still carries today.

My life during the years when Gary was around is full of happy memories. He taught me to love hockey, took me for rides on his Harley, and let me watch wrestling even though my mother preferred my mind not be polluted with such rubbish. He was an amazing father.

I've struggled to decide how to describe my mom. I can't say I've ever felt an abundance of love from her. I have a hard time recalling many big hugs. I don't remember hearing her say "I love you," nor do I remember receiving special treats from her.

When I was four, I went to my friend Sheena's house. My mom had instructed me to be home for dinner at five o'clock, but Sheena's mom accidentally sent me home about a half-hour late. For some reason, my mom didn't believe my story and accused me of playing on the nearby highway. This was a strange accusation because it would never have occurred to me to play in traffic.

I didn't understand why my mom dragged me by my little arm up the stairs to the bathroom, but I was to receive a harsh punishment for my supposed lies. I vividly remember crying as she forced a bar of soap into my "dirty" mouth. She then shoved me into my room and slammed the door shut. I cried and screamed in agony as my mother left the house to "get to the bottom of this."

I hid under the desk in my room, desperate to get away from my maniacal twenty-three-year-old mother. I remember hiccupping, crying, and feeling confused.

When my mom came back into the room, I recoiled from her. She apologized for what had happened, remorse and shame taking the place of her hate and anger. It turned out I wasn't a liar; Sheena's mom had indeed just lost track of time.

But the hands of time could not be turned back. My innocence was permanently stained that afternoon. The damage was done. My mother had given me a reason to fear her.

Chapter Two

KING OF THE PLAYGROUND

As my five-year-old mind developed, I played with my dad on the regular and finally enjoyed a somewhat stable family life. But for some reason I had an insatiable appetite for danger, always putting myself and other children in harm's way. I remember fitting myself into a box and having other kids push me around our neighbourhood, a public housing project, on a skateboard. I relished the feeling of not knowing where I was being pushed, knowing that I could fall or run into something at any time. It was a thrill.

I also remember having a strong desire to fly. I would strap a kite to my back and jump completely horizontally off the tallest fence I could find. Needless to say, I didn't fly around the neighbourhood like Peter Pan; instead I learned my first lesson about gravity. I hit the ground astonishingly hard.

My fascination with sex also emerged at the age of five. All the neighbourhood girls would show me theirs if I showed them mine. I was the cool kid on the block, inquisitively seeking out girls who would bare their privates. I taught everyone I knew my conception of sex!

I started going to a daycare close to my mother's work, and it was way better than playing in the public housing parking lot. It had unlimited toys, a playground, tricycles, and musical instruments. I was king of this particular playground. I played with all the best toys, developed a close circle of followers, and had my pick of the girls. I would have my friends stand guard by the playhouse window, inside of which were the best toys and one chair: the king's throne. As I sat, the girls would reveal themselves to me. I felt supreme in my perverted childish ventures.

One day, the daycare took us on a field trip to a local swimming pool. Instead of us changing in the gender-appropriate bathrooms, the staff put us all together in a group change room. A weird feeling came over me as I watched everyone change. I proudly displayed my erection to the other kids like a five-year-old stallion, only to be quickly hustled out of view by the daycare staff. This should have raised a red flag. Nonetheless, this made it clear to all the kids who the alpha male was. I was the lion king, all four feet of me.

Crystal was the only girl in daycare to have enough self-respect and maturity to know this was wrong. She wouldn't show me her goodies.

Another day, the daycare staff took us all to a playground down the street and paired everyone up. When Crystal and I were paired off and told to hold hands, she squeezed so hard that she almost popped my fingers off. But I didn't care; she was my great white buffalo, the only girl not cowed by my provocative flirtations.

I put up with her torture that day without saying a word.

Back at the daycare afterward, I went with my friends into the "band room," which held all the instruments. It was a small room with a curtain for a door.

Suddenly, Crystal walked through the curtain like a five-year-old princess, bent down, and whispered in my ear, "'Do you want to have sex?"

I left my friends behind as Crystal and I walked outside to the playhouse. I ordered a couple of other kids to stand guard and put pillows in the window to keep us out of view.

Once inside, I whipped out the goods.

"What are you doing?" she asked.

Confused, I replied, "Sex…"

"No, no. You need to lie on top of me."

Realizing I might be over my head on this one, I cooperatively lay down on top of her with my pants on.

"Now you need to move around," she said.

I did as my tutor told.

As we were collaborating on our idea of sex, a woman poked her head through the pillows in the window.

"Crystal, are you in here?" the woman asked.

It was Crystal's mom.

Busted, I jumped off the lady's daughter and ran away without looking back. This was my very first run from the law, and it was thwarted by a four-foot chainlink fence.

Unfortunately for me, my booty house was now a crime scene.

After this, I still managed to continue my reign, but I noticed that a strange phenomenon was beginning to take place in all the girls. Their sense of morality and dignity was maturing to the point where they could distinguish right from wrong. With this change, my toddler sex life came to an abrupt end.

My mom soon took me out and put me in another daycare only a few blocks from my house. I don't remember liking or disliking the new daycare, but one thing was sure: I wasn't king there. As one of the youngest kids, I just tried to have fun and adjust to my new surroundings. But I didn't like being at the bottom of the hierarchy.

My stint there was cut short when I pushed a kid into a steel-barred fence. His leg got caught in the bars and ended up getting severely mangled. The skin from his kneecap to his lower leg had unrolled. It was disgusting, and for the first time I had really hurt somebody. I didn't like that feeling.

Well, I got the boot. Bye-bye, daycare!

I soon started Grade One at Lake Bonavista Elementary. I was hyperactive and not a great student. It was the same school my cousin was attending, so I got to spend a lot of time with her, which made me happy. I don't remember any friends from this school, but for some reason bullies took a liking to me—and not in a good way. It was my first experience of getting picked on, and it made me want to disappear.

One day, the bullies came at me and my cousin on the playground. She protected me, making them all cry. Under her watchful eye, I continued through the rest of Grade One bully-free.

Because of hyperactivity, my teacher came up with a program designed to meet my special needs. I had a daily journal in which my teacher filled out a daily progress report; my mom had to read and sign it every night.

At home, my failure to behave at school resulted in getting grounded, losing my TV privileges, and being deprived of precious toys. On some occasions, I was even sent to bed on arrival from school at four o'clock in the afternoon. Those were sorrowful times. I would cry and sob, pleading for my punishment to come to an end, but for some reason I always repeated the actions that had gotten me there in the first place.

Unbeknownst to me, these experiences were paving the way for far more malevolent and destructive patterns of behaviour.

CODY AT FOUR YEARS OF AGE.

Chapter Three

STAINED

In Grade Two, my mom and Gary moved us to the Ranchlands, a suburb north of Calgary. It wasn't quite as fun as subsidized housing, but we had our own house and the school was just a short block away.

My best friend Glen lived just up the street and we went to school together at St. Rita's Elementary. Glen was very intelligent, and he wasn't much for trouble. He and I were inseparable at that age.

His dad once took us to see the movie *Cliffhanger*. It was awesome. I was awe-struck by the foul language falling out of the movie stars' mouths. F-bombs filled my eardrums like music. Glen's and my language took an odd turn that day. We went to school the next day dropping F-bombs like we were in a race to see who could say the most. The rest of the kids marvelled. After that, swearing became the way the cool kids interacted. I became quite popular at St. Rita's.

My first experience with crime came when I was seven. My dad took me and my friends Caleb and Heather to see the movie *Hook*. When we got home, my dad and I walked Caleb home. On our way back, my dad suddenly broke into a run, and I did my best to keep up. It turned out that our home had been the victim of a burglary. I remember my confusion as I walked into the house. All of our valuables had been stacked by the door; the culprits had been thwarted just in time. If we would have been twenty minutes later, all our stuff would have been gone.

It had never occurred to me that you could take something that wasn't yours. I felt thrilled to be in the vicinity of a crime. Although I had seen this kind of thing in the movies, I hadn't realized it actually happened in real life. If it was so easy to get away with theft, why didn't everyone steal?

In the coming years, I thought back often to that night. I wondered if those burglars had ended up in jail or if I would ever know who they were.

With the burglary incident still fresh in my head, I went into my mother's purse one day and took a twenty-dollar bill. The thrill of taking it was exhilarating. Do you know how much candy twenty dollars can buy? It felt like I had the whole world in my hands. I could do anything!

My mother realized the money was missing and came up with a pretty clever trick to make me confess. Because I had just received an invitation to Glen's birthday party, my mom claimed that she had no money for a birthday present. Therefore, I was to attend my best friend's party empty-handed.

Well, I couldn't go without a present! I presented the twenty dollars into her hand, unknowingly walking right into her trap. I tried to explain that I'd been saving that money for some time… I know, stupid. That was my first lie. Unless you're the Wayne Gretzky of deception, I'm pretty sure no seven-year-old would stand a chance in a battle of intellect with an adult.

Surprisingly enough, my mom wasn't mad. She lovingly told me that it was wrong and then gave me my punishment: I couldn't go to the birthday party. I was pissed. It was my best friend!

Getting through that punishment was fairly easy. The next time, I wasn't so lucky.

I got sent home from school one day because I had the flu. I had learned the trick that if you hold your tummy and say "It hurts," you would get sent home from school to watch TV and play with toys. My mom had caught on, though, and my plan to relax was rudely upended by my mother coming home early and sending me to bed at one o'clock in the afternoon.

For some strange reason, she soon roused me to head to the store for milk. My mom gave me a five-dollar bill and said over and over again that she knew how much a carton of milk cost; she would know if any change was missing. I was to go straight there and back.

Looking back at it now, I can only figure that she was trying to goad me into stealing. Why else would she send me to the store for milk at two in the afternoon, making me walk directly past the school that had just sent me home sick? I think she was pissed that she had to miss work because of me, so she concocted a plan to make me never want to come home from school early again.

So I walked to the store, passing by the school. I remember thinking it would be a great idea to walk up to my classroom window and gloat to my classmates about how clever I had been. Looking back at it now, my mother probably walked outside the house to watch me head toward the school. Plan in motion. Surely I would come back short on change in order to be taught the lesson I clearly needed.

When I eventually arrived at the store, I easily acquired the milk my mother asked me to get. But as I was paying for milk, something else caught my attention: some twenty-five-cent Mr. Big chocolate bars, strategically placed to entice hungry change-carrying customers such as myself. With my mother's words ringing in my head, I figured that I could just tell her that I had dropped a quarter on the way home. That sounded plausible.

I walked through the door of my house, where I was met by my mother, her hand out, asking for the change.

"Where's the rest?" she questioned calmly when she saw that I was short. "Where's the rest of it, Cody?"

Her composure quickly left her, replaced with deafening screams. Before I knew what was happening, I was being punched and kicked into the corner. My mother beat me mercilessly. She pulled my arms away from my face, demanding that I put my hands down so she could have a clear shot of my face. When I finally cooperated, I was met with blows to my young mug. Terrified, I put my arms back up. This enraged my mother. She grabbed my boots and ripped them off my feet, turning them into weapons. She hit me over and over with them, screaming in a blind rage.

I remember trying to get to my feet, protecting my face as I ran, but my mother caught up with me as I crossed the kitchen. I tried to stop before falling down the stairs into the basement, but she seized the opportunity to inflict more pain, shoving me down the eight-step flight of stairs. I crashed to the carpeted floor below. Surprisingly enough, nothing was broken.

I scrambled up on shaking hands and knees, hurtling toward my bedroom door, my mother kicking me hard in the butt as I crawled. With a surge of adrenaline, I thrust myself through the bedroom door and into the corner of my room. The punishment not quite drawn to a conclusion, she picked up one my hard plastic toys and threw it at me as hard as she could. It smashed into the wall above my head and shattered.

The carnage finally came to an end with her slamming the door. I sobbed as I picked up my broken toys. One thing had been made clear: I was a bad boy. My mom had gotten her point across without having to say it.

Chapter Four

YOUR SON'S TEARS

My drug addiction began at the ripe age of eight, when I was given Ritalin in school. At the time, the drug was very effective in counterbalancing my hyperactivity. My grades improved and my behaviour became easier to control.

But no one considered the drug's long-term effects. If someone who doesn't have attention deficit disorder (ADD) takes Ritalin, that person will feel stimulated. Years later, cocaine had the same effect on me. I felt invincible whether I was on Ritalin or cocaine.

I moved to a small town called Turner Valley when I was nine. My mom and Gary had just found out they were going to have another child, so they decided to leave the hectic pace of the city. Turner Valley was quiet and budding with the promise of happiness.

At first I loved the small town atmosphere. Turner Valley was full of great things to do, like cliff-jumping, rock-climbing, hiking, swimming in the river, snake-hunting, and hockey. This place gave me the freedom to do what I pleased.

My grandparents on my stepfather's side took me shopping for school clothes, and I was determined to get Power Rangers stuff—to make a statement on my first day at school. Power Rangers was the big thing at the time. In Grade Three, I spent every single lunch hour playing make-believe battles between good and evil. I was always the Red Ranger, the lead ranger of the pack. Once again I was the boss, and I planned to keep it that way.

My first day at Turner Valley Elementary was interesting. I recall standing with my mom at the front desk by the principal's office. I was wearing my new Power Rangers sweat suit, picked out by my wonderful grandparents. I watched the kids walk by and felt determined to make my mark here. As the other children passed, though, I began to notice I wasn't getting the response my sweat suit had been meant to evoke. The kids were snickering at me.

"What is he wearing?" one girl said to her friend.

The girl had obviously been living under a rock.

It turned out that Power Rangers weren't cool in Turner Valley. What the heck was wrong with these people? They were just a bunch of rednecks not watching the best show on the planet! I would need to find another way to win these hicks over.

Unfortunately for me, that day never came. I never ended up fitting in with my new town.

It didn't help when my mom's rage was put on display for the first time for all to see. I had cleverly snuck a Pepsi out of the fridge one morning despite strict instructions not to drink pop because of my hyperactive nature. I don't know what else was going on in my mom's world that day, but she met me in the school hallway and grabbed me by the neck, slamming me into the lockers in front of all my teachers and friends. She held me by my throat and squeezed, cutting off my airway.

Finally, a teacher intervened and my mother tried to act as if manhandling her kid was completely normal. Before storming off, she made sure everyone knew I was a thief.

Tears swelled in my eyes from pain and embarrassment. I dropped my head and walked away, my stare glued to the floor. If I didn't look at them, maybe they wouldn't see me.

I kept asking myself why no one helped me, and my conclusion was that I deserved it. After all, I had stolen the Pepsi.

I pretty much only hung out with one friend, Kent, who lived with his grandparents down the alley from my house. We were truly the best of friends, hanging out all day and every day. Kent was a couple years younger than me, but he ended up being the first true friend I ever had. Our bond was a brotherhood.

One night, my mom came into my bedroom and asked me if I wanted to sleep over at Kent's house. Getting her to agree to a sleepover was usually a battle royale, so I was suspicious at this request. That's when she told me that Kent's dad had died that evening in a car accident.

I had never known anyone who had died. I just didn't understand. My young mind couldn't quite wrap itself around the idea of never seeing someone you love ever again. Although I didn't understand death, one thing was clear: I needed to be there for my best friend in his time of need.

I didn't ask questions when I visited Kent that night. Instead we tried to play as if nothing was wrong—but something *was* wrong. His family all wore the same pain-stricken expression. They cried and hugged. I watched this amazing family come together in a time of great need and noted that my family never joined together for anything other than celebration and drink. I witnessed a family carrying each other's burdens.

This helped me to grasp a deeper understanding of compassion. I was grateful to be a part of something so cherished.

My struggles at school continued as I tried to find my place in Turner Valley. I was tight with all the guys after school, but during school I had a different personality due to my medication. It killed me inside. I couldn't fit in, and the more I tried the more I felt separated from the pack. I yearned for my glory days at daycare and St. Rita's Elementary.

The further down the popularity scale I slid, the more I tried to compensate by acting out, which only pushed my cohorts away. I began to focus on instant gratification, which kicked off a destructive cycle that would last for decades.

While standing in the library one day, I noticed another boy my age. Since I had been struggling to make friends, I decided to say hi to him before someone else tried to influence his opinion of me.

"Hi man," I said. "I'm Cody."

"I'm Alex."

I can confidently state that Alex has been the most influential friend I've ever had. I loved Alex with all my heart. He exuded confidence the likes of which I hadn't seen in anyone else. He managed to accomplish in a few short days what I had been trying to do for months. He was hilarious and everyone adored him. His comedic charm and contagious laughter lured everyone in.

I felt a lot better after meeting him. Maybe Turner Valley wouldn't turn out to be so bad.

One day while reading Spiderman comics in my room, I wondered what it would be like to be a superhero. How would it feel to save innocent civilians from bad guys? I liked the thought of helping people, of being the person everyone could count on to keep them safe from people with no sense of morality. My brain sparked at the thought of saving girls, being in the newspaper, and kissing babies.

When I had jumped off the fence with the kite strapped to my back as a five-year-old, my motive had been to make my friends jealous, to show them I had figured out how to fly. But I had also wanted to help people.

I could get lost in these comics all day. The Spiderman comics Gary had given me shaped me in a positive way, teaching me to put others first and help those who are weaker.

As I fantasized about being a righteous superkid, my mother walked into my room with a stern look on her angry face. What the heck had I done now?

When I asked what was wrong, she told me that my dad wasn't sending her enough child support. She had come to hurt me—in order to hurt my father. She angrily told me that I wasn't allowed to see my dad again until he caught up on child support. At the time, my dad was a struggling painter but also a master of wood-graining. He had even been flown to Japan for work. But there wasn't a lot of employment for skilled wood-grainers, so he was close to bankruptcy.

My dad was a very gentle and kind man, and I knew that seeing his son get hurt at my mother's hand would devastate him.

I broke down and shed the tears my mother so malevolently desired. She did hurt my father, but at the cost of losing another piece of her son's soul. She left my room victorious, but I was in pain and didn't understand why. Why was it that I was to be the target of her vindictiveness?

After my mom left, I escaped out the basement door, got on my bike, and started the long ride from Turner Valley to Calgary. I wanted to see my dad. He was sixty-five kilometres away, but my mom made me feel as if I was a lifetime away from his safe arms. I didn't want to be around my mother. It felt like she hated me, like my tears meant nothing to her except as a manipulation tactic to coerce my father. How could you love someone and so easily hurt them?

In my mind, my mother knew best. I must have done something to deserve the punishments I received. She regularly reminded me of what a bad boy I was with spankings, groundings, and hateful remarks. I see it now for what it was: emotional, physical, and psychological abuse, manipulating and shaping my thoughts and personality to suit her selfish needs.

My stepfather caught up with me about ten kilometres out of town. As Gary pulled over, I felt a small sense of relief that my mom wasn't in the car with him. I stared down at the pavement as he approached, trying to hide the tears that stained my face. He walked up to me, his head hung low. To my surprise, he wasn't mad. He was hurt—on my behalf. When Gary asked me if I'd come home with him, my soul was so damaged that I couldn't say no. I needed to be loved, and I could see that he knew that what was happening to me was wrong.

That day, my mom warped my mind in a very dark direction. I learned that it was okay to hurt the people you love the most, even if they don't deserve it. But at least Gary gave me love when I was most desperate. I believe in my heart that my tears led him to feel grief, knowing that he was powerless to reverse the profound psychological damage my mom caused me that afternoon.

Chapter Five

SCREAMING SNAKES

In 1996, my baby brother came into the world and changed our family dynamic forever. He was a blond-haired, blue-eyed bundle of joy. He took up much of my attention, and he always put a smile on my face.

I didn't have a lot of experience with babies, so I was loaded with questions. He smiled at me an awful lot in the first four months, which I understand now through my studies in child psychology; those smiles were merely reflexes. And yet his smiling face cemented a bond that played a huge role in terms of extending compassion and love in my life. My brother was my world and my reason to change many years later. My love for him runs deep.

Grade Five brought about a whole new set of struggles for school. My Ritalin prescription was switched to Dexedrine, all my friends treated me like crap, my mom's abuse stayed consistent, and my parents went through serious problems.

My life also took another strange turn that year. I became obsessed with killing small animals. That whole year, it's all I did for extracurricular activity. I enjoyed the rush of catching small rodents, killing them, then collecting their tails. My friends all joined me in this, so I didn't think there was anything wrong with it. Farmers told us they were a menace and that their rodent holes broke horses' legs.

I didn't see them as living creatures. It escaped my psyche that I was causing them pain. At that point, my mind was utterly corrupted by self-hate, Dexedrine, and my mother's abuse. I wasn't able to have empathy for these poor animals.

I came up with some ingenious ways to catch the critters, getting handy with a slingshot. I shot down birds, gophers, fish, and even deer if given the chance. I took it one step further when I discovered rat traps. I would buy peanut butter with the change I stole from my stepdad and cake it all over the traps, then sit back and watch the destruction unfold. Usually the traps would break their necks instantly. If they didn't die instantly, I would enjoy watching them die. The control I had over these creatures gave me gratification. I could also work two snares at a time, with rat traps all over the place and a slingshot in my back pocket as a last resort. I was a juvenile killing machine.

I hunted snakes as well. At the halfway point of the trail connecting Turner Valley and the neighbouring town of Black Diamond, there was a rock that was home to hundreds of snakes. They would burrow little tunnels into the rock to hide in, then come out and bake in the sun on the hot rocks in the summer. We used to catch them and bring them to school the next day. My mom wasn't inclined to have stinky snakes in the house, so they would sometimes freeze to death overnight in ice cream pails outside.

One day I caught twenty snakes and brought them home as usual. I became a bit of a fire bug around this time, so I got the idea in my head to set all these snakes on fire. I don't think I understood that it would hurt them; for some reason, I just pictured the pails melting and all the snakes slithering out in different directions.

Why was it so easy for me to take the lives of twenty snakes? I still can't explain it.

I doused the snakes in gasoline and turned the pail upside-down, thinking that would make it easier for them to escape. What happened next will forever haunt my dreams. I lit the pail on fire and backed off as though expecting to see a fireworks show. But the pail didn't melt, creating holes for escape. No, it melted onto the snakes, creating an enclosed inferno. The snakes actually screamed as the plastic melted into their bodies. The transparent ice cream pail illuminating the shadows of the poor creatures climbing up the walls, letting me see their mouths open in painful shrieks. I'll never forget what those snake screams sounded like. It was almost human.

Something strange happened to me in that moment. For the first time in my life, I felt empathy. Hearing the screaming snakes made me identify with them not as objects but instead as living creatures that felt, thought, and understood what was happening to them. I watched them burn to death at my hand and felt an abundance of confusion and hate toward myself.

The walk home was a quiet one.

Chapter Six

BONDING TIME

As I walked through my school at the beginning of Grade Six, a daunting reality became clear: I would never be a cool kid in Turner Valley. I hated myself and my family life was deteriorating by the second.

Right before my sister had been born, I remember my mother freaking out daily on my stepfather. In retrospect, Gary was probably the only other person on the planet who truly understood how manipulative and dark my mother could be. He started working later to avoid being at home. My mom would say the meanest things she could think of to make him suffer, and she would involve me in it. I would sit with my mother while she unleashed all the hatred she carried inside but couldn't vent because my father wouldn't answer the phone when she called. That was the only way I ever bonded with my mother, and it came at the cost of hearing her tear down one of the only people who ever loved me unconditionally. It hurt me immensely.

One such conversation occurred after I broke my collarbone. While I was in the hospital, she told me that Gary wasn't coming because his work was more important than me, that he didn't come home anymore because he didn't love his family. It was a lot of hate for my twelve-year-old mind to endure, but I sat through it. I listened to this sinister pollution and even tried to help her figure out different ways to hurt my loving stepfather.

My youngest sister was born on Valentine's Day 1998. Even as a baby, she showed the same passion and tenacity she has today. I didn't know at that time how significant a role she would play in my life. She and I relate to each other the most in our family, even though she has never been an addict, never been violent, and never died.

My stepfather was thrilled about my sister. On the outside, we were a picture perfect family, all with big smiling faces—but the smiles were a mask covering our shame, hurt, guilt, resentment, and hatred. I hated myself, my dad hated that he was getting in deeper with my mom, and my mom hated anyone who opposed her or got in her way.

At this point in her life, after working hard to build a business around herself, my mom began to be successful. She became very independent in the looming breakup of her marriage. Because she confided in me so much, I knew that she saw it coming from a mile away.

I found myself grounded an awful lot. Looking back now, I can see that my mom used me as a full-time babysitter. My groundings would last months at a time for such things as coming home late, stealing petty change, and smelling like smoke. I was never allowed to go hang out with my friends after school, something I desperately needed. But my mother wanted me at home taking care of my siblings. It was very self-seeking. I guess she thought that it was for the greater good, providing for her family.

I remember the 1998 Nagano Winter Olympics. It was the peak of my parents' fighting and hostility. I recall sneaking up the stairs from the basement in the middle of the night and hearing the TV. I would creep around the corner of the living room and see my stepfather there, watching the screen with a blanket draped over him a foot away from the TV. He was hurting. I caught him like that many times; it was like he didn't sleep at all. He was stuck between a rock and a hard place—his love for his kids keeping him in this volatile marriage with a woman who had nothing but vengeance on her mind.

He was a victim of abuse as much as I was, but he finally chose not to be a victim of her malignant control any longer. He left shortly after that, although he continued to make child support payments for me—even though I wasn't his biological son.

I spent the early mornings by myself in my private bathroom getting ready for school. The smell of Axe and heavy cologne permanently lingered in that bathroom. I was in Grade Seven and had budding pubic hairs, a thin moustache of peach fuzz, and pesky zits. This all needed to be dealt with each morning.

One morning, I walked up the stairs and found my mom still in bed, as usual. Since Gary had left she had been staying up late drinking wine and smoking cigarettes, which meant she got up even later. My brother was usually watching cartoons in his cute little pyjamas. My sister was just a wee baby so her alarm was on my mother's watch.

I creeped into my mother's coat, as I had done a hundred times before, to steal a couple of cigarettes to smoke on my way to school. A younger kid who lived across the street would partake with me, making me feel like the cool older friend. This was the only time I felt that way.

As I opened her pack of cigarettes, I was greeted with a little surprise. On the downside, there was only one smoke left, no doubt saved for a hangover morning. On the upside, there was more than just a cigarette; there was also a joint. I felt blessed with the opportunity to get high. My friends were always talking about it. Some of them had older brothers who regularly smoked pot with them. Why did they have to make it sound so cool?

My mom had clearly been smoking weed last night. I was no expert, but I was positive that weed made you forget things, so it only made sense to me that she would assume she had smoked all her weed and cigarettes and not realize I had taken them. Meanwhile, I'd get to be the cool kid on the playground for once.

I met my buddy in the middle of the road excited to divulge my ace in the hole. We started walking and I confidently asked him if he wanted to get high, as if I had done it a hundred times before. He was in the sixth grade, a year younger than me, and he respectfully declined my generous offer, thus delaying the forfeiture of his innocence. My innocence, on the other hand, had been stained long before. I couldn't talk the big talk in front of my young friend and then jam out, so I had to do it. I put the joint to my mouth and lit it up.

I remember the harsh taste down my thirteen-year-old throat. It was painful and I felt scared, so I didn't take massive inhales. Nevertheless, I was stoned.

The only way I can describe the feeling is one of serenity. I felt at peace with myself as well as my surroundings. Despite it being the reason for stealing the weed in the first place, for once being cool didn't enter into my mind. That day, I didn't care how ugly my acne made me. And I didn't care what the girls at school thought of me. All I knew was that all my cares disappeared. It was uncompromised, incomparable, unprecedented bliss.

And to get it, all I needed to do was light the flame. Oh my God, I had found the answer to all my problems. Who could've seen this coming?

When I was thirteen, I had been so manipulated and abused that the implications of smoking my first joint evaded me completely. Drugs became my solution, my answer to everything that was wrong. I was a drug addict before I even picked it up, the predisposition having been forged in me many years prior.

I had no worries or cares that day at school. I enjoyed every second of the enlightenment, feeling fearless from the bursts of pleasure in my brain. Once class started, the teacher asked me if I was okay.

"I think so," I replied. "Just feeling a little sick."

I was sent to the principal's office for a quick assessment and the consensus of the staff was that I must have a virus. Nobody suspected that a thirteen-year-old could be stoned. They called my mother, and I sat in the principal's office, absorbed by the colourful paradise in my head.

Suddenly a shadow loomed over me. My mother was there to pick me up, and she looked pissed. I guess she hadn't received the memo telling her that she was supposed to be too stoned last night to remember anything. At the same time as she smiled at the school staff, I felt her threatening looks in my direction. Dang, she was good. The principal released me to her care.

I got into my mother's minivan and crawled all the way back to the third row. She got in the driver's seat and politely asked me to come sit up front.

As we began driving up the street she coolly asked me, "Where is it?"

"It's gone," I replied.

She asked me once more, this time concurrently with the van turning the corner away from the school. Her voice raised. "Where is it!?"

I put my arms up to protect myself against her fingers and nails as she struck me over and over again.

"Put your hands down," she shrieked.

The beating I received that day didn't deter me from my newfound solution.

Chapter Seven

BAD BOY

I fell in love with marijuana. The problem was my lack of funds. My friend's older brothers proved to be our suppliers, but they were only in Grades Eight and Nine and not a reliable source.

My mother became darker and darker toward me as time passed, but I didn't care because I had finally found an answer. Even if I wasn't high in the moment of a trauma, I knew that I'd be able to get stoned as soon as I had money. It felt like always having a light at the end of the tunnel.

My mother began relaxing the rules with me around this time. She didn't care as much about curfews, and she even gave me back a pack of cigarettes she had confiscated from me. All of this was no doubt a ploy, a reward for listening to her vent and letting her pollute my thinking. I didn't even realize there was anything wrong with that. She was grooming me with gifts, making me believe I deserved my punishments.

I sometimes think back and wonder if anyone or anything could have intervened and saved me during my adolescence.

One occasion does come to mind.

On a normal chaotic afternoon at the house, my mother once again vented to me, only this time it wasn't in a cordial manner. She was upset about something that had nothing to do with me and I somehow became the object of her rage. I was washing dishes and keeping my fourteen-year-old opinion to myself. She was flying off the handle about my stepdad, and for some reason she had it in her head that she didn't want to be a mom anymore. She coldly threatened to leave all of us kids behind—"like your dad"—so she could go off and enjoy her life.

She was a very angry woman—angry at her situation, angry about her life, and for some reason angry at me. To say that my relationship with my mother was toxic would be a gross understatement.

On this day, she claimed that she was going to leave us kids and start a new life in British Columbia.

"I'm successful now," she said. "I don't need kids. I'll leave you all, just like him. I'll go party and have fun. I don't need you guys. I'll drink wine and live on the beach. I'll be good, I'll be really good."

When my mom got mad, she flew into a sarcastic rage, acting like she was on stage putting in an Oscar-winning performance. Her screams were all coupled with hand gestures and head movements. It is a full-on production.

As she was yelling, something came over me—anger. Maybe I was a bad boy and deserved punishment, but she was threatening to leave my three siblings as well. What had any of them done? I tried to grasp what she was saying, and I tried to say something.

My mom cut me off. "Shut up and do your job," she hissed, referring to the dishes I was washing.

"Then you keep doing your job," I barked back, referring to her role as mother to four kids.

What happened next I will always have seared into my mind. It's like it happened in slow motion. I told her to keep doing her job, and before the sentence was finished, in the blink of an eye, she grabbed a glass beer mug off the counter and hurled it directly at my face from less than five feet away. With less than a second to react, my arm shot up holding the plate I had been washing.

Glass flew all around me, showering me in shards. My eyes wide, I glanced down at my hand; the skin of my middle finger was torn open, scaring the ever-living crap out of my fourteen-year-old self. I had never seen so much blood.

I ran from my mother as fast as my juvenile legs could carry me. In the bedroom, I cowered in the corner of my bed, bawling. Why did this keep happening to me? And why was nobody stopping it? Was it because everyone could see what a bad boy I was? Did it show that much?

To this day, I don't know how I stopped that mug from destroying my face. Something greater than me must have been looking out for my young, broken soul.

I sat on the bed shaking, not yet fully comprehending what had transpired. What had I said to her? I'd told her to keep doing her job as a mother.

I guess this is what I get for talking back, I thought to myself. *I won't do that again.*

My mom burst into my room, her rage replaced with shame.

"I'm sorry," she said, her face reflecting how mortified she felt. She glanced around my room, her gaze falling on my blood-soaked bedspread. She tried to come closer, but I recoiled from her. "We need to go to the hospital."

At the hospital, it dawned on me that maybe someone would be able to help me and tell my mother that what she had done was wrong. Then I wouldn't have to be so scared all the time.

We approached the counter together and the receptionist politely asked what had happened. Right as my mouth opened to respond, my mother cut in.

"I did it," she said, her voice full of shame.

I couldn't believe it. My mother was taking responsibility.

I don't know what was said between my mom and the doctors fixing my hand, but no one asked to hear my side of the story. Being so young, it never occurred to me that my mom would once again be deploying a manipulative tactic to redirect the situation to her benefit. My hand was severely mangled by a vicious assault, yet the police weren't called and social services weren't notified. No one from my school even asked what had happened to my hand. My mother again dodged a bullet.

Nobody helped me. Nobody asked me. Nobody batted an eye.

I'm a bad boy, I concluded. *I need to be hurt because that's the only way I'll listen.*

In my immature thinking, I assumed that everyone knew what was happening. How could they not see it?

The truth is that no one knew the extent of the torment she was subjecting me to. But I thought I deserved it, so I said nothing.

CODY AT FOURTEEN YEARS OF AGE.

Chapter Eight

SHELTERED

That same year, I got more heavily involved in stealing. Drugs helped make my hurt subside, so I poured every ounce of strength and mental exercise into getting my next high. I collected change, stole cigarettes, and lifted anything I could that might provide the serene bliss I craved. I would roam the neighbourhood at night checking every car door. Sometimes I had an accomplice, but most times I did it alone. Weed was always on my mind.

This is also when I tried alcohol for the first time. Unlike marijuana, alcohol was easy to procure. One day my neighbour and childhood friend Lisa wanted to come over and play on our trampoline. I was grounded, so I wasn't supposed to have people over. In a tempting proposition, she offered to bring Maria along; Maria had been my crush ever since I'd moved to Turner Valley in the fourth grade. She was absolutely gorgeous in my eyes.

As Lisa and Maria made their way down to my house, I became extremely nervous. I had zits all over, I felt unattractive, and my personality was that of a greasy weasel. I hated myself. I needed to figure out a way to prepare myself so I wouldn't act like an idiot in front of my pretty friends. Since I was lacking in the money department, I turned my attention to alcohol.

Well, I had known this day would come.

My brain sparked at the thought of the girls walking up and seeing me sun-tanning on the deck with a wineglass full of vodka. Lisa and Maria were the popular, well-behaved girls in my school, though, so why the heck would they think me drinking by myself was cool? I clearly had some self-esteem issues.

Needless to say, Lisa and Maria didn't think I was cool with my wineglass of vodka. And they didn't think it was cool when I puked everywhere and rambled at them drunkenly.

But I loved it. I didn't care who thought I was cool or how stupid I made myself look. I was hammered, my mind lost in the euphoric state I'd brought upon myself. I had found yet another solution to my pain. I didn't enjoy puking my face off, and my head spun round and round when I lay in bed that night, but it beat the hell out of being me, the grotesque loser I had come to see myself as.

When I was fourteen, I also had my first interaction with violence from someone apart from my mother.

My childhood friend Glen invited me to come visit him up in Calgary for the weekend. We started by going to a Flames game. I was dying to show Glen my new-found solutions. I hadn't seen him in a few years and we had barely talked. I made certain to bring weed for the occasion, but I didn't bring it up with him in advance. I wanted it to be a surprise.

For the first time in a long while, I felt cool. Glen and I picked up right where we had left off. It was unreal to again spend time with my far removed compadre. Glen was way beyond his years in terms of intelligence and street smarts, and he was really good-looking, too, with all the hottest girlfriends. The only thing he lacked was size, being just a little guy.

I was barely able to control my excitement as I whipped out the joints. He coolly informed me that he had never tried marijuana, but he was happy that his first time would be with me. We happily blazed up. I immediately got that euphoric pleasure rush I wanted. Coupled with sharing the experience with a good friend who didn't make me feel crappy about myself, I was on top of the world. This was going to be a good weekend.

I was baked. Glen, however, was not. I knew something funny was up.

We got back to his house and he introduced me to his sweet Doberman Pinschers. I loved dogs more than I did humans, so I always made special connections with my canine friends.

Glen and I proceeded to his basement and into his room, and when we walked inside I saw that the walls were plastered with weed posters. What the hell? For a guy who hadn't ever smoked pot before, he sure had an amplified interest in the subject.

He ushered me into his private bathroom and locked the door behind us. Suddenly, he pulled out the bottom drawer under the sink. I watched as he reached into the darkness.

"I don't smoke weed," he said, slamming a quarter-pound of marijuana on the sink counter. "And I don't sell it." He slammed a second quarter-pound on the counter.

What was going on?

The mischievous guy had played me like a dang fiddle. I loved him for it. Glen had more weed than I had ever seen. What had I been missing out on because of my sheltered existence? Country life sure had kept me on the conservative side of things. The most I had seen so far had been a half-ounce.

We sparked up a joint the size of my skinny arm and I proceeded to get higher than I had ever been in my life.

When Glen's cell phone rang, we had to go out and make a sale. I guess it made sense, him being a weed dealer and all. Anyway, we couldn't smoke that entire half-pound in one weekend. So we bundled up and headed into the cold to the same store where my mom had sent me on that diabolical milk run in Grade Three. I loved being back in the old neighbourhood.

I had never been part of a drug deal before or purchased or sold narcotics. My friends back in Turner Valley had always played the middleman for me. I was nervous... but I couldn't let Glen see how nervous I was. And yet it was a little too late to act as if I was used to this.

I was also incredibly stoned. Although I was bigger, my tiny companion could clearly smoke me under the table. I decided that I had better follow his lead into this unexplored experience.

We arrived at the corner store around 9:00 p.m. I was shaking, but I managed to keep my cool in front of my friend. I didn't need anyone thinking I was a coward on my very first drug transaction.

As two guys strutted toward us from around the corner, I felt the sweat clamming up my palms.

"Waz up?" Glen said.

The first guy reciprocated the greeting and immediately asked to see the goods. Glen then pulled it out.

Something strange happened as Glen pulled out the ounce of weed; these fellas weren't going to pay for it. They snatched the weed out of his hands faster than I could blink and went running back around the corner. What the heck had just happened?

I just stood there with the most dumbfounded look on my face. I didn't know what to do. I'd never been in a fight, never been in a drug deal, and never been jacked. My senses were very much overstimulated.

We watched them jump into a car and take off. Glen got his phone and started talking to someone about what was taking place. Within two minutes, we were being picked up in a truck by two strangers.

"Hop in, boys," said Tom, the older of the two. Clearly he was the boss.

Tom was in his early forties, balding, and he wore years of stress on his face. No doubt every one of his wrinkles had been earned. I could tell he loved Glen, though, and in turn he treated me like a brother. I now find it a little weird that he was hanging out with a couple of fourteen-year-olds, but Glen was a prodigy of sorts; he was capable of stacking dollars. It doesn't surprise me in retrospect that he was treated with the utmost respect even by people much older than him.

Corey was Tom's driver. He was a good-looking chap in his mid-twenties and very talented behind the wheel.

We cruised around for hours, looking for the men who had robbed us. Tom, Corey, and Glen commenced smoking more weed than I had ever seen. Tom and Glen were on the phone nonstop trying to figure out who the thieves were, where they hung out, and even where they lived.

Eventually, we parked in front of one of the guys' house. That's when it dawned on me that I might be in over my head. Back in Grade Three, I had been the one to lead the way; this time Glen had the reins. I was so high that it hurt my head to think about what could happen.

"Let's get them tomorrow, guys," Tom finally said.

Thank God. I would be back in Turner Valley by then and could read in the paper whatever the end result was. I didn't want to be involved.

But God has a funny sense of humour. As we were driving away and I was doing my Hail Marys, Glen pointed at a passing car and yelled, "That's them!"

We did a U-turn over a cement median and gave chase, bombing through roadways, blowing red lights, and even flying into oncoming traffic. Absolute insanity was taking place right before my eyes, but Glen wore the biggest smile I had ever seen.

Finally, Corey got the better of the other driver and cut him off. My heart pounded out of my chest so hard I could hear it as Tom jumped out of the car, baseball bat in hand. He approached the driver's side of the car as the guy inside rolled down the window; maybe he was just trying to save his window from being broken.

I watched as my new friend beat the crap out of these guys with the bat. It turns out they hadn't smoked much of the weed yet, so we got almost the whole supply back.

But most importantly, a message was delivered that night: you don't mess with Glen. He likely wouldn't get jacked again for a long time to come. Word would get around.

What I learned that night is that you don't need to be a killer for people to think you're a killer. Everyone would think Glen was a crazy lunatic when really he had been in the back seat with me the whole time!

Chapter Nine

A FATHER'S LESSON

Age fifteen was a very dark time for me. Criminal charges were falling upon me almost daily, and my mother's rage was growing. I acted out more and more. Rules and laws became but an obstacle.

My dad had recently started a restaurant in Turner Valley, and I cooked and washed dishes for him. He loved me so much, but I seemed incapable of loving him back. In fact, I figured out a way to steal money from my dad's brand-new business venture. I stole thousands of dollars right out from under his nose, even though I knew he was a hard-working man who had struggled for years to make ends meet.

I spent a lot of the money spoiling my friends, buying them gifts and giving them a ton of weed. They in turn would steal it from me, constantly make fun of me, and take advantage of my generosity. I didn't care; I was so desperate for acceptance that I put up with their afflictions.

Later in life, my friends divulged that they hadn't agreed with what I was doing to my father. Even I hated myself for doing this to my dad. I couldn't blame them for looking at me with disgust.

One day, my dad came into the restaurant while I was mid-theft and caught me hiding in the closet. He started to cry as it dawned on him that I was the one killing his business. His own cherished son, inflicting the gravest of wounds.

How could I be capable of hurting my dear dad? My own pain consumed me so much that pushing out the only blood parent who actually loved me was a risk I had needed to take. Otherwise I would have had to live in my own skin, something I couldn't fathom. I felt as though I didn't even deserve a father; he would be better off if I was dead.

Many things happened that summer. My mom kicked me out and I was forced to live at a campground, my access to weed dried up when my father caught me stealing, and my friends kept up a steady flow of insults against me.

One day I purchased a brand-new snowboarding backpack. I loved showing off the way it converted into a seat. I was so unbelievably proud of it. Soon after I bought it, though, I left it at a friend's house. When I retrieved it the next day, it reeked of urine. My friends had pissed in my backpack. I was heartbroken—not because of my attachment to the bag, but because of what it represented.

Pain and anguish consumed my entire life, and living in the campground only made it worse. My seclusion caused my addiction to worsen, but my constant desire for drugs overshadowed much deeper and darker manifestations. I knew if my mom let me come back home, I would be permanently grounded and spend the summer painting her fence, babysitting, and listening to her constant talk, the prospect of which terrified me.

To add to the trauma, my mom got a new boyfriend who had stepped in as my disciplinarian. This man I barely knew would put me over his knee and spank me like a child, with my mother watching. They sometimes even did it in front of my friends. When those punishments didn't thwart me, the boyfriend's punishments got more creative. He would sit me at the kitchen table for the entire night, not letting me sleep, and force me to stay awake the entire next day. Sleep deprivation is a painful punishment; it's one of the ways the authorities extract information out of prisoners at Guantanamo Bay! I screamed bloody murder from the mental anguish and exhaustion, pleading for my mom to wake up and save me from this man. All the while, he sat on my back with his knee pushing my face into the ground when I tried to sleep.

When my screams finally got my mom's attention and she came down to see what all the commotion was about, he just told her to go back to bed.

"Just get him to keep it down," she said on her way back to her room. "Everyone is sleeping."

The campground was better than that.

Finally, my dad offered me a place to stay at his house. The only problem was that my father was completely dependent on my mother for parenting advice. Being the narcissistic personality she was, she thrived on being able to control the situation from afar.

As if things couldn't get any worse, I had another run-in with my father. I don't recall exactly what I did, but it most likely involved stealing again. My father, crushed once again by something his only child had done to him, ran away from me, screaming from the heart-crushing realization that his son was a monster. He dive-bombed into his bed and buried his head in his arms, sobbing. In that moment, I felt more pain than at any other time in my short life. I stood in his bedroom doorway, watching the scene unfold. How could I do this to the only person in the whole world who seemed to love me? I ran back to my bed and cried.

Something happened to me that day. I felt empathy. My dad's heartfelt tears washed my corrupt mind with feelings of love, compassion, and benevolence. That was the last time I ever stole from him.

Although the hands of time would soon prove that there existed in me much darker and more sinister ways to hurt the people I loved. Soon my dad was forced to watch his only son make the slow decline into the pits of hell.

Chapter Ten

KIDS

My buddy James and I were kicked out of Oilfields High School early in Grade Ten, so we started a new school together in Okotoks. The bus would pick me up first in Turner Valley, and I would already be high when James got on the bus in Black Diamond. Every day was funnier than the next; as soon as his head would pop over the seat when he got on the bus, we would gauge how high the other was. We'd laugh as he walked with a grin down the bus aisle.

In a time when I was in an enormous amount of pain, James helped me feel like a person again. But I was probably smoking half an ounce per day, splitting it with my comrade. We shared everything. We hung out during every break and often skipped the whole day to get high and figure out ways to supply our weed habit.

One day we decided to go to a random stranger's door and ring the doorbell. We were going to pretend we were looking for someone specific if someone answered the door. But if someone didn't answer, we would check to see if the door was locked.

When I walked into that unlocked house, I felt something new. It was like having a credit card with no limit. We stepped into the house gazing at everything. I could take some nice wall decor, or some electronics; if a young guy lived there, he probably had some nice gear. And of course we didn't forget to check for a liquor cabinet. My senses were in overdrive.

We soon got kicked out of school for skipping classes. But instead of tapping out, we got home before our parents did that day and erased the messages from the school. We then continued to get on the school bus every day in Turner Valley and get dropped off at the school, even though we didn't go inside. Instead we'd spend the day breaking into houses. This went on for quite a while, at least two months, breaking and entering all day, every day.

James and I left our mark on that poor town.

One night, however, something out of the ordinary happened. We had broken into the Turner Valley town office to see if they kept any beer in the fridge, and that's when we came across the keys for the town's dump trucks. I'd never driven a standard transmission before, but I decided to give this dump truck a try. I may not have been the brightest crayon in the box, but somehow I got it into gear—and almost took out the post office in the process.

Turner Valley is a very small town with only one four-way stop to this very day. When I pulled the truck to a stop and tried to start it again, I blew the clutch.

James and I jumped out. Should we go home? Logic only dictated that James should get a chance to drive. Not to mention that there was a whole cache of keys and trucks at our disposal. So we jumped into another truck and laughed as he drove us out of town.

"What should we do?" I asked with a massive smile on my face.

"Let's go four-by-fouring," he screamed excitedly.

That sounded like a great idea, so we revved up the truck to see what it was capable of. Clearly my partner in crime had more experience behind the wheel than me. There were enough buttons in the truck to overload one's senses, and I was determined to push each and every one.

With country music blasting and rolling down the road at sixty kilometres per hour, one of the buttons I pressed triggered the back of the truck to lift up and dump its load. Dirt poured out over the street as the truck's lights flashed. Talk about a trail of destruction.

After abandoning the truck, we walked to Bailey Hill and started rummaging through cars. In an alley behind the main drag of Bailey Hill, we were blessed to discover a vehicle with the keys still in it. As we reversed out of the owner's driveway, I politely informed my narrow-eyed driver that we were going the wrong way; there was a dead-end ahead of us followed by a seven-foot drop. James didn't respond except to press down harder on the gas pedal. He was in the zone.

I braced myself, pushing my feet against the floor and gripping the handle with all the strength I could muster. I screamed as we flew off the drop and landed on the road. The car must have looked like a mobile teeter-totter as it shifted from front to back and back to front again.

"Oh my God, what the heck just happened?" I asked in shock and dismay.

"We just drove off a cliff, that's what happened."

Since it was nearly four in the morning, we decided to ditch the smoking car and call it a night.

As we were returning from Okotoks, however, the car suddenly broke down. We had to hitchhike home as the sun came up.

What a night! We said our goodbyes and parted ways around six o'clock. For some reason, I held onto the keys and threw them into a deep freeze where I'd stashed the rest of my stolen goods—a mistake I would pay for.

A couple of weeks later, my mother notified the police about all the stolen goods she'd found in the freezer. I was then arrested on a multitude of charges. The cops knew I had an accomplice, but I couldn't bring myself to give up the only friend I had at the time. They put me in jail and offered me deals, and my fifteen-year-old mind really wanted out of jail. But my inner sense of loyalty, respect, and brotherhood kept me from naming James, even if it meant doing time for my crimes alone.

I don't know where that sense of loyalty came from. It certainly wasn't something I learned at home or from my friends who were stealing from me all the time. But I knew I was capable of love; I just hadn't received a ton of it to this point, even though I had given it out in the form of gifts and selfless actions. Maybe staying solid with James would get me the respect I craved.

At least it would allow me to actually look at myself in the mirror.

Chapter Eleven

SUMMER CAMP

Juvenile delinquency landed me in the Calgary Young Offender Centre. The funny thing was, I didn't even realize at first that they were sending me to jail. I thought I was headed for a kind of summer camp for struggling kids. I thought it was weird when I got there and they put me in a holding tank while they processed and admitted me. I thought it was even more strange that all the staff laughed at me when I asked if there was a swimming pool. It didn't dawn on me that I was in prison until they put me in a cell and I heard the lock snap closed behind me.

Oh my God, I'm in jail.

I looked around at my six-by-nine cell and let my surroundings sink into my psyche. There were two beds, one on either side of me. At the back of the room stood a desk. There was no toilet, just a scratched-up plastic sheet of some material for a mirror on the wall, and a big, thick window.

I sat on the desk and looked out the window for hours. I daydreamed about running across the grass, jogging all the way back to Turner Valley. I was sad. My actions showed that I did not belong in society.

I remember going to the recreation yard for the first time. A bunch of Asian kids approached me, and I later found out they were members of a gang. I recall the lead kid taking a disliking to me. He slapped me in the face and the whole yard roared in laughter. My place on the totem pole was cemented that first day. After that, I faced a steady flow of problems: not being able to use the phone, getting beaten for my meals, and more often than not getting punched in the face. I hated prison.

One day, a new kid showed up, Devon, who would play a significant role in my life. He was young, thirteen at the time, and a really good-looking kid with short hair and an infectious laugh. He had been charged with fifty-odd counts of breaking and entering. He was also an addict.

He and I became close over the following months, and one day Devon informed me that he was getting released to enter a long-term drug treatment program, apparently the best of its kind with the highest success rate in the country. It just so happened to be in Calgary. Wow! I both felt sorry for Devon and thought he was lucky, although I knew he needed help. He had told me of his experiences and they more than rivalled my own. I gave him a hug and said goodbye, and I was sad at the prospect that I would probably never see him again.

My mom came to visit me a week before I was supposed to be released on bail. I had a nice visit with my mom, and we agreed that I would stay with her upon my release. As bad as it was with her, I would rather be grounded there than stay in this hellhole.

A psychologist named Peter also came to talk to me, by court order. He asked me a ton of questions, all of which surrounded my childhood, my drug addiction, and my life story. I never said anything to him about my mom or my self-hatred; I thought that bringing these things up would make me look worse, not the other way around. I didn't want my mom to suffer because of me. After all, I thought I was the problem.

When the date of my release arrived, August 15, it turned out that I was first supposed to go talk to a counsellor at the treatment centre Devon had gone to. This caught me out of left field. It was strange to think of myself as a drug addict. I'd only ever smoked weed.

Upon release from prison, my parents took me out for lunch before my so-called meeting at the treatment centre. My parents had said they would bring a T-shirt for me to wear to lunch, since the only clothes I had were the signature blue sweat suit from jail. When my dad passed the shirt to me, I opened the neck to put it over my head and noticed my name was on the inside of the tag. My dad had just told me that it was his own shirt, so I thought this was a little strange.

The other thing I remember about that day is how I felt when I saw my reflection in the mirror. I looked absolutely hideous, with pop marks and blood crust littering my acne-infested face. I hated my appearance, but at least I would be high again soon.

I wasn't that nervous later as I walked into the recovery centre, I wasn't nervous when I was greeted by four large men, and I didn't even lose my cool when they led me into a basement room and sat me down.

But my nerves tweaked when those men told me that I wasn't going to be allowed to leave.

Chapter Twelve

NEW BEGINNINGS

When I was first told I wouldn't be leaving the recovery centre, I felt upset, to say the least. But I didn't pipe up or make a scene, mainly because I was scared that the men would overpower me. That wasn't why those gentlemen were there, however. From the first day I stepped foot in the treatment centre, the staff showed me nothing but compassion, love, and understanding. Although I was scared, I felt safe.

When I entered the group room, I remember seeing clients seated in three rows on either side, separated by gender. The first row was for newcomers, seated in order of how far along they were in the twelve-step program. The second row was reserved for "old-comers," those who were in steps four through seven. In the third row sat the "old-timers," those going through steps eight through twelve.

Those in the first two rows engaged in group therapy sessions together, although they also made time for recreation; the facility was equipped with a full-size hockey rink, a volleyball court, a basketball court, a fitness centre, and a lunch room. We were given a workbook for each respective step, and in order to progress we needed to have the workbook for the current step completed.

The steps were outlined in the book *Alcoholics Anonymous*, otherwise known as the "big book." I remember seeing the steps outlined on a poster hanging on the wall in front of me as I was politely asked to sit in the first chair in the front row. As I sat, I noticed ten guys in the front row with me—none of them had styled hair or wore jewellery, and most had pretty big smiles; I didn't know what they were so happy about.

The second row was a different story. When I looked behind me, I saw a guy I recognized from my assessment interview. He looked great. Although I could see the darkness in the men in the front row, the eyes of the men in the second row radiated freedom.

I was introduced to the group, then stood up, waved, and sat back down. I felt as though everyone was staring at me, and I later found out why. I was the first fresh face they had seen in a long time.

One of the first things I noticed, though, is that Devon was nowhere to be seen. I would later find out he had run away soon after getting there. It looked like I was on my own.

The treatment centre had a specific scent that I'll never forget. Every time I walked into the building, I detected the aura of safety, freedom, and love. A strange euphoric peace came over me as I let the smells take me away, allowing my anxiety to subside. I intuitively knew things were going to be okay.

Slogans adorned the walls in the group room: "First things first," "By the grace of God," "One day at a time," and "Thy will be done." Most people would be put off by such forward God talk, but I was drawn to it.

The second step in the program says that you must come to believe in a power greater than yourself. You might think that my spiritual growth was minimal, considering what I had been through, but I was open-minded. The thought of a higher power stimulated me. I was done being the repulsive human being I'd become. I was willing to believe in God if it meant having even a one in a million shot of feeling better. I was ready to try something different.

After dinner that night, I experienced my first "night rap," a group therapy session run by a peer counsellor who would bring up topics for discussion. For example, we'd discuss times in the past when we'd felt like we had no one left, or times when we'd hurt someone we loved, etc. The list of possibilities was endless. After the topic was declared, a song could play and all the clients would corral in their minds an incident from their past that related to the topic at hand. When the music tapered off, people would raise their hands to speak.

That first night, I left my hand down. I just wanted to listen. I felt gross in my own skin and didn't want anybody to see what I saw in myself.

The rap leader started by choosing the guy who I'd noticed in the second row earlier, the one who had done my intake. As he shared, more hands raised and the group leader called on another client. Eventually, the leader wanted someone from the front row to share something from their life, and he picked a girl who had been sitting near me. She stood with her back against the wall and shared a tragic story about her drug use. As she shared, I looked around to watch everyone listening intently, on the edge of their seats. She began to cry, her tears showing the hardship and pain she had faced.

"What are you feeling right now?" the leader asked.

"Just hurt," she replied as she wept harder.

Everyone raised their hands, eager to support her. It was the most amazing thing I had ever witnessed. The other clients shared benevolence, clemency, condolence, kindness, tenderness, and sorrow for the girl's pain. They rallied to make sure this suffering soul knew she wasn't alone in her battle. My heart ached for her.

At the end, the leader asked everyone to give the newcomers a hug.

Oh man, that's me! I thought, half-expecting everyone to recoil at the idea of giving me a hug. But that's not what happened. Every single guy hugged me, and hugged me tight. My throat hurt from the lump that swelled as each person gripped me and told me they cared about me.

Why was this happening? Why did these guys care so much? Didn't they know I was hideous? Didn't they know I was a monster who hurt the people I loved most at the cost of a wee bit of bliss?

I sat down after all the hugs, overwhelmed with emotion. *They just don't know who I am yet. Wait until they find out who they're being asked to wrap their arms around.*

At the end of the night, I was surprised to learn that we didn't sleep at the centre itself. I was to go to the home of one of the old-comers. When a person got to step four, they got to return home to live with their families again, and take in newcomers. This was mind-blowing.

When I stepped into the old-comer's home, I could feel the bond between the people there. Everyone hugged everyone. People welcomed me, told me I was safe, and squeezed me tight. The lump in my throat had yet to dissipate.

That night, as I lay in an unfamiliar bed, I reflected on how incredible this place was. But I wasn't convinced it would work for a disgusting piece of trash like me. People would see me for who I was soon, and then they would pick on me. They would point out how gross I was.

I brought my hand to my face, tracing my fingers across all the zits and potholes from my years of stress and toxins.

They will see what I see soon, I thought. *I guarantee it.*

Chapter Thirteen

JUST MAYBE

My first week was mostly spent getting use to the structure and customs the program was built around. Step one stated that we had to admit we were powerless over alcohol and our lives had become unmanageable. As the newest member of the pack, I was told that I was the most important person in the room. Not because I was in any way unique, but because I was newest. That first chair in the group room symbolized one's need for love and compassion.

It flabbergasted me that I was receiving so much kind-hearted attention. I wasn't used to the feeling of benevolence. Why did these strangers so badly want to help me find freedom? I was so used to being manipulated that this tenderness was unexplored territory.

A day after getting there, I was pulled for a one-on-one therapy session with my primary peer counsellor, Conner. He was one of the most genuine and gracious people I ever met and it didn't take me long to feel an abundance of love toward him. We sat in his office and talked for at least half an hour. He closed his doors, gauged me for a few seconds, and then asked me how I was feeling. Over time, I opened up to Conner more and more, and to my surprise he didn't recoil. Instead he would lead the session according to his professional opinion, slowly chipping away at the emotional wall that I had put up.

I hadn't cried in years at that point. It was very difficult for me to express emotions since my mom and my so-called friends in Turner Valley had messed with them for so long.

I would get frustrated when Conner brought up the subject of getting to the deeper levels of pain in my life. Conner needed to realize that I wasn't like everyone else. And yet he started to break down the invisible emotional barrier I had built for myself. He helped me to realize that I was capable of feeling love.

Truth be told, it took a while for him to break down that wall. But session by session, I was able to open up and honestly feel and share the pain I had been living with for so long. It was a small start, but it was a start. Maybe, just maybe, this could work.

Friday night was a very important night of the week because the parents would come and sit on one side of the room with all the clients sitting on the other. It was also the night of my first official AA meeting. I remember sitting in a circle with all my fellow brothers and sisters watching a scene that would be replayed hundreds, if not thousands, of times in my lifetime. It started with a moment of silence to remember those who were still suffering. I glanced around at my cohorts and saw that they were all bowing their heads as if in prayer. I followed suit.

Someone was chosen to read a passage that gave me my first opportunity to hear about spirituality and God. I wasn't able to wrap my head around the idea of a greater power. However, the book didn't say the greater power *had* to be God. I thought I might be able to start believing in something greater than myself, but I was getting ahead of myself. I was on step one.

But I related to the passage read that day, and it was hard not to feel bewildered. It started to sink in that I might not be unique in my desperate battle to feel better.

When the AA meeting ended, I was the first one to walk into the dimly lit group room where our families were waiting. A staff member led me past the fifty family members on the left, bringing me to the first chair in the front row. I looked across the room and saw my dad.

The guy sitting beside me reached out to hold my hand. I was little put off at first, but a quick glance around the room reminded me that everyone else was doing it. Not being one to draw attention to myself, I held another man's hand for the first time in my life.

As the clients sat in their respective rows, a man in a suit walked to the front of the room holding a piece of paper. He glanced down at me as he passed, his scent wafting into my nasal cavity and forever imprinting on my memory. His presence commanded attention. Clearly this man, Doc, was the boss.

The depth of Doc's gaze was unlike anything I've ever felt. He scrutinized each one of us, penetrating our expressions. Then his gaze darted to the parents' side of the room. He smiled and nodded at them, as though to say, "Welcome. You are in the right place." He certainly didn't offer them the same intrusive stare we'd gotten. He could say things to you without even opening his mouth.

A smile appeared on his face, he flashed a bit of teeth, and began to speak. His voice was loud and had a poetic cadence. His passion poured out, one sentence after another. He must have been in his fifties, but he moved like he was in his twenties. He didn't skip a beat when he spoke and his tone expressed passion and genuineness.

I decided that I was going to pay attention to this man, and I wasn't short of company; everyone in the room listened intently to him, hanging on to his every word.

Finally, he wrapped up his opener and moved on to the part of the meeting devoted to the subject of "earnings," the time when people who were two or more weeks along in their respective step and had grasped it could request to move on to the subsequent step. He called a name and a boy two seats down from me stood up and walked up to face the audience. He had finished the first substep of step one and had "earned" step 1B. His family stood as well, all wearing smiles although I could tell they were pained, masking a hurt that had clearly been years in the making. But there was also pride in their eyes as they stared intently at their son.

Doc informed the boy that he had a long road ahead but that he should be proud of himself. He was absolutely certain there wasn't a kid in the room who couldn't be helped.

I wondered if he would still think that way after he'd gotten to know me a bit.

I was grateful that I wouldn't have to stand up there for at least a couple of weeks. It scared me to think I would have to stand in front of everyone and have that entire room looking at me. I pictured myself nervously rocking from foot to foot, standing across from my disappointed parents and letting what may as well have been the whole world see what a disgrace I was. Sweat stains would begin to form as the lump in my throat returned. People would whisper to each other, possibly about my acne.

It made me want to vomit.

Doc went on to go through all the earnings that week. As he got further along, his smiles grew bigger and his attitude became more jovial. I couldn't help but feel a brief sense of hope. I would do anything to share the love these people appeared to have for one another.

I turned around and stared at the twelve steps listed on the wall.

What if?

Those two words played over and over in my mind. I needed to feel better. I hadn't felt content in a long time, and seeing Doc and the love in the room made me feel good. Maybe I didn't need to get high anymore.

Just maybe.

Chapter Fourteen

HAPPY DESTINY

The next few weeks were filled with trial and error. The centre's rules were difficult to follow, and all of them were in place to protect me from myself. I wasn't allowed to talk to anyone else in the first row unless I first asked someone from the two rows behind us to listen in. I also had to have an old-comer or staff member shadow me absolutely everywhere I went. So if I needed to go to the bathroom, I had to ask someone to take me.

One thing that was made abundantly clear was that I no longer led the pack. In fact, it had been a long time since I'd led the pack anywhere. I was so destroyed inside that I was incapable of asserting dominance. I walked around the treatment centre with my shoulders tucked in, my head hung low, and I avoided eye contact wherever I could. If I was standing still, I'd have my hands in my pockets and my shoulders to the wall, a shell of the extroverted personality I had once been.

After my first couple of weeks, I faced my first stool presentation. The way this worked is that on each Friday, the old-comers decided whether each newcomer had demonstrated their step through their actions the previous week. They also discussed the likelihood of that newcomer being able to express enough knowledge and discernment to move on to the next step. Then each newcomer would come in, sit on a big stool in the front of the room, face the group, and divulge their soul.

My first stool presentation wasn't supposed to be that hard. They hadn't let me wear shoes for the first couple of weeks because I had come from jail and was likely to run away given the first opportunity. Since my parents had signed me in, I wasn't allowed to leave. So I was under the impression that at my first stool presentation, to earn step IA, I could have my shoes back.

While I was doing my stool presentation, which was run by peer counsellor Aaron, I remember staring shyly at all my new brothers and sisters. Aaron was a heavyset blonde man and his laugh captivated everyone. He wore his five years of sobriety on his sleeve, and I could see the freedom in his eyes from a mile away. Tenderness adorned his compassionate face, making it easier for me to make a small connection with him. I couldn't tell if he cared about me the same as my own peer counsellor, Conner, but he certainly appeared to have some level of affection toward me.

At the end of my presentation, Aaron proclaimed that there was to be a change to my treatment plan. He said that Conner would no longer be my peer counsellor.

The words hit me like an iron bar to the throat. For the first time in years, I began to cry. Tears streamed down my face as I looked upon my cohorts. Aaron's face was filled with wonder and compassion as he assessed the broken boy before him. My heart beat loudly in my ears. I was a monster and didn't deserve to be loved. I had known this place was too good to be true.

"What are you feeling, Cody?" Aaron asked.

The words pummelled my damaged heart, his tenderness striking home.

"I don't want to lose Conner," I said, barely able to form the words my heart was yearning to convey. In that moment, I felt as if the world stood still.

I think back to that day and remember clearly the look on Aaron's face. He realized that he was looking at a very damaged young man.

"It's going to be okay," he said.

He then picked a raised hand in my group, and a boy began to share about how much he cared for me. Then I started to see other hands begin to rise. Slowly, the whole room had their hands raised.

"Look around, Cody," Aaron said. "People care about you."

I looked around at all my brothers and sisters with a tear-stained complexion. I felt love, peace, and tenderness for the first time in a very long while.

Aaron closed by informing me that he would now be my primary peer counsellor, with Conner taking the role of my clinical counsellor. I wasn't going to lose Conner at all.

Gratitude and benevolence warmed my beating chest. In a split second, I had gone from losing someone I loved to finding someone new who cared for me immensely. The day ended with every guy in the room embracing me as a brother. I looked to the future, trudging the road to a happy destiny.

Chapter Fifteen

NEVERLAND

The compassion I felt from my group grew on a daily basis, but my insides made me want to throw up every time I heard someone tell me they cared. My guts stirred like a witch's cauldron smouldering with steam that reeked of corruption. I wanted so badly for people to see that I loved them in return, that there was more to me than the animal inside, but I struggled to convey how I felt.

I never brought up what my mother had done to me. I still wasn't able to decipher the pain she'd bestowed on me, not at my young age. In fact, she had manipulated me for so long and so deeply that I actually yearned for my cruel mother's arms.

Most of the time I sat in silence while counsellors tried to get me to participate in group therapy. They dug from every angle, trying to help me find a way to release my pent-up pain, but there seemed to be no way to penetrate the emotional barrier I had created. I fought and fought, almost as if my subconscious mind wouldn't allow me to dig that deep.

Yet somehow the whole experience became so frustrating that Turner Valley didn't look so bad anymore. I seized the next opportunity I could to escape from the emotional justice that was treatment.

One Saturday morning, my old-comer left me in the bedroom by myself to shower and get ready for the day. Jumping on the opportunity, I managed to manoeuvre myself through the chained window and onto the roof of the house. This was the easy part. I looked down to the ground and paused. I had jumped off fences nearly this high as a five-year-old, so I decided this ten-foot drop would be fine. I hit the ground with the grace of a cat, and in one smooth motion sprang back up into a trot. I had no shoes, no shirt, and no problems.

About halfway down the alley, I stopped. This was the first time I had been free since going to jail. I spread my arms and looked up at the sun, my half-naked body cooling from the biting chill of October wind. I sucked the chilly breeze into my mouth, closed my eyes, and let adrenaline warm my body. I focused on what needed to be done.

I needed shoes. There was a Walmart across the highway from the neighbourhood I was escaping from, so I skipped across the road shoeless, wearing only an undershirt to keep me warm. I think about what that must have looked like to someone driving by. If I had seen that now, I would have to conclude that it was exactly what it was—an escape of some kind.

Imagine you're a Walmart greeter saying hello to all the lovely Saturday shoppers. It's beautiful outside and you expect it to be a busy day. People are very kind to you. Then something catches your eye—a half-naked, shoeless young man hurrying through the doors.

"Excuse me, ma'am," the young man asks. "Can you tell me where your shoe department is?"

Three minutes later, that same young man waves goodbye, still half-naked but at least wearing a pair of shoes. As you watch him disappear into the parking lot, something holds you back from calling security. That young man looked very dark, and you make the educated decision not to add to his despair by getting him arrested for a fifteen-dollar pair of shoes.

My heart didn't skip a beat as I walked back across the parking lot—unafraid, calm, collected, and methodical—and approached the highway to hitchhike home. The winter breeze chilled my exposed thumb as I hooked it on the side of the highway. Before too long, a lady pulled over and picked me up. She was older, sweet, and kind, but confused by my appearance. Nonetheless, she dropped me off and gave me a collared dress shirt to go with my sweatpants. I wasn't sure if that made me look better or worse, but I didn't care.

I had one thing on my mind: I needed to get high.

I showed up at a buddy's house in Turner Valley, and to my delight the boys had some weed. They gave me the honours as I lit the joint up. Euphoric bliss was once again mine. The shame I felt slipped away. I lay my head back on the couch and closed my eyes, losing myself in dreamland as rushes of ecstasy consumed me. For the first time in a while, I was content. The ugliness faded to black and I was at peace.

Take me to Neverland, Peter Pan. And if God will it, never make me go back.

Unfortunately, God didn't will me to stay in Neverland. After all, what goes up must come down. I crashed hard. Something happened to my mind and body that had never happened to me before. When I came down, the mental and emotional anguish was excruciating. All I could think about was how much I hated myself.

What was I doing? Where would I go next? Why had I run?

This was the first time in my life I had gotten high while knowing about another solution to achieving happiness and freedom. It devoured my thoughts and made my pain twice as bad.

I need to get high again, to escape the pain—and then I needed to stay high.

Somehow I ended up at my childhood friend's house. While chatting and reminiscing, we heard a knock at the door. It was an authoritative knock; anyone who has ever heard the police knock on your door will know exactly what I'm talking about.

I don't know how they found me, but they had and they were going to take me away—not in handcuffs, at least. I had dealt with a lot of RCMP at this point and I could tell these officers felt for me. They handled me softly as they escorted me to the detachment and informed me that someone would be picking me up shortly. Instead of a cell, they placed me in a room with a comfortable chair.

As I sat there, I started to cry. Why did I keep hurting myself like this? This was my doing, and I had no one to blame but myself.

Suddenly, a peer counsellor walked into the room. She looked at me with tenderness. The scolding I had braced myself for never came to pass. I could tell she knew she was looking at a young boy in the midst of a painful detox.

I never stood up, and she didn't make a move toward me. The hands of time stood still.

"How are you doing, Cody?" she asked.

Her words brought back the familiar lump in my throat. I felt so ashamed. I had once again hurt the people I loved most. What was wrong with me?

Chapter Sixteen

UNREACHABLE

Back at the centre, I sat once again in the first chair. My parents sat across the room from me; they had also been shifted back to the first chairs in their row, my humiliation being passed on to them. I was putting my family through hell.

My mother looked the least impressed, her eyes scolding me from across the room. She made certain that I knew the pain I had caused her—pain I had caused her ever since I'd been that precious child. I was a gift from the devil himself, sent to the world to make her life a living hell. She was like Doc, able to tell you things without opening her mouth: "You stupid kid. Doesn't it occur to you that my life is on hold right now?"

My father's eyes evidenced a much different disposition. He wore his pain in his hurting expression. I read it as hopelessness. I felt that my dad was giving up on me. But I knew my mother very well and could almost guarantee that she was manipulating the way he viewed me. She had been making me seem like hopeless garbage ever since I was very young.

She was claiming her place as the biggest victim of my thoughtless actions, pushing herself to the top of the totem pole. As long as I kept thinking I was a bad boy and that she was the only person who wasn't bailing on me, her place would be secure. She focused entirely on my addiction, because if my addiction stood prominent then everything she'd done to me would remain overshadowed.

Indeed, my mom was praised around the centre for her strength, allowing her to bask in what narcissists desire most: recognition. This cemented her malevolent plan for my future.

It occurs to me now that this wasn't an inexpensive treatment centre, and it wasn't funded by the government, so it shouldn't have made sense why my mom would put her life on hold given her selfish actions in the past. But I realize now that she wasn't paying to get her son back; she was paying to rationalize her corrupted take on the situation. I think she felt that if I didn't stay sober, she could justifiably push me away and still look like a hero. Because she did indeed look like a hero to everyone at the treatment centre. But all she was doing was methodically weeding me out of her life. I was the only reminder of the poor and desperate life she had traded for riches and a good reputation.

I was pleading with her from across the room with tearful eyes, hoping against hope that she would come to my rescue and be my mom.

It didn't happen.

Suddenly, the door at the back of the room opened and Devon walked in, wearing newcomer clothes. My friend from jail had lasted a lot longer than I had on the run, but here he was again, joining the circle. As I gave him a welcome nod, he wore such a mischievous smile. I loved it. He always looked like he was up to something.

He and I displayed many antisocial traits as we teamed up, struggling to make much progress through the program. Other clients began to come and go, passing us in our stunted treatment. Our families forever bonded on the other side of the room, as they, too, were passed by newer families.

Devon's parents and sister were beautiful people, and they treated me with fondness. I was usually the kid other parents didn't want their children to hang out with, so this was a nice change. In the meantime, Devon's and my friendship blossomed into something much more meaningful, and over time it even became healthy. We rooted, supported, and constructively criticized each other. We fought the good fight together. He became my rock, and I in turn became his.

I felt love for Devon. True, unconditional, compassionate love. We carried each other's pain in times of sorrow and always had each other's back in group. I trusted him more than I had trusted anyone else. He had never once wronged me, and he'd taught me the true meaning of friendship and brotherhood.

After five months of treatment, we finally arrived together at step IC, a process that usually takes clients just five weeks. It was because we were initially incapacitated by our youthful trauma. His revolved around getting involved with drugs at the exceptionally young age of seven; he had been using hard drugs by the age of twelve. My trauma, on the other hand, had to do with my mother. Although different, these traumas had stunted our growth, hindering our ability to reach the required honesty needed to reach the point of surrender.

We were both very sick.

When a person goes through their IC stool presentation, they are seeking to earn the entirety of step one. If they don't get it, they need to wait another week to ask again.

Most people need to ask two or three times. Devon and I, however, asked thirteen times each, the most in the centre's history. We sat side by side to the bitter end.

Devon never shed one tear while trying to earn step one, and neither did I. It seemed the only thing that could make me cry was when I thought about how ugly I felt. And I had to focus on myself as I worked with staff to round out step one, slowly but surely facing deeper levels of honesty.

I realize now that my struggle didn't so much lie with looking at myself and my addiction honestly as it did with working through my mother's manipulation and not seeing her as the reason I couldn't seem to *feel* anything. The truth is I was never taught compassion or empathy from my mother. Instead she taught me to hate and how to take advantage of people. I had listened to her intently and hunkered down through her countless hours of psychological, emotional, and physical abuse. At this point, I was only a handful of manipulations away from saying goodbye to my feelings forever.

Those feelings were still inside me somewhere, however, and one fateful night Doc brought them out of me like a nuclear explosion.

On a Friday night open meeting in front of the families, Devon and I settled into our seats—the last seats in the front row. It had been a long journey for both of us, for we had been in the front row for nine whole months, the same amount of time it took many clients to finish all twelve steps.

On this evening, Doc was being Doc, the charismatic and benevolent personality he was. He worked down the row, from newer clients to older ones. I eagerly kept my hand raised throughout the evening, even when others were sharing. It was a sign of willingness to get better and do anything to get there.

The hours wore on, as they always did. The clock usually ticked past midnight by the time we got to the deepest part of the session.

Finally, Doc called on me. I stood against the wall and began to share an incident from my past. I don't remember the specific one, but I recall that my head hung low as I spoke; it always did when I was trying to push past my emotional barrier. But Doc told me to look up at my family. I glanced up and saw my mom, my dad, and my sister.

"What do you see, son?" he asked.

"I see my family. They look like they're hurting."

Doc's voice was low and deep. "They're *here*. How do you feel?"

"Hurt."

Everyone in the room was on the edge of their seats, the silence making the noise in my head seem as loud as a trumpet. It was deafening.

"Now look up, Cody," Doc said. I slowly tilted my head upward. "You feel ugly."

Those words landed on me like a cement blanket. I glanced again at the crowd, almost as if I wished they hadn't heard them. But they had.

My head hung low again as I tried to make myself feel the honest, gut-wrenching pain. I felt like I was losing it, that it was getting away from me.

"Look up, Cody," he whispered.

I did as instructed, and immediately made eye contact with my baby brother, his innocent little face staring at me with compassion and empathy. His look of concern hit home, and all the darkness inside me rose to the surface. I cried out in pain.

The staff rushed my brother out of the room. I sobbed loudly, thinking about my siblings and the damage I had caused. My little brother's expression was seared into my mind.

"How does it feel, Cody?" Doc asked, pushing further.

The pain almost brought me to my knees and I screamed at the top of my lungs. The crowd was dead silent.

"How does it feel to be a drug addict, Cody?"

"It hurts." I could barely form the words.

Doc took a step back and made eye contact with my parents. "That's why your son does drugs," he said matter-of-factly, referring to my unmasked pain.

I glanced up through my tear-soaked vision and saw the looks of anguish on my family's faces. I could see that they wanted to save me.

"This is why your kids do drugs, everybody," Doc said, addressing the whole room. "It's their way of dealing with the depth of pain this young man is showing you." He turned to me again. "How do you feel, son?"

In that moment, a wash of peace flooded over me like a tidal wave. My tears and hiccups subsided and transitioned into deep breathing. The tears transitioned into clarity. The pain transitioned into surrender.

For the very first time since I was young, I felt happy. Truly happy. A smile spread across my face.

"I'm an alcoholic," I said.

"And how does that feel, Cody?" When I looked into Doc's eyes, I saw an uncontrollable, uncontainable fire. "Tell us how that feels."

The smile on my face grew larger. "I'm okay with it."

"This is why we go to war with your kids' addictions every day here," Doc said.

He then chose Devon to give some feedback. When my thirteen-year-old friend got to his feet, he bowed his head silently.

After a few seconds, Doc broke the quiet. "What are you feeling, Devon?"

Devon had been struggling even more than me with getting to deeper levels of honesty, so what happened next caught everyone in the room, including myself, off-guard. He raised his head, and in his eyes I saw tears. He struggled to form words as he said that he loved me and that he was proud of me.

My heart swelled as our brotherhood became cemented in time, a brotherhood between two kids who were supposedly incapable of experiencing emotions.

That night, I hugged him tight—tighter than I'd hugged anyone else in my life. I loved him.

I surrendered to my disease that night. My alcohol and drug addiction no longer controlled my life. I heard the paradox ring loudly in my head: only through complete surrender can you rise victorious.

During the closing song, Doc stood in the middle of the room with the parents and clients all holding hands. He had accomplished that night what doctors, psychiatrists, and psychologists sometimes go through their entire careers without achieving. He held his head high, and I saw the pride in his expression. This man lived to save kids. He did it every day—sometimes quickly, sometimes slowly—but he kept grinding away, going to war across enemy lines to battle the darkest of demons. This man thrived on being a soldier for God, and I was left speechless.

Chapter Seventeen

HOMECOMING

Step two states you must come to believe that a power greater than yourself can restore you to sanity. Note that this step doesn't specify God, and for me, at this point in my life, my higher power became Doc, Conner, Aaron, and the rest of my group. But looking back, I've come to the understanding that far greater powers were at work the night when I made my breakthrough. The fact that Doc had helped us so much to feel honestly the tragedy of our lives tells me that he had some hard-hitting angels behind him.

It was nice not feeling like the centre of attention anymore. The focus for me now lay in putting to action my process of growth. I had to build a solid foundation for myself to stand upon.

Step two went by without a hiccup, and so did step three.

Except that I can say now that I didn't really grasp step three at the time. It says that a person must turn their will and life over to the care of God, however they understand Him. I was so focused on God's will that I never fully developed a relationship with God. I never said it out loud, but I didn't actually believe in God. It didn't make sense to me that there could have been someone watching over me through the tragedy of my life.

No, I didn't believe in God. I just did and said the things that I thought would make the staff and everyone else happy.

One day while I was in group, Aaron pulled me out of rap. We sat down in his office and I could tell he had something serious to tell me.

"Devon ran away this morning," he said. "During chores. That's why he wasn't in group today."

For some reason, it was hard for me not to take it personally. Devon was the best friend I'd ever had, and it hurt a lot that Devon had left. But I didn't deal honestly with the pain, because the anguish I felt from Devon leaving directly correlated to the pain I had yet to talk about regarding the abandonment issues I had from my mother.

So I acted as if it didn't hurt at all.

I was going home soon. Once I earned step four, I would be able to return to my family and begin my life as an old-comer, taking newer kids into my home. I would be the one kids asked when they needed to go to the bathroom. I would also carry more responsibility in the form of doing chores, helping lead raps, and becoming a beacon of hope for the kid on the first chair.

I was over-the-moon excited. This would be a position of love and respect, all I'd ever wanted in life. I was becoming a man, a good man, and I was truly happy.

But I wasn't working the steps properly or for the right reasons. I was working the steps so that people would like me and look up to me. I didn't go to the deeper meaning of each step, instead staying near the surface.

Still, in the process I developed an enormous number of meaningful relationships.

But the night I went home for the first time, I felt the consequences of my choice to work the steps only on a surface level. Life came crashing down on me.

When kids get sent home, after earning step four at an opening meeting, it's always a surprise for the parents. They have a general idea of approximately what week it's going to happen, but they don't know for sure. Doc would take every opportunity to help change a kid's life for the better, so parents wouldn't find out until the Friday night in question. At this point in the process, clients were intentionally kept in suspense. Doc lived for those moments.

I can't remember what crazy scheme the group came up with to maintain the secret that I was able to be sent home, but I'll never forget the looks on my family's faces when they were told. My dad had on a wide smile as he stood up to embrace his homecoming son. His cheek pressed against mine and I felt his tears mingle with my own. Those are the most meaningful hugs, when your cheeks are pressed together.

Then I hugged my sister. She was crying as my young siblings came screaming out of the back of the group room. I went down to my knees and scooped them up in my arms.

A song began to play as the staff wheeled out massive chairs for our whole family to sit in at the front of the room. This was the first time since being there that I didn't mind being the centre of attention.

I could tell that my mom relished every moment of this. She was the star of the show. She had made it, finally made it. As a single mom with four kids, everybody looked at her in awe. The funny thing is, I think my mom got more feedback than I did that night. She truly looked like the hero in everyone's eyes.

She was the hero in my eyes, too. I was so proud to give her that moment. For me, it was more about her getting her son back than it was about me going home. She was the one who had been forced to sit waiting for her kid to get his act together for the last eleven months, suffering the humiliation of having other, newer parents pass her over and over again. On this night, she was finally in her glory, being recognized for being such a strong mom. A narcissist's dream.

Driving out to Turner Valley with my family after being away for almost a year was surreal. It brought back many memories—some good, some bad. I remember seeing the sign for my dad's restaurant as we rolled into town, driving home the fact that these were my stomping grounds.

As I walked into the house, my memories took the place of better judgment and common sense. I remember the battle starting in my head as I checked out my house, my mom proudly displaying to me how she had converted the house into a host home.

It felt good to be back, but being in my old environment brought back a sense of lost power. I had been grounded here for years straight, so I remembered the feeling of not being allowed to leave. With it, I felt the old urge to sneak out. I had sneaking out down to a science.

I didn't have the urge to do drugs, but I had the urge to see my old friends.

That night, my heart didn't skip a beat as I creeped out my bedroom window. It was exhilarating to emerge into the warm summer air. Turner Valley was my oyster.

What did I want to do? I really wanted a cigarette. I crept across the street to see if my friend Taylor was awake. I knocked quietly on his window, hoping against hope that he would be up. He wasn't, but his mom was.

Busted.

I calmly explained that my treatment centre had let me out at three o'clock in the morning to find a smoke. It must have been the stupidest thing to ever come out of my mouth.

But the damage was done, so I decided that I may as well find a cigarette and enjoy my last hurrah.

Déjà vu came over me as I skulked through the alleys of Turner Valley. I thought about trying to get high, but I already knew the gig was up. And I still remembered how clouded my mind had gotten after I'd taken marijuana while running away the previous October.

I was in damage control mode, but I didn't think a cigarette would make my punishment worse; after all, I already snuck out on the day of my homecoming.

Thinking about what I would have to face the next day was crippling. What the hell was wrong with me? It was like I couldn't wrap my head around long-term consequences, or even short-term ones. I was the instant gratification type, something that has handicapped me on more than one occasion.

I rummaged through some cars and soon found the cigarette I was looking for. As I lit it up, I closed my eyes, hoping to feel something close to a weed high. Instead it just made me sick.

I went back to my house and snuck into my room. Maybe Taylor's mom wouldn't rat me out. It was all I could hope for.

The next morning, I woke up to find Aaron in my room with me. I knew what was happening before he even opened his mouth. I walked out of the house, past my family at the kitchen table, and out to Aaron's waiting car.

It was time to start over again.

Chapter Eighteen

GOD'S WILL

S o once again I was sitting in the first chair. Devon had been caught, too, and he was sitting right beside me. I was ashamed of myself. Everyone who walked in and saw us that Saturday morning wore a different look of calamity; they all expressed the same disappointment, however. I felt like a failure. Once again I had pushed away the people who were trying to get close to me. I didn't understand my own thinking. I couldn't make sense of why I kept doing this to myself. Why was I so selfish?

When Conner entered, I could tell he was upset. As I approached him, though, I saw that something else was wrong. We walked silently down the stairs to the staff offices, then stepped into his office and closed the door. My stomach began to flip. He looked so sad, and I knew he was trying to figure out how to tell me something important.

"How was your little excursion last night?" he finally asked.

"Sh*tty."

That was literally the best I could come up with. I hated saying using that word—it was so vague. I wanted to snap my own neck every time I said it.

"Cody, your dad has decided to leave treatment."

The words hit me like a smack to the face. My father had finally given up on me. And how could he not? I had shown him over and over again that I was incapable of putting myself in others people's shoes to consider their perspective. My sole focus was me. Nothing else seemed to matter.

I didn't understand it, but the reason was that had an inability to feel empathy. My mother had robbed me of the ability to feel love, compassion, or empathy in a normal way. When I had the opportunity to consider the consequences of my actions, I never followed through.

And now my dad was gone.

Conner sent me back to group after a short chat, where I just sat down and recoiled into my quicksand-like thinking.

Step three had asked me to turn my will and life over to the care of God. At that point, I had needed to make the choice to commit to following God's will. Well, what would God do? I had to ask myself that question in every situation I was in. I needed to start checking the motives and outcomes of every decision I made, hundreds of times a day.

I was stunted, but very intelligent, and the AA program taught me a lot about emotion and how we can develop our relationships with each other by simply doing what God would do.

Going forward, I became an advocate for following God's will. When I faced a problem, instead of relying on primal instinct I decided to check my motive, adjust, adapt, evolve, and then proceed. I wouldn't look at struggles as setbacks, but instead see them as opportunities to develop my thinking and grow. And every time I conquered something, I would learn more about emotion and carry that with me. I would even teach people who struggled in similar situations and help them to grow. I wanted to be a good person.

I cruised back through treatment, achieving each step in the minimum amount of time. I consistently questioned my actions and in turn developed significant relationships.

Devon moved along as well. It was almost as if our thinking was in sync.

I went through step four again, taking a fearless moral inventory of myself. For a guy who had endured as much as I had, my list of resentments wasn't that long. I don't know where it came from, but I was a man of forgiveness. I didn't hold grudges. It was hard to identify my worst resentments, because I had lost all anger toward those who had wronged me. The main reason might be that I was so lonely from pushing people away that I hated it when anyone was upset with me. I was widely known as a people-pleaser. If someone was upset with me, I would go miles out of my way to make it right, even putting myself in discomfort.

However, the list of people I had harmed was rather long. Most of this was the result of me not thinking through the consequences of my actions. I felt bad about the things I'd done, but it was more about objectively knowing I shouldn't have done those things. If an action didn't cause myself or another person anguish, I didn't feel remorse—even though I knew those actions were wrong, too.

Step five was a big one: I had to admit to God and to myself the exact nature of my wrongs. I sat down with Conner and Aaron and divulged all the horrible things I could think of having done. But I still didn't bring up my mother. I still thought bringing up her actions would only make me look worse. I didn't realize how much freedom I would gain from disclosing these closely guarded secrets.

Still, I received a profound amount of freedom in step five. Releasing the pain that constricted my defective heart, I started to think like a human being. The process helped me get in touch with the withering strings of my emotions. My feelings were minor and small, but they were there. Only time would tell how many of them I'd be able to bring to the surface.

Although I may never be able to feel like a normal person, treatment saved me from the dark and sinister path along which I was trudging.

I was sick of being a weak, broken boy, so I kept trudging the road to my happy destiny, all the while completing the steps. Life gradually became meaningful, sobriety paramount. I desperately fought to be whole again. I felt that I finally had an answer to the void drugs and alcohol had filled for so many years: God's will.

Despite my constant teachings about God's will, I had yet to fully develop a conception of God. I was taking actions, but they were merely objective actions to my subjective thoughts. I didn't have a relationship with God outside of what I thought was His will. The step about turning my will and life over to Him continued to elude me. In fact, I completed treatment without ever making that connection.

I consistently told people that if I kept doing the right things, everything would work out. I wasn't too far off, because doing the right things did get me where I wanted to be emotionally. But as treatment taught me, without God you leave a massive gap for fear to creep back in.

I will never forget my graduation night. My family, minus my dad, all stood proudly on the podium with big smiles on their faces. They were beacons of strength. Devon spoke at my grad, speaking fondly of our bond. I loved him so much.

Afterward, I was elected to speak at four other people's graduations as a peer. Most grads went on to speak at one or two other graduations. My many invitations to speak for other people spoke highly of the impact I'd made on them. I was loved, a pillar of strength to those I had helped, a far cry from the shell of a human being I'd been when I walked in.

Treatment saved me in more ways than I could possibly comprehend. The teachings of AA and its twelve steps pumped life back into my soul. I now had a reason for being: help the still-suffering alcoholic and live in the divine paradox of giving away what you have in order to keep it.

After I graduated, I once again became secluded from my peers. I returned to school, although my experience this time was very different. I walked around with my head held high, proud of my accomplishments and content with myself. I met girlfriends and made new friends.

But these relationships were different from the attachments I'd forged in treatment. They held less meaning to me, because it was hard for me to understand people whom I hadn't watched divulge their souls. Now I had to interpret what people were thinking and feeling. It was difficult to read people in the real world, but I knew I would likely enjoy favourable outcomes if I continued to do God's will.

I worked for my dad at his restaurant on the weekends. I'd been cooking and eating there since he had started it five years prior, so I was good with a skillet. The cooking line became my domain for mindless peace. I also worked at the hotel in town every night—except Thursdays, when I hit the local AA meeting. My life was structured and content.

My mother helped me get a car. I was to pay $200 every month to rent my car, and I had to pay my own insurance, which was another $300 a month, plus gas. I was working six days a week at two different jobs, so it was hard, but the car would help me get to the treatment centre as often as possible, allowing me to give back and see my sober cohorts. To me, it was worth every penny.

On top of my two jobs, I had a busy schedule at school, trying to catch up from all the time I had missed. Although everyone else my age was in Grade Twelve, I was in Grade Ten. I worked until midnight every evening to pay off the car, for without it I would surely lose the connections I had built, so I was tired a lot. I struggled to jolt out of bed in the morning.

After about eight months of being graduated and sober, and after turning eighteen, my mom's patience with me sleeping through my alarm finally ran thin. Since I was "of age," she kicked me out of the house. By secluding me from my family, I think she was trying to propel me back toward a state of perfection.

I once read about a scientific study that looked at a large group of rats. As part of the experiment, half of the subjects were isolated and the other half were socialized. In addition, the subjects were all given an unlimited supply of heroin. The test would see how severe the rats' heroin addictions became, comparing the socialized rates to the isolated ones. The obvious hypothesis was that the isolated subjects would develop stronger addictions, and this proved correct. The socialized rats were more content, more fulfilled, and in general happier rodents given their capacity to connect with one another. The isolated rats, on the other hand, depended on heroin for their only means of self-fulfillment; they became agitated, restless, and irritable when their heroin supplies ran low.

Interestingly, the researchers found that once the isolated rats were integrated back into the social rat population, their need for heroin dramatically declined.

What this study tells us is that human connection is the key to happiness. If we aren't loved and cherished, we rely on substances to fill the gratification void. This results in extreme self-hate.

My mother's isolation of me from my family, along with my inclination to blame myself, led to my condition getting worse. I lost all the connections I'd made, and my mom even took away the car, my only means of maintaining those connections.

Soon after getting kicked out of the house, I relapsed in a moment of hopelessness and despair. During this period, I was introduced to the drug that would in time become my only companion, my only reason for living: cocaine.

Chapter Nineteen

GARBAGE

About four months after my mom kicked me out, I once again sat in her house. I had stayed sober the whole time. She probably let me back in because of how ridiculous she'd looked for kicking me out over the issue of sleeping in. Her position on the pedestal as greatest mom had been threatened when I'd need to go asking the families of other graduates clients if I could stay with them. My mom needed that glory. It's what she lived for.

I sat at the kitchen table with a bottle of booze in front of me alongside a shot glass full of spiced rum. I stared intently at the glass, having a hard time pushing myself to take the drink.

When people relapse, the usual goal is to get drunk. But I wasn't looking to get wasted this night. I had one purpose: I *needed* to relapse—not for the bliss of being wasted but for the comfort and peace of mind of knowing I would be relapsed, so I could go out tomorrow and get higher than I'd ever been in my life. By taking the fateful plunge, I would have pot-committed myself. I just needed to take one shot. After that, it wouldn't matter what happened. I wouldn't be able to turn back the hands of time.

My hands were sweating, my heart beating loudly in my ears, as I eyed the glass. I craved the release I could get from pushing myself back to not caring about consequences. My mom had shoved my addiction problem so far down my throat that I had myself convinced that I could blame all my problems on being an addict. I had the perfect excuse to be reckless and go back to the worry-free creeper life I'd once had.

The pain I felt was intense. All life stood still as I locked my gaze on this drink.

All you have to do is one shot. Then you'll be relapsed, Cody.

No longer constrained to God's will, I knew that I might hurt when I came down—but I didn't want to think about that. I wanted to think about how good it would feel not to care for a few minutes. A couple of minutes of complete and utter bliss in exchange for a lifetime of sorrow.

Why did it sound so worth it to me? Was I in that much pain? Yes, I was. I wanted to die. I wanted blackness.

Don't you remember what it's like to get high, Cody? Don't you remember how good you felt?

I was also tempted to try cocaine. I'd heard so many stories about it in treatment. Yeah, those stories had ended badly, but...

How you think those people felt when they were able to forget everything for a few minutes? They felt amazing, Cody. Don't you want that? Aren't you sick of caring so much? Wasn't life easier when you gave zero cares?

One thing was holding me back. I knew I would end up hurting by this decision.

I thought about my mom, how I could never make her happy. It was hard to think of anyone else outside my mother, because she had made herself so prominent in my life. I didn't think of my dad, of my siblings, or anyone else. Just my mom and how I didn't want to displease her. She had been through enough at my hand, hadn't she? And she had just taken me back. Was I going to disappoint my poor mother again?

After you relapse, you don't have a mom anymore. You'll be left alone, because she'll make sure everyone you love stays away from you.

But I couldn't be as perfect as she needs me to be. I wasn't capable of perfection. So what was I staying sober for? I couldn't live up to her impossible expectations. She would kick me out soon enough, sober or not. I couldn't win. I didn't think I deserved a family. I didn't think I deserved to be loved.

You're a monster, Cody! You deserve the most excruciating pain. Why would your mom love you? Why would anybody love you? You just disappoint and disgust everyone you love. You're garbage.

Tears streamed down my face as I gripped the shot glass. One time. That's all it would take.

Nobody loves you. You're garbage.

The thoughts seemed to be whispered in my ear. I could smell the rum spilled on my hand. My eyes were blurry with tears and fog. So much devastation would be left in my wake if I woke the beast—the beast that didn't care, that had no remorse, no compassion, no love.

Do you know what you're doing, Cody?

I need the pain to stop!

I jumped to my feet and let out a crippling scream, shrieking as loudly as my lungs would let me. The strength it took to do it paralyzed me and I fell back into my chair. I looked up at the ceiling through blurry vision, tears flowing down the tracks on my cheeks. My arms dangled lifelessly. My head lolled back as I let out painful sobs.

No one loves you Cody. Quit torturing yourself and just end the pain. You're garbage, sober or not. Damned if you do, damned if you don't. You may as well feel better, even if it's just for a second.

With that thought, I raised my arm, tilted my head back, and took the shot of spiced rum.

There you go, buddy. Doesn't that feel better?

PART
II

Chapter Twenty

FORKS

When you look back at your life and see all the forks in the road, how often do you find a decision that shaped the path of your whole life? These are split-second decisions that ripple through time. Did those decisions correct your course, or ultimately change your life for the worse?

I finally came to the night I had daydreamed about so many times. I didn't understand my primal urge to do cocaine, but it had been instilled in me ever since treatment. There, I had decided that if I ever relapsed, I would do it with cocaine.

My heart beat loudly as I pulled out the bag to show Alex. He and I had a big plan to meet up with some girls and have some fun with a drug we knew nothing about.

This night, the first time I ever did cocaine, is probably the most pivotal moment in my life. Alex and I stood together, bound by our brotherhood and ready to take a leap of faith. Our thoughts were as one, both of us understanding the gravity of our choice: instant gratification in exchange for long-term sorrow.

After taking the cocaine, I tilted my head back and let it settle on my brain. It hurt, but it was also so, so good. I closed my eyes and let the feelings explode like an erupting volcano. It was too much. My heart was playing a harmonic melody the likes of which had never been sung before.

Then I opened my eyes to a massive tidal wave of deafening joyful, soundless peace consuming me. My pupils dilated, my thoughts shaping themselves to razor-sharp points. It was as if I could cut a brick in half by just propelling the thought.

I looked at Alex. It seemed as though he could hardly breathe; he wore the determined expression of a marathon runner infused with adrenaline. He looked at me back.

I needed to do push-ups. I needed to somehow disperse this uncompromising energy before it swallowed me whole. But I collapsed into the push-up position, Alex following in sync with me. Together, we were harmonizing, doing push-ups together, our eyes locked, neither of us daring to break the connection, as if closing our eyes would cut off the majestic flow.

Our intensity rose with every push-up. The spiritual wind was deafening in my ears as we reached the summit of our team effort.

After the climax, we rolled onto our backs as the serene blast of ecstasy dissipated. We were speechless. As we looked at each other now, sadness adorned our stunned faces, possibly from knowing on a subliminal level that we were full-blown cocaine addicts.

More than likely, the sadness was a result of us being out of cocaine.

As my heart came down, I made an instinctive life choice—that I would chase that blissful rush to the ends of the earth.

Again consider the matter of spiritual forks in the road. The day I found cocaine, the void inside me that my mother had created was filled to the brim. But my inability to feel empathy or remorse had caused me to make the biggest mistake of my life.

For me, there didn't seem to be a fork, only a singular path, the foundation of which had been masterly crafted for me. It was like a beautifully flowing river, ever maintaining its loud and unpredictable current.

With cocaine on the brain twenty-four hours a day, I moved out of my mother's home and took up residence at the home of my childhood friend. He was a skater like myself, loved smoking weed, and didn't mind doing the odd line of coke. I liked living at his house, because his mom didn't have any rules. Still, we had to keep our cocaine habit secret.

I loved introducing every one of my friends to blow, since no one had seen it in Turner Valley before. Cocaine made everything better. I loved getting my hands on it and doing the biggest rails I could possibly take. I pushed myself to the limit many times. I remember going to parties and feeling like the coolest guy there, because of the bags of blow I had on me. Everyone wanted to try it, and in turn everyone wanted to hang out with me.

I also introduced people to another new drug—ecstasy, which were little pills of different colours with different stamps. I mixed my beloved cocaine with a steady flow of E. That became the only fun way to do it.

As my powder habit skyrocketed, it stopped working as well and my comedowns grew worse. I developed paranoia and life's sole purpose became chasing the unspeakable rush, only it became more difficult to achieve the rush. I tried to stay high for as long as I could, but my income wasn't high enough to meet my lofty ambitions. I became desperate.

One day, in the midst of a furious comedown, I got an idea. Instead of my usual car-creeping ploys or burglary strategies, I would go directly for the hard cash. I had tried to pawn merchandise, but it always took forever and never came with satisfaction guaranteed. Instead I could just rob a store of cash. It would be so easy. Perfect. It sounded like a concrete idea.

I needed a plan. First of all, who was to be the lucky target? There was an antique shop down the road from my house. Wouldn't they have to carry extra cash? Done deal! Secondly, I needed a weapon. I didn't have access to guns, thank God, so I was forced to get creative. I found a pool cue.

The plan seemed flawless. I would go in, get the money, get the hell out of there, then get my drugs. It was so simple. I couldn't believe everybody wasn't doing this.

On a snowy day in October with a wind chill that made it feel like it was thirty-below, I walked up to the store. The weather actually worked in my favour, since wearing a ski mask didn't make me look suspicious.

Then something out of the ordinary happened. I walked right past the store, feeling nervous. I would have to try again, pushing myself a little harder on the second walk-by.

On the second passing, I got up the nerve and walked into the store.

When I went to counter, the clerk, an old lady, wouldn't take me seriously. When I asked her to open the register, she replied, "No." What the heck? When I asked her a second time, this time smashing the pool cue into the counter, she just said, "You do it."

"Listen, woman," I said. "I don't know how to open it. You do it!"

This was crazy. I wasn't about to hit an old lady! I felt a lot of pent-up frustration over the unravelling of this simple task.

"This is how," she said, popping open the register. But faster than I could blink, let alone react, she slammed it shut again. Her tenacity was boundless. Can you believe the guts of this old woman?

"Open up the register!" I screamed.

When she wouldn't do it, this time I reached over, opened the register, and took out all the money. Home-free, baby. Cold, callous, methodical.

I ran back home and called my drug-dealer.

There was another part of my genius plan that I hadn't thought through. Turner Valley had a total of 1,200 people. It had zero traffic lights and only one four-way stop. So when my drug-dealer rolled into town, it appeared as if the entire town was in complete lockdown, complete with more police cars, officers, and canine units than the town had ever witnessed before. It would be a cold day in hell before my dealer was going to drive into my hometown.

The next flaw had to do with the weather. As I said, there was snow on the ground. For some reason, I never thought to throw off the police by covering my tracks through the snow. So they literally followed my footprints right to my house and arrested me, charging me with armed robbery, unlawful confinement, and disguise with intent. I was given $500 bail with the condition that I reside at my father's house.

There was only one problem with that: my dad wasn't paying my bail.

Chapter Twenty-One

HELLHOLE

I sat in a holding cell, watching the wall—staring at it as if it was going to all of a sudden do something if I looked away. I didn't take my eyes off it, and yet my eyelids felt heavy.

I couldn't believe that I'd just carried out an armed robbery and gotten caught.

There was nothing in the cement room but a mattress, so I paced over to the window and looked into the dark hallway. The lights were off and it smelled like piss. I hated the smell of piss; it reminded me of jail.

Because I was eighteen years old, my mother couldn't be held culpable for my actions any longer. She may have traumatized me, but she had also paid for my treatment. I would have to take responsibility for my actions.

Treatment had taught me that there was a clear difference between right and wrong. It also gave me the ability to look honestly at myself. My mom hadn't committed the robbery; I had. I had thought of it, planned it, and executed it. And now I would have to pay for it.

I had known it was wrong before I did it. I'd gone through the motions, even walking past the store without going inside. I'd had to push myself to go in there the second time because I hadn't innately wanted to go through with it.

I released my mom of responsibility. There was no one else to blame for my deplorable actions. I had known when I took that first drink of spiced rum. Now I needed to stay sober and contain the heartless beast inside, for its rising was as sure a thing as the sunrise. The beast was out of the cage.

Good luck putting it back in, I thought.

The RCMP knew me really well. A bunch of the officers had even made a point to come say hi when their shift started. They had gotten in a pretty good laugh about following the footprints to my house and catching me dumbfounded.

An officer I knew suddenly appeared to unlock my cell. "You ready for big boy jail?" he asked.

Yes, I was ready, although I wished there was a way to serve out my sentence in this holding cell, reeking of piss. I was nervous. Scared.

The drive to Calgary went fast, faster than usual. It was usually an hour and twenty minutes, but we did in forty-five minutes. Mind you, we were in a police cruiser; cops can almost do as they please.

As we pulled into admission and discharge, I watched the heavily fortified garage door close behind me. Welcome to big boy jail, Cody Bates.

The airlocks at Calgary Remand did their thing, guiding me through a set of doors like a cow being whisked to slaughter. An odd feeling of familiarity came over me. I can't explain how, but I knew this wasn't going to be my last time here.

My intuition told me it wasn't going to be easy convincing my dad to pay my bail and get me out. My pops relied on my mother for knowledge on how to deal with his drug-addicted son, and her method would be to let me find my pain in jail. Everyone seemed to rely on my mom for advice.

But this was my fault, not hers. I was forced to endure the consequences of my own actions.

They herded me to the back of the building to fit me with the signature blue coveralls, size fifty-two. First, they strip-searched me. I had to hand over one piece of clothing at a time, all the way down to my birthday suit.

"Let's see behind your left ear," the guard directed me. "Okay, now your right. Now run your hands through your hair. Turn around. Now the bottoms of your feet. Wiggle your toes. Okay, turn back around and lift your nuts. Turn around again. Now bend over. Spread your cheeks and cough."

It's a process I would end up going through hundreds of times.

Then off I went to unit one. As I walked onto the medium-security unit, a bunch of inmates were out of their cells for dayroom time. Dayroom time is the small amount of time every day when you get to use the phone and socialize. Every head turned my way as I walked in. I was one hundred forty pounds, had bad acne, and looked like a crackhead. Needless to say, my time in remand wouldn't be enjoyable.

I was picked on constantly. My self-esteem and self-respect faded more and more by the day. My sandwiches were taken, I was never allowed a turn on the phone, and I was targeted by a steady stream of convicts looking to release a little pent-up frustration. Half the time I didn't even get to eat. I despised leaving my room, and in turn I looked like a massive coward. Everyone fed on it.

One thing my first stay in Calgary Remand taught me is that convicts will feed on inmates who show weakness. The old familiar feelings of self-hate returned, and I once again felt like the repulsive creature I had been before treatment. Everyone was involved in my humiliation. How could they all be wrong about me?

I begged and pleaded with my father to get me out before I got seriously hurt, but he wouldn't do it—on my mother's educated advice.

This torment went on for a couple more months. I never said anything to the guards, since I didn't want to be labelled a rat. Not snitching was a moral standard of mine, one that went back to the break-and-enters with James. I had been praised back then for keeping my mouth shut. This time, I decided to just endure my horrible remand experience.

One day, I finally convinced my dad to bail me out of this hellhole. I was so grateful when I walked out the front doors. My dad's loving embrace providing a much-desired safety blanket. I was to go live on his acreage on house arrest. The place was out by Longview, a town about an hour away from the big city. I was way out of my element there, amongst horses, cows, chickens, tractors, hay bales, and barnyard cats.

That was no problem, though. I was just grateful to be around someone who loved me.

Chapter Twenty-Two

THE LEAFLESS FOREST

A wise man once told me that the scariest thing about me was my tolerance for emotional pain. The amount of psychological torment I could endure was astonishing. I had been trained to hunker down and suffer through crises from a very early age. It didn't feel good, but I took the malice and lived in it for years.

It's a daunting feeling when you realize that your sanctuary of peace—your mind—is full of torture and dangerous things. Perhaps you could think of it as a forest—a leafless forest with foul and evil creatures lurking behind every tree, stalking and studying you, calculating when to launch a vicious assault.

The animals of this forest are not of the world, but messengers sent from hell to take turns teaching lessons of brutality, hate, and violence. They wait in the shadows until your guard is down so they can pounce when you're at your most vulnerable. These creatures are patient, always waiting in a battle stance, their salivating mouths open to expose fangs of unthinkable cruelty.

These beasts don't care if you're tired or hungry. They don't show mercy when you're beaten down and broken by the real world. You can't even defend yourself, because you're not really there. It's just these demons and your thoughts. They show no tolerance, compassion, empathy, or remorse. They're animalistic and primal and only show their grotesque faces in those rare instances when you can't handle what's happening in the world around you. Then they tear you apart while you scream in pain, rip you to shreds piece by piece. They suck your blood until you're empty, nothing left but your bleeding heart for the devil to torment as he wills.

If you've spent as much time as I have in this "sanctuary," you'll learn lessons only another addict could understand. If you're an addict, you do things in times of hopelessness and despair you never thought possible. When you do these things, the things you dare not speak aloud, you create an opening for the forest creatures to attack, capitalizing on your weakness.

Addiction is the devil's window into our thoughts. We hurt ourselves, demean ourselves, and destroy ourselves as we travel over and over into untreated and unexplored depths, always looking for a means to get high. In this place, the devil plays his demented mind games. The more pain he can inflict, the more fulfilled he becomes. He doesn't break, for when you're not using substances—engaging him—he's doing push-ups, getting bigger, stronger, faster.

Sobriety bestows freedom from his heinous mind control, but he is forever waiting. Cunning, baffling, powerful and patient. When we finally slip, he cripples us.

When I moved to my dad's acreage on house arrest, I was very grateful to be out of jail. One thing I've never understood is why I never leaned on my dad more growing up. He was successful and he loved me more than anyone else in the world. It's just that he never understood what was wrong with his son.

Recently, while sitting with my father, he asked me how I learned how to use guns. I informed him that I was self-taught.

He pondered this with a questioning look in his eyes.

"I've always had guns," he finally said. I hadn't ever known that about him. "I don't know what it was, but I never showed you how to use them. I never even told you I had them."

Perhaps some sort of spiritual mandate had been guiding my father in my younger days. I can only imagine what would have happened if he hadn't trusted his gut and put a gun in his disturbed son's hands. This implies that my father knew that his son was disturbed. After all, most fathers where I'm from dream of the day when they get to place a gun in their son's hand. Everyone has them out here. It's a rite of passage from father to son.

But something inside my father had figured out that I wasn't a worthy candidate to hold a gun. Perhaps these thoughts were subconscious on his part, but his intuition was right; I was a very dangerous kid, living with dangerous thoughts. Putting a gun in my hands and making me comfortable with it would have been a mistake of unthinkable proportions. Instead of introducing me to firearms, he fell back on such activities as fishing, camping, and sailing to try and forge a bond with me.

I worked painstakingly at my father's ranch while I was on bail. My previous twenty months of sobriety stood like a pedestal in my mind. I fought so hard to get back to that point. But I felt shame and despair after every day of sobriety at my dad's acreage, for it seemed as a small bucket of water in contrast to the flowing river of sobriety I'd enjoyed before.

It was hard to look in the mirror and be proud of my short-term recovery. I associated those twenty months with failure, a constant reminder of what a piece of garbage I truly was.

I made my father crazy with my uncontrollable spaz attacks. At one point, I wanted a stereo to play music, but he declined my request. I had a full-out tantrum in Walmart, like a three-year-old, in front of countless midday shoppers. It seemed as though I acted like a child twenty-four hours a day, perhaps to make him sick of me enough to let me get my own place where I could do as I pleased—and finally get back to my destiny: cocaine.

I finally got approval to move in with Alex, who lived in Black Diamond across the street from the high school. My probation office cleared it and my dad rightfully serenaded it.

But my life only got worse from there, and within weeks I was back to the state of mind I'd been in before the armed robbery. I tried every drug I could get my hands on, and one in particular commanded my attention. Crack cocaine. I ended up falling into that because my cocaine dealer ran out of powder, and all he had for me to buy was crack. I was jonesing so bad that I said yes. When I tried it, I knew I was in trouble. It was far more intense than the powder I was used to snorting, and the high didn't last nearly as long.

About one month later, Alex and I were left out in the cold. All of our stuff had been tossed onto the front lawn and we were so focused on getting high that we just left everything there. We scurried around Black Diamond with a crack pipe and took turns taking blasts in the alleys. We didn't care what happened to us. We were disgusting.

At 2:00 a.m., he and I were sitting in the cold foundation of a house that was under construction. The temperature was twenty-below, but at least we were out of the wind and our flame didn't keep getting blown out. We sat in the dirt, huddled together trying to stay warm. Our teeth chattered as we sucked as hard as we could on the little glass pipe; it just seemed to make us feel worse. There was zero bliss.

Alex and I were homeless now. Hopelessness and despair only strengthened our connection.

When the drugs ran out, we walked through town at five o'clock in the morning, on the verge of frostbite. Alex worked at a local fast food restaurant, so he had a key to the store. A warm blast of heat rushed into our cold faces as we stepped inside.

We hated ourselves for what we'd become, and my relapse was all I could think about as I tried to get comfortable in a booth against the window. I wanted to sleep, but the pain of coming down hadn't yet subsided. It's impossible to fall asleep when you're still coming down.

By the time I woke up, Alex was serving customers. I sat up feeling hungry, cold, and tired—a recipe for catastrophe. I didn't have anywhere to go or anything to do. I had the simple life of a homeless crackhead.

I started to ponder whether I even wanted to go on living. Instead of propelling me to get sober, these thoughts pulled me toward total blackness. I didn't want to be me anymore. The battle in my head between good and evil had faded away, and evil seemed to have won.

I left the restaurant without telling Alex. There was a drugstore down the street where I spent the last bit of money I had on three bottles of extra-strength Tylenol. It was the best idea I had to kill myself. I'd never been a fan of pain, so I didn't think I could cut or hang myself. I wanted to go out in peace. If I didn't make it easy, I didn't think I'd go through with it.

Although I did honestly want to die, taking all 150 Tylenols wasn't likely to have done the trick. Perhaps I was yearning for someone to come and save me.

I returned to the restaurant and sat in a corner booth with a cup full of water, swallowing ten pills at a time until all three bottles were completely empty. It took about ten minutes.

My body started to feel funny after a bit and my mind became numb to the outside world. I lay down in the booth and thought about my family. Would they miss me? I honestly couldn't answer that question. This just seemed to verify the decision I'd made. I was truly a monster, incapable of putting myself in other people's shoes. The only thing I could see was the pain.

I let the Tylenol carry me off into a peaceful, thoughtless slumber. I didn't even cry or feel sorry for myself. It was cold, callous, and methodical. No emotion attached whatsoever.

But it wasn't enough. To my dismay, I woke up in a hospital bed in Calgary. My liver was toast, though, and I wouldn't be allowed to drink for a long time. The doctors told me this like I actually cared. Everything they said went in one ear and out the other. As if I was going to continue living through my gruelling torment without drinking or doing drugs. These guys were obviously drunk themselves.

They kept me in the hospital for a week and a half. During that time, I regularly snuck off the property to get high and drunk with my Calgary friends. I was literally sitting in bars while wearing my hospital gown. Everyone thought it was hilarious, even though they knew I was in liver failure.

Soon after my hospital release, the police apprehended me at a train station on a warrant for having missed my court date for armed robbery. While being escorted to the waiting cruiser, I took a swing at the officers and took off. This resulted in me being chased and violently taken down by the understandably angry police officers.

They sent me back to prison, and this time I wasn't getting off easily. A message would be sent.

Chapter Twenty-Three

REBIRTH

The daunting reality of being back in jail sank in as the police van pulled up to Calgary Remand. Jail hadn't been fun for me the last time, and I was sure it wasn't going to be any better this time. Having new charges added to my old ones, including trying to escape lawful custody, I was looking at around two years.

It didn't take long for me to be transferred to Spy Hill Correctional, located right across the parking lot from Calgary Remand, which itself was across the parking lot from the Calgary Young Offender Centre. In two years, I had managed to have a bed at one point or another in all three. I was clearly a career criminal in the making.

Spy Hill Correctional proved to be important stop in my jail journey. I found that these inmates, serving time rather than waiting for impending doom, were a lot less hostile. I partially survived there by lying about what I was in for. I didn't tell anyone about the armed robbery, or about being caught after the police had following my footprints in the snow. Instead I told people I was in for beating up an RCMP officer. In fact, that crime was true, only I hadn't been the perpetrator; my friends had been. Knowing the real details of the crime allowed me to give the story the ring of truth.

Being in for a cop-beating caused my rep points to go through the roof with the other inmates. Everyone showed me respect, and nobody messed with me. When weed and cigarettes came in, I always got cut in because I was the cop-beating psycho kid. The older inmates thought I was cool. I even changed my voice while I was there and wore fake glasses. I probably even damaged my eyes from never taking them off.

I started believing a lot of my own BS, confusing myself from all the lies I spun. Soon I couldn't tell the difference between truth and fact. The voice I created for myself became the one I spoke with for years to come.

Finally, I didn't have to be me anymore. I invented a fake Cody to help live with myself.

I took my GED exam and passed high school without even studying. After all, I was an intelligent kid, and becoming more so all the time.

I didn't get into one fight in jail, because the other inmates were scared of me, even though I was a total coward. I socialized with gang members and lied about fake drug deals and shootings.

The more entrenched I became in this fake persona, and the more I fell in love with him. I started to think like a gangster rather than a junkie. I grew to despise crackheads, as if I had never touched the drug in my life. The gang members, killers, and psychos were the ones who ran the jails—and they were the ones who brought in the drugs. If you control the drugs, you control the prison population.

My fake persona didn't quite elevate me to those higher levels, but I studied those people. I read their demeanours, personalities, and behaviours like a fine-tuned human-interpreting machine. I became a student in other people's emotional states.

Everything I did was focused on transforming myself into someone new. I hated the old Cody and wanted him dead. So I killed him, burying the hopeless crackhead junkie so deep that no one would ever remember him.

About two-thirds of the way through my sentence, I was granted a transfer to Lethbridge Correctional. I claimed that my family in Turner Valley would be able to visit me more easily there, helping me to build stronger community support for my eventual release. Corrections Canada ate it up; they strongly encourage family support.

I had ulterior motives for going to Lethbridge, though. I knew I couldn't live in this house of lies forever. Eventually it would come crashing down around me. So I wanted to try out the new and improved Cody Bates in a fresh setting where I could test my newfound gangster confidence with people who didn't know me.

My transfer enabled me to start fresh and tell the truth, although I stated the truth with a lot of aggression and authority. I fit right in in Lethbridge and everyone there accepted my persona.

But I began to worry about my dormant drug addiction. I didn't want to be that person ever again. I had been sober for about a year at this point, and it occurred to me that I might be able to carry my newfound confidence into a life of sobriety. I remembered the feeling I'd had when I was surrounded by friends and family who truly cared, and with my new leadership skills I hoped to be able to help people again.

It was an overwhelming realization.

Now that I wasn't dodging all the lies I had concocted at Spy Hill, I realized that my old life didn't need to follow me back onto the streets if I didn't want it to. All I had to do was follow the AA teachings and reach out for help. This was possible, and that life looked way better than one where I was a disgusting homeless crackhead.

I made the decision that I wanted to be sober. I wanted to live in truth and honesty. I wanted meaningful human connections. I wanted the solace I had found once upon a time at a place where miracles happened daily, at Doc's treatment centre.

In October 2005, I walked out of Lethbridge Correctional a completely changed person. I had gone in as a one-hundred-twenty-pound junkie and came out a two-hundred-pound man. I was calm, collected, and sober. I had been writing Doc again, and he had agreed to let me come to his centre for a residential refresher course.

My big book in hand, I walked beck in through the doors of the place that had saved my life. Doc decided to start me off on step eight, since I had been working the previous steps from my prison cell.

I was to go back to work as soon as possible, an opportunity I was grateful for. Living in recovery homes again was a blessing. Perhaps my time in jail had actually helped me. I didn't want to tell lies, though; I relied solely on confidence and self-love to help propel myself into the leadership role Doc wanted for me, and which I yearned for.

It felt amazing to be loved again. I took my role as a leader very seriously, and I once again always questioned my actions and motives. I was still an undiagnosed sociopath, but I was at least aware of my inability to feel empathy. Being in prison had taught me many skills which I could use to help people. I could read human emotion very well, a gift I used for good while back in treatment.

Every once in a while, my mother stopped by and said hi. She loved the label she wore at the treatment centre, where everyone still thought she was the strongest, bravest mother to ever go through the process.

I got a job as a clothing store manager, which allowed me to dress nicely every day, be the boss over some employees, and be honoured and praised for surviving my hardships.

The times when I struggled most in life were the times when I thrived. When I was in the gutter, I always fought with tenacity to get better. But when I got better, I'd go back to thinking that it wasn't enough—that I needed more.

When I left treatment again, my job at the clothing store fell apart. I had started stealing and living my life dishonestly. I found myself wanting to try out my newfound leadership abilities on the other side of the tracks.

CODY AT TWENTY YEARS OF AGE.

Chapter Twenty-Four

DRUG-DEALING 101

I stood at a light rail station, waiting for my friend Blue to pick me up. He had contacted me hours earlier with a proposition to help him build a dial-a-dope operation in the poverty-stricken neighbourhood of Forest Lawn, known throughout Calgary as "the hood." I had never spent an abundance of time there, but I knew from stories that it was the city's hub for crime, prostitution, and drugs.

When Blue pulled up in a black pickup truck, I reflected on the fact that I hadn't seen him since our time together in Spy Hill. He had an athletic build, always smelled good, and usually wore a tracksuit. He was also bald and looked more or less identical to actor Jason Statham. Despite his monster addiction, he was a good-hearted guy. He treated me as a brother and I in turn gave him loyalty.

The first thing he said to me as he pulled the vehicle to a stop was, "You like your new truck?"

What the...?

This was going to be a good time. Blue and I drove into the hood and immediately my senses were tweaked by the clear animosity and sketchiness in the people stalking the sidewalks. Addiction was everywhere in this neighbourhood.

We pulled up to a house one block off the main drag. When we walked in, we were greeted at the door by a massive Pitbull named Kilo. He was a big softy, licking my hand.

I was also introduced to Bruce, a real naïve kid. The way Blue talked to him, I could tell Bruce was in way over his head. He didn't know the first thing about being a gangster. I knew right away that this would be Blue's and my operation, despite Bruce putting up the funding, the house, and the truck to make the operation happen.

I was two years sober and had grandiose notions of being a gangster. I was so determined to never go back to the old Cody that staying clean was a priority in my mind.

But I was quickly greeted with a quarter-pound of crack cocaine, right there at my disposal. I was supposed to sell it, earning a profit. The point of selling drugs, after all, was to make double what you'd paid for the drugs in the first place; if you were good, you'd triple it. And we already had a burner phone set up with a flow of customers.

I sat down with Blue and bagged the crack into half-gram and one-gram bags. Blue liked to partake, but for some reason I didn't crave it at all despite having at one point given the shirt off my back in the cold for crack cocaine. I was so keenly focused on making this work that I didn't use.

I don't know where it came from, but Blue called me Hollywood, a nickname I grew to love. The moniker was to thwart would-be snitches and police detection. We couldn't rely on our customers to keep their mouths shut. A dial-a-dope operation needed to be set up in such a way that it could all vanish at the drop of a hat if anything went down.

The first thing I did was get myself a burner phone, set up under a fake account, and loaded it with contacts for customers in my social circle. Because Bruce didn't know the first thing about drug-dealing and Blue was high 24/7, I was in charge of everything. I drove out in my new truck, my Pitbull sitting in the passenger seat, waiting on my phone to ring. It did, and soon I had a steady flow of customers and a pocket full of green.

I was ready for this. I was going to make this my life.

I never said much to my customers and always kept the deal as objective as possible. One thing I learned quickly about crackheads is that more than half the time they didn't have money. So I started getting into the habit of starting every interaction with one question: "Full paper?" If they answered yes, meaning they could pay, I would head out in the direction of the call. But asking the question only weeded out the problem to a certain degree.

I was rocking a bleached blond buzz cut around this time, a product of me dying my long hair blond and then shaving it right away; after all, I was a twenty-one-year-old man now, not a teenager. It ended up looking pretty good. I usually rocked black jeans, a leather jacket, and sunglasses. My look matched the role I was playing, and it made me feel like a million bucks.

Blue insisted that I treat everyone like a friend except the customers who didn't have "full paper." It didn't take me long to get a hang of the lingo. I would ask people how much they wanted before the drop so I could have it out instead of having to dig through my massive bag in front of the junkies. In determining how much they wanted, I would ask, "How long you looking to hang out?" A half-hour equalled a half-gram, one hour a full gram, etc. If they asked to play a game, it meant they needed an eight-ball, which was three and a half grams. The more they bought, the cheaper it was. Most drug-dealers I've met hate meeting people for only one gram, but I figured out that the largest profit was made in the area of small sales, so I happily met every single call.

Back at the house, we kept ourselves armed to thwart off any would-be kick-ins. We had a shotgun in the couch, and the safe was in the bedroom. The operation itself wasn't as tight as it could have been, but this was drug-dealing 101; I was sponging up every shred of info I could get.

I started to move the operation as much as I could out of the hood. The police in Forest Lawn weren't dummies, and I was feeling the heat. I hustled in my old neighbourhood of Shawnessy, where there a mix of powder cocaine and rock cocaine customers. Always having my own set of wheels, and always being sober, gave me a strategic advantage. I was a drug-dealing machine living off cat naps instead of sleep.

I spent my days driving through the hood, my right hand on Kilo's head and my left on the wheel of my nice black truck. The hot summer heat radiated up from my leather seats. I liked the hot leather; it reminded me I was a baller. My dark Versace shades kept my wandering eyes hidden from the world. I had three phones in my lap, all steadily ringing the song of money.

The old junkie Cody was a thing of the past. I was a drug-dealer now.

Chapter Twenty-Five

6/6/6

Sinister evil does exist. It walks with us, seduces us, and plays with us until the satanic endgame is upon us. Being a drug-dealing gangbanger is all I had ever wanted, at least since I'd seen it in movies. But real life wasn't as glamorous. In *Scarface*, Tony Montana had looked like he was on top of world. But how did he feel inside after doing all the horrific things it took to get him to the top? He felt nothing. Why? Because *Scarface* is just a movie. Films can't depict what happens to a person inside when they're waiting in a car with a loaded shotgun, knowing that the shell is marked for the death of an unknowing father, brother, friend, or son.

On June 6, 2006—6/6/6—my life was forever changed when my friend and I took another man's life. I hadn't been prepared for the transition from drug-dealer to cold-blooded killer. I will never be able to put into words the evil that took over my heart that day.

When my friend Brad asked me to help him make some money by robbing a dealer, I didn't even need the money. I was already making lots. But my thirsty mind was soaking up every experience this new life had to offer. A mere taste of the Tony Montana lifestyle wasn't enough to satisfy me.

When Brad asked if I knew anyone we could set up to rob, a name crossed my mind. One of my old friends from treatment, Jimmy, was now a customer of mine, and he'd recently brought it to my attention that another Shawnessy cocaine dealer, Lewis, had been asking around about "Hollywood." I realized that this was my opportunity to set an example and make myself stand prominent in the underworld. I wanted people to know that although I might only be twenty-one years old, I didn't screw around—and I could help out a friend at the same time.

Brad was a sad case. He was the older brother of my old friend James, who I'd stolen the dump trucks with in Turner Valley. I respected Brad, as he always hyped me up for having taken the heat for James after all the break-and-enters. I loved Brad and he was a good friend, but it was hard watching his decline into addiction. When I agreed to help him make some money, I agreed to let him keep all the drugs and cash. I didn't need any of that. I just wanted to teach this other dealer a lesson about who owned the southwest neighbourhood.

Well, it turned out that Lewis had been wanting to teach me a lesson, too. Jimmy brought me up to speed about Lewis, who wanted to end this turf war before it began. This just validated my plan. I had learned that gangsters always had to defend their home turf, and this would be a test of how far I was willing to take this new lifestyle.

I asked Jimmy if he'd be willing to help me out, to help me put a gun in Lewis's face and take away all his pride in one fell swoop. I offered Jimmy an eight-ball to be the point man in the setup and call Lewis for what was supposed to be just a simple transaction.

That night, I picked up Brad at his house. He was about my size and almost looked like he could be my own brother. He hopped in my vehicle, wide-eyed, and without a word we were ready to roll. We pulled into Shawnessy, where we picked up Jimmy in the public housing complexes. I explained to him the plan: I would pull in behind the 7-Eleven and Jimmy would walk around from the back to use the payphone to call Lewis for a sale. I cautioned him about the surveillance cameras I had previously scoped out and told him exactly where to walk and precisely what to say: "Keep your hood up, head down, and wipe the phone when you're done."

After the call, Jimmy jumped back into the car and explained that Lewis was going to be at the drop-off point in two minutes. I had to act fast, but stay smart. We screamed toward the drop-off and dropped Jimmy off in the parking lot. Brad and I then pulled into a nearby alley.

When we got out of the vehicle, Brad took my gun and slipped it up his sleeve. I was so focussed on the task at hand that I didn't give it a second thought. In hindsight, this was a fatal error—a critical fork in the road.

We trotted out of the alley and approached the parking lot just as Lewis's silver Mustang was already starting to pull away. Fate wasn't on his side. Jimmy had shorted him the money, according to plan, and Lewis stopped the car to yell at his customer.

Suddenly, Brad and I found ourselves right in front of him. We walked up to the side of his car, my heart not even skipping a beat as I reached for the handle to the driver's side door. That's when I heard a loud bang, accompanied by a flash, right beside my head. It blinded me for a second. With my ears screaming, my vision came back into focus to see Lewis slumped behind the steering wheel. The blast of a sawed-off shotgun, at close range, had killed him instantly.

Brad had shot him.

As Brad and I ran back to the alley and got in the truck, Brad was losing his mind, punching the dashboard. I told him to calm down. We needed to find a place to bury the gun.

We drove out of town, toward Turner Valley. Brad was in tears, but I kept reassuring him that everything would be fine. But things weren't fine.

The two of us got rid of the shotgun outside of Turner Valley. I then dropped off my distraught friend at a known drug-dealer's house in town. I don't even think we said goodbye.

The drive home was quiet and thoughtful. I pondered what the next step would be. Since both of my accomplices were drug addicts, I knew the odds of us getting caught were high. It would be solely up to me to clean up this mess. I was careful, calculated, and methodical. As long as everyone kept their mouths shut, there was absolutely no way this would come back to us.

I walked into my house and took off my muddy shoes, deciding to throw those away in the morning. As I turned on the light in my bedroom, though, I had forgotten that I had a guest over—a beautiful petite French girl. She was probably the most sincere, honest, and innocent girl I had ever met and this was to have been our first sleepover together; she had asked me earlier in the day if she could stay at my house. My apartment was close to the bar and she'd planned to drink that night.

As I stood in the doorway, she asked me why I had dirt all up my arms and on my clothes. I sat on the edge of the bed, giving her a view of my back. Coldness adorned my beating heart as I came up with a lie: I had been at a campfire. Well, I couldn't tell her that I had been in the country burying a murder weapon. I took off my shirt, revealing a stab-proof vest. She asked me why I was wearing it.

"It was just a precaution," I lied again. "Someone was going to be there who had a problem with me."

I unstrapped my vest and laid it down without even washing my hands. She rolled over and I put my arm around her, holding myself tight to her warm body. She buried her head between my neck and my shoulder. I stared at the ceiling, holding her, while darkness flooded over me.

This was real. It had actually happened.

I needed to decide whether I could take the chance of trusting Jimmy. He was young, naïve, and had never been involved in something like this. I hadn't either, of course, but I had taken the plunge now and there was no turning back.

Would I have to kill Jimmy? I had watched Jimmy pour his heart out at the treatment centre, so I had to prepare myself for the worst. But it was pointless to think about it until I met with him the next day and gauged whether he could carry such a heavy load.

I figured Brad would be fine, although his reaction had scared me a bit. But who wouldn't react that way after blowing someone's head off? He wouldn't rat, but there was a high likelihood that he'd kill himself with drugs, trying to bury his burden. I was worried for him.

But what about me? Was I okay? Was I going to be fine?

Yes, I would be. I closed my eyes and fell asleep almost instantly, dreaming of the laurels and riches ahead of me. I proved to myself that night that I could go as far as I had to in order to be a gangster.

Chapter Twenty-Six

HORSESHOES

I met up with Blue the morning after the homicide. Being a gangster himself, he told me to get rid of Jimmy. I was conflicted; I had spoken at Jimmy's graduation at the treatment centre. He was one of my good friends. I loved him, but I selfishly didn't want to get caught. It didn't help that Blue was high all the time and in a constant state of paranoia. I couldn't trust his judgment.

But we at least needed to talk to Jimmy. As we drove around looking for him, the plan went from simply talking to him to another murder plot. I tried to focus and remain sound-minded despite Blue's invitation to do some crack. What had happened the night before had made me stronger and more seasoned.

I loved who I was becoming. People were scared of me, even some of my friends. In a few short months, I had gained a reputation as a drug-dealer, gangster, and now killer. It's fair to say my moral compass had shattered.

Blue's high turned out to be Jimmy's saving grace, as he started thinking we were being followed by helicopters. Now even he didn't want to kill Jimmy. I dropped him off somewhere and continued my search alone.

Jimmy finally answered my call later that night and I met up with him at a coffee shop outside Shawnessy. I arrived early and waited for Jimmy to arrive. I spent the time looking at the front pages of the newspapers, which were covered with images of the previous night: yellow police tape wrapped around Lewis's silver Mustang as homicide investigators scoured the scene.

When Jimmy came in, his eyes were wide. He had insisted on meeting in a public place, probably sensing that he might be next. But instead of trying to instill fear in my friend, I went in another direction. I brought him close and told him that I loved him, that if we went down we would do it together.

I didn't tell him that Brad had been the one holding the gun. I figured the less he knew, the better.

When I got back to the house, after meeting some customers and picking up some dinner, I noticed that the front door was off its hinges. The house had been robbed before, so this much didn't surprise me.

I walked inside, carrying a pizza box with my favourite Hawaiian, to find that the place was destroyed. All the plates from the cupboards had been smashed onto the floor, the cushions had been ripped inside out, and even the food had been dumped out of its packaging. This had been the work of one ballsy crackhead.

I put the pizza down and started to look around. The bedrooms had been torn to pieces, too, and the safe was gone, along with the shotgun that had been stashed in the couch. But the worst thing was that the dog was gone—and the clean-up, of course.

As I surveyed the damage, taking inventory, I heard a knock at the door. It was the landlord. He asked where he could find Bruce, the leaseholder of the house.

"I have no idea," I said truthfully.

"Well, tell him the police raided his house. The warrant's on the table."

I suddenly realized I had to get out of there. I gathered up a few of my possessions and put them in a backpack. It hadn't even occurred to me that this had been the work of cops. If they had found that shotgun, they might think it was the murder weapon. It wasn't, but they wouldn't know that.

I grabbed my pizza and jetted out the door, only to be greeted by about twenty armed officers with their guns out. I put my arms in the air, lifting the pizza box and noting the presence of a police helicopter circling above.

This was it. I didn't even care that I had a couple ounces of cocaine in my crotch.

They screamed for me to get to the ground, and I did as I was told. If I ran, they would let that snarling German shepherd of theirs off its leash and turn me into a pork chop.

A couple of officers handcuffed me and informed me that I was being detained. They found the three phones in my pocket along with a ton of cash. When they patted me down, they didn't feel the $3,000 worth of cocaine I had stashed in my crotch, but that must have been the least of their worries.

As I sat in the back of the police cruiser, I looked around at all the attention I had brought down. Red and blue lights illuminated the whole neighbourhood.

I had been busted.

Suddenly, an officer opened the door and pulled me back out of the car. They unlocked my handcuffs and gave me my money and phones back. They weren't going to arrest me after all; they had merely executed a drug search warrant. The person they were looking for was Bruce.

I'm pretty sure my jaw was on the ground.

"Yeah, no problem," I said as they returned my backpack and sent me on my way.

I wasn't allowed to take the truck, because it was in Bruce's name, but I otherwise walked away with all the money, all the phones, and all the cocaine. What was happening here? I had thought I was going down for murder, at the very least for gun or drug charges, but apparently their warrant hadn't contained my name. So I walked away scot-free.

Chapter Twenty-Seven

RUSTY FAUCET

The next month, my business boomed in the southwest, no doubt with a flood of clients from the man in the silver Mustang. Word was starting to get around about what had happened. Silent whispers were shared about Cody Bates, the kid who was getting away with murder. The more people began to realize there was something dangerous behind my crooked smile, the more the rumours spread. I became infamous, which was exactly what I wanted.

One thing I've learned over the years is that there's a big difference between fear and respect. Someone who's scared of you does not respect you. They will hate you and spread their fear of you to others. On the other hand, when a person respects you they will brag to others about your friendship. That's how meaningful human connections are made in the underworld.

People didn't respect me; they feared me, something that would end up costing me countless relationships over the years.

The more violent I got, the more detached from reality I became. I buried my emotions so deep that almost nothing could bring them to the surface. I didn't see my family anymore, as they had all written me off. My heart was heavy, but it was like I enjoyed the afflictions. It might have appeared to people that I didn't feel anything at all, but the truth is that my self-hate ran so deep that I felt I deserved to suffer.

Darkness followed me everywhere. My eyelids were low and heavy, making me appear psychotic to anyone who looked into them on the rare occasion when I took my sunglasses off. I hated people looking me in the eye, because I was scared they would detect the intense resentment I had for the world and myself. When I looked at a person, I could tell exactly who they were. I could see their strengths and weaknesses. When people looked at me, I wanted them to see that I didn't care about anything anymore—to see how dangerous I truly was.

One day in July, I woke up to a telephone message from a friend from my treatment days. I thought it was weird that he would call, and I delayed replying to him because I tended to avoid people who could try to resuscitate the old Cody.

That evening, I woke up and did a line of coke while I watched the five o'clock news. I sat back, letting the cocaine take me away for a few minutes, a release from my pain and anger. While I was good and high, I figured it would be the best time to listen to my old friend's message.

"Cody, this is Paul. I have some bad news. Make sure you talk to someone. Devon died yesterday. He hung himself. He's dead, Cody. Reach out for help."

His words landed like a truck on my throat. My best friend had taken his own life—and he had only been eighteen. He'd been incarcerated at Stony Mountain Penitentiary in Manitoba, one of the roughest jails in the country. I once heard that when you walk into Stony Mountain, the first holding tank they put you in has these words carved out on it: "Keep your head low white boy, you're in Indian country now!" I can only imagine the suffering my best friend must have gone through to push him to suicide by hanging.

I lay back on the couch almost as if I was trying to make myself cry. I objectively knew I should be devastated, that I should shed tears, but I couldn't dredge it up. Not even my best friend's death could stoke emotions in this heartless monster. I hated myself for appearing to feel nothing for Devon. I felt as though I were letting him down for not being able to show my hurt. Did I even have a heart anymore?

I put my sunglasses on before my roommate got home. I didn't want him to walk in and see me.

Devon's funeral was a few days later, and I spent every one of those days high. Then I walked in to view his body, stood over his coffin, and stared at him intently. Again I found myself trying to force out tears for my friend. Surely he was seeing this… his best friend standing idle and cold over his body, showing no love for him at all. I hated myself so much for that. I wanted to hurt for him, I wanted to cry for him, but I couldn't. I touched his cheek. Still nothing. I was an abomination from hell.

My head hung low as I walked away from him for the last time. I would never see him smile or laugh again. I had failed him.

I sat in the front row next to my mom, with his parents and sister sitting on the other side of the aisle. Everyone there knew I had been his best friend, and I could feel their silent questions landing on my shoulders: *Isn't Cody even sad? What's wrong with him?*

I listened to the speakers and thought about all the good times I had treasured with my friend. I thought about when we'd earned step one at treatment, that magical night Doc had reached our lost souls. I remembered the emotion I'd felt when Devon shed tears for our brotherhood after watching me bare my deepest, darkest self.

Why couldn't I do it for him? What was wrong with me?

At the end of the funeral, a song was played over a slideshow of his life. It started with pictures of Devon as a baby. He had been a good-looking kid, always wearing a massive smile. I watched each picture fade in and fade out, and it somehow dawned on me that this really was goodbye. I stared into his eyes in picture after picture, bracing myself as something deep inside started to bubble up. I was remembering holding him in treatment, remembering the freedom we had found together, the solace we'd shared as we continued through treatment, loving and supporting each other as brothers, his parents loving me as if I were their own son.

His parents. They would never hold their boy again.

I looked around the room and saw that people were looking back at me.

Don't you love your brother? their gazes demanded. *You monster.*

I desperately wanted to hurt!

Please God, let me show him that I love him now, before he's gone forever, I thought. *I love you, Devon. I'm so sorry, brother. I love you.*

As the slideshow came to an end, my throat constricted with the force of a vice clamp. The last picture was one of Devon and me, with our arms around each other at his treatment graduation. Smiling, free, and sober!

In that moment, five years of pain came exploding to the surface. I was never going to see my best friend again, and it hurt so bad. I heaved as an enormous gush of tears poured out of my eyes. I sobbed for my friend.

I could barely stand as I walked to the front with the other pallbearers and lifted his casket, carrying his body out to the waiting hearse. I almost fell down from the pain pouring out of me. I wasn't able to see as I put the front end of his casket onto his last ride. I balled and sobbed like a baby, years of pain pouring onto the cement.

My mother gathered me into her arms and I buried my war torn face into her chest. I couldn't remember the last time she'd held me like this. Maybe she never had. But now was when I needed her most.

CODY AND DEVON. THIS WAS THE PICTURE USED IN DEVON'S FUNERAL SLIDESHOW.

Chapter Twenty-Eight

THE HUSTLE

After Devon's funeral, not much changed for me. I moved into the housing complexes in Shawnessy, living with my good friend Mel. Mel was sweet and kind and had no idea what living with me would entail. I kept my drug-dealing secret and she didn't ask many questions.

But I became really sad after Devon's passing. Being so in tune with my emotions brought on a whole new set of obstacles. Sometimes I had a hard time controlling my tears. Not only that, I was now living in the same neighbourhood where Lewis's murder had taken place. My cocaine habit got worse as time went on, even though I promised myself I would never smoke it again. But sometimes I would snort whole ounces of the stuff.

My business took a hit when I started suffering psychosis from the lines of cocaine I was doing. Impossible realms suddenly peeked their ugly heads into my life. Also, my paranoia soared. I always thought there was someone in the house with me, and I sometimes walked around with a gun. I even killed all my fish once, dumping $500 of blow into the tank when I thought the cops were raiding my house.

The murder had done something to my mind, which became fractured with delusions. I was losing my mind, but I slowly got my psychosis under control by balancing my alcohol intake.

One day, my childhood friend Alex called to ask me if I'd be interested in buying his car. Heck yeah! It was a '91 Mazda RX7, black on black. I had loved that car ever since I'd seen his older brother driving it when I was little. He wanted $1,500 for it, though, and I was broke at the time. But I was a hustler. I could wake up with zero dollars in my pocket and end up with $5,000 by the end of the day. I did it all the time.

Alex needed the money for rent that exact day, so if I wanted the car, it had to go down now. I told him to meet me at Walmart in an hour.

I had a quick-cash scam at my disposal. You see, the Walmarts in Calgary all had an electronics section with cashiers inside it. But Walmart, being as accommodating as they are, allowed customers to either pay in the electronics section or at front checkout. If you paid for something in electronics, you could just flash your receipt to the greeter at the front on the way out.

Let me apologize now to Walmart for the hundreds of flatscreen TVs I stole in that two-year span.

That day, I went to Walmart and casually stole three $150 electric toothbrushes. Then I returned them ten minutes later at the same place. Because I didn't have a receipt, they wouldn't give me cash money but a gift card instead. Exactly as I had expected.

So I rolled into another Walmart where I found Alex and his girlfriend waiting in the parking lot. I asked the girlfriend to go into the store with the gift card and buy a $450 LCD flatscreen. She did as I asked. Alex was confused about why I was spending that money on a TV, but I told him to relax.

Before his girlfriend was back, three vehicles pulled in beside us. The buyers were here. She came out with the TV and I put it in my trunk. I then strolled into the store and went straight to the electronics section. I grabbed a $2,000 flatscreen and put it in the cart, then wheeled it to the front of the store and flashed the receipt to the greeter. Easy as pie. I wheeled the TV to the first buyer and got $500. A happy buyer, to say the least.

I then went back in and repeated the process, this time exiting through a different door with a different greeter. It went off without a hitch. Another happy buyer drove away with his new TV.

There were only two ways into the store, and I needed to do this a third time, so I implored Fate to help a brother out. Sure enough, she was on my side and I walked right by the same distracted greeter with the third $2,000 TV in a row.

Alex and his girlfriend stood there with their mouths on the ground as I collected the money for the final TV. When the third happy customer left, Alex signed over the registration for my new sports car.

I'd driven a standard transmission once before—the dump truck. But now was as good a time as any to teach myself. I drove away from my friends with a big smile on my face, grinding the gears of my new wheels. I didn't care. If I broke it, I'd just get another.

On the way home, I swung into another Walmart, returned the original TV I'd bought with the only receipt I'd used, and got my $450 gift card back.

Life's easy for a guy with no conscience.

Chapter Twenty-Nine

COOLER HEADS

This was the year I turned into a bar star, selling cocaine and building my business in the clubs, partying all hours. I had a different club to go to each night of the week. I partied steadily with my old crack dealer from Turner Valley, and together we hung out with some pretty dangerous dudes. Because I was working with them and bringing in money, I became a member of their gang. They were all ballers, and a few of them were killers. Most knew about my homicide through the rumour mill, so they liked me.

As soon as I walked into a bar, I'd fill up a table full of shots and make my presence known to everyone there, even if I couldn't afford it. I broke bread and gave out tons of free blow, building my clientele. I always taught my guys that giving out their number didn't mean anything; getting people's numbers in return was where the true value lay. The more numbers we had, the more business we retained, leading to more money to fund our cocaine- and alcohol-fuelled nights.

As the business grew, I had to get people working the phones and making drops around the city to keep customers happy while I was building friendships at the bar. I was a boss, drunk and high all the time. But I didn't go many nights without sleeping, because that's when my mind started to split from reality. I developed a sound bedtime of about 7:00 a.m., after nights of crazy sex, booze, and drugs.

My favourite bar in Calgary was The Back Alley. I knew all the bouncers, and there were always lots of friendly gang members there—friendly toward me, anyway. Life as a gang member had its ups and downs. I had to wear a bulletproof vest, since my new friends were in a full-out war with a rival gang. They were getting shot at continuously.

I didn't get involved in the war, and neither did the guy I was working for. We liked money, we liked girls, and we liked to party—but we were strapped most of the time, just in case. I had a .22 handgun in my waistband everywhere I went.

One day, a hockey player in town for training camp asked to meet in a back alley to cuff an eight-ball. "Cuff" is lingo for accepting the product upfront, without cash, with the promise of payment by a specified date. He had bought five eight-balls in three days and was enjoying the sad reality of a severe cocaine comedown. A state of mind I was all too familiar with.

Unfortunately, it was cash on delivery only. He begged and pleaded, claiming he was getting paid the next day. No can do. He whined, moaned, called back, and then finally said he had the cash. I gave him directions to my house, since he would be leaving town soon. I wasn't concerned about disclosing my location.

When he got to my house, he was with a friend. I chatted with the boys on the deck and for some reason left them out there for a second to do something in the house. Dummy. They ran off with the drugs without paying me.

This told me they had been planning on jumping me in the first place, but I'd given them an easy opening to leave. I was furious. Common sense flew out the window as I pulled my gun, got in my car, and began to hunt.

I called the number from where he had called me, but it was for a hotel a few miles down the road. I drove there and staked out the hotel, periodically driving to the adjacent train stations since I knew they were cashless and on foot.

Next, I picked up a buddy to help control the situation if things went sideways. We sat in front of the hotel doing lines of cocaine until about four in the morning. Finally, sleepiness took hold and I went home, promising to myself that I'd return.

As we drove home, I decided to take a detour past a train station close to my house. Unbelievably, guess who I saw walking through the empty train station parking lot? You guessed it: my hockey player friend. Alone.

I ripped into the parking lot, peeling the tires of my rear-wheel drive and making it seem like I was going to run him over. I wanted to, but I had bigger plans for this goofball. I got out of the car, forced him to the ground at gunpoint, then put him in the trunk of the car. He was sketched out from all the blow he'd done, so this probably scared him half to death.

I took him back to his hotel, where he showed me his room. I made him pack up everything he had there, and then I took his clothes, his wallet, even his toothbrush, which he begged me to leave. I thought that was odd, given the situation. He still claimed he was getting paid the next day.

I left him the clothes he had on and said that if he paid me $500 the next morning, I would give him all his belongings back. He said he would comply... mind you, he still had a gun in his face. Worst-case scenario, I figured I would get my money back through identity theft.

When I left, he was thanking me for having mercy on him.

Turned out he was speaking a little too soon.

The next day, he called me and claimed he had his cheque; he just needed a ride to go cash it. I then asked him if he wanted to go back to our old friendly relationship.

"Absolutely," he told me.

I told him that I knew of some hot girls who would love to get their hands on a sexy hockey player. He was all for it, so I picked up some girls and swapped vehicles with a friend for the day; this larger car was a four-seater.

The plan took shape as I drove along.

I also picked up a good buddy of mine, to provide a little extra control in case it came to that. And as a final thread to my mischievous plan, I called my friend Steven, telling him to be parked at a specific gas station at a specific time; when I drove by, he was to follow me out to the country—and bring a friend or two along for the ride.

When I picked up my hockey player friend, I introduced him to my friend and the women in the back.

"They love you," I whispered to him. He happily parked his butt in the back seat between them. "Do you want a little weed?"

"Oh yeah."

"Awesome. I got the perfect spot outside of town. You'll love it."

As I drove by the gas station, Steven pulled out behind me and proceeded to follow me out of town.

Suddenly, one of the girls asked me to turn down the music.

"Yes, honey?" I asked.

"Did you find that guy from last night and break his legs and leave him naked on a dirt road in the country yet?" she happily asked.

In the ensuing silence, I adjusted the rear-view mirror so I could stare down my victim. Beads of sweat broke out on the hockey player's face.

"No, my love," I answered, stoking his agitation. "We were about to rendezvous that objective presently." By now, the hockey player was petrified. "Don't say anything, buddy. You embarrassed me last night. Keep your mouth shut and you might live through this one."

I flashed my teeth in a smile, letting him know I meant business.

We pulled up to a spot I had chosen, and Steven and his carload of boys pulled up behind me. Then I got out of the car and asked the girls to step out.

"Not you," I said to the hockey player as he started to step out. He sat down again, stuck in the back seat of a two-door car.

The girls backed up as I began to talk.

"Take off your clothes," I told the guy in the car. My lip raised in a sinister snarl. When he started begging me not to do this, I cut him off. "You embarrassed me last night. I don't handle that kind of stuff well. Now take your clothes off. That's the last time I'll ask you."

I whipped out an extendable police baton and brandished it in front of me. He cried as he took off all his clothes, then reached for the pocket where his money was.

"No, no, you won't be needing that," I said. "I think I need it more, and I need new clothes and a toothbrush." I smiled, implying that he was getting nothing back.

I had been planning on breaking both his legs, but something came over me as he extended his first knee outside the car. The only person who didn't look terrified was Steven, and he was ready for anything. That's when I made the educated decision to spare the hockey player's knees. That would ruin his career, and likely his life. My point had been made.

As I drove away from our abandoned, naked, but otherwise unhurt friend, I asked the girls in the back seat to go through his pockets. A few moments later, one of the girls let out a shriek. I turned around and saw that she was holding a stack of hundred-dollar bills as thick as a softball. Hollywood was getting paid!

I pulled over and tossed Steven and his boys a bunch of party cash.

I drove back to Calgary feeling ruthless and looking like a Pitbull, my gaze low and my shoulders hunched forward. I was unstoppable.

The excitement of the money wore off within an hour of returning home. I didn't really care about cash, and I spent every last dime of that massive stack at the bar later that night. Just another day in the life.

The next day was a rollercoaster ride, to say the least. The hockey player called me again, this time out of fear since he figured that I knew where he lived now that I had his ID. I left a message for him at his parents' house and he subsequently offered me money in exchange for peace.

Soon after, I got a phone call from a well-known Hell's Angels gang member, someone who had apparently grown up with the hockey player. He insisted on a face to face meeting, and my curiosity was piqued enough to agree to it.

With a vest on and the .22 tucked in my waistband, a friend and I made our way to the foot court at a downtown mall. As we came up the escalators, I saw the Hell's Angel guy. We shook hands and I introduced him to my friend before going off to a table to chat by ourselves.

My new friend informed me that I was making quite a splash around town.

"Thank you," I said, calm, collected, and straight-faced.

Then he asked me for the hockey player's stuff back. I wasn't about to disrespect a man who had shown me nothing but respect, but I told him I had to respectfully decline; his friend was lucky that I hadn't killed him. But as a goodwill gesture, I gave him the hockey player's wallet.

"I know he's your friend," I said, "and I'm not looking for trouble, but he messed up. He's lucky cooler heads prevailed in the heat of a very intense moment."

My new friend was inclined to agree. We stood up, shook hands, and parted ways. I never saw him again.

One thing was very clear after this: Cody Bates was a boss. Word of my ruthlessness quickly spread through the underworld.

Chapter Thirty

UNWANTED VISITORS

The more distracted I got with the bar scene, the more people I needed to work the phones. Cocaine profits were pouring in, but most of the money was going up my nose or into the bars' pockets. I was the most generous tipper in the city, always needing to stand out from the rest.

The nights got crazier and crazier as time went on. I would take cocaine, pile on the ecstasy, then follow it with a ton of alcohol. It got to a point where I was constantly getting into fights. I had a favourite alley that I went to on Wednesday nights, behind one of the clubs, for bar brawls. I dropped so much money at the club that they would always let me back in.

One time, a guy was really upset that his girlfriend had taken a liking to me. It wasn't my fault, but he didn't care. After about ten seconds of trying to calm the situation, my patience ran out. My lip curled and decided to take the altercation to the next level. But it turned out that one of the guys with me was also friends with my would-be victim; he turned on me, giving me the wildest head butt I've ever had the pleasure of receiving. My face exploded with blood.

When the bouncers sorted out the mess, I noticed that all the guys I'd been fighting were gone. I was wearing a white collar shirt with stripes and white jeans, but it was all crimson with blood by now. I had a gigantic hole in my face, too, where my teeth had bit through my upper lip. It was disgusting.

The bouncers wouldn't let me go outside until they knew the guys I'd been fighting were gone, out of fear of what would follow once I got to my car.

I couldn't drive myself to the hospital with my face hanging off, not to mention the fact that I was wasted. As luck would have it, a friend of mine from treatment days, Mark, happened to be outside the bar with his girlfriend. He agreed to take me to the emergency room. But I told Mark if the wait was long, I would just leave. Sure enough, the three-hour wait time sent me in the opposite direction.

Instead we scooted over to a drugstore and bought a sewing kit, where Mark proceeded to stitch shut the massive hole in my face, using cocaine as a numbing agent. Well, the coke didn't make it numb at all. In fact, it had quite the opposite effect. I let out a shriek of agony, but we were committed at this point.

As Mark threaded the needle and I reclined in my seat to give him a better angle, his girlfriend stepped in and said that she had let this go far enough.

"If you let him do this, you'll be deformed," she said.

Well, I didn't want that. Thank God cooler heads once again prevailed.

Mark and his girlfriend dropped me off at a friend's birthday party at a nearby pizza joint. I can't explain why, but the staff agreed to serve me despite being covered in blood. Perhaps they didn't want to tell the faceless man that he wasn't allowed to have a drink. I got high and wasted there, then retreated to a house party without even changing my clothes.

I woke up the next day in a ton of pain. I had passed out on a massage chair that had been left on for who knows how long. My head hurt, my body hurt, and oh yeah, my face was still hanging off.

I had somehow ended the night in Turner Valley, so I was close to the Black Diamond hospital. The look on the face of the receptionist was priceless. The doctor couldn't believe I had dumped cocaine into my massive open wound and then let it sit for fourteen hours without seeking medical attention. They must have thought I had a mental disorder.

The doctor proceeded to reopen my wound with metal mesh. After scrubbing it clean, he stitched it up and I was able to walk out of the hospital on two feet. Another day in life of a psychotic animal.

What I didn't know is that several people had seen me go through the night missing half my face. This only added to the reputation I was building. From that day forward, I had a massive scar to go along with my lip snarl.

―――――――――

One day I got a call for a drop in the Marda Loop neighbourhood. It was pretty far, but one of my uncle's restaurants was in that direction so I figured I'd make some quick cash and get a free bite to eat in the process. I put my puffy white coat on and headed out the door.

Before I got out the door, I was met by a bunch of police officers who put my face in the snow.

They put me in the back of their police cruiser when they found the bag of cocaine on me. They didn't tell me which one of my crimes to this point I was being charged with. I hoped it was merely possession; worse-case, it could be trafficking, kidnapping, or murder.

Obviously I'd been set up, but why?

The cops drove me toward the parking lot of a nearby fast food restaurant. I was very confused. He parked, turned around, and opened the sliding window separating us. He made eye contact with me then as he rolled down his window and poured out my bag of cocaine into the snow.

"Do you know what this is?" he asked

"I don't know. What is this?"

"I helped you. Now you need to help me." Was this guy serious? I stared at him in disbelief. "I need to know who's bringing in all the drugs around here."

This guy actually thought I was going to help him. I couldn't believe it. He went on to say that he knew I was connected and that he wanted me to help him take down the Shawnessy drug-dealers. He wasn't even offering something in return. It was literally the stupidest interrogation I'd ever had the pleasure of being a part of.

I just told him that I didn't know anything. He countered by saying he'd have to bring me in for cocaine possession.

"What cocaine?" I asked with a mischievous smirk.

He kept insisting that he wasn't going to let me go, so I finally decided to give him something.

"Fine," I said. "You want to know who's bringing the drugs in?"

His eyes and ears almost perked through the roof of the car. He even pulled out a notepad and pen. "Yes, I do."

"The Jamaicans!"

I had a big smile on my face as he wrote it down in his pad. This guy was nuts.

"Yeah man, the Jamaicans," I continued, my face barely being able to contain itself.

"Do you got a number for them?"

His idiocy had no bounds. I gave him one of my old soft phone numbers. He then got out of the vehicle, opened my door, unlocked the cuffs, and told me that I had to walk home since he didn't want anyone to know I was helping him.

It was by far the weirdest interaction of my life.

Around this time, my friend Jimmy crashed my car during a night ride. I was in the passenger's seat with a girl I was bringing home from the bar; preoccupied with the girl, I had let Jimmy drive so I could get acquainted with my new date. That's when Jimmy drove his drunk self, and my black sports car, right into the median. When the cops arrived, it turned out that they had a warrant for my arrest—for an unpaid transit ticket, of all things. I didn't remember the ticket in question, but try telling that to a cop bound by his duty of service.

They brought me downtown and put me in holding.

While there, I made friends with my cellmate, a guy named Rob. He was a nice enough guy, easy to talk to. He had shoulder-length black locks and had a solid build. We laughed and chatted and ended up getting released at the same time. He asked for my number and I gave him a fake one, since I didn't know him from a hole in the ground. He seemed a little out of his element, like he was a family guy or something.

At home, Jimmy was begging for forgiveness. I just responded that I really didn't care about the car. I'd just go get another when I had time.

But that time never came. I was too high to put in the time and energy to go get one.

Without a car, my addiction took off. My binges went on for days, just one steady line of cocaine after another. I secluded myself at home and stopped taking calls; I was too messed up. I got myself into debt and slowly drifted away from the drug-dealing game. I couldn't run my business. I stayed drunk constantly, unhappy from being in a psychotic state. It was almost like I'd decided to take a vacation from my crazy life.

One night while sleeping on my couch, my eyes snapped open. My heart beat loudly and my eyes darted around the room. Something was wrong. I felt it with every fibre of my being. Despite my adrenaline spiking, however, I was unable to move. I looked around frantically, unable to move my head. What was going on? Why couldn't I move?

All of a sudden, the cushion covering the hide-a-bed started to lift, slowly. There wasn't enough room for someone to have been hiding in there, but the cushion just kept moving upward.

I wanted to run, but I couldn't move a muscle.

Suddenly, with a crazy burst of speed, I shot up and lifted the cushion. What I saw there would haunt me for the rest of my life. A human hand shot out.

I screamed at the top of my lungs, flying off the couch and out the door with no shoes on. I backed off the property, flailing my arms and yelling that there was something in my couch.

Mel came bolting onto the porch, begging me to come back inside before I woke up the whole neighbourhood. I didn't care.

"Cody, get in the house!"

After about fifteen minutes of negotiation in front of a growing crowd of neighbours, Mel finally convinced me to come inside. I bolted past the living room and up to her hopefully safe bedroom. She told me the next day that I shook violently in her bed for hours.

I slept there for a few days, in the safety of my roommate's presence, until I finally got the guts to be by myself in the living room at night again.

I just couldn't figure out what a hand had been doing in the couch. I searched and pondered, but there was no explanation. My only guess was that it might have been the spirit of Lewis, come to haunt me. That was probably the only thing that could actually scare me.

Less than a week later, I was again sleeping on the sofa, although I was sober now. The fear of seeing another ghost hand was all I needed to stay that way. And sober I stayed, to keep that crazy demon hand at bay.

That night, my eyes blasted open again with the same sinister feeling. Instinctively I knew something was again wrong. I was frozen, unable to move. My eyes darted around the room, looking for the cause of my primal fear. The TV was on, dimly lighting the otherwise dark room.

My gaze landed on my lamp at the foot of the couch. As my eyes slowly adjusted, I saw a hooded figure about seven feet tall looming over the lamp. I became paralyzed with fear.

Realizing that I could finally move my hands, I pulled the blanket over my face. *Maybe it will go away*, I told myself.

Fear made me check again five seconds later, and it was still there, not moving. I pulled the blanket back up.

At that point, I lost my mind. I jumped and screamed and ran out the door for the second time in a week. It was déjà vu for the whole neighbourhood. Mel, now a seasoned veteran in dealing with her shrieking, shoeless roommate, talked me back inside after half an hour.

Completely sober, I knew that something evil was coming for me. It was no joke.

Once again, I shook violently in her bed for hours. I found it even harder to calm down the second time around, and I knew I would have to move out. I prayed it was just the house that was haunted, and that the spectre would leave me alone if I left.

I moved out the following day.

Chapter Thirty-One

THE OLD CODY

I found a new place, still in the southwest corner of the city, sharing a house with two guys. They were both super weird to me, but it was affordable and the location was perfect. I stayed away from cocaine as much as I could during this period, but I dabbled. My phone still rang, too, pushing me to get my addiction under control so I could get back to hustling. The guy I had been working for told me that he had a place for me to stay as soon as I got back on my feet.

My ghostly encounters became a thing of the past, but they were still extremely fresh in my mind every time I went to sleep. I couldn't wrap my head around it. It put into question everything I knew and understood. I had never believed in ghosts, but now they became a stark reality.

One morning, I had to get on the train to make my way home after a long night of drinking at a friend's house. It was March and the spring air still had a bite to it. I stood at the light rail station, barely able to remember the previous night.

Suddenly, I looked up and saw a freight train passing on the other side of a fence. For some reason unbeknownst to me, I thought it would be an absolutely fantastic idea to sober up by jumping on a moving train. These trains went super slow through the city, so I figured I could just jump on the back and relax for a while.

Genius.

I ran off the platform and around the fence separating the tracks just in time to catch the caboose of the freight train. It was travelling at maybe ten kilometres an hour, so I managed to jump on with no troubles at all.

My senses tweaked as I let the cool air sweep over my face. It was wonderful.

Why doesn't everybody do this? I asked myself. *I'm never taking the light rail again.*

The liberating gush of pleasure faded, though, and I needed to get high again. I noticed a ladder leading to the top of the caboose, and it was the only thing separating me from my destiny. When I'd climbed to the top, I spread my arms wide.

Laughing, I gave everyone the middle finger as the train moved, passing through one intersection after another. Flipping everybody off gave me the greatest feeling ever.

The train jolted, picking up speed, and I almost fell off. The first thing that went through my mind was surprise at how quickly the train sped up. That didn't matter. It was time to get off.

By the time I got to the platform at the bottom of the ladder, the train had accelerated to at least sixty kilometres per hour. Scrambling for an idea of how to get off, I looked off the side and took a quick inventory—all I saw were rocks, grass, and debris. If I jumped, I would likely impale myself on a steel pipe or smash my head on a rock.

I thought about where the train would likely stop, and that's when I got worried. These things went all the way through the mountains to British Columbia. Being early March, I wasn't exactly dressed for the occasion. I'd more than likely freeze to death.

It was going at least seventy kilometres per hour now.

The thought crossed my mind that I could climb to the top and walk the train all the way to the front, taking refuge with the engineer. But these things were at least a hundred cars long and it would be traveling at a hundred thirty kilometres per hour by then.

That left me with only one option. I grabbed the vertical bar on the back of the caboose and jumped down, landing on my feet and sliding along the rail bed.

In that split second, I realized that I was probably going to die. My shoes were skidding across very large rocks and the locomotive wheel screamed right beside me. My legs weakening by the second, I knew there was a chance they would go under that unforgiving wheel.

I tried to get my feet under me, to run, but I lost both shoes in the first two steps. Now I was being dragged barefoot, my legs skidding over the rocks. I don't know how I managed to keep gripping that vertical bar, but I did.

With every ounce of strength, I pulled myself back to a barefoot standing position. Big mistake. My feet planted and I in turn went flying, doing somersaults.

I don't know how in the world I didn't lose any limbs, but I hit the ground after a couple of flips and continued to roll for twenty feet. I don't know how it happened, but I ended up in a standing position, stunned. I raised my hands to my face, half-expecting them to be missing.

Something physiological happened when I noticed that all my limbs were intact: a rush of blood to the head. Then I dropped to the ground, knocked out.

Now, just imagine everything I've just described to you, except imagine that you're watching it unfold from your car on the road. You hear a scream and see a stupid kid skiing behind the back of a freight train. He tries to run and he loses both shoes, then proceeds to plant his feet which results in him flying through the air. Through the cloud of dust, you see him stick the landing, then collapse in a heap.

Crazy kids these days. Maybe you should call an ambulance.

Well, as my luck would have it, such an observer did exist. A man witnessed me fall off the speeding train and did me the favour of getting me much-needed medical attention. I woke up in an ambulance unable to speak of the horrors I had just endured.

In the hospital, the doctors hooked me up to IV bags and got me high as a kite. I'd never tried morphine, but it felt nice. I looked down the bed at my damaged feet and the massive cuts atop them. I couldn't believe I was still alive.

No one was around when I woke up the second time, so I grabbed my cell phone and called my buddy Steven. He came straight to the hospital and helped me escape. I figured I would probably have some broken bones in my feet, so I decided to keep the morphine drip bag. I left without talking to doctors or getting X-rays.

We roared with laughter as we sped away, me in a hospital gown. I was embarrassed about my adventure, so I just told my friends it was a hit and run.

They dropped me off at my house, and that's when the pain really started to kick my butt, possibly trying to tell me I should have stayed in the hospital. In my delusional state, I decided that I needed cocaine. So I called my boss and he dropped off a package big enough to get my drug-dealing career going again.

That night, I once again wanted to die. My life was insane.

My boss had brought me twenty-eight grams of cocaine, which would have made fifty-six bags to sell at fifty dollars apiece. That would bring me $2,800 if I sold it all.

However, I didn't sell any. I snorted every last bag that night. All fifty-six. I would open one, crush it into a massive line, snort the whole thing at once, then lay down until I passed out from my overdose. Twenty minutes later, I'd wake up, wipe all the blood off me, then crush up the next bag and snort it. Repeat until every last crumb was gone.

I don't know how I didn't die. It seems as impossible as a ghost hand coming out of the couch.

I was trying to kill myself, but somehow I kept waking up.

Once again I was left penniless, with no more drugs. The excruciating physical pain of coming down, coupled with my physical injuries from the train, was more than I could bear.

The old Cody was back.

Chapter Thirty-Two

DIVINE PREMONITION

I stayed in bed, sick from how depressed I felt. I didn't want to look in the mirror. My family was long gone at this point and I honestly felt like I was the loneliest person in the world. I tossed and turned for days on end, wishing my heart would stop. I considered hanging myself from the stair banister.

One night while watching TV from bed, something caught my attention to the right of the screen. I ignored it at first, but it kept moving. At first I thought I was seeing tracers, even though I was stone cold sober, but then I realized that it had to be something real; tracers would follow my gaze, but this thing stayed put.

I moved closer, and then I realized what I was looking at. Devon was waving his arms as frantically as he could to get my attention.

"Devon?" I screamed.

He bobbed his head up and down, confirming that it really was him. I wasn't tripping out at all. I knew instantly that he was there, standing in front of me. This was no hallucination, no illusion.

Devon couldn't speak, but we spoke through gestures. He was transparent, making it hard to see him well, but I could at least make out what he was trying to say.

After five minutes of screaming at the top of my lungs, no doubt leading my roommates to conclude that I had serious problems, Devon cut to the chase. This was no average ghostly house call. He had come with purpose.

He started showing me visions of myself doing lines of cocaine. After they faded away, I apologized to Devon for being a cokehead. He just shook his head, pointed at his own chest, then at the sky. He then pointed at me and pointed downward.

I had never believed in any kind of afterlife, but his was message was clear: he was in heaven, and I was going to hell.

I'd like to say that I believed in God before this, but that would be a lie. This was definitive proof, though. My dead best friend was standing in front of me playing charades while I was five days sober. This was real.

When I asked if I was going to hell, he nodded with a look of urgent sadness on his face.

He then started pointing at all the pictures on my wall. A *Scarface* poster, pictures of weed and cocaine… Devon made motions of tearing them up. I asked him if he wanted me to rip down the posters and he bobbed his head excitedly. He got very animated every time I guessed correctly.

I hesitated for a second before getting up to rip the poster. It crossed my mind that if I moved, I might cause Devon to disappear, and I wanted to spend every last second I could with him. Just as I thought this, as if he could read my thoughts, he walked across the room in front of me to the closet. He was trying to tell me that he wasn't going anywhere.

I got up and gladly ripped every one of my posters off the wall and stuffed them in the garbage. When I sat back down on my bed, he was nodding at me as if to tell me I'd done a good job. He then pointed at the Tony Montana clock hanging above my door, followed by a vision of me doing cocaine in my Versace sunglasses.

His message was ringing loud and clear. I put my beloved clock in the garbage with the posters.

Devon then leaned over my nightstand table and pounded his finger overtop a photo album I had sitting on top of it. He was telling me to open it up. I did so without hesitation, and in the album I saw pictures of me getting high. In some of them I was doing lines and in others I was smoking weed or drinking. There were also pictures of me holding pounds of weed and big bags of blow. The whole photo album was dedicated to my sad addiction, and Devon was telling me to rip the pictures.

I understood why he was here. I asked him for forgiveness and then made a commitment to him that I would stop using. I would put everything in the garbage.

This wasn't my imagination. It was real. And if this was real, and I knew it was, then it meant I was going to hell.

Devon started showing me more visions of me doing lines of cocaine. Only this time, the visions continued, showing me as I put a rope around my neck and jumped off something. I watched myself die by hanging.

The vision then took a very strange turn. In it, I wasn't dead—in fact, I looked very much alive—but I had a look on my face of terror. I looked deathly afraid, and I was running. I could tell I was in a forest, and there was something weird about the forest that I couldn't quite put my finger on.

I tried to hide myself behind a tree, and that's when the thing I was running from came into focus: dogs—not normal dogs, but massive, vicious dogs. They had gigantic mouths with huge folds over their snouts, exposing monstrous fangs. Their eyes were demonic as they chased me to do God only knows what.

The vision ended with Devon pointing at his own chest again, then to the sky again, then to me again, and then to the ground again.

I was going to kill myself.

The forest thing was strange, though. I didn't understand it.

I don't remember falling asleep, and I find it hard to believe that I would be capable of falling asleep under those conditions, but somehow I passed out.

That was the last time I ever saw Devon.

I woke up in the morning to see my buddy Eves in my room. He had never even been in my house before, let alone come into my bedroom to wake me out of bed. Well, I lost my mind when I saw him. I screamed in his face.

I tried to calm down while taking inventory of my torn apart room. All the walls were bare, the paraphernalia smashed, and my broken Tony Montana clock was in the garbage. Eves was really confused. He sat down with me and listened to my story. I left nothing out, even the confusing part about the forest and the dogs.

By the end, Eves was white as a ghost. He explained to me that his girlfriend was in the middle of reading a book about hell. The book was a written account of a lady's real-life experience in which Jesus had appeared to her and taken her down to hell so she could write a book about it and tell the world that it exists. According to the book, when you kill yourself you are taken to a leafless forest and are tortured by animals for eternity.

That's what had been weird about my forest, the thing I hadn't been able to put my finger on. It had been leafless.

Chapter Thirty-Three

CALL FROM THE NORTH

My perception of the world had been shaken to its core. I had always acted like I believed in God, but this hit me like a baseball bat to the face. I couldn't wrap my head around something like this, but Devon's appearance had been tangible. Just like that, heaven and hell, angels and demons, were real to me. I became one hundred percent certain of it.

I never asked Devon's family, but I know now that he must have found God before he passed. To this day, Devon is my angel, and his message was divine. Untold horrors awaited my soul if I lived for evil. This meant that I needed to make a drastic change or be condemned to an eternity of pain and sorrow.

The first thing I had to do was escape Calgary. Moving in with my parents wasn't an option since my mother was still keeping me detached from family life. Those connections had been dislodged long ago at this point. So I decided to give Alex a call. I ended up needing to beg him, but he loved me and my desperation moved him to want to help. His girlfriend was also on board.

Off I went sixty kilometres south to High River, Alberta.

Upon arrival, I told them what had happened. When they heard about the vision, they both thought I was nuts, and justifiably so. Still, they blessed me with a place to live and Alex even helped me get a job: cleaning a meat-packing plant on the night shift. I literally had to clean up guts and blood all night.

Manual labour really wasn't my forte, so I accomplished very little every time I went to work. Alex, on the other hand, was a master in the art of purging entrails. I would just sit around smoking a joint. It was literally the only way I could push myself to go. I would proceed to smoke as much weed as I could to make my time there tolerable. This didn't sit well with Alex, since I was supposed to be out there to get sober.

One day, Alex told me he couldn't afford to pay for all the food I was eating. I could tell he and his girlfriend were a little upset given that I hadn't contributed anything to the household. I just ate their food and smoked their weed.

The two of them gave me a ride to the local grocery store. When we got there, I asked his girlfriend to go inside and tell the workers that she had just gotten approved to pick up a donation from the local food bank—but she had to supply her own bags, which she didn't have. I figured they would be more than happy to oblige her by giving her a whole bunch of empty grocery bags.

Five minutes later, she came out with the bags.

After handing them to me, I trotted into the store, grabbed a cart, and started cruising through the aisles. I loaded the cart with far more food than was needed for three people. Pretty soon it was towering with delicious grub. I even grabbed a bouquet of flowers for Alex's girlfriend. I then pulled into a secluded part of the store and began placing everything into the empty bags. A few items didn't fit, and I just hid those in the middle of the cart where they weren't visible.

A few minutes later, I rolled the massive shopping cart out the front door, walking by all the busy clerks and even waving at them with a big innocent smile on my face.

I walked out with about $600 worth of groceries that day.

I ran with the cart toward the waiting car, but as I hurried through the parking lot the cart tipped, leaving a condemning trail of groceries in my wake. Good Samaritans all began helping me pick them up off the ground. "Thank you so kindly," I said to them. They even helped me pack everything into the trunk of the car.

Alex and his girlfriend lost it when we popped the trunk at their house to the sight of hundreds of dollars in stolen goods—fruits and vegetables, bread, drinks, snacks, frozen goods, meat, and even the bouquet of flowers, which I presented to her with a hug. They loved me.

My intentions were good, but clearly my psychopathic traits were still very much in control. I'm sure God was shaking His head at me.

Around this time, Steven joined me out in High River. He was having a rough go in the city and wanted to get away for the summer. Every day we bought a pack of twenty-four beers and went down to the sandy beach off the Highwood River. There we jumped off the bridge, had campfires, and drank beer. Steven and I talked, laughed, and got hammered there all summer long.

As the summer came to an end, something was calling us back to the big city. Calgary was constantly on our minds. Steven was the first to go back.

But my vision of Devon weighed heavily on my mind. What did I want in my life? Was I capable of staying sober? I had been a constant failure in sobriety and I couldn't picture life with or without substance.

I was at another fork in the road.

Chapter Thirty-Four

THE TEST

One day, while walking out of a convenience store in High River, someone on the way in recognized me.

"I know you from somewhere," the guy said. He was a big guy with long black hair.

It took a second for my drug-addled mind to catch up, but I soon figured it out. This was Rob, the man I had met in the holding cell after Jimmy had crashed my car. I was more than a little surprised to bump into him all the way out in High River. He explained to me that he had been out golfing with some friends and was seeking out a local watering hole.

"I got a handle on all the good spots," I told him.

When he asked if I wanted to tag along, I was happy to oblige.

We got into his truck and I met his friends, both of whom looked like bikers. The shorter one was Brett and the taller one was Walker. I'd spent a lot of time in the underworld at this point and could sniff out a gangster from a mile away. These guys were serious. But I didn't bring it up and didn't ask questions. I knew it would be rude to ask about gang affiliations.

I guided my new friends to a local pub and we spent the entire evening drinking, laughing, and breaking bread. These guys loved me. They kept provoking me to share hilarious stories, my favourite of which was my attempt to depart from a moving train. We shared pitcher after pitcher and story after story. By the end of the night, I had forgotten completely that I had thought these guys were gangsters. It was hard to cast a dark shadow around such benevolence.

When it came time to go, they picked up the bill, and it didn't escape my drunk consciousness that Rob pulled out a massive wad of hundreds. He also tipped the waitress about fifty percent of the tab. I watched, silently intrigued.

But I followed the gangster mantra: don't ask, don't tell.

They dropped me off at home and I gave Rob my real phone number this time.

———————

After some time had passed, I retreated back to the city, my gangster ambitions heavy on my mind. I went right back into my old life, running a small dial-a-dope operation with Steven, although it wasn't much more than a means of supplying our own monster habits. We spent countless nights doing lines together.

One day I got a phone call from Walker, who wanted to know if I could help him with something. No problem, I told him. I didn't even ask what the favour was.

He picked me up from the house I shared with Steven and we proceeded to leave the neighbourhood. We got some good laughs in, picking up right where we'd left off. For some reason, I bestowed a lot of trust in this new friend. He seemed like a loyal guy, which made me want to get closer to him.

As we pulled into a busy mall parking lot, I frowned. At last he disclosed the favour he needed: he needed to retrieve a briefcase from a locker inside the mall, but he couldn't be seen on camera taking it. My mission was to discreetly and nonchalantly pick up the briefcase and bring it back without looking inside.

My heart began to race, but I shoved aside my anxiety. I didn't see this as a setup; I saw it as an opportunity to take what was mine and reclaim my rightful place beside some real gangsters. This was my chance.

I walked into the mall with my hat low over my eyes and my hands in my pockets. A million thoughts raced through my mind. What was in the package? Money? Cocaine? For all I knew, I might be walking out of there with a bunch of cut-up body parts. I had no idea, and I loved it.

I opened the locker and there it was—a medium-size black briefcase. I took one last look around as I reached in. My first thought when I picked it up was that it didn't feel heavy enough to be body parts.

Closing the locker, I turned around, half-expecting to be tackled by a cop or security officer, but there was no one in sight. I strutted out into the busy mall, on a mission, every step solid and aggressive. I didn't know what I would do if I was grabbed, but I knew I wouldn't go down easy. I would protect whatever was in the briefcase with my life

Once outside, the sun hit my face and I took a gulp of fresh air. My confidence skyrocketed as I approached Walker's jeep. I coolly opened the door and climbed in, passing him the briefcase and smiling.

He smiled back at me. "Let's go for beers."

After a few pitchers at the bar, he leaned in to whisper something into my ear. "Rob wanted me to test you today. We want to bring you in on something big. You didn't ask questions and did exactly as you were told. We all like you, brother. Rob wants to meet with you tomorrow and discuss a business opportunity. You cool with that?"

I replied with a nod.

My outer expression of calm didn't correlate with my inner excitement. I felt like I was going to explode.

He dropped me off after a couple of hours.

"Good work today, brother," he said as he passed me a handful of hundred dollar bills.

"See you tomorrow, dude," I replied.

As I approached my front door, I pulled out the cash and stared at it for a second. That was literally the easiest money I'd ever made. I laughed out loud. These guys had it locked up tight.

Time to be a gangster again.

Chapter Thirty-Five

THE CLEAN-UP MAN

The following day, Rob took me to a restaurant for a bite to eat. As we chatted, I once again didn't ask any questions. I was just happy to be a part of this.

He soon explained that he didn't ever want to speak inside a vehicle, in the event of police surveillance. I knew a fair bit about how that worked and knew that vehicles could be bugged if they had been impounded recently.

We then drove to a bar in the north end where Rob was to meet with someone. But he had a bad feeling about this guy. He needed me to watch their interaction and then figure out what vehicle the guy was driving, and retrieve his plate number. Sounded fun.

I went into the bar first, found a table, and ordered some food and a pitcher of beer to take the edge off. Rob came in ten minutes later and sat down about thirty feet from me. We both played it cool. Rob's unsuspecting friend joined him about ten minutes later.

I watched intently as the men conversed about who knows what. Once again, my mind raced at a million miles an hour. What the hell was I involved in? I couldn't ask; one of the things they liked about me was that I didn't ask questions. So I played it cool and waited for my opportunity to jump into action. At some point, the man got up and walked out of the bar.

Showtime.

I walked outside and followed this guy through the parking lot. Without a clue, he jumped into a vehicle where someone was waiting in the driver's seat. As they drove off, I memorized the plate number.

Laughing to myself at how easy this was, I strolled back into the bar and joined Rob. I gave him the information and we proceeded to get drunk. Later that evening, he presented me with another fistful of hundred-dollar bills.

These guys were obviously pros. This was organized crime.

As the months passed, I got deeper into their organization, which involved gun-running, stolen goods, dirty deeds, and countless other illicit activities. But one thing we weren't involved in was drugs. Even though I did cocaine fairly consistently, I could tell that my new friends frowned upon it and they wanted to help me get clean.

When I wasn't with them, though, I continued my life as a cocaine trafficker. Steven's and my little operation picked up momentum as we built our clientele. We were a dangerous team and partied hard every single night. We were both paranoid, too, and had a cache of firearms at the house.

Steven was uninterested in meeting my new friends, and I remember thinking he must be a little jealous. But that wasn't it. Steven just didn't trust anybody but me. We had each other's backs and I loved him with all my heart. Everyone knew that if you messed with one of us, the other would be coming for you with murder in his eyes.

As time passed, my friendship with Rob and his crew flourished. I loved the way they cared about me and encouraged me to better myself. They even asked me to get a real job so I could thwart police detection and keep myself busy and off the blow.

Steven and I got jobs at a gourmet burger joint on the south side of town. We were drunk and high most of the time, but the work helped.

Every time Rob and the boys gave me a new assignment, I felt a rush. I was making tons of money and getting hammered with them at strip clubs almost every single day.

One day, my new friends informed me that I was a suspect in a capital crime. Nobody knew what it was, but I instinctively knew that it was in connection with Lewis's murder. This jeopardized my position in their organization, as it would bring too much heat on them.

I was crushed. These guys were my brothers. I told them I would do anything to stay in the organization, even offering to kill if necessary. They told me that I could talk to one of the guys who specialized in "clean-up." I agreed to the meeting.

When I sat down with their so-called clean-up man, I told him that I didn't have any idea what the cops might have on me. I then lied, saying that I had been the trigger man in a complicated homicide that I had callously planned and executed. Of course, I hadn't really been the trigger man, and in fact Lewis's murder had been an accident, but I needed to sound ruthless. After I told him the story, he agreed that I had cleaned up the murder nicely and that I should be fine as long as everyone kept their mouths shut. My job was safe for now.

Not only was it safe, but I was going to be moved up to more significant tasks, such as possibly serving as a hitman. I was on top of the world. Kill people for a living? That was next level.

Chapter Thirty-Six

FUNNY GUY

I had managed to shove aside my concerns about Devon's divine message, telling myself that I would stay alive long enough to change my destiny later—if not, I would just claim my place in hell when all was said and done. I was oddly accepting of that. As a seeker of instant gratification, I couldn't square short-term pleasures with long-term consequences. I had tunnel vision.

The next step was for me to move out of my house with Steven. They were in universal agreement that I needed to get away from the cocaine I had surrounded myself with. They wanted me out of the dope game.

They helped me get a place with a friend and colleague from the burger joint. It was a nice house overlooking Fish Creek Park in the quiet neighbourhood of Deer Run in south Calgary. I drifted away from Steven during this period and focused entirely on my life with my new friends, who set up one task after another for me complete. I felt content and satisfied with my new life.

One day, an old cocaine customer of mine offered me tickets to a Keith Urban concert. The seats were incredible and he told me that I didn't even need to pay him; the tickets were a gift. They also included backstage passes.

I was stoked and wanted to invite a girl I had been trying to connect with for some time. She had a boyfriend, but my lack of empathy didn't let me care about that. I persisted in my venture, and on this day I had tickets to go see her favourite country singer and even go backstage. She excitedly accepted my generous offer.

When it came to women, my strategy was always to get them drunk enough to dull their decision-making abilities. I wasn't much of a ladies man, so alcohol was pretty much the only way to get me a sleepover. I didn't mind being a girl's mistake. I was very selfish.

The night of the concert, I picked up two mickeys of Crown Royal and took the light rail to the concert, knowing full well I wouldn't be in any state to drive home. Hopefully, I'd have some female company for the ride back—if God willed it.

But God did not will it. It turned out my hot date didn't drink.

The first half of the concert was a blast, but it became increasingly obvious that this girl had way too much self-respect to cheat on her boyfriend. This realization propelled me to imbibe drink after drink, downing both of the mickeys I'd brought and finishing off seven beers from the concert vendor. To this day, I don't think I've ever been more drunk in my entire life. I was slurring and tripping over everything. I remember drunkenly asking if she wanted to come home with me, and I don't think the words were even in the proper chronological order—"Home with me come?" Needless to say, my hot date wasn't too inclined to share my bed that night. She probably went home and squeezed her boyfriend tight.

Well, she wasn't the first and she wouldn't be the last. It took a very specific breed of human to keep up with me.

I woke up in the morning to the sound of my phone ringing. I answered it after the very first ring to thwart off the looming second ring.

"Can you work later?" Rob said after asking how my night had gone.

"Sure can. But I need at least four more hours to sober up."

He agreed to give me some time to sleep. "You at home right now?"

"Yuppers." I was desperate to end the phone call so I could pass out again.

"Okay, see you later."

He quickly hung up and I immediately closed my eyes again, thanking God that I could go back to sleep.

But our Lord has a funny sense of humour.

Two minutes later, I heard the loud crash of people breaking through the door, followed by screams and a series of bangs. I knew right away it could only be one thing.

"Calgary Police, get on the ground," someone yelled at me.

The SWAT team entered with guns drawn, then pulled my naked butt out of bed and slammed me to the floor, lights flashing in my face. And I had thought the ringing phone was bad for my hangover!

Eventually they pulled me to my feet and one of the officers was kind enough to toss me some underwear. As they escorted me up the stairs at gunpoint, I tried to figure out what this was about. I assumed it was for drugs, as I hadn't always been careful about how I networked. But I had no cocaine or guns in the house—my friends had insisted on that. After the police executed their search warrant, I figured I'd be released.

The officers walked me into the kitchen and sat me down at the kitchen table.

I laughed to myself as I took in the scene. There were about twenty-five police officers in the house and nearly as many cars packing the street out front. Through the window, I could see cops posted all over Fish Creek Park. I could hear helicopters flying low, too, just in case I made a dash for it. This was a full-out police raid. Overkill.

Once I had the chance to think about it, I knew I had nothing to fear. Their search wouldn't turn up anything. I would walk away with a big smile on my face, as always.

As the uniformed officers helping me into a pair of sweatpants, a plainclothes cop approached us. I recognized him instantly—it was that crazy cop who had been trying to get me to cooperate with him the previous year. This seemed to confirm that this was a drug raid. I breathed out a sigh of relief. I had never been so happy to see a cop in my life. I could have kissed him!

"Remember me?" he asked.

I returned his smile with one of my own. "Oh yeah. Did you catch those Jamaicans yet?" I thought that was the wittiest retort in history.

"You're a funny guy. Cody William Bates, you're under arrest for first degree murder."

First degree murder carries the maximum sentence in Canada, life without eligibility of parole for twenty-five years. But the thing that rang in my thoughts while waiting in the police cruiser outside the house was that Lewis's murder had been an accident. Why were they charging me with premeditated murder? I wondered if Jimmy or Brad had been picked up, too.

My heart squeezed inside my chest as I let the full weight of what was happening land on me. I stared at the trees in the nearby park, watching them blow in the light September wind. It hit me that this might be the last time I looked at that park.

I soaked up every last image of scenery as we drove away. Everything looked so gorgeous to me. The trees, the houses, the stores, the cars, the people... Perhaps because I figured I might not see any of this again until my late forties. I didn't want to miss a second.

I felt numb—not sad, not angry. I didn't think I was getting out of this.

We pulled into police headquarters downtown, where I was escorted inside and taken up the elevator. Instead of stopping at the holding tanks, which I had expected, we continued up. When we stepped out, the first clue about where I was turned out to be small rectangular sign on the wall reading "Homicide."

I was in the big leagues now.

They sat me down at a desk inside a locked interrogation room and removed my cuffs. The wheels in my head worked overtime as I tried to piece together exactly what had happened. If they thought I had committed premeditated murder, how had they come up with that?

As I came to a startling realization, I felt like a cement blanket was crushing me. Rob, Walker, Brett, and the clean-up guy I'd confessed to had all been cops. I had been tricked into confessing to a murder I hadn't even committed.

My throat crushed from the hurt and betrayal. I had considered those guys brothers. I would have given my life for them, and they hadn't even told me their real names.

The scope of the investigation slowly dawned on me. These detectives' lives for the past several months had revolved entirely around me. They had been setting up fake crime after fake crime to dupe me into believing they were heavy hitters in the criminal underworld. No doubt they had me on video saying that I had been the one to plan and execute a heinous killing.

I started to think about my options. They knew about Jimmy, because I had told them, but they didn't know about Brad. I had kept that part to myself.

It crossed my mind that I could escape this whole situation by just telling them about Brad, who was the real killer. The murder charge would be gone, just like that.

I can't explain where it comes from inside me, but I just can't rat another guy out. The thought of snitching to save my own ass is enough to make me want to puke. I couldn't do something like that and still look at myself in the mirror.

I brushed the thought aside. I was a gangster through and through.

Besides, I wasn't innocent. I had let Brad use my shotgun on a man I'd decided to rob because of a turf war beef I had with him. And I'd been the only one sober on the night of the murder.

Perhaps I wasn't guilty of this precise murder charge, but I was culpable. I would be going away no matter what.

I sat in that chair, with my feet on the desk and my hands behind my head, for what felt like days. Detectives would come in and sit down, but I wouldn't talk except to insult them. I made myself very hard to talk to. These guys didn't scare me. They told me that the jury would end up watching this video recording and everyone would see what a cold-hearted monster I was. I just smiled and told them to get me my lawyer—and not to come back without him.

I stayed in that chair for two days. I wanted to lay on the ground and rest, but I didn't want to show weakness. The dirty floor wasn't worthy of Cody Bates.

They finally took me down to the holding tanks, where they put me in with Jimmy. Right away I put a finger over my lips, indicating for him to stay silent. No doubt they had put us in a bugged room. He got the message right away.

When I asked him if he knew what had tipped off the police about us, he confessed that he had confided to an AA sponsor. Jimmy didn't know the truth about who had pulled the trigger that night, but I had told him that I did it—and that's the story he shared with his sponsor, who had been wearing a wire and acting as a police agent. Jimmy felt just as betrayed as I did.

Unfortunately, this meant that my false confession had been corroborated. That's how the police had justified the expense of their operation against me.

I wasn't mad at Jimmy, though. I told him that I loved him and that I would take care of him in jail. We would face the future together.

PART
III

Chapter Thirty-Seven

DEEP MORAL CODES

Walking into Calgary Remand at 3:00 p.m., I knew from the bottom of my aching heart that it was time to step into my big boy shoes, for I was being put on a unit designed to hold accused murderers. Murderers aren't separated in maximum security, as one might think. They live together, eat together, play together, and plot together, all day long.

I passed through a big airlock door labelled "Maximum Security." Inside, unit five was on the left and unit six on the right. I was to be housed in unit six. Between the units was the guards' bubble, fortified by shatterproof glass and a thick cement wall. Across from the entrance to unit six was a weight room for inmates who wanted to work out during their designated times.

When I walked onto the unit, a quick glance around told me that there were twelve cells upstairs and twelve cells downstairs, all of which had double bunks. The upper and lower tiers were never allowed out of their cells at the same time.

I knew that my gang owned this prison, so I was going to be fine.

As I stood at the bubble, the guards assigned me to a cell on the upper tier. The upper tier prisoners were out of their cells at the moment, on "dayroom," and an Asian man sized me up from his card table as I walked in. It turned out that everyone here had been waiting for me, since word had gotten around that I had been arrested. I had been in the newspapers for a couple of days.

I brought everybody up to speed on what had gone down, and I was quickly informed that I had succumbed to a Mr. Big operation. Apparently countless accused killers had fallen victim to it over the years, leading me to wonder how many others had confessed to crimes they hadn't actually committed. But at least I wasn't a unique case. These operations still take place across Canada all the time.

I chatted with the guys, who filled me in about all the gangs that were currently housed in the jail. Not surprisingly, the guys in the Max called all the shots.

My short and stocky Asian comrade "had the floor," meaning that he was the boss, and since my gang controlled the prison, this was the guy to know. He was a natural leader, seasoned in prison and gang politics, stuff I didn't know very much about. I knew how to make money, but in here you had to know about territorial control. Our gang needed to maintain the highest level of control. This was accomplished through intimidation and stiff-arm tactics on both inmates and guards. We stayed unified as brothers and in turn controlled the population.

All of the gang members on unit six were tattooed from head to toe, and we are all in for murder. Some of the others had multiple killings under their belts.

There are certain rules to follow when living on a maximum security unit. Number one, if someone asks you to leave, you don't go. The only way you leave a unit is on a stretcher. That's the only way to maintain your reputation as a solid guy. If you walk off a unit, you're considered a "hideout" and a "check-off," which will follow you everywhere you go after that. You could change cities and eventually someone would recognize you and tell the population that you were a check-off. The whole unit would then come after you and you'd be in a constant state of terror, afraid of getting knifed in the back while you're lining up for dinner one day.

Another rule is that you don't talk to the guards. They aren't your buddies. Unless you're deploying some sort strategic ploy to get a guard to pass you something, you thoroughly ignore them.

In the Max, your word is everything. If you give your word about something, then it needs to be gold. If it's not, you will meet the blade. The only lower form of life in a prison than a liar is a paedophile.

Lastly, if you got called in to a cell to fight someone, you went in, win or lose. Failure to fight led to a beating—or a blade in the neck. You'd be leaving whether you wanted to or not. The nerve-wracking thing about going into a cell to fight someone is that the airlock would snap shut behind you and you'd be trapped in a cell with someone for the next thirty minutes until the door cracked again. That was a long time, especially if you were on the losing end of a fight. I saw countless people go out on a stretcher for that.

As dayroom ended, we were called into our "houses" (cells). I walked into the cell and saw the familiar steel toilet and desk adjacent to the bed. The airlock snapped shut behind me and I rolled my coveralls down to my waist, using the arms of my jumpsuit to tie it off like a belt. I lay on my bed and closed my eyes, hoping for a bit of sleep.

This wouldn't be so bad. I was a member of the most powerful gang in the prison, rubbing shoulders with one of the founding members.

As I was drifting off, I heard the unit door open and shut. I jumped, peeking through my window to see what was going on. At the bubble stood a monster of a man. He stood six feet, five inches, weighed three hundred forty pounds, wore a skinhead mohawk, and was tattooed from head to toe. This was by far the meanest-looking individual I'd ever seen—and he was pointing at my cell.

It seemed I had already been assigned a roommate.

The airlock cracked as the mountain of a man stepped inside, filling the entire doorway. He rocked his goatee, a sign that he was affiliated with a biker gang.

He stuck his hand out. "Name's Rolly."

The name rang my bell of recognition. This man was the founder of one of the most well-known white supremacist gangs in the country. When I shook his hand, it was like trying to shake a baseball glove. I offered up the bottom bunk, not really feeling like getting into an argument with him. But we ended up getting along. I told him about myself and he laughed at me for telling undercover cops that I had killed someone. He responded by showing me newspaper clippings of the operation that had taken him down, a multimillion-dollar sting.

The day was definitely bringing to light some interesting characters.

After getting to know each other, he asked if I wanted to get high.

"Definitely," I said with a big smile.

He told me to jump up on my bunk and turn away. I thought this was weird, but I did as he asked. I listened as he discussed the structure of his prison gang, and that's when I started to smell poop. It was so bad I could taste it. I tried so hard to keep the mental image of this big man pooping out of my head.

"Okay, done," he finally said, signalling for me to come down.

As I jumped down from my bunk, I realized why it had felt like I was snacking on a piece of crap. Rolly held out a piece of toilet paper containing a wrapped package the size of my forearm, and it was covered in faeces. I guess I hadn't really thought too hard about how people smuggled drugs from prison to prison.

He rinsed the poop off in the sink and then started to unwrap the package. As he got through the layers of saran wrap, I realized this cucumber-sized anal bead contained more than drugs. There was also a ten-inch blade. And this guy had just crunched it out like it was nothing.

"Let's get high," he said.

One of my deeply buried moral codes took effect at this point: I would never turn down bum weed from a man more than three times my size with a faecal-covered shank in his hand. We got good and ripped together, laughing and having a good time getting to know one another. He was looking at twelve years for a laundry list of charges.

He then asked me if I'd be interested in joining his white supremacist gang. I respectfully declined his generous offer since I was already a member of the crew that ran the jail.

Suddenly, Rolly went silent. I was so baked that I didn't even notice it at first.

Dinner was being served, so I walked out of my cell, stoned off my face, to grab my tray. We were supposed to take our dinners back to our cells, locking the doors behind us and eating in our rooms. But one of the other inmates invited me over for dinner at one of their houses. As I walked into this guy's cell, I met a white guy named Caleb and an Asian guy named Phuc who didn't speak English. We all sat down and began to dine.

The food… wasn't great. If this was the kind of food I'd be enjoying for the next twenty-five years, I wanted to die right now.

Just as I was poking my mystery meat, the leader of my gang walked in.

"By the way, don't tell Rolly you're with us," he said to me. "While he was gone, we stabbed up his second-in-command. If you tell him anything, he'll probably kill you."

All I could think about was that huge blade he'd pooped out. I guessed that explained why he had gotten so quiet when I'd told him which crew I was with.

"I already told him, right after he passed a shiv the size of a remote control," I said.

"Don't worry," the boss said. "We'll just deal with it right now."

I smiled. "That's perfect."

I went back to prodding my ball of meat, suddenly feeling like I'd lost my appetite. Would I be snacking on Rolly's bowel blade in a minute for desert?

One thing I forgot to ask as we walked out of the cell was what I was supposed to do. I returned my dinner tray, realizing that this was life and death. If I walked back into my cell with that man, I might as well flip a coin on my life expectancy. Clearly that sword he'd brought in his rectum was meant for payback.

But then I remembered a key part of the inmate's code: never refuse to go into a cell with someone. So I calmly walked to my cell.

Just go in, I told myself. *It'll all be over soon. This is your first day in prison. Don't mess it up.*

I can't begin to describe what was going through my head as I walked to the back of my cell and turned to face the door, waiting for my dreaded roommate to cast his gigantic shadow. But I was no coward.

I put my fists up and breathed heavily, listening to the boss man yell at Rolly down the hall, telling him that his second-in-command had been a rat. He was trying to make Rolly understand that his guy had been a check-off. But Rolly was having none of it. As I watched, he gave the boss man a violent shove and backed into our cell, slamming the airlock shut behind him.

He turned to face me with murder in his eyes. His veins bulged, his upper lip curling over his nose to expose colossal yellow teeth. He reached under the mattress under the top bunk and pulled out his imposing weapon.

"You going to kill me in my sleep," he screamed at me, taking a battle stance and pulling back the blade in preparation for launching the death blow.

That's as close as I'd ever come to pooping my pants. My stomach flipped as I bared my teeth back at him, not really having a plan. I just let my aggressive lip snarl do its thing. I stood ready, not daring to blink, as I calmly told him that I was new on the unit and hadn't known about what happened with him or his guy until just now. We stared each other down. I knew I was way out of my weight class, experience, and age. Oh, and I was unarmed. But I stood firm, feet planted, shoulders forward, and fists clenched.

The boss man was screaming at Rolly from the door, begging him not to kill me, to turn around and talk this out between bosses. I can't remember everything that was said because my heart was about to explode in my chest, but eventually Rolly put down the shank and said that everything was fine. He even asked if I wanted to get high.

My moral code was tested again, and I agreed to smoke some more bum weed with him.

My heartrate eventually slowed to normal and I brought my heavy breathing under control. It looked like things were going to work out.

That evening, the boss man took a slap from Rolly—a compromise for the action taken while he was absent. I would never have taken an open-handed slap from anyone; it was a major sign of disrespect. But it did save my life. I respected the boss man for that. I had a lot to learn about being a leader.

I lay in bed with my hands behind my head and pondered the last twenty-four hours. It was my first day in prison and I had already being shoved in the middle of gang and prison politics.

I would have to kill the last of my feelings if I was to survive in this hellhole. This was my new home, and these men were accustomed to reading people. They could smell fear and would eat you alive if you let off even the smallest pittance of it.

I spent that night murdering my old self—again. Afterward all I had left was hate, brutality, vengeance, and aggression. Primal evil. I was willing to do whatever it took to survive.

I had shown my fellow inmates that Cody Bates wasn't scared of anything. I had stepped into a cell with a man twice my size, a man armed with a blade, and stared death in the face. This did wonders for my reputation.

Now I just needed to live up to the hype.

Chapter Thirty-Eight

PRISON POLITICS

As the days and weeks passed, I read the Calgary newspapers. Almost every criminal worthy of a column in the paper was either on my unit or the cell block next door. I got to know them all, as well as the other gangs—there were Native gangs, biker gangs, white supremacist gangs, black gangs, Mexican gangs, and Islamic gangs. But my gang ruled the prison population with an iron fist. We snapped people's limbs, filled them full of holes, or stomped heads into the floor on the regular. Anyone who stepped out of line earned our wrath.

Our main enemy was a well-known rival group. Many of our friends had died at their hands, and vice versa. It had started on the streets long ago and raged on in the newspapers almost daily with shootings, killings, and never any arrests. Calgarians lived in constant fear of this thoughtless war. The police were up to their necks in killings.

In prison, currency came in the form of illicit substances. I can't think of a single day in jail when we weren't plotting how to get packages into the prison, and only about thirty percent of the packages ended up in our hands. When we did get a package, we would turn the drugs for at least ten times their street value. Prison trafficking was a cash cow. We'd move heroin, morphine, cannabis oil (honey oil), and liquid crystal meth.

But the more drugs we moved, the more the prison caught on to our methods. We were forced to evolve our thinking all the time. None of us used drugs other than substances with THC (tetrahydrocannabinol, the active ingredient in marijuana); it was frowned upon to belittle yourself in that way. We were soldiers, not junkies. Staying clean wasn't such a big mountain to climb for me, since I was enjoying the power I had as a high-ranking member of my gang.

The money-makers on the street had built a system for us in the form of a fund designed to pay the top guys in jail. Rewards were given for vanquishing prison enemies; hospitalization of a known enemy would be rewarded with cash. Large-scale trafficking, guns, gambling, prostitution, racketeering, murder for hire, chop shops, stolen goods, white collar crimes, and extortion were just a few of the money-generating activities of our gang.

As the war picked up on the street, I started to become more seasoned in the ways of jail politics. We maintained order through violence, and I was regularly asked to take care of certain political issues throughout the prison. I did it objectively without thought, compassion, or remorse. If someone owed money, or if someone had ripped off a package or ratted another inmate out, I would help plan and execute the punishment to preserve order. The boss man used me regularly because not only was I a ruthless combatant, but I was intelligent in the ways of how people's minds worked. I was well read and able to make clear-headed decisions that would further our empire.

Because I had been a member since my days on the street, I had a higher stature than those who had been recruited in jail. I had proven myself in the ways of money-generating and violence. It also became well known that I was looking twenty-five years in the face for something I hadn't done. I was as solid as they came.

Meanwhile, Jimmy and I were attending regular court dates. The guards wake me up at 4:30 in the morning and take me to a holding tank to wait for the prison bus to escort the inmates to the city courts downtown. Going to court was always an interesting ride. A lot of justice was dealt out in that bus, because the driver wasn't allowed to stop for anything, even if an inmate was getting his head stomped the whole trip. All the guards could do was watch. The other nice thing about going to court is that no matter how many people you stomped or punched, the guards wouldn't be able to reprimand you, because it had happened outside the centre. It was basically a free-for-all.

Because I had been charged with first degree murder, I got to wear my own nice clothes to court instead of wearing the standard blue prison coveralls. As I gained weight over the months, my clothes were exchanged for better-fitting gear. In fact, I used the clothes exchange to bring drugs in. My shoes were modified to contain a compartment in the sole that was invisible to the naked eye.

The morning after one of my court dates, I woke up to a newspaper article on the third page with a huge headline: "Murder Suspect Smiles in Court." At first I thought the article was about some other idiot, knowing full feel the person must live with me on my unit. When I scanned the article, I cursed. The article was about me!

If people hadn't thought I was psychotic before, they sure did now.

The more I spoke with my lawyer, David Chow, the more hopeless I became. My mind went to some really dark places. I felt very lonely, especially since I hadn't spoken to anyone in my family since the arrest.

In prison, I had built a reputation for being a certifiable psychopath. Violence became my everyday calling. I had acquired a taste for the power that came with violence. I was neck-deep in gang politics and helping to keep up the flow drugs and money in and out of the jail.

I made a best friend in Luke, a tall and handsome guy with short black hair. He was a certifiable psychopath like myself. He and I became roommates, and we provided each other with all the company we needed. He was a well-known gangster at the time and was feared by absolutely everyone. He had also been charged with murder, along with a slew of other serious offences.

Not only was Luke charismatic, but he was very intelligent. Our conversations required an above-average intellect. He gabbed one day about wanting to be a bigtime fashion designer, even going as far as to draw some of his more imaginative ideas. He also had an enormous collection of books on the go, not just fiction but psychology, religion, and politics. He and I were both very metrosexual, spending abundant amounts of time on our hair, questioning each other nonstop about how we looked and spending hours at a time in front of the mirror.

We didn't talk about how extremely violent we were. Whenever it was necessary for us to release our inner beasts, we just did it then went back to our cell to fix our hair. The inmate population was terrified of us.

A few weeks after Luke and I moved in together, we got word from the street that a kid on our unit possibly had some info about a murdered gang member. As this kid's bad luck would have it, he was placed in the cell next to us. It didn't take much planning to decide how we were going to get said information out of him; it would be as easy as walking into his house and closing the door.

As we stood at our cell door, waiting for it to unlock so we could scoot over to the adjacent cell before he had a chance to vacate, we laughed and fought over the mirror to check our hair. Our hearts were as cold as ice.

When the airlock snapped open, Luke walked through and calmly entered the cell next door. The kid was taking a piss as we came inside. Luke snapped his jaw sideways, knocking the kid unconscious. I closed the door behind me and put toilet paper over the window so no one could see in.

We had thirty minutes to ourselves.

The kid woke up to Luke and me looming over him, two vicious individuals locked in a room with a kid who had been involved in the murder of a friend. I would have rather walked into a cell with an armed three-hundred-pound white supremacist.

We took turns propping his limbs on the seat of the toilet and stomping on them. Our main focus was his arms. We made sure to get every single finger, both wrists, and every inch up the forearms to the elbows. We relished in the sound of bones snapping, one after another.

Once his arms were one hundred percent destroyed, we went to work on his face. We took turns bashing it in with different makeshift weapons, every blow showering us with blood from his lacerated face and head. After that, we toyed with our victim, taunting him while he begged and pleaded for his life. Our plan wasn't to kill him; it was to extract information.

Despite thirty minutes of gruelling torture at the hands of two psychopaths, he didn't break.

Perhaps he didn't know anything after all.

When the cell cracked open, Luke and I walked back home, both of us covered in blood. We laughed and joked as we watched the kid get taken out of the unit. Everyone had seen the damage we inflicted.

Despite how cruel we could be, we shared our feelings with each other. Luke missed his family dearly, as he had come to Calgary by himself with nothing but a bicycle. He'd then built an unstoppable dial-a-dope operation downtown, a real money train. When he got arrested, he had two Cadillacs, a condo, several people working under him, and more fear and respect than anyone could imagine. He ruled his empire with an iron fist.

He'd gone a lot further than I had to protect what he'd built. If you messed with Luke, he'd burn your house down and possibly take your life. It was a manifestation of the hurt he felt inside. I could see it written all over him. But this man could do anything he put his mind to, good or evil.

One morning, after having returned from court the previous day, I woke up to discover that I was being transferred to Edmonton Remand—three hours away.

The guards had found a list in another inmate's cell containing the licence plate number of every guard. This rattled the correctional officers to their core, so they'd decided to execute a big shakeup.

My goodbye to Luke was short. I loved my friend with all my heart, and he in turn loved me. But there was no way in hell they would ever let the two of us live together again. We'd left nothing but blood and broken bones in our wake.

Chapter Thirty-Nine

SHOT-CALLER

I was mildly nervous upon my arrival at Edmonton Remand. I was way out of my element here, where the Native population was so large. Native prison gangs ruled in the north part of the province. This jail had three maximum security units, every one of them dominated by the Natives. Gang politics were tricky in the Max, and everyone was aware of the repercussions of an unauthorized hit on a high-ranking gang member like me. But my gang didn't have any members here. This worked out okay, because I could be their eyes and ears in uncharted territory.

I walked onto a unit called 4B, which was jointly ruled by a Native gang and a well-known biker club. The biker members were few, but a friend of mine had connections within their ranks. When I walked onto the unit, I was greeted with canteen and weed. They had been well aware of my impending arrival.

After being assigned to a house, I proceeded to set up camp while I smoked the weed supplied by my new biker friends.

During my weeks at Edmonton Remand, I spent a lot of time by myself and talking on the phone with the main boss of the entire gang. He ran everything, inside and out. I don't know how he always had time to talk to me considering how busy he was, but he accepted my calls several times a day. Although he was kind, I could tell he had been psychologically marred from many years of battle.

On one of our calls, he suggested that I pay my lawyer to write a stay order so that I could be returned to Calgary. He needed me back because the guy who had the floor in Calgary would soon be shipped out, leaving me as the only incarcerated member of the gang capable of being left in charge. None of the other members carried the appropriate leadership skills.

I managed to get my lawyer to get me sent back to Calgary. I remember walking back into Calgary Remand with leg and iron shackles. Walking slowly, I held my gaze low and raised my scarred upper lip. My chains rattled with each step. I was walking in as the boss of the prison. No one held a higher stature.

They placed me back on unit six, where I was met with a gigantic cheer. The boss man had caught me up over the phone, informing me about the hierarchy to be imposed upon my arrival. Lieutenants and soldiers were soon assigned.

I unpacked my things and proceeded to smoke the weed given to me. Most of the drugs and money through the prison now rested on my shoulders. I was in charge of making everything happen, and all calls for violence ended with my okay. I sat back on my chair and stared at the ceiling as my brain's pleasure centres erupted.

I was now the shot-caller. The high I was experiencing was unmatched by any drug I'd ever tried. I was ready for boss life.

For my twenty-third birthday, my brothers cleverly made a cake for me from canteen items they'd put together. I remember the birthday cards I received—one from unit five and another from unit six. They were both signed with love from all sorts of underworld characters, every signature coupled with the author's gang sign. The birthday cards meant the world to me.

I felt like I'd finally found my place in the world. I was part of something huge, and I was the boss. Other gangs didn't take orders from me, but because I was head of the most powerful gang in the prison I was treated with the utmost respect. To do otherwise was to be dealt with swiftly and harshly.

I had fun as the boss, and I treated all my brothers with the same level of respect they showed to me. They looked at me with loyalty, and I in turn would have died for them. We fought together, bled together, and if necessary would have even killed together.

At one point, I created a fun game for us. The goal was to see how many people in a row we could assault to the point of making them poop themselves. I took the title, making four grown men poop themselves in a row. I could hit harder than anybody, and I had found that soft spot just above the liver. When I rolled into another man's cell to deliver justice, they usually just turtled and waited out the attack. Once my victim curled into a ball, I'd drop my thunderous right hook on that spot above the liver that couldn't be protected against unless they dropped their hands from their face. I just kept drumming on it until I smelled poop. It usually took two or three shots. I taught all my comrades how to make people crap their pants. After the attacks, we added insult to injury by making the victims clean up the mess themselves.

At some point, we convinced a guard to bring us in a Phillips head screwdriver bit, which gave us the capability to get into the overhead light fixtures in our cells. Inside we accessed an arsenal of metal supplies. Not only that, but it was the best hiding place in the jail for weapons. After that, our boys were carrying around swords in their coveralls. Jailhouse snitches were paralyzed in fear of us.

During one search, the Phillips head bit was uncovered and the guards immediately figured out what we were using it for. When they unscrewed the lights and uncovered our caches of weapons, I don't think they were able to believe their eyes. We'd sharpened countless pieces of metal. We didn't toy around.

The prison's means of punishing us was giving out institutional charges. When we received a charge, we were presented to the upper chain of command, where an outside decision-maker would decide whether we deserved to have our privileges taken away. The worst punishment was being sent to the hole, and the maximum legal amount of time we could be sent there for was two weeks. In the hole, you got nothing. No clothes, no bedsheets, no mirror, no pens or pencils, no books, no radio, and no paper. You literally sat in an empty cell wearing a massive fireproof dress. I got very accustomed to it during my time in the Max, since I regularly got caught with shanks.

I was always angry at the guards. I think they started their own demented game to see who could set me off and get me sent to the hole. I regularly threatened their lives with violence. They became my worst enemies during my Calgary stay.

I came up with ingenious methods of smuggling large amounts of narcotics into prison, the most foolproof of which involved corrupt guards. I would woo female nightshift officers with my charismatic charm, and they'd often help me bring drugs in off the street.

The other main method I used had about a twenty-five percent success rate. I would find inmates with bails that they couldn't afford to pay. I would offer to pay their bail and give them the night of their life with alcohol, drugs, and willing women, all on my dollar and under the gang's supervision. In exchange for their one night of bliss, they would pack their rectums with drugs, then breach their bail conditions, and get rearrested, bringing the drugs with them back into the system. Generally they went into medium- or minimum-security units where I had impatient soldiers waiting on every floor. When the packages were received, they would make their way back to me through medium- and maximum-security prisoners. Then the unit leaders each got a quantity of the drugs, which they could sell. All the money came back to me and consequently went toward another man's bail to keep the flow of drugs steady.

One time, a package came in that contained a quarter-pound of weed, some morphine, cocaine, honey oil, and tobacco. I didn't like bringing marijuana in. I much preferred honey oil, as it was easier to conceal and it didn't stink. My solution to this problem was to give away the entire thing to my brothers so we could get rid of the damning contraband as fast as we could. When the guards came on the unit that day, the entire upper tier was engulfed with a hazy cloud of weed smoke. We were scooped up and taken to dry cells, which were holding tanks without a toilet or running water. We had to poop into buckets and wait for officials to inspect it for contraband.

When we got back to the range, I went a step further in my abuse of power, telling the guards that I had to be rehired as the unit cleaner, the one responsible for cleaning the unit and keeping it pristine. They refused, and in reaction everyone in the unit started trashing the place. Before long, garbage, food, board games and dirty laundry completely littered the place. I relished the devastation.

The cell extraction team had to be brought in to quash the uprising. They tackled me to the floor and cuffed my legs and hands together behind my back. The unit roared as they carried me out.

One thing was made abundantly clear through this exercise: I was the boss. They took me struggling across the hall to my new home, the Special Handling Unit, also known as the Super Max.

Chapter Forty

WAR

Super Max had a mix of general population and protective custody inmates. The protective custody inmates, people like serial rapists and paedophiles, were only in segregation because they themselves couldn't mix with the rest of the prison. The general population inmates on this unit were the most dangerous individuals you could imagine.

We were released for phone and shower privileges for thirty minutes once per a day, and we had to wear belly shackles to constrain our movements. You knew someone was really dangerous when you saw them taken to visits in belly shackles.

Another inmate in Super Max was Luke, and this reunion with my best friend was more than worth the trip. They even put us in cells next to each other, which enabled us to talk through the vent. He was in good spirits despite the intense confinement. His charges were all getting dropped and he was taking a plea deal in exchange for a sentence of ten years for a single manslaughter conviction.

If I could only be so lucky, I thought.

We laughed and chatted for weeks on end until finally the guards told me I was going back to the Max. It turned out that the inmates on unit six had trashed the place for five straight days, until the guards let me come back. All I had to do was ask my brothers to stop the revolt. I hesitatingly accepted their offer.

Meanwhile, Luke was being shipped to Edmonton Max, the most dangerous jail in the country. I told him I'd see him soon. Considering my looming first degree murder conviction, I knew I might end up there.

I walked back into the Max to a big cheer. I was more than happy to be housed again with my brothers in arms. I quickly took up my rightful position as the shot-caller.

One day, the dynamics of the system changed in a flash. I was called to the gang coordinator's office to be brought up to speed on some news that would shift all of our lives. Edmonton Max was in flames from a massive gang war that had taken place in the yard on Canada Day. About fifty inmates had armed themselves with homemade knives and brawled for hours; in the aftermath, they'd set a large blaze. The gang coordinator informed me that the war had been fought between two gangs—ours, and the largest Native gang in the province. Apparently several men had gotten their faces cut up with razors blades and one inmate had been shot by the guards for refusing to stop stabbing his victim.

They didn't have information yet on who or what had started the riot, but one thing was made clear: we were going to war. The official pleaded with me to hold off my men until we sorted everything out. All of our gang members in the prison were housed on the same units, and we were armed to the teeth. The Native gang had a lot of people here in Calgary, but they were mostly low-level junkies.

We were not going to lose this war, I decided.

When I was returned to the unit, I passed on the news to my brothers, explaining why we were in a state of lockdown. Everyone was furious. They wanted blood.

The tension was so strong, you could cut it with a knife. The rival gang's leader was next door to us, on unit five. I spoke with him through the door, and we agreed that bloodshed would be held off until we could find out more about the melee that had taken place in Edmonton. His crew was mostly kept on unit five, while most of us were on unit six, but the gangs were completely mixed on the medium-security units.

My biggest concern wasn't for my safety, but for Jimmy, who I knew was housed on unit five. It was terrifying for him to come talk to me through the door, since everyone on his unit could then study him the whole time. Jimmy was just a little guy, five-seven and a hundred forty pounds. He was happy-go-lucky and lived like a little prince in jail, mostly because of the way I took care of him.

Now he was clearly marked. He would be the first target, since he was the only easy way for the guys on unit five to get to me. Everyone knew that Jimmy would be used to send the message of war.

The guards all knew that Jimmy's life was at risk, so I told him to get caught with a shank and get himself sent to the hole. That would enable me to talk some sense into the guards who refused to recognize the looming danger. Their idiocy was going to get my brother killed.

Jimmy did as commanded and went to the hole when the guards uncovered a blade I had sent him. This bought me a week to figure things out. The problem lay in the fact that the inmates at Edmonton Max were in complete lockdown now and no one there could even shower or use the phone. So we couldn't get any information about the riot other than what we saw on TV. It greatly impeded my decision-making process. I didn't want to send the troops directly into battle and in the process lose the opportunity to avoid unnecessary bloodshed. I may have been a little psychotic, but I wasn't impulsive when it came to gang politics.

As the days passed, we found out more about what had happened. To my surprise, I learned that my gang had ambushed the Native gang, not the other way around. Apparently they hadn't seen it coming at all. They had walked right into the ambush in their flip-flops. After the ensuing riot, every last one of the rival gang members had been sent to the hospital.

My friend Otto, who was serving a sentence there for torturing a biker for three days by stuffing him in a dog kennel, was the one who had led the charge. I knew Otto well, and I thought he was about the scariest man you could ever meet, a true psychopath through and through.

Well, it turned out that Otto had started this riot for one reason: he was bored. Not a lot of consideration had gone into it. But he was one of the original gang members, going right back to the beginning, so his decisions were gold in most everyone's eyes. He had earned people's respect long before the riot.

As I learned more about what had taken place, it became abundantly clear to me that there would be retribution from the Native gang. A war was definitely looming. I just had to keep my head straight in case the officers released Jimmy straight back onto unit five. I was pushing for him to be sent to my unit, but the guards hated me.

Indeed, when Jimmy was released from the hole, he went right back to unit five. I remember waking up in the morning after Jimmy was placed back on the unit. Right after breakfast, a massive swarm of guards went storming onto unit five. I knew instinctively what had happened.

My anger soared to a whole new level when I saw Jimmy get pulled out on a stretcher, looking unrecognizable. I beat on the glass of the bubble, screaming at the top of my lungs. Had the guards' incompetence killed my friend?

Not only did a full-out gang war spread throughout the province, but I started my own war that day—against the guards. My good friend was in the hospital because of them, because they hadn't wanted to put us together out of spite. I told myself that I was going to make them pay for it.

My impending life sentence was the maximum penalty a person could receive in Canada, so my life couldn't get worse. Anything I did now would be a freebie.

Stretchers became a daily sight as the gangs warred. Most of the bloodshed could have been thwarted, but the officials in charge of the jail refused to recognize that there was a gang problem. They continued to mix the gang members on units, in court, and during visits. Their delinquency resulted in us carrying blades strapped to our arms everywhere we went, with orders to kill our rivals on sight.

One day, a discussion with my second-in-command brought about a plan that could possibly bring the war to an end.

Because of how well liked I was, I still had some friends on unit five who weren't gang members. I called one of them one day, sending them a message to come over to the window between the windows to talk to me. When this guy finally came over, I asked him to book a visit between the units for the next day, for 7:30 p.m.

My plan, along with a couple of my finest soldiers, was to wait until 7:30, when the door between the units would be cracked open. Then the three of us would rush into the unit five dayroom, catching them off-guard and unarmed, and kill as many people as possible.

As the day unfolded, I thought about how many men I could send to the afterlife. I knew we weren't going to get away with it, but the consequences mattered very little to me. I paced back and forth in my cell, fantasizing about the bloodbath to come. My two cohorts and I felt invincible.

But as the hour drew closer, I heard a commotion outside my cell. When I walked to the cell door, I saw twenty combat-ready officers standing outside. They commanded me to lie down on the floor with my hands behind my back. Then they led me off the unit while the other inmates kicked their cell doors in protest.

It turned out they had received a tip about a would-be murder plot.

I eventually figured out who had ratted me out. My friend on unit five, the one who was supposed to have scheduled the 7:30 visit, had gotten cold feet when he realized what he was about to be involved in. So he notified our rivals of the plan and they in turn told the guards out of fear, breaking a common jail rule in order to save their own lives.

I wish prison life could always be that simple, but it's not, especially when you live by an unwritten code of ethics. Because they had ratted me out, I was sent to Super Max for an undetermined amount of time.

But this didn't lessen my power. I merely had to adjust, adapt, and evolve to my new circumstances. I continued to run everything from Super Max. I plotted to kill the rival gang members there, and I would go to visits armed just in case the guards gave me an opening to kill my enemy.

I led my troops in unit six from afar as they continued to battle, with casualties falling on both sides. It was the most dangerous time that prison had ever seen, and all the shots were being called from my cell.

Chapter Forty-One

HABITUAL

Days turned into weeks, and then weeks into months. I was always alone, with periodic stints in the hole for threatening guards' lives. I knew what the punishment would be every time, but I did it anyway. Maybe I was just bored. I had come to terms with the fact that this was going to be my path for the rest of my life.

To help with the loneliness, I created a structure for myself. I worked out three times a day—once at eleven, then again at four, and one last time at seven. Obviously I didn't have access to a gym in Super Max, so I created handmade weights out of tomato juice boxes and bunched them together using bedsheets and towels. I regularly received institutional charges and time in the hole for this, but at least it kept me sane.

I eventually figured out which guards cared about me using weights and which ones didn't. I would watch each shift change to see who was coming on. If it was a guard who I knew would issue an institutional charge again, I would simply take my weights apart until the next shift.

When one of the guards did take my take my weights away, I would threaten their life. It was a full-out drama production every time. I'd call out every single guard to come and fight me, pissing and moaning like an inconsiderate jerk. They would eventually send me to the hole, but I didn't care about that. It didn't matter where I went and how much time I spent there.

I figured I had twenty-five years of this to look forward to, having already accepted the reality of my life sentence. It seemed like a foregone conclusion, since I wasn't going to rat Brad out and ruin the reputation I had built thus far. At least I had people's respect, something that had been hard to come by growing up.

Strangely, I started to miss my mom. I hadn't talked to her in well over a year, but I was going through a really hard experience by myself. My heart felt cold as ice and I didn't have anyone to speak to for a long time. I became accustomed to the darkness which consumed my existence. Missing my mom gave me a needed jog down memory lane.

Eventually I decided to call my mom. It felt good to speak with her again. Hearing her voice provided me with a sense of comfort I hadn't felt in a long time. She even did something completely out character: she sent me money, and not just a little bit but $100 per week, the maximum an inmate could spend at the canteen. I didn't need the money considering my gang position, but I couldn't tell her that. Besides, I could sense that sending me the money made her feel good.

Looking back, I've come to the conclusion that she felt partially responsible for me being in prison. I think it pained her to see how dark I had become.

She soon started coming to visit me, and she didn't display any of her old narcissistic traits. Her thoughtful and selfless actions affected me in a positive manner, and I started to realize that it might not be too late for me to reconnect with my family. The opening she had created was small, but it was enough for my hate and anger to recede. Slowly, the old Cody emerged, a little bit at a time.

After six months in solitary confinement, the prison finally sent me back to the Max. I was over the moon. Despite all the happy feelings my mom had provided me, they were still a pebble compared to the mountain of benevolence I received from my brothers.

I packed up my things as they cracked my airlock to take me across the hall. Just like that, I walked back onto unit six, my muscles bulging out of my jumpsuit from all my workouts. I strutted onto the unit a hero. The lion king had returned.

They placed me in a cell on the lower tier just as the upper tier got let out for dayroom. My brothers immediately came to my cell to greet me, catching me up on current events.

"Did you bring goodies?" a friend asked.

I smiled. "Sure did."

I pulled out a bunch of honey oil and an arsenal of blades I had kept taped under my door in Super Max. All my friends freaked out, overjoyed at the sight of my widow-makers as I caked the honey oil onto some torn-out Bible pages to disperse among the men. Then I rolled up a joint, lit it, and passed my package of weapons to a friend outside the cell. I needed to get the weapons out of my house; the guards were keeping me on a short leash.

As I strutted to the back of my cell, I heard the unmistakable clinking of metal shanks on the cement floor. I turned back to see that all the weapons had been pushed back under my door. My confusion only lasted for a second. The cell cracked open and I saw about twenty guards outside, ordering me to lie down. I did as they told and watched them pick up the weapons off the floor, taking it into evidence.

With my hands recuffed, the guards led me straight back out of the Max as the other inmates raged in their cells. I had lasted no longer than ten minutes after six months away. That had to be a record.

I figured they were never going to let me out of Super Max ever again after this. I was way too dangerous, and their recovery of weapons cache was all the proof they needed. By sending me away, they were taking a key piece off the chessboard. It turned out that when I was gone, the men on unit six were a lot more peaceful. They just focused on smoking weed.

Chapter Forty-Two

LIMBO

Back in solitary confinement, I got my entertainment from taunting my enemies on the unit. I made sure everyone around me felt my wrath, and paedophiles and rapists got it the worst. I was under the belief that any man who hurt a kid deserved lifelong torture and cruel punishment—and I made myself the executioner of their punishments.

I was such a disruptive force that I was taken to court by myself. This became necessary after some incidents. They had made the mistake of mixing me with the inmate population a couple of times when I was being taken to court, and I made them pay dearly for their grace. I vanquished my enemies at any opportunity, even while wearing leg irons. I would smash people in the head with the cuffs adorning my wrists; they could inflict some serious blunt force trauma.

I couldn't be trusted at all, and I laughed at how it took them so long to figure it out. Without a doubt, I was a menace to the prison population.

On New Year's Day, Calgary was rocked to its core when a gunman burst into a restaurant in the early afternoon hours and opened fire, killing several people inside the eatery. The target was a high-ranking rival gang member who died at the scene. It became known as the New Year's Day Massacre.

The tragic part was that an innocent bystander who had been fleeing the bloody scene was shot in the head. He hadn't had anything to do with the war. He was just in the wrong place at the wrong time.

Because of my crew's widely known disregard for lives, my friends became targets of the police's most sophisticated operation ever. There had been a public outcry and people wanted justice. Rightfully so.

A couple of weeks after the massacre, two top members of my gang were taken down by the police while they were hunting rivals. These were my friends, and the police found them with guns, body armour, throwaway shoes, a change of clothing, and masks—all the ingredients for a "kill kit." This is the main reason why body armour is still illegal in Alberta today.

The guards walked onto my unit that night, delivering my two friends. I even got a roommate in the form of my friend Mitch. Because these two guys were both founding members of the gang, I was relieved of my leadership role. I didn't mind. It's not like I was capable of doing much from solitary confinement anyway.

The next day, they were both transferred to the Max and I was once again left alone.

I was sent to the hole for a while after that for threatening a guard's life. I had felt that this guard was abusing his power—a regular happening, to say the least. Once in the hole, I paced my cell until I heard my name being called through the vents. Because the hole was next to Super Max, I could clearly communicate with the inmates there. I quickly figured out that the person calling my name was a friend of mine.

"What's up?" I hollered back, half-expecting to hear back that he was just bored and in need of some social stimulation.

"You're in the newspaper today."

"For what?" I asked, my curiosity piqued.

"Someone else just got charged for the murder you're in on."

It took a second for the totality of that statement to sink in. It could only be one person: Brad, the one who had pulled the trigger.

All of the evidence so far had pointed to only two people being involved, me and Jimmy, with me being the killer. A third arrest meant that the truth had been revealed. Did this mean my own murder charge was going to be dropped?

Suddenly, I wasn't looking at twenty-five years anymore. Maybe I would get my life back.

I sat heavily on the edge of the bed, staring off into space and letting the full weight of this revelation fall on my shoulders. Since I was in the hole, I wasn't able to use the phone. I had no way of finding out what was going on.

I listened as my buddy in Super Max read the article to me.

It was true. Brad had been picked up the previous day and charged with manslaughter. And if they had arrested him, they obviously knew now that he was the shooter. They couldn't charge us both!

I was still culpable, of course, but getting a sentence of four to nine years, which suddenly seemed likely, was a lot better than what I had been facing.

For the first time in a while, I looked up at the ceiling and questioned the higher powers above. I knew that hell existed, because of what Devon had showed me, but I still had my doubts about heaven.

Perhaps the good Lord did exist. But if He did, why had He just given freedom to one of the most ruthless individuals alive?

Chapter Forty-Three

PSYCHOLOGICAL ASSESSMENT

When David Chow came to visit me, he explained that Brad had made a full confession to police officers during an interrogation. He had admitted to being the gunman in the crime I was accused of, thereby relieving me of that culpability.

David then said that he was going to ask for a psychiatric assessment to be done on me to give the courts an idea of my recidivism risk. I was a well-spoken and well-read young man, so how bad could it go?

Time passed at a snail's pace as I planned my return to the street. There was a small possibility, given all the time I had spent in solitary confinement, that I could request extra credit for time served and be immediately released. In anticipation, I worked out for longer hours to get my body in top-notch shape.

The day arrived when I needed to visit the Southern Alberta Psychiatric Centre and convince the doctors there that I was just a very misunderstood young man and a victim of circumstance.

"Bates, you're being transferred," I heard a guard say over the intercom as my cell door cracked open.

I smiled and laughed as the staff loaded me onto a prisoner transport van in the usual belly shackle.

As it turned out, this place was basically right across the street, so my excitement about getting to go for a car ride was cut very short.

They brought me in slowly, my anklets only allowing me to take quarter-foot-steps. I waddled through some bay doors where some nurses and security official were waiting for me. When they asked the sheriffs to remove my constraints, it dawned on me that I might actually be mixed with other inmates here. Surely they wouldn't allow that!

After my intake was complete, I was stripped and given a grey sweat suit as they apprised me of the rules of the hospital. They made it abundantly clear that I was here for an assessment to determine my risk to reoffend, and also to determine how likely it was that I could be reintegrated into society.

I was then escorted to the facility's one and only unit. Carrying my bedding, I walked through the heavy door and waited for it to close behind me. I looked around. Guys and girls were mixed together here, playing cards, watching TV, and gathering over board games. Many others were pacing around, something that I soon learned was very common on the "psych ward."

We also had access to an outdoor yard. I walked out and saw that it was a cement pad with nothing but a single chain-link fence blocking me from the traffic on the road a few hundred feet away. I almost felt free.

The shock of being given so much freedom stunted my ability to socialize here—that, plus I thought everyone there was a rapist. I withdrew to my new room and picked up a book. I'd always hated reading and writing, since my ADD made it next to impossible to immerse myself in a book.

To my growing surprise, we weren't even locked in our rooms here. The cells didn't have toilets, so the guards let us go to the bathroom whenever we needed. I couldn't believe it.

But I didn't make any friends there. In fact, I kept my gaze low and refused to talk to anyone but the nurses, whom I continuously flirted with. At Remand, I had only been able to flirt with the female guards who worked the night shift, and I could only do it through the intercom.

The doctors there wanted to speak to me one day. My behaviour was apparently very concerning, with me being antisocial and semi-hostile with the rest of the population. I explained to the doctors that I was just focusing on having a good assessment and didn't want to run the risk of getting into it with these other would-be creeps. And I didn't want to say anything to anyone that would later be used against me in court.

One doctor then informed me that my assessment was to determine how likely it would be for me to reintegrate into society. For him to write a good report, he would need me to be forthcoming and honest about certain aspects of my life. I agreed to share filtered pieces of my life.

The prison drug trade had come to consume my thoughts. From the moment I walked in, I could see how easy it would be to bring packages in here. There was hardly any security at all! So I began formulating a drug-smuggling scheme that would fill my pockets with cash. I walked around the unit and figured out that the best course of action would be to receive packages through the fence outside. It wouldn't work just to have someone run up to fence in broad daylight, so I would get a friend to come at night and place a package a couple of meters from the yard, attaching it to a transparent fishing line that needed to be threaded into the fence. That would help to avoid detection by the guards doing their perimeter checks. I scoped out all the camera angles and found the best approach for my accomplice to take. This was going to be a cakewalk.

While on the phone with a friend one day, I asked them to check my social media profile to see if I'd gotten any messages there. I didn't usually get messaged, since everyone knew I was in prison, but something inside me that morning urged me to check. After looking at my profile, my friend said there were some messages from a girl named Anna.

Anna was an ex-girlfriend of mine from a couple of years back. She was absolutely stunning and I had found it odd that she wanted to talk to me at all. Ultimately, though, she had broken it off with me because of how dangerous my lifestyle was. Now that I was in jail for murder, I was surprised to hear from her.

I called her, feeling over the moon when her lovely accented voice answered the phone. As we spoke, it became clear that she still genuinely cared about me. She was concerned about everything going on in my life and insisted on hearing everything. We talked for hours and she asked if it was possible for her to come visit me. My head almost blew off my shoulders. Of course she could visit! I helped her through the process of booking a visit, and she said that she would come that very night.

To say I was pumped would be a gross understatement.

As I walked into my visit with Anna, it occurred to me that this was my first visit in a very long time without shackles adorning my hands, waist, and feet. I strutted in to find Anna already waiting for me on the other side of the protective glass. An uncontrolled smile creased my face as my gaze fell on the most beautiful woman I had ever seen. She had long brown hair, a petite figure, and two of the deepest eyes I had ever seen. I could barely breathe when I looked at her.

I sat down, my heart beating fast. The next step should have been to pick up the telephone so we could hear each other, but we didn't do that. Instead we just sat and stared at each other for a couple of minutes, studying each other, trying to gauge what the other was thinking and feeling.

Finally we picked up the phones and started talking. I just didn't get her interest in me. What did a girl like this want with a monster like me? It's not like I had a lot to offer a classy woman such as her. But I accepted her kindness for what it was.

I made a promise to myself in that moment that I would do anything for her. She would become my sun and my stars. And if God willed it, I would leave the life I had grown accustomed to for even a chance at happiness with her. She was worth it.

As we said goodbye, I kissed my hand and touched the glass with it. With my heart singing in my ears, I watched her walk away.

While leaving the visitors area, I noticed that they had another room, a place where prisoners could meet with their lawyers. I peeked inside and saw that the only thing separating the prisoners from the lawyers was a table. No glass. If someone were to slide a package under the door on the other side, I could literally dive over the table to retrieve it.

That night, I called Steven and told him about my brilliant plan, and he was inclined to go along with it.

The next night, Steven came to visit me. Five minutes before the visit was supposed to end, before the guard returned to bring me back to the unit, I got up and head-faked toward the lawyer room. Sure enough, Steven had left a package there for me. Just like I'd planned, I dove over the table, picked it up, and then returned to the inmate side. I walked out without missing a step, knowing that I had gotten away with it.

As I strutted out of the visitors area, I saw Steven through several plates of glass. We smiled at each other. I loved that man with every fibre of my being. He knew I would have done the same for him.

I got back to the unit and immediately went to the bathroom to inspect my package. Transparent honey oil. This stuff was the best of the best. I could easily make over $15,000 on one vial alone. But that was only if I didn't smoke it, which I couldn't resist doing.

I cracked open the vial and smelled it. This was the best honey I'd ever had. The smell was so pungent that I began to get worried the aroma would make its way down the hall, down the stairs, and over to the nurses station.

I couldn't wait to let it take me away.

"Bates, open up," a commanding voice said from the other side of the bathroom door.

Had I already been found out?

I looked at the five-gram vial and realized that I was about to get strip-searched. I had never put anything in my bum to this point, as I'd seen that as being beneath me. But I was on my own now.

I closed my eyes, held my breath, and penetrated my virgin butt for the first time. It hurt—my pride more than anything.

When the staff opened the door, I quickly flushed the lighter I'd been holding in my hand. They just assumed that I had gotten rid of whatever it was I'd been holding and didn't bother to check me too closely.

However, the guards escorted me to a holding tank and called for a ride back to Calgary Remand. I was being kicked out after lasting just six days in psych, cutting short what was to have been a thirty-day assessment. I wondered if they had gotten everything they needed from me for a proper diagnosis.

Wearing my shackles again, they loaded me into the sheriff's van and drove me back across the street.

I knew that the assessment had been meant to determine how long of a sentence would be needed to rehabilitate me—and I had just cut it short by smuggling in drugs. I'd failed to grasp that my life was on the line and that I had needed to take the psychological evaluation seriously.

But even if it added years to my sentence, I couldn't resist the pull of instant gratification.

Chapter Forty-Four

NO OUTWARD
EMOTION

To my surprise, the guards brought me back to the Max. Everyone was happy to see me and got a good laugh from the story of my short-lived visit across the street. Even the killers on the Max thought I was crazy. But I had a good time breaking bread with them while stoned out of my mind on the honey oil. I didn't care about the money I could've made; the true value lay in sharing it with my brothers. I ended up not making one dime.

After two days of being content and happy, though, one of the guards got bored and decided to push my buttons. When I threatened to kill him, I got dragged right back to Super Max. That was standard procedure at this point.

A month went by as I waited to head back to court for sentencing. I had spent twenty months in custody by now without accumulating any new charges—a miracle, to say the least.

The day finally arrived. The sheriffs brought me down to court one morning to receive judgment. My shackles clanked as I walked into the lawyers room where David Chow waited to brief me before we went before the judge.

He informed me that he had gotten my assessment back. A smile crossed my face as I pondered the outcome of my six-day assessment.

"You exhibit an abundance of antisocial traits, Cody," he said, not smiling back.

"That's because I thought they were all rapists and paedophiles in there. I didn't want to socialize with that scum."

I had really been making life difficult for him, and suddenly I saw that he'd had enough of my BS.

"You've been labelled a high-level intelligence functioning sociopath," David said, raising his voice. "Good job!"

That word—*sociopath*—landed hard. I had never considered that something might actually be wrong with me. To this point I had honestly thought I was completely normal.

I refused to accept it. Maybe it just hadn't looked good that I had been caught smuggling drugs so they'd decided to classify me as high risk. But a sociopath?

I walked into the courtroom that day feeling dumbfounded. As I sat down, it dawned on me that this information was in the hands of the judge staring at me from the bench.

Court was in session.

Victim impact statements were read by Lewis's family. They cried as they read how my crimes had altered their lives for the worse. I held their gazes as they read to me. I felt that they deserved my full attention, despite how much it pained me to see their innocent faces.

After that, the Crown prosecutor went into a long spiel about how firearm homicides are on the rise and how gang members everywhere need to be shown an example of what justice looks like—in the form of harsh sentences. It was also noted that I had been under a lifetime firearms prohibition at the time of the murder. The prosecutor further stated that I should be the one held most culpable since I was the one with something to gain from the murder.

The Crown was seeking ten to twelve years whereas my defence lawyer was asking for a sentence in the range of six to eight years.

The judge asked me to stand up, which I did.

"Cody William Bates, I hereby sentence you, on the conviction of manslaughter with a firearm, to eight and a half years."

I felt nothing as he passed judgment on me, showing no outward signs of emotion. With time served, he ordered that I serve five more years. I was given two-for-one credit for my time in solitary confinement.

After it was all said and done, I looked around for the last time at the courtroom. With any luck, I would never see the inside of it again.

I was officially a convicted killer, which meant that my time in Calgary Remand had come to an end. I would soon be assigned to the penitentiary I would call home for the next five years.

There were two options in my mind. Always the optimist, I hoped to be sent to Bowden Penitentiary, which was medium-security. Since people convicted of first and second degree murder had to be sent to maximum-security jails, and I had only been convicted of manslaughter, I figured there was a chance I would get away with Bowden.

The other option, of course, was Edmonton Max, home to some of the vilest human beings in the country.

The placement guards laughed at me when I asked to go to Bowden—not just an under-the-breath snicker, but a full-out roar of hysteria. They were barely able to get the words out of their mouths because they were laughing so hard.

"No, Mr. Bates. Your new home is Edmonton Max."

Chapter Forty-Five

WELCOME HOME

As Edmonton Max came into view, a daunting feeling washed over me. I'd heard rumours that it was the only prison in the country where inmates were required to put an $80 deposit down on a body bag as soon as they walked through the gates; they got their money back if and when they were released or transferred.

My gaze landed on all the gun towers, manned with guards holding loaded assault rifles. Two massive fences circled the prison, their tops shrouded with razor wire. The red-brick building had huge enclosed cages at the end of each wing where inmates could get thirty minutes of sun per day—if you could call it that.

The place had a dark aura.

A large gate opened to let the van between the fences. After the gate closed behind us, a couple of guards with mirrors on extended sticks walked around the van, checking the undercarriage of the vehicle. Another guard walked around with a sniffer dog, signalling the dog to pay special attention to certain spots on the vehicle.

After that, the second opened and we pulled up in front of a building marked "Admission/Discharge."

When I stepped out onto the pavement, I inhaled deeply, filling my lungs and raising my eyes to the fences and gun towers. Guards were looking down at me from their eagle-eyed view.

I'd never felt more ready for anything in my entire life. My chains rattled as I was escorted inside.

Welcome home, I thought to myself.

A week prior to my arrival, there had been another small riot in the recreation yard (which everyone called the rec yard) between my gang and the Native gang. It had been an ambush, much like the big Canada Day riot the previous year, only this time my crew had been the unsuspecting targets. My friend Luke and another gang member had fought off a whole gang of Natives by themselves; they had managed to defend themselves with some shovels until their attackers had retreated back into the gym.

Because of this, my whole crew was in the hole.

The wing where I was placed consisted entirely of killers. Each range had six single cells, and the characters occupying them were absolutely insane. Everyone there felt the need to come by my cell and gloat about how many people they had killed, and since only one cell was allowed out at a time I was forced to introduce myself five different times.

One thing was prominent in my mind: if you control the drugs, you control the population. I had saved some honey oil just for this reason. I gave everyone on my range a free sample of the honey oil I had, and by the end of showers I had a massive accumulation of clothes, canteen, electronics, CDs, and pornography in front of my cell waiting to be let in by a guard doing his hourly shift walk to make sure there were no dead bodies.

The guards at Edmonton Max had a much different demeanour than the ones at Calgary Remand. They didn't take crap from the prisoners, but they were respectful. After all, they were dealing with cold-blooded killers with absolutely nothing to lose. At least I only had five years, compared to the ones on my range who were serving life sentences. A couple of these guys had started their twenty-year sentences over a few times after killing inmates or rubbing guards the wrong way.

Needless to say, the guards here were very aware of the risk they ran working in such a volatile place. They weren't stupid.

It must have been obvious to the guards—indeed, anyone with half a brain—that these gifts were the result of a transaction, but they opened the door and let me acquire my new belongings. There were no dead bodies around, so they didn't object.

I donned the new tracksuit Luke had sent over and left my cell. I found out that Luke was in the range on the other side of a cement wall. We yelled back and forth at each other for a couple of hours. My range-mates probably would have been pissed off from all the yelling if I hadn't just given them drugs for the first time in who knew how long.

Someone else had given me a stereo, which I plugged in to listen to some rap music. I lay on my bed, my fingers intertwined behind my head, and stared at the ceiling as the music blasted. The other killers must have turned their TVs up to drown out my inconsiderable volume, but they didn't say anything.

I had drugs. Therefore, I had the power to do as I pleased.

A couple of weeks after my arrival, the guards put all my fellow gang members on two ranges. We had enough members to fill them both, which meant we had enough soldiers to fill half a general population unit. It was only a matter of time before we got our own personal wing.

The prison officials here didn't mess around with gang politics. They housed all the gang members with their respective crews to avoid bloodshed. To do otherwise would have been to flirt with death; everyone here was dying to prove how crazy they were by killing an inmate.

But some of the guards didn't handle disrespect very well. If you pissed them off enough, they would "accidently" crack your door while an enemy was on the range. One time, despite prison policy, members of rival gangs had their doors cracked at the same time. The result was fatal. When one particularly irate inmate's cell door slid open, he was killed on sight.

Suddenly, the body bag policy made perfect sense.

But our range was packed with friends, and we partied like crazy. Luke was housed next to me and our light switches provided the perfect ear hole through which to talk quietly to each other. We chatted almost all day every day.

Something occurred in Luke during this time that caught me off-guard. He had been reading the Bible, and suddenly he started preaching the word of God to me. I was somewhat familiar with God from my days in AA, but he wasn't preaching the God of my understanding.

At first I thought it was just a phase, but over the next few months Luke proved me wrong. He completely immersed himself in the word of God. He told me that he could feel God's love filling him to the brim with joy and freedom. I was awestruck as I watched my convicted killer best friend transform before my eyes. He quit watching R-rated movies and stopped swearing. I was proud of my brother, knowing full well that it had to have been a divine intervention. Nothing else could have changed him.

So I listened to my friend through the light switch. His fiery passion for the word of God made him very interesting to listen to. He was one of the most dangerous individuals I'd ever met, but you wouldn't guess that from listening to him now.

Whenever I got the chance to get on the phone, I called Anna to update her on the many poems, letters, and pictures I was creating for her. I thought about her constantly throughout my stay. I was always concerned about her and looked forward to hearing her singsong voice. She gave me hope that this wasn't going to be my life forever.

The only other person I talked to on the outside was my mother. She was being abnormally supportive given her track record. She accepted my phone calls, sent me money, became a listening ear when I needed to vent, and even came to visit me periodically. She even built a relationship with Anna. The love of these two ladies gave me an enormous amount of hope for the future.

But the future remained distorted. I didn't know if I wanted a bulletproof vest with a .45 in my lap or a white picket fence with a swingset and a kid. In my sick, demented mind, both options looked good. I considered having a double life, leading my mother and Anna on with promises to leave the gang behind while at the same time building a criminal empire.

Anna and I fell deeply in love as time passed. We talked about raising a family together and possibly moving to her native Quebec to get me away from the gang life in Alberta. I started to desire this. Luke even said that he would come with me and build a legit business together in Montreal. We would find him a beautiful French girl and all four of us would live happily ever after.

Anna was very spiritual, too, and believed in God. Between her and Luke, I listened to what they had to say and started praying again. I didn't know if it would be enough to save my lost soul, but the people I loved most still believed in me. That was enough to bring me to my knees.

Chapter Forty-Six

POSITIVE INFLUENCES

I started having ghostly encounters again, this time in my cell. Although I never saw anything concrete, I regularly woke up out of deep sleeps in a state of paralysis. It was super scary. My eyes would snap open in the middle of the night to a blast of adrenaline and I wouldn't be able to move.

When I'd had my demonic visits in Shawnessy, I had instinctively known they were sinister. When Devon had come to me, I'd felt love and joy.

These new encounters certainly did not fill me with love and joy. While lying in bed paralyzed, I could sense someone or something standing in the corner of my room or outside the window. It happened almost every night.

The prison itself had claimed countless lives through murder and suicide—Edmonton Max had a very dark energy—so these encounters petrified me. I thought maybe I was going nuts.

At one point, I was moved to a new cell, and then the encounters stopped. I knew for certain there had been a dark entity in my old house. I was very grateful when these hauntings came to an abrupt end.

Once all the members of our gang were housed on the same unit, we were a happy bunch of killers. This meant we could be employed on the unit together, enjoy rec yard privileges, and play abundant amounts of poker.

It also meant we could have roommates. Luke was obviously my first pick, but something held me back from moving in with him. My friend Mitch, who had recently been charged with three counts of first degree murder from the New Year's Day massacre, had been tattooing himself with a homemade tattoo gun and ink. He was getting really good at it, and I convinced him to cover me with tattoos, too. So he and I got housed together.

He covered me in jailhouse ink in just two weeks. I had two full arm sleeves and a chest cap. The full-patch gang tattoo, only to be donned by gang leaders, went under my arm just above the tail of the dragon that was wrapped around my bicep. When I looked in the mirror and saw myself covered in tattoos, my pleasure centres exploded in ecstasy. They were completely black, with no colour at all, and I felt fully deserving of them.

My stay with Mitch was short-lived, though, and I moved in with Luke shortly after.

We only got out of our cells for an hour per day, coupled with extra shower time and gym time every second day. Going to the gym was always a show. We all wore brand-name tracksuits and sunglasses, and we got our hair done.

When you walked into the gym, after passing through a metal detector, you looked up to a very large ceiling. Near the top were seven gunports where guards trained their firearms at us; they could also deploy tear gas and non-lethal ammunition if the situation warranted it. The back of the gym had a door that led to the rec yard. When you stepped out into the open air, you felt more imprisoned than when you were inside, ironically.

The yard had once been much larger, but the space had been cut down over the years. There were basketball courts and a hockey arena that we couldn't access anymore. As the violence and bloodshed had gotten worse, the yard had gotten smaller and smaller. Now the prisoners were only allowed in a quarter-section of the original yard, and we were surrounded by razor wire and gun towers.

While in the rec yard, you could just feel the violence that had taken place there over the years. It was very dangerous, very uncomfortable.

The boys and I played soccer all year round, whether it was outside or inside. That was our main gym activity, and we got pretty good. Mind you, it was the only thing there for us to do. All the weights had been removed, and there were only a couple of machines. A pull-up bar had been bolted to the ceiling, and if you were really good you could ask for a basketball. We made the best out of what we had.

One day, the prison moved a Native jail gang from Saskatchewan to Edmonton Max. We agreed to let them come onto the lower level of our unit after some supervised meet-and-greets to make sure we would get along.

We finally had people to sell our drugs to, and they spent every dime of their reserve money to get high. My friends and I would sit on the upper level of the unit, playing poker with all the street cash we were making. It became a regular thing for a few thousand dollars to exchange hands. There were never any problems with payment, and we strapped blades to our arms in case the gang downstairs ever got out of line.

Months turned into years as my crew and I stuck to structure and habit to make our time go by as fast as possible. My mom helped me to enroll in university and I studied psychology in the confines of my cell. My main interest was psychopathy, although to this point I wasn't far along enough in my education to get to the course covering this subject: abnormal psychology.

My diagnosis as a sociopath greatly intrigued me, and the more I learned about it through my studies the more I began to identify with the label. I remembered stroking Devon's cheek while he lay lifeless in his coffin, feeling incapable of drumming up any emotion whatsoever. I also recalled asking to earn step one in treatment thirteen times in a row because of my difficulty feeling my pain honestly.

However, after both of those circumstances I eventually had been capable of hitting deeper levels of emotion. This confused me.

One of the things I was reading about sociopaths was that they had charisma and the ability to fake emotion despite not actually being able to feel it. Had my tears at Devon's funeral been fake? I didn't think so. Love did exist somewhere in my cold, black heart. I just needed to figure out a way to resurrect it.

With Luke's help, I gradually focused on my desire to clean up my life. He entrenched himself in Bible scriptures, something I was sceptical about, but the radical change that had taken place in him was undeniable. He had become a living example of God's greatness.

Soon, Luke was granted a transfer back to Ontario to be closer to his family. I was extremely sad to say goodbye to him, but I understood that he was a new man. He had to leave Alberta and leave his old life behind.

Once Luke was gone, the transition for me was very difficult. I was left with no one to help jog my deeply buried feelings. At least Anna and my mom were just a phone call away, and Anna even got approved for conjugal visits—or as the prison called them, private family visits. This meant that every sixty days, she could come and stay with me in a trailer onsite for a whole weekend. I needed an almost spotless institutional record to receive these special visits, but my attitude had changed dramatically since my arrival.

I had picked up just a single institutional charge in all that time—for attempted escape. But I certainly hadn't done anything of the sort. I had made a dummy, placed it on my bed, and covered it with a blanket. Then I stayed in a friend's cell for the evening so we could clock a few tattoo hours. That was all, and I was pissed off that I even got the charge.

Eventually, after some grievances that went all the way to the Ottawa, I was granted these private visits with Anna. She and I would be alone for three whole days together inside a trailer equipped with a kitchen, bedroom, living room, and bathroom. For one weekend, it would be like I wasn't even in prison. We got a camera and took pictures together, dreaming about what our life would be like together outside the prison walls.

The weekend activated in me a deep desire for change. I was drifting away from my gangster ideals and leaning toward my white picket fence fantasy. Anna had purchased a house for us and was setting up a life in anticipation of my impending release a couple of years down the road. My heart beat loudly in my ears for this woman who loved me so unconditionally.

My mother and my siblings joined me for another one of these three-day private visits. We all laughed and hugged. Once again, I had a family who loved me.

At one point, my family and I sat on the couch watching a movie together. Anna, the love of my life, nestled under my arm while my family spread out around the room. My new baby sister, who at four years old was new to me, was playing with toys on the floor. I watched her just be a kid, talking to herself and letting her imagination take her in all sorts of joyful and peaceful directions. She was happy, and I in turn was grateful and proud to be her big brother.

I watched my other brother and sister intently and could find no trace of darkness in them. They laughed and joked constantly.

My mom proudly surveyed her children, then turned her head and caught my gaze. I remember my eyes filling up with tears as our eyes connected. I felt close to her. We shared a silent smile, a demonstration of our love for each other. We had both made mistakes and were moving past them together as mother and son.

All my siblings had grown up content and grateful for the beauty in life. My mom had done a good job with them, and I even concluded that she had done her best with me. She had given birth to me very young and had been unprepared for motherhood. I certainly hadn't been an easy child to raise.

I love my family and didn't mean to cause them so much anguish. Perhaps there was still a chance that I could join them one day and take my rightful place by their side.

Cody at age twenty-four in the Edmonton Max conjugal visit house.

Chapter Forty-Seven

LONE WOLF

Because of the ongoing gang wars, our crew recruited heavily inside the prison system. This eventually bestowed a lot of knowledge and power to many untested individuals. Our unit started to fill up with men from Bowden who had been played as dumb pawns, carrying out dirty work and getting sent to the Max as a consequence. These Bowdenites came in strong and all were eager to prove themselves.

A lot of red flags went up regarding these new arrivals. First, they didn't understand why they weren't allowed the full-patch tattoos that were only given out to leaders. They were rather distraught over this issue. Second, I noticed that these guys all gossiped like children. It was enough to drive everyone nuts. But our gang's main boss on the street said that we had to accept them. Our rivals were winning the numbers game, and we needed more soldiers.

I can't remember how it started, but one day we came to the collective decision that it was time to make the guards to pay for their maltreatment of us. It began with them keeping us locked down one day when we were supposed to be let out to socialize with each other. They gave us excuse after excuse, which rubbed us the wrong way.

We came up with a plan: the next time they let us out of our rooms, we were going to start a riot. But this wasn't going to be an average riot, with us lighting fires and refusing to be locked up. We wanted to send the ultimate message. So when they cracked us out this day, someone was going to ask to speak with one of the corrections officers in the prison office. When they opened the barricaded door, as they always did, the population would rush the office, cover the gunports with mattresses so they couldn't shoot us, and pour syrup over the cameras so they couldn't see or record our sinister plot. The guards would then be beaten and dragged up onto the unit and into the laundry room, where we were would torture them by cutting off their faces with razor blades.

The plan was almost unbelievable, and it would end with the killing of three guards.

But one of the Bowdenites felt he was in way over his head and slipped a message to the guards, foiling our plan. Our gang's top five members were then scooped from the unit and put in the hole, leaving me in charge of everything back on the unit.

After a lockdown of a couple of weeks, everything went back to normal, only I was running the show now. I was in charge of the drugs, the gambling books, and all the soldiers on the unit. I didn't get a good feeling off the Bowden guys, but there wasn't much I could do other than exert the power given to me. I made sure they knew they were lower-level soldiers. I was respectful to them, but I found myself regularly needing to reel them in. They didn't seem to understand that they weren't trusted. We all knew one of them had ratted out our plan on the guards, and it was only a matter of time before we found out who it was.

Being back in charge didn't come with the same great feeling as it had before. In Calgary Remand, I had been in charge of a bunch of ruthless gangsters, but these new Bowdenites were cowards. Edmonton Max was notorious for weeding out the weak.

One day while in the laundry room doing my usual thing, folding people's clothes and switching over the inmates' gear from washer to dryer, I heard all the cells crack open for evening dayroom.

Then everything went black.

———————————

I awoke to find myself handcuffed to a bed in an Edmonton hospital. I could feel that my face was swollen, and it hurt to make any facial expression. What had happened? I tried to gather my memory of the events that had unfolded. I could remember being taken off the unit bleeding profusely from the head. Whoever had attacked me had been targeting my neck and cranium.

Surely this must have been an ordered hit. Did my friends think I had ratted them out for the guard plot? My head hurt so bad that I could hardly think. Fortunately, they were all superficial wounds. Nothing was broken except my pride.

Everything I'd fought for had come to an abrupt end, for reasons I couldn't understand. I had bled and fought for the gang. Whatever had gone on, I hadn't deserved it.

But that's just the way prison politics go. I would be a lone wolf fighting to survive on my own from now on. The only good thing was that I hadn't broken the universal prison code—don't walk off the unit. This was the only solace I could muster.

I needed to get to the bottom of what had happened. Maybe there was still hope, a way to somehow be redeemed.

While being escorted to the bathroom by the guards assigned to watch me, I looked at myself in the mirror. My face was unrecognizable. It swelled in every direction.

When I got back to prison the next day, the guards put me in the hole for my safety.

The first thing I did was call Anna. She was beside herself, as she had gotten a call from the prison saying that I had been severely beaten but was in stable condition. I tried my best to calm her down, reminding her that she didn't need this kind of stress. She promised me that she would be all right, but I wasn't so sure. It was one of the most difficult phone calls of my life.

Shortly after being locked up again, my buddy Mitch came to my door. As the cleaner here in the hole, he was allowed out sometimes to clean up garbage and the showers. The look in his eyes radiated anger, but not toward me.

He told me that I had fallen victim to an unauthorized hit and that I was to go back to the unit to reap my revenge with the help of my brothers. An example needed to be set.

I had been jumped by three Bowdenites who were pissed off at me for being put in charge of things. Their jealousy had been the main factor in the ambush. My brothers in every institution were apparently sending love my way as well as messages to hang in there.

I sat back down on my bed, feeling mixed emotions. What was I fighting for? I couldn't answer that question honestly. I had been fighting for so long that I had lost track of why I was doing it. Maybe it was because I always desired people's respect. But I couldn't wrap my head around throwing my life away for this lost cause. And yet I had made a commitment to my brothers, and there was no backing out. So I would go to the unit and get my revenge.

Mitch had informed me that all three men were to suffer a beatdown for their crime against me, and I was going to personally teach this particular lesson. I went to bed that night dreaming of ways to crush them.

It took about a week before I was able to convince the institution that my safety wasn't in jeopardy back on the unit. The three men who had jumped me were also in the hole and slated to go back the same day. A couple of my brothers who had gotten scooped for the guard plot were going back as well. Our empty unit would be filling back up this day.

I walked back onto the range with my heart beating loudly in my ears. This time, there were no cheers. It was dead silent. I planted my feet at the top of the stairs leading to the upper level, looking down at both wings with fire in my eyes.

After I'd returned to my cell, people started coming by to make sure I knew they hadn't been involved in the plan to kill me. They voiced their concern and noted that if I needed anything, I could ask them. They couldn't give me the one thing I desired: my attackers' blood.

I got on the phone and immediately called Anna to make sure she was okay. My call ended up confirming my worst fears. Anna was in the hospital because of her heart condition. The stress of what had happened to me had been too much for her beautiful heart to handle. She sobbed uncontrollably on the other end of the call and my heart constricted with pain the likes of which I hadn't felt since Devon's funeral.

I hung up and put my head against the wall. When I opened my eyes, I found myself gazing down at the tattoos covering my arms. My lifestyle had brought pain to the one person in the world who loved me most. She represented the only happiness I'd ever had, the only pure thing in my life.

I walked back to my cell in a state of dismay and confusion. I didn't know what the answer was, but something inside me was telling me revenge wasn't it.

When the door cracked for dayroom, I immediately went to the house of the guy who was in charge of the unit. The door closed behind us as we sat on the bed to talk through the punishments that were to be handed out.

He told me that beatings weren't enough to send a message to our new recruits. Rather, these three men needed to die.

His plan was similar to the one he'd come up with to kill the guards. We would start a riot, cover the gunports, and disable the cameras. Then he and I would lead the three individuals into their cells for a beating—and we would kill them one at a time. In the aftermath of the riot, three dead bodies would be discovered and the message would be sent.

I concurred with the plan and went back out to the dayroom.

I laughed and chatted with my attackers as I showed them fake forgiveness, after which I returned to my cell early. I was so uncomfortable with what was about to happen the following day. I sat on the bed and let the reality of the last few years sink in. I thought about how much blood I had spilled for my so-called friends. I thought about the automatic life sentence that would result from this massacre. I knew from the bottom of my heart that if I went through with this, I would never see the streets again.

My relationship with Anna and my newly rejuvenated relationships with my family weighed heavily on my mind. Did I want to throw my life away for a cause I didn't even fully believe in anymore?

When my door opened next, with Anna and my family forefront in my thoughts, I walked by all the cells, through the dayroom, downstairs to the office, and for the first time in my life I did the unthinkable—I asked to leave the unit.

Once again I sat in the hole, feeling perplexed. My decision to walk off the unit had gone against everything I believed in, but I didn't feel bad about it. I could see that the direction the gang was going in, and so I had taken my chance to jump ship.

Now I would have to live in shame. I knew I would have to fight an awful lot, and I would be standing alone without any friends to back me up. I was okay with that. I had stood alone many times before and walked away unscathed. I would just have to, once again, adjust, adapt, and evolve.

Mitch approached my cell and asked me if I would go back. I updated him on the boys' plan to kill everybody. He pleaded with me to go back and even asked me to call the boss man on the street and talk to him. No one wanted me to leave. I respectfully declined his offer and told him I was done.

I had chosen the white picket fence. Anna and my family were my priorities now. I had nothing left to prove in prison, and everything to prove to the people I loved. I wouldn't let their faith in me be destroyed by selfishness any longer.

If I walked back onto the unit I had voluntarily left, I would be risking my life. Besides, it was full of untested kids from Bowden now. I wasn't going back.

My first phone call with Anna was a powerful one. I told her that I had left the gang. Being the genuine angel she was, her first reaction was concern for my safety. I knew right then that I had made the right decision.

Less than a week after I left the unit, my concern about going back was validated with the utmost certainty. A man had accidentally left a pair of blue jeans in the washing machine, thus ruining another inmate's whites, and ended up paying with his life. They found the man dead from fifty-six stab wounds. Someone I knew described the scene as the detectives investigated the scene. Cackling laughter had filled the unit. Every single person thought it was the funniest thing they had ever seen in their lives.

Even though I wasn't there, that scene haunts my dreams to this day.

My validation only grew more secure when five men were arrested on charges involving that murder. Two of them were charged with first degree, and three others with accessory after the fact. They were all ratted out by Bowden kids who couldn't take the heat.

Those five men had been dying to kill someone for months. I was grateful not to be involved with that. If I had stayed, I have no doubt that I would have been next.

Chapter Forty-Eight

GETTING COMFORTABLE

I was going nuts in the hole, so I was glad to finally get some answers about where I would be placed. The prison officials approached me with an ultimatum: I could take medium security and get shipped to Grande Cache Penitentiary in northern Alberta or stay here and go onto a range designated for ex-gang members. They gave me the night to decide.

I had wanted to go to medium security for a long time, but that had been because I wanted to live the easy life in Bowden with my friends there, one of whom was supposedly making $100,000 a month in the drug trade. I had wanted a piece of that action, but that life was no longer in the cards for me.

I weighed my options. I could travel ten hours away to Grande Cache, but then I would be even further away from the people I cared about. Anna wouldn't be able to come see me. Or I could stay in this hellhole.

With that, I made my decision. Anna was worth dying for. I would stay in this murderous penitentiary, hoping that my charisma and people-reading skills wouldn't fail me now.

When I got to my new unit, I was surprised by the friendliness of the inhabitants. They all introduced themselves and I got to know who ran the show pretty quick—a skinhead named Neil. He and I hit it off instantly, as he had heard of me through some grape vines. Since it was his show and he clearly had respect for me, the rest of the unit followed suit.

I decided that life on this unit wasn't going to be so bad.

When I inquired about who ran the drugs and gambling books on the unit, Neil looked at me in surprise.

"No one," he replied.

I laughed to myself, reminding myself that these guys weren't exactly well-funded gangsters. Well, that was going to change. I respectfully asked him for permission to step into that role, as long as I gave him a cut. I think this caught him off-guard, but he smiled and nodded in agreement.

By giving him respect, I made a best friend in a position of power. He was a good guy.

As I said before, I didn't have anything left to prove to anyone. I was sick of having enemies everywhere I went. This was a chance to start over and make meaningful connections, not just in prison but also out on the street.

I dedicated myself to treating everyone with the highest degree of respect possible, unless they gave me a reason not to. The great thing about this philosophy was that everyone thought I was a savage killer, which led people to be grateful for my respect. My legend implied what would happen to them if they didn't reciprocate it. I didn't need to be a killer anymore for people to think I was a killer. I just needed to carry myself a certain way and let them draw the inference on their own.

Within a day or two, the guards asked me if I wanted to be the unit cleaner. This meant taking care of the dinner trays and spending extra time out of my cell cleaning the unit. It also meant I could spend more time on the phone with my loved ones. After asking Neil for his thoughts on the matter, I accepted the offer.

Being on my own, with no gang to coordinate with, I needed to figure out how to make money. A healthy option would be to run a store, which meant keeping canteen supplies of all different kinds on tap, charging for anything I had in stock. It was a steady but small income stream.

I wasn't finished there. Funded by my store revenues, I started gambling lines for the NHL, NBA, and NFL. I was the first person on the unit to get the paper in the morning, so I'd collect all the point spreads from the paper and make up a ticket for every single person on the unit. Their ticket would contain their name and what they were up or down from the previous days. I politely told the men in the unit that they didn't need to bet, but I would slide a ticket in their slot on their lunch tray every morning. If they didn't like the games, they could just throw it in the toilet. Like drugs, though, I figured once a person made their first bet, they'd be hooked.

They placed bets by writing them down on the back of the ticket. The denomination was pop, my jailhouse currency. People could make as many single bets as they wanted, including parlay bets. In sports betting, a parlay bet is when you pick two teams to win; if both win, you get paid back three to one, but if one or both teams don't win, you lose. I also allowed for triple parlays, which I paid out at five to one. These were much more difficult to hit, but when you did you got paid.

Everyone loved gambling.

As for payday, you could only order twenty-four cans of pop at a time. This meant that people occasionally won more than their allowed pop purchase. I would then give them store credit for the equivalent dollar value.

Canteen day happened every two weeks, so the cut-off for gambling fell on the day when we had to place our canteen orders. If a person owed me more than the $100 they were allowed to spend on canteen purchases, they needed to send cash on the street to a specified account by a certain day. Failure to do so would result in a fifty percent tax, meaning that the debt went up by half. This also applied to anyone who owed me money through the canteen.

The Edmonton Max guards all agreed that it was unlike anything they had ever seen before. After I collected the goods on canteen day, they would get stacked to the ceiling in my house until I sorted everything out and dispersed it around the unit for people to hold for me so I didn't draw too much attention throughout the week. It quickly got to the point where everyone's canteen was coming directly to me. I lived like a king.

Chapter Forty-Nine

PRETEND I'M HOME

One day I received a phone call my mom. It consisted of our usual banter, until she brought something up that hit home for me. She said that she had been talking to a woman I knew from my treatment centre days named Tanya. Tanya had mentioned that it was a shame I hadn't stayed sober because I really could have helped a lot of people.

That simple statement awoke something magical inside me—a part of me that had lain dormant for years. The groundwork had already been laid when I left the gang and chose to be on my own so I could stop hurting the people I loved most. I just needed this extra boost to propel myself to a larger purpose.

I ended the call, walked back to my room, turned off the stereo and TV, and thoughtfully pondered what Tanya had said. I was at a point where I could lay the foundation for my new life. Tanya was right. I could help a lot of people. My story would turn heads and people would listen.

But the story wasn't fully written yet. I needed to put in some serious legwork to be at a point where I could deliver it.

I knew where I needed to start, though. I crawled onto my floor and prayed to God for deliverance. It wasn't a recitation, but rather a conversation with the Big Man. I told him that this was going to hard, but I was ready to put in the work. I asked Him to come into my heart and fill it with love and light. Finally, I begged Him to help divorce me from my evil thoughts by working His will through my actions. I wanted Him to use my body as a vessel to bring about His will.

I was sick of being alone and trying to impress people. That part of my life was over. I made the conscious decision to commit my life to God.

I wanted to write to Doc from my old treatment centre, but I knew the man well and a letter from me would be better received if it was filled with the actions I had been taking instead of my lofty intentions. I had an AA big book in my cell, something I'd come across weeks prior when someone had discarded it. This told me that there were people on the unit who desired a better life, just as I did.

Over the following weeks, I built a routine around simplicity and structure. I would wake up in the morning and drop to my knees in prayer as soon as I got out of bed. I always started my conversations with God by reciting the step three prayer, the step seven prayer, and the step eleven prayer. Then I would talk with Him about my day. After wrapping it up, I'd toss a fist pump to the Big Guy as I got to my feet.

The beginning of each day began with serving out the breakfast trays. After that was wrapped up, I opened the daily paper to catch up on current events and collect the point spreads for upcoming games. Next, I'd call Anna. Each morning we fantasized about our white picket fence life. After about an hour of that, I would go into my cell to start the shower rotation around the unit. I'd read AA scriptures to pass some time, then create my tickets to pass around at 10:30.

In the late morning, I would strip down to my shorts, put on some music, and work out in my cell. I played CDs while doing push-ups and running on the spot between sets. The number of push-ups I did increased over the months. I started with sets of forty, and within a few months I progressed to ten sets of one hundred.

After the one-hour workout, I would go back to my knees and pray until the cell cracked open at noon to serve lunch. While serving the lunch trays, I'd hand out all the tickets for that night's games. Almost everyone on the unit utilized my gambling line. With lunch served, I proceeded to clean the unit—and call Anna a second time.

One o'clock was always my signal to resume afternoon showers, after which I'd go into my house and write letters to loved ones, work on my psychology degree, and wait for my favourite show to come on, *Dr. Phil*. I usually turned on my TV a little bit early so I could catch the end of *Ellen*; it always made me smile to watch her light up the crowd with her boundless generosity. It made me want to be a better person. I identified with her giving and in turn wanted to make people that joyful in my own way. Except my desire was to help suffering alcoholics and give messages of hope to the hopeless.

I loved watching Dr. Phil, because his show applied to my studies in psychology. Something about the man also reminded me of Doc. Perhaps that's the reason it became such an integral part of my daily routine. In the final year and a half before my release, I never missed a single episode.

He once said something to a guest that made me roar with laughter. A struggling man asked Dr. Phil if there was any way he could be helped. Dr. Phil's response was gold: "Well, of course you can be helped, son. You can't fall off the floor." Applying this statement to my own shortcomings put me in hysterics. Here I was, sitting in cell in the most dangerous jail in the country, surrounded by psychos and murderers, and I couldn't help but wonder, *Can life get better for me, Dr. Phil?* I could almost hear his voice telling me that I couldn't fall off the floor.

I needed to take some action. It was good to pray and read from the big book, but I wasn't doing everything I could. I was on a unit full of the sickest individuals in the country. What a testament it would be if I could help even one of these lost souls.

A plan began to unfold. I would put in a request to the warden, asking humbly for an AA meeting for our unit. It was a long shot, but it would be a good start along my path of redemption.

Back to my routine. Once *Dr. Phil* went off the air at 4:00, I again stripped to my shorts and did my daily ab workout. That consisted of a routine I had developed over time to strike every area of my abdomen. My sets were coupled with running on the spot, just as I did during the morning workout.

About fifteen minutes before my cell would open to serve dinner, I'd snack on some protein bars from my store. I would follow that with a fist pump to give thanks to the Big Guy, again, and then strut shirtless to serve dinner.

People would have their bets ready to slide to me through their open tray slots at dinner, and afterward I would call Anna for the third and final time, then take dinner and all the extra food trays to my cell to fuel my starving, overworked muscles. While eating, I wrote down everyone's bets for the night. There was usually about $500 on the line, cumulatively, sometimes more. And then I'd turn on the TV and check the scores, all the while watching my bank account get bigger. The most money was always riding on hockey, so I had a second screen devoted to that.

Doors would crack open for an hour of gym time at six. I would roll down under the watchful eye of the armed guards in their gunports. I tried to be the first one to the gym, because they had a light medicine ball that I liked to use, but there was only one. I could do jump squats, lunges, work my shoulders, and on occasion even do pull-ups.

I quickly got to be the heaviest I've ever been, at two hundred ten pounds. I was completely shredded from all the resistance training.

At the end of each gym session, I walked out to the middle of the yard and took a second to myself. I would look up at the stars in the night sky and stand on my tip-toes so that the fences seemed to vanish. For that split second, I was free. I would stare into the big sky and pretend that I was home, with my family by my side.

It was brief, but it was all I had.

When I came back down onto the flats of my feet, the razor wire fences and gun towers dropping back into sight, I reminded myself that this would not be my life forever. On October 19, 2012, I would walk away from here and never look back. For I was walking with God, and He loved me. I could feel it in every bone and muscle in my body.

I hardly ever wavered from this simple routine, doing the same things day after day, and lo and behold, my thought life began to clear of wrong motives. I began to consider others and figure out how I could improve the lives of the people around me.

While this change in my thinking was occurring, I made the conscious decision to make a big splash in Edmonton Max. For the first time in my life, I would be a soldier for God. It was time to devote myself to the daunting task of making a positive difference.

Chapter Fifty

MAXIMUM SOBRIETY

The prison didn't accommodate my request for an AA meeting on our unit. Indeed, there hadn't been a meeting there since the Canada Day riot a few years before. Ever since then, with no mixing of the unit populations allowed, the jail didn't have enough staff to move inmates around to meetings. It was too big a risk.

At first, this failure brought my spirits down. But with some leaning on God, I pressed on. I couldn't give up. I was going to make a difference in these people's lives, with or without the warden's blessing.

One Sunday evening, while serving dinner and collecting people's bets, an idea occurred to me. At each cell, I told the occupant that I was a recovering alcoholic and had been to many AA meetings in the past. In fact, I was well versed in running one. I explained that everyone was invited to join me in the rec yard during gym time that night for a meeting. The only requirement to taking part in the meeting was a desire to stop drinking. There would be no dues or fees, and I would supply some snacks from my store for the people who came and had a desire, no matter how small, to make something of themselves.

I disclosed my plan to every cell on the unit. Now it was time to see if these people, living in the darkest place in the country, would follow me to the light.

I walked out into the hot summer air of the rec yard, my gaze falling on the armed gun towers and twenty-foot razor wire fences. I slowly stepped toward the middle of the yard and sat down, looking at the gym's exit. I was the only one there, but I had been the first to get to the gym. I started to pray, asking God to fill me with His love and to guide my thoughts and actions so that His will, not mine, be done.

I stared intently at the open door. What if no one came? What if everyone thought I was stupid for wanting to help these monsters? What were the guards going to think? My fear emulated the absence of God, for there was no room for God when

I was filled with fear. I asked Him again to make me strong as I waited for inmates to start walking through the door.

I breathed heavy as the prisoners began to flood into the yard, every one of them in for homicide and covered face to toe with tattoos. Most of them were large and very intimidating, but I wasn't scared; God had filled me with the light I had prayed for.

Most inmates immediately took to the well-tread path that circled the yard. But as I watched the men come out, one inmate came out the door and started walking directly toward the middle of the yard where I was sitting. Our eyes met and I bowed my head a few inches. Then I raised it back up and offered a small smile.

You're in the right place, I communicated without saying a word.

He smiled back as though to say, *I want something better.*

Behind him, several inmates followed suit and walked toward me. My heart beat loudly in my ears as they began to sit in a circle with me. As that transpired, inmates circling the yard began to step away from the beaten path, joining the rest of us on the grass. I watched in awe as my circle, starting with one, grew to more than ten. It was very powerful.

I stood up and asked everyone to join me in a moment of silence to remember why we were here, still suffering. I said a quick prayer and sat down. I had the floor.

This was going to make or break someone's life. I needed to stay focused and let God direct me with these broken men.

I opened the meeting by reciting the responsibility statement that I knew by heart from the hundreds of meetings I'd attended in the past. I then asked a couple of individuals to read the fifth chapter from the big book, as well as the twelve traditions. I needed to be careful in choosing who I asked to read, as many of these men didn't know how and I didn't want to embarrass anyone.

When that was completed, I decided against asking if anyone was attending their first meeting or if anyone was coming back. But I continued to let God direct the meeting and followed the procedure that I knew worked.

Several individuals had never been to a meeting before, and almost every single person was coming back. I was the only one who had worked the steps prior to this.

I then read the chapter on step one. Everyone listened intently as I informed everyone that step one was to be the topic that day. I was sure to also mention that they could discuss anything that was on their mind as it related to their problems with alcohol. I did this because I wanted everyone to feel comfortable sharing.

I knew that everyone was relying on me to make this work, so I came to the conclusion that I needed to set the tone by sharing first. I let God work His magic as I described how I felt living in this awful place and how much trouble I'd had staying sober in an environment so overflowing with hate and violence. I talked about my family, and how proud they were of me for working the steps in such a dark place. As I shared, I paid attention to how everyone responded to my preaching. They were all listening, nodding in agreement and showing signs of empathy.

I decided to touch on the topic of God, making a statement and following all the AA members who had come before me. I discussed the God of my understanding. I needed them to hear this so they would know that my beliefs shouldn't dictate their own. After all, AA doesn't show prejudice toward one God. All you need to do is believe that a power greater than yourself can restore you to sanity. This power carries no label, although it's widely known as God.

For this AA meeting to work in a maximum security setting, with all these stone-cold killers, I needed to follow the book to the letter.

I finished sharing and went around the circle, asking to hear from people. While this was happening, I remember looking up at one point and noting the dumbfounded expression on the face of a sharpshooter in one of the towers. I loved it.

As people in the circle shared, it dawned on me just how hopelessly lost these men were. All of them had taken a life, some a lot more than one, and in turn they had lost theirs. This meeting brought about some of the deepest honesty I've ever heard divulged.

Most of these men would never breathe free air again, so they weren't fighting to better themselves in anticipation of returning to the street or of earning a lower security rating; they were just sick of the twisted existence that had engulfed them in prison.

I watched grown men cry as they talked about the prospect of never seeing their families again. They spoke of their children, many of whom would never see their fathers or feel their warm embrace. These men weren't getting out, but they wanted something better. They wanted to be able to look in the mirror.

At the end of the yard time, as the guards called for us to go in, I wrapped up the meeting by asking everyone to stand up and say the serenity prayer. I had no expectation that they would do it, but as I stood with my hands out the men all held hands in a circle, the chain joining together. We looked at the sky, the sun beating off our faces as if God's glory was illuminating the entire yard, and under the gun towers and razor wire this group of alcoholic killers said the serenity prayer.

That day will forever go down as one of the best of my life. I have never been more proud of myself for anything. It produced in me a more powerful feeling than money or drugs ever had and it cemented my purpose. If I was capable of doing this with a bunch of murderers, imagine what I could do on the streets. I decided on the spot to chase this warm feeling to the ends of the earth. Helping people, I realized, is where true happiness comes from.

As we walked out under the stunned eyes of the guards, I told everyone that this was an official AA meeting, for it says in the AA scriptures that any group of two or more alcoholics, when they gather together to fight for the common purpose to stop drinking and discuss the steps, can call themselves an AA meeting. I would chair this meeting every single Sunday until I was released.

Our meeting name, I told them, was Maximum Sobriety.

Chapter Fifty-One

HIGHER POWER

I found myself sponsoring a handful of people as I took the inmates through the steps. Although I was only two months sober, I saw it as spiritual mandate to not refuse any man who asked for help. I wasn't there to judge men for their crimes; I was there to be a messenger of love and light.

In addition to the meetings, I held regular big book studies in my cell for those who showed interest.

As we discussed scriptures together, I saw a change take place around the unit. For example, we slowly put into effect a no-violence policy. When people didn't pay their gambling debts, I just cut them off. The gambling was just for fun anyway; it wasn't supposed to be life or death. I happily told people that if they couldn't pay, they should just stop betting and not worry about it.

A funny thing happened as a result of this: almost everyone always paid. I treated all the inmates with the utmost respect and in response they respected me. It was un-believable how much farther I got by being nice to everyone.

The prisoners greatly respected what I was striving to achieve by hosting those Sunday AA meetings. No one disrespected it a single time, despite not everyone being involved; they were happy to see hopeless individuals create purpose in their lives.

It's not like I got struck by lightning and became perfect overnight. My temper, for example, continued to be a major defect in me. Once while on the phone I got impatient with another inmate who was trying to get on after me. When I slammed the phone down, I told him to quit acting like a b*tch. He called me the same name back, and before long the devil inside me took over. I fed him quite possibly the hard-est one punch I've ever given anyone in my life. His nose exploded and the back of his head smashed against the wall, splitting it open. When I looked down at the man I'd attacked, he was unconscious on the floor, a pool of blood spreading around his head. I swore at myself for falling to such cowardice. This was not the man I wanted to be anymore.

At lunch that day, the guards moved me to lockup and recruited a friend of mine to serve the trays.

It later turned out that this man had suffered a broken nose and needed to get stiches to the back of his head. Feeling horrible, I got down on my knees and asked God for forgiveness and guidance on how to make things right. When I was done praying, I instinctively knew how to handle the situation. Probably for the first time in Edmonton Max history, an inmate wrote a well-thought-out letter of apology. The letter was well received by the injured man, which came with a care package of fifty dollars for him to use at the canteen. I never let myself disrespect him ever again.

The only other time my temper got away from me was when the guards took the second mattress I'd been using to make my bed feel more like a pillowtop. I got really pissed and pounded my fists into the metal doors, screaming that I had scoliosis and they were sentencing me to nights of torturous discomfort. That, of course, was a lie.

Steaming mad, I rolled around the unit rubbernecking every single house for a second mattress. When I came to the cell of a guy I didn't like because of a debt he owed me, I saw that he had two mattresses piled on top of each other. I lied once again and told him that I needed the extra mattress because of a painful back disorder. He lied right back, telling me that he only had one mattress even though I could clearly see he had two. I smiled sarcastically and told him I was sorry for taking up his time. When the doors all opened for gym, I walked straight to that guy's cell, stepped in, cracked him in face, and knocked him unconscious.

When he came to, he scurried into the corner, scared to set me off again. I was in the process of untying the double mattress, but I couldn't undo his stupid knots. He finally asked if he could help me with them, and in frustration I let him. I then stood back, waiting for him to deliver the mattress, which he soon did and I left.

I later felt like an idiot for what I'd, but my pride kept me from writing an apology letter this time.

God, however, has a funny sense of humour. A couple of weeks later, I went to the health clinic complaining about back pain. The doctor informed me that I suffered from a double curve in my spine and that the malady was a disorder called scoliosis. With an unimpressed frown, I told the good doctor that I was aware of what it was.

I walked back to my unit, shaking my head as I walked past all the gunports. What planet was I living on? Had I just gotten disciplined by God? I truly had gotten what I had asked for.

From that day forward, I never again used violence in prison.

My anger was tested a third time one Sunday evening on my way to the meeting. While going through the metal detectors, a guard grabbed my big book and said I wasn't allowed to have it in the gym. It was a power trip. I don't know who that guy was trying to show off for, but I got nose-to-nose with him rather quickly. As I stared into his eyes, unblinking, my fists clenched, a sort of higher intuition took hold of me. I unballed my hands, stepped back, and pressed on into the gym.

I walked outside to the disappointed circle of my fellow alcoholics, knowing that we were all feeling the same thing. The institution wouldn't give us an official meeting, and now the guards seemed to be trying to thwart us from even meeting privately. All we wanted was to feel better.

But I saw through the actions of that single guard. Even if the prison was trying to thwart us by taking away our big book, God had His hands on us and I wasn't going to let that advantage go to waste.

That day, I asked everyone to rise for a moment of silence to remember why we were there. I stood up with my brothers and silently recited a prayer to the Big Guy. When we finished, I sat down on the grass with everyone following suit. They all stared at me, waiting for my reaction to the guard's attempt to ruin our meeting. I smiled and told them that the guards could try and take away our spirits, but God was with us and the show must go on.

Every one of my cohorts' mouths dropped open when I went on to recite the fifth chapter word for word, from memory. I had been to so many AA meeting in my life and read the chapter so many times that I knew it like the back of my hand. Perhaps God had caused me to memorize it, knowing I would need it one day.

Needless to say, the meeting continued as if we had the book right there in front of us, thanks to our higher power.

Chapter Fifty-Two

BEARING FRUIT

My relationship with my mom was growing into something beautiful. I treasured our visits and phone calls and could tell by her passion for me to succeed that she loved me dearly. I knew this with certainty.

While this was going on, my relationship with Anna was growing ever more unconditional. I had long since lost any fear that she might be realizing that she'd made a mistake by getting involved with me. She encouraged me to develop and grow through my struggles. She taught me not to look at my problems as setbacks, but as opportunities to develop and learn from.

I continued to hold my weekly AA meetings while keeping up my fight to speak with the warden about an official meeting. I couldn't tell if I was getting anywhere, but before long a whole year had passed with us holding our meetings.

In my personal life, I found that when I stuck to simplicity, life kept getting better. I grew in my role as a soldier for God, and He showed me His greatness by filling my cold heart with the blessing of giving.

As I pressed on in my newfound healing, I approached the end of my sentence. It was an unbelievable feeling when the clock counted down and my days left to serve dropped to double digits. I was so close to breathing free air again in the presence of my loved ones. It had been six long years of serving the hardest time imaginable.

A few months before I was to be released, I got called to the interview room to see the warden. I was confused by the summons, for I hadn't tried to talk to her in quite some time. When I got to the room, she was waiting for me and politely asked me to sit down. She enquired about the weekly AA meeting in the rec yard I held every Sunday, and I proudly told her that it was called Maximum Sobriety and that there were about fifteen participants on the unit. She smiled as I gabbed on about the positive changes that were occurring in everyone. Apparently she had been watching us week after week, and she wanted to know if I understood why I wasn't getting any official help. I told her that I was very aware of the issue.

Suddenly, the warden got up. "Congratulations, Mr. Bates. Your unit is now the only one in the prison that will get to have an outside AA meeting in the chapel, every Thursday night at eight o'clock."

With that, she walked out of the room.

I sat there, stunned. It took a while for what I'd heard to sink in. It seemed as though I had achieved the impossible. The prison wasn't staffed to facilitate this, but obviously my hard work and integrity had paid off.

I laughed to myself. For so long, I had lived by the code of hate and violence. Never had I dreamed that I would be doing this, and that it would bear fruit. My legacy in this prison would be one of joyful reckoning. With this new AA meeting, outside members of the program could host and chair meetings. That meant my friends would receive help long after I was gone.

I was in tears as I stood up and thanked God out loud.

As I walked slowly back to the range, I pondered what to do next. I was grateful for the Thursday meeting, but I didn't want to put aside the Sunday night meetings we'd already been running. So I looked at it as a second meeting, not a replacement meeting. A year ago there had been no way on God's green earth that AA was ever going to come to Edmonton Max, and now my unit had two meetings, my big book studies, and the promise of outside help.

I truly felt as if I was capable of moving a mountain.

Chapter Fifty-Three

MADE IT

With three days to go before my release, I was saying goodbye to all my friends on the unit and spreading well wishes to all the cells. One of my stops was to approach the man who knew the most about AA next to me and ask him to keep Maximum Sobriety going. He told me that he wouldn't give up on it.

This man then gave me a gift. It came in the form of a tattered but thick sheet of paper, the edges of which had been burnt with charcoal. The words "Maximum Sobriety" were written across the top, with the twelve steps and the date established on the bottom. It was beautiful. My friend smiled at me and thanked me for everything I had done on the unit.

Emotion swept over me as my legacy sank in. I was very proud of myself.

I gave away about $2,000 worth of canteen credit to everyone on my unit from my store and gambling line, and I left the store to Neil. He was the hardest person to say goodbye to, for he had been the one who started this change in me by urging everyone to listen to me and show me respect at the beginning. Surely things would have been very different if it hadn't been for him.

I walked off of the unit with my head held high. I could honestly tell myself that I had done everything I could since I'd been sober to impact the lives of those around me there. I smiled and waved at all my friends who came to see me off.

I may have technically had three days left on my sentence, but we had timed it so that I could spend this last weekend on my final private family visit with Anna. As I walked through the courtyard toward the trailer, my heart leapt in anticipation. When I opened the door, Anna attacked me with the biggest hug I've ever received. It felt like I had just gotten out of prison—and I had.

For those last three days at Edmonton Max, we enjoyed good food, movies, and the best company we could ever ask for. When the weekend ended, the guards would come and take Anna to the front and check her out. And then I would follow her out the gate a few minutes later.

I had been worried that after serving six years in prison, I wouldn't be able to sleep the last few nights out of sheer excitement. Everyone knows that when you're excited for something, time slows right down. I'd spent twenty-three hours a day surrounded by murderers and psychos for years, at one point believing I would never again breathe free air. To say I was excited would be a gross understatement.

But being in the trailer with Anna for the final weekend was a great transition. It didn't feel like I was in jail at all. We talked excitedly about the house she had gotten for us, my plans for a job, and all the fun things I needed to catch up on after spending the better part of my twenties locked away.

When we talked about what I would do for work, I told her that I wanted to work at a gym. I had put on a lot of muscle in Edmonton Max and I thought it would be healthy to have a job that helped people feel good about themselves.

The three days went by pretty fast, to my surprise.

I remember the morning of October 19, 2012 as if it was yesterday. I walked out the back door of the trailer with a coffee in hand and looked up at the gun towers for the very last time. I smiled to myself, savouring each sip. The air was cool but warm for October and the sun was shining down on me. It was the most beautiful day God had ever made.

Anna joined me out on the back step and wrapped her arms around me. She squeezed me as if it was for the very first time. It almost felt as if it was, for this was the beginning of the rest of my life. Prison would soon be behind me, and I would never darken the door of Edmonton Max ever again.

God is great, I said to myself, looking up at the sky. *Thank You for today.*

The guards came and took Anna and her things to the front offices to check her out. My blood was pumping at lightning speeds as I waited for them to return for me. About ten minutes later, I heard the front door open and the guards asked me to come with them. I walked with my belongings to Admission/Discharge. I didn't carry much with me, just the letters from Anna and a couple of outfits; I had left everything else behind for my brothers on the unit.

But my bank account was fat from my time in prison. Cody was going to be all right.

I signed my release papers and they escorted me out toward the front gate. Apparently that's how you leave—the exact same way you came in.

The massive razor wire gate started to slide open and I looked over to see that Anna was recording a video on her phone. I walked through the middle of the two fences, waiting as the first one closed behind me with an unmistakable click. Then the gate in front began to open.

I stepped out, free of leg and belly shackles, unattended by armed guards, and not paranoid that I was about to get stabbed in the neck by an inmate. All these burdens fell off my shoulders as I embraced Anna.

Holding her tight, I looked up again at the sky.

Thank You, God. This is truly a miracle.

PART
IV

Chapter Fifty-Four

LEARNING CURVES

I struggled to sleep that night. My mind was alive and wandering uncontrollably about what would be waiting for me when I woke up in the morning. I was free! I could go for a walk. Take a hike. Eat whatever my heart desired. The possibilities for my day seemed endless.

After six years in a locked room, my senses were overstimulated. I wanted to experience the world and all the beautiful things God had to offer.

I jumped out of bed, kissed Anna on the forehead, and allowed my heart to swell as I watched her sleep. None of this would have been possible without her. She had so much faith in me. I felt complete with her by my side and God in my heart.

I had a few plans for the day. The first was to hit my first outside AA meeting in eight years. The second was to get my driver's license renewed. In fact, it had been so long since I had driven that I would need to get a learner's permit first. The only thing that I had to do after that was pass a written test. I had studied the driver's book in prison, so that wouldn't be a problem. I planned on buying a car and start driving by the beginning of the next week.

I also needed to find the time work out and maintain my physique. There was a gym just down the street from our place in south Calgary. I walked out into the early morning sunshine at six o'clock and trotted down the sidewalk. I was wearing the only set of clothes I had, so I also needed to hit the mall and fill up my wardrobe.

As I made my way to the gym, I started to realize how institutionalized I must have appeared. As people got close to me, my shoulders naturally slumped forward into an aggressive stature. I didn't even mean to do it. Also it was October and there was snow on the ground, yet I was rocking an unzipped tracksuit with a tank top underneath. My chest cap tattoos clearly showed and the sunglasses prevented people from seeing where my gaze was landing.

If I had seen me, I would have known I had come straight from prison.

I wondered how a passing mother with her child would react if she knew that the man who had just graciously stepped onto the grass to let her and her child pass was a convicted killer, fresh out on parole from a maximum security prison.

This made me think carefully about the way I dressed. What message was I hoping to send by looking like a gangster? It was okay to dress that way in prison, because people needed to perceive me the right way there and know what I was capable of. I no longer needed to make a point with my clothing.

I decided to let God direct me, and I figured He would want me to dress nice. Looking like a gangster would take me in the opposite direction of my goals. As I looked around, I could see that wearing dress clothes was apparently the new fad anyway. I was the only person around wearing a tracksuit.

I pulled my sunglasses down as I walked in the door of the gym. I paid a drop-in fee and headed for the change room. It didn't escape me when I was changing that everyone in the locker room kept secretly stealing glances at me. After six years in the Max, I had learned to develop eyes in the back of my head. Nothing got by me. But I let them look and ponder what kind of story could be behind this tattooed man changing in front of them.

As I walked out of the change room, I took a quick walk around the gym to figure out what kind of routine I would start with. I wanted to bulk, but I needed my muscles cut. In order to facilitate this, I drifted toward resistance training, running on the spot the entire workout. I hadn't quite figured out how to work Anna's iPod, so I'd brought my old discman and a big book of CDs. It didn't bother me that the CD constantly skipped. Everyone was looking me like I had a second head when I pulled that discman out. It dawned on me that no one had likely seen one of those in about a decade.

I worked out like a beast. When my mind was set to a purpose, nothing could stop me. It was the one and only time I let the old Cody come out to play. I started off my workouts by doing 1,500 sit-ups in various forms, running on the spot between sets. Every time I stood back up from pushing myself to the limit, my heart rate picked up speed.

I was angry and I didn't know why.

I am a soldier for God, I reminded myself. *My enemies are demons and addiction. The devil has nothing on this worthy combatant.*

As I pushed myself to the breaking point, anger exploded out of me. I shadowboxed the air with weights in my hands. I then turned to the free weights, which I hadn't seen in years. My balance needed a little touching up, but I was amazingly strong. I could have worked out all day.

I went at it for about an hour and a half. At the end, people approached me to ask what I was training for. One guy said that he'd had a better workout just from watching me push myself, almost as though the energy I was burning was somehow contagious.

I realized that I was helping people just by being me in the gym. That made me feel incredible.

I wasn't even tired when I left. In fact, I ran as fast as I could all the way home to try and bring my energy down. I felt like I could conquer the world.

As expected, I passed my learner's test on the first try, which officially allowed me to drive. I was excited to get behind the wheel of Anna's car, but I was even more excited to buy my own. I had no idea what I was going to get, but I was pumped to start looking. The world was my oyster.

Up next was an AA meeting. My energy levelled out as soon as I walked in the door. I felt relaxed as I sat on the couch with a coffee in hand. I recognized a fair number of people from my time in AA many years prior.

As we stood up for the opening moment of silence, a wave of serenity washed over me. It was exactly how I had felt at the meeting in Edmonton. I felt at home. I needed these meetings; they were a consistent reminder of where I had come from and how I would keep on the right path.

I was asked to share shortly into the meeting. As I contemplated where I was going to go with it, a wave of emotion consumed me. I couldn't help but let the tears stream down my face as I tried to vocalize the gratitude I felt and the long road I had trudged from that fateful day of my arrest. I could feel my blood coarse through my veins. I could barely speak, but I managed to get out what I had gone through the past six years. I talked about Maximum Sobriety and the meeting under the gun towers with all my convicted murderer acquaintances.

Every person's jaw hit the floor. I smiled as it really sank in how this was affecting the room. I was showing that the program worked in even the darkest places on the planet.

After the meeting, several people approached me and said that my story had touched them in a profound way, that what I'd shared had been exactly what they needed to hear. This is what God put me on this earth for. As I looked into each person's eyes, I felt their sincerity. I could sense their compassion without even hearing them speak.

My mother and siblings came for dinner that night. My mom was beautiful as always and wore a massive smile as she stepped through the door with my brothers and sisters. It was surreal for everyone that I was out of prison. We almost had to pinch ourselves to make sure we weren't dreaming.

I think it was a surprise to everyone in my life that I had come out the other side of the darkness I had shrouded myself with. At one point I had been a killer, gangster, and sociopath. Today I sat at the dinner table as a son, brother, and loving boyfriend. I truly felt blessed.

As dinner was served, something unanticipated happened. In the Max, the cleaner would go from cell to cell handing out trays of food. As soon as he was done, he would go back to the beginning and pick up all the empty trays. The inmates literally had only about five minutes to eat their food.

Well, as I looked around the table I noticed that everyone was staring at me in silence. My cheeks were puffed out, full of food, and my plate was empty. A piece of spaghetti hung from my tomato-sauce-covered mouth.

It dawned on me what had happened. My plate was empty and not a single person had even taken a bite yet.

You're not in prison anymore, Cody, I told myself.

This wasn't going to be an easy learning curve.

Chapter Fifty-Five

NEW PHILOSOPHIES

I passed my driver's test on the first try, two days later. I was now able to drive around and explore on my own. But exploring was the last thing on my mind. I wanted to change the world, and I knew my dark past was the greatest tool I had. I wasn't ashamed of it.

As I walked into my old treatment centre, I was met by Doc, who introduced me to some wayward youngsters who were struggling with the steps. I wanted to help them so bad. As I shared with them, I saw that they were grasping onto every word that fell from my mouth. I was a tatted-up reformed gangster from the most violent prison in the country. But for some reason, that's what drew people to me. They wanted to know how I had found myself in such a dark place. Their eyes lit up as I described my relationship with God and utilizing the steps to propel my recovery. I was a pillar of strength and led by example.

I asked Doc and the other staff if I could train the kids further in the centre's gym. They were more than happy to accommodate my offer. For me, it was another way to help myself by sharing what I knew. My teachings in the gym would facilitate more growth for all of us.

So I worked out with the kids, moulding and shaping their young minds toward the love and light my heart had found. I became infatuated with watching them learn and grow spiritually. My spiritual cycle was coming full circle.

It was hard to imagine the dark places I had once gone in my mind, such as the leafless forest. I was grateful to not be consumed with that darkness. I never wanted to be that person ever again. He was slowly becoming a relic. As long as I remained grateful, I knew the beast would stay dead—but never forgotten, because I needed him. I needed to remember.

One of my biggest fears walking out of prison had been whether I would find employment. I had experience in cooking and mowing lawns, but that was about as far as my work history went. One thing I did have going for me, though, was my physique, so I decided to try and get a job at a gym close to the treatment centre.

I walked into the gym wearing nice clothes. I had been cautious in prison about where my tattoos were placed, strategically locating them in areas that could be covered. When I spoke to the manager, I learned that I needed to take specific courses to be a personal trainer. I felt let down at first, although it turned out there was a position open selling memberships.

I could be a salesman, I thought, recalling my drug-dealing skills. I'd been told by more than one person that I would make an amazing salesman.

Just like that, I had a job. The manager said I could start two days later. I walked out of there employed and full of gratitude. The smile on my face proclaimed the peace I had in my heart. I already had a license and a job.

I called my mom to share the amazing news and she joined me in a happy dance. Then I notified my dad and Anna. Next, I made my way to the treatment centre, which was becoming like a second home. I shared the news with Doc, and everyone was overjoyed.

As the days passed I continued with my routine of prayers, morning readings, daily AA meetings, and lots of worship to the Big Man upstairs in the form of singing, fist-pumping, and spiritual walking.

I walked in for my first day of work, through the roof excited to begin my journey toward eventually becoming a personal trainer and helping people through fitness and positivity. I was wearing a tracksuit, which was appropriate under the circumstance. I approached the front desk and the secretary informed me that someone needed to talk to me. This seemed strange, but I was in no state of panic. The manager then came out and informed me that the trainer for the membership sales job was out of town and I would have to come back in two days.

Though a little disappointed, I had faith in God's timing and process. I just smiled and joined the staff for a group workout. It was a blast getting to know my co-workers while learning the different methods for teaching fitness. Everyone seemed excited to have me on the team. I gave the workout all the intensity I could muster. I loved this stuff.

A couple more days passed and I returned, ready to work and eager to please. But once again they asked me to come back in a couple more days. I didn't think anything of it. I joined in for another group workout and cherished the new connections I felt like I was building.

The third time I walked in, things went differently. The training manager was present this time, so it was time to sell some memberships. I beamed as I sat down and took my rightful place at the desk, ready to take on the world. This whole city was going to be buying memberships off me in no time.

Without warning, the training manager called me into the back office. A look of concern crossed my face as I walked in. As soon as I sat down, four rather large men joined us. I knew exactly what was happening. The biggest personal trainers were all standing behind my would-be boss. They were letting me go—and using a show of force to do it.

"Due to unforeseen circumstances, we have to let you go," the manager said assertively.

My throat felt like it had taken a punch. I was mad. More important, I was hurt. I felt like crying as I looked her in the eyes.

One of the trainers I had become closer with over the week could see how crushed I felt. He stepped forward compassionately and told me I was welcome to continue to join them for the group workouts.

"No, he's not," the manager said. "He has a lifetime ban from the property."

A second hard blow to the throat. Even my personal trainer friend was taken aback by the coldness of her comment. I stood up and exited her office to pack my things and leave for the last time.

As I walked out of the building, tears streamed down my face. I wasn't scared to show how I felt; it was honest. But making myself vulnerable had led me once again to pain. The manager hadn't said why they were letting me go. What "unforeseen circumstances" had come up? I was heartbroken.

The realization of how they perceived me crushed my heart. Is this how it was always going to be? Would people only ever see me as a killer? For just a second, my dangerous thinking returned.

I got in my vehicle and let my shoulders slump. I lowered my head onto the wheel. The demons that had lain dormant in my mind began to whisper: *What are you going to do? Be a cook?*

I started the engine and began driving toward Doc's treatment centre. I needed my mentor. More than that, I needed God.

While driving, I tried to put myself in that manager's shoes. I reminded myself of where I had come from and considered how daunting it must have been for her to sit across from me and try to get me out of the building as quickly as possible, knowing that she was talking to a killer paroled from the Max.

After I spoke with Doc, I walked out of the treatment centre with my passion fired up again. He always knew how to ignite me. I've never met anyone who has been able to read me as skillfully as he could.

I drove home and cleaned myself up, giving up on the idea of working at a gym. They hadn't asked if I had a criminal record on the application, but I figured the gym world was a close-knit community and word had gotten around.

I had an alternate idea, though. I don't know what exactly drew me to this precise place, but when I prepared my resume I knew where to go with it. With my new dress clothes on, I drove to a car dealership in south Calgary. Over the years, many people had suggested that I could be a great car salesman—and the thought of selling these particular cars, expensive imports worth $50,000 apiece, excited me.

Well, I tried not to get too excited. But if this was God's plan, it would surely unfold.

I felt nervous as I walked through the doors and my gaze fell on the amazing showroom, packed with countless vehicles, all polished and sparkling in the sunlight. I don't usually feel nervous, but this was a daunting sight.

I walked up to the reception desk with a big smile and asked to speak with a manager. She politely asked for my resume and said that someone would get back to me. I kindly thanked her and started my way toward the door.

Just as I was pushing on the handle to leave, the receptionist called to me as a heavyset and clean-cut man walked by.

"This is Cody," she reported in the man's direction. "He's applying for a job."

He took my resume and gave it a quick study. He then asked me if I'd ever sold anything before.

Crack, I could have answered. Thank goodness, I didn't.

He asked if I had time for an interview right then and there. Startled, I said yes and followed him toward the used car building across the parking lot.

At this point, I let God take over. I smiled, nodded, and let my interpersonal skills take over. I was very good at making people like me. I was well-versed at striking the right emotional chords with people and in turn developing personal attachments. I openly shared with this man that I was in recovery, and he reciprocated by informing me that he was ten years sober. I couldn't believe it. He then told me that he wanted me to start the next day. He passed me a hiring package and asked that I be there at nine o'clock the next morning with everything filled out.

I walked out of the dealership cradling the hiring package under my arm. To think, only a few short hours ago I had been decimated. Now I had a sales job, possibly the start of a solid career, and I was just a few days out of prison. If my original plan had come to pass, I would have been selling gym memberships over the phone all day! Once again, my higher power had come through.

In the morning, I was going to start a new chapter of my life—moving metal, cashing cheques, taking names, and helping people find God's light.

Chapter Fifty-Six

SECOND CHANCES

"**D**o you have a criminal record?"

That question in the hiring package obviously made me nervous. In hindsight, a lot of hurt could have been avoided if they had asked that to begin with, but I trusted that God's plan had unfolded the way it was supposed to. I was a man of faith. Because of what had happened at the gym, I made a commitment to always disclose my criminal history before I got too deep into an opportunity.

That morning, I walked into my boss's office dressed in a nice suit and a completely filled-out hiring package. I sat in front of him and took a deep breath.

Your plan, God.

I placed the papers on his desk and asserted that I had something to tell him. He was a compassionate man and listened keenly as I told him that I had a criminal record from something that had happened when I was twenty-one.

He laughed out loud when I said it. Clearly sensing how uncomfortable I was and striving to lighten my mood, he said, "Everybody has a record in this industry. What's it for?"

His jaw hit the floor when I was done telling him the story of where I had come from and what I'd done since to better myself. He could clearly see that I was now a better man.

"I'm not going to let you go," he finally said. "But when the general manager comes in tomorrow, I'll have to tell him, and you might not have a job."

At least this man was giving me a chance. But if I could sell a car half as well as I could sell myself, I would surely have a fruitful career. He assigned me to a desk and showed me how to start the online training.

One thing that struck me was how far behind in technology I was. He showed me how to work the computer, but I was completely lost after he left. Determination arose in me that this guy had faith in me and I wanted to prove him right. I didn't want to ask him for help and make myself more trouble than I was worth.

Later that morning, my manager asked me if I could help a customer. It was a kind lady and her son who were looking for a vehicle for him. He was only seventeen and needed something safe, reliable, and fuel-efficient.

That's the moment when I realized I knew absolutely nothing about cars. I hadn't seen a car for the whole six years I'd been in prison. What did I know about fuel economy, engine sizes, safety ratings, Bluetooth connectivity, or interest payments? I literally couldn't answer a single question they had. I had to laugh at myself.

As the customer and I looked over the cars, my enthusiasm for newly developed technologies like heated seats and built-in navigation became contagious. By the time the test drive was done, even though I hadn't been able to answer any of their questions, they were more than willing to move forward with the purchase I had gotten them excited about.

I had sold a car to the first customer I'd talked to.

With the next customer, I followed the same approach and sold another car.

It turned out I didn't need to know much about vehicles, I just needed to provide exceptional service and enthusiasm. I was forthcoming about being new and not having an abundance of knowledge. I couldn't even tell them how to pop open the gas cap on these futuristic machines, but by the end of each test drive I could tell you about where my customer was from, how many kids they had, what they did for work, whether they liked it, and where they pictured themselves in five years. I learned that building meaningful connections with people and creating a foundation of trust is more important than product knowledge.

After three days, the general manager finally had a chance to have a conversation with me about my criminal record disclosure. I sat down at his desk with a pit in my stomach. I liked what I was doing, and I was clearly really good at it. In three days I had sold six cars.

The general manager told me that he wanted to give me a chance, but the owner of the dealership would have the final say and he wasn't back for the better part of two weeks.

At least I still had a job for now. I had survived two tiers of hierarchy, and bought myself another two weeks to prove myself. God's plan was unfolding. I had been blessed with a very unique gift; God had given me the gift of gab, passion, and the ability to evoke emotion in people.

I continued to defy the odds, learning quickly the fundamental tools of a salesman. I wanted to know everything. If I stayed open-minded and willing to learn, I would surely have a fantastic career here.

When the owner of the dealership called me up for a meeting at month's end, three and a half weeks after I'd been hired, I walked into his office feeling honoured and humbled. I knew I was good in my newfound calling, but my career was in his hands.

He asked me about myself and I happily shared my story of redemption and the spiritual principles that had guided me. He was fascinated and explained the risk he was taking in considering me for a role on his team. At the end, he told me that he believed in second chances and felt that my words were genuine.

We shook hands as he welcomed me to the dealership. My heart swelled with gratitude as I exited his office. I was grateful that this man believed that my history didn't necessarily reflect my present character. He was a good man.

But I'm sure it helped that I had walked into his office with twenty-two car sales under my belt, having outsold his entire staff that first month.

Chapter Fifty-Seven

FULL CIRCLE

One day, I was asked to share my story at an adult treatment centre. I had never been asked to share my story in front of a group, but I decided to do it if this was the path God had destined for me. Sharing my experience, strength, and hope was a passion.

When I told Doc about the opportunity, he was very happy for me. I was a walking example of what God's greatness was capable of. I worked hard at helping the kids there. The biggest thing I could pass along to the kids was this: without God, I wouldn't have gotten sober or been placed in a position to help people.

I developed strong relationships with some of Doc's clients, and several of them asked if I would sponsor them. Of course, I had to run those sorts of big decisions through my own sponsor—Doc. He thought it was a good idea, though, so I started to help these kids through the steps that had saved my life. I worked out with them, took them to meetings, and attended all their graduations. I was a beacon of hope and a pillar of strength in the treatment community, a far cry from the psychopathic gangster I had once been.

As I walked into the adult treatment centre later that week, I asked God to give me the words to say. This place was a lot bigger than Doc's centre. From what I understood, it had at one time been a hotel.

The man who had invited me to share greeted me and led me down to the group room. I felt love as I stepped inside to see all the recovering addicts in attendance. My new friend informed me that it generally wasn't this full, but word had gotten around that I was going to be there, through some people from my past who were current clients.

I greeted everyone and asked if they would join me in a moment of silence to pray for the still suffering. I then led them in sitting down and started from the beginning. As I spoke that day, I watched everyone as they listened to me, nodding in agreement, shaking their heads in astonishment, and fist-pumping when I struck an emotional chord. Indeed, I had a hard time controlling my emotions when I spoke about the gratitude I now had.

It was an incredible feeling to bear my soul for these men. I shared about my experience with addiction, which had ravaged my life until I had almost no soul left to save. I related to the pain and hardships of early sobriety, acknowledging that my thinking had been my worst enemy in the first little while. But if I could achieve sobriety in one of the darkest places on the planet, surely these guys could pull it off in a treatment facility. That was the most powerful component of my recovery. It took away all the excuse and invalidated all fears. I told them to be brave and strive to be great.

"God works, you guys," I concluded. "Cry out to Him and I promise you'll see miracles."

After my story was done, I hung around and took part in some fellowship. One guy after another approached me and express how much my story had touched them. My heart beat so loudly that I could barely hear people talk. I walked out of there later and danced to my car. This was what God had saved me for.

As I walked into the house that night, Anna was patiently waiting at the table for me. She hugged me, and I embraced her back with all the love in the world. She was so proud of me, and I felt honoured. I loosened my grip on her and looked into her eyes, telling her that she was my world. She gave me that beautiful smile I had fallen head over heels for.

If it wasn't for her, who knew where I would be?

The following months were spent working, preparing for the next chapter of my life, and getting acquainted with healthy people who I hadn't seen in six years. Alex was one of those people. He had started a family by now and couldn't wait to introduce his six-year-old son to his uncle Cody.

As I pulled up to his house in High River, my excitement amplified. I hadn't seen my best friend in years. He was working at a meat plant, supporting his young family, and had stayed away from cocaine ever since. I couldn't have been happier for my friend. He truly deserved happiness, and it appeared that he had attained it on all fronts.

I had brought Alex's little boy a present, and the kid loved it. I almost spent more time playing with him than I did catching up with my childhood friend! But when I glanced at Alex watching me and his son play, I could see the pride in his eyes. I'm sure he had wished many times for my safe return.

Playing with his little boy put into perspective what I had to look forward to. I wanted to someday be a dad. I admired the look of unconditional love Alex wore when he looked at his boy. He would do anything for his little man.

———————

I was doing well at work as the months passed. It was rare for me to sell less than twenty cars in a month. My product knowledge was steadily improving, but I was careful not to drift too far from what worked for me. Getting to know my clients on a personal level was the most important part of making a sale. People loved to work with someone they trusted.

Less than a month out of prison, I had bought myself a brand-new car with the money I made from the gambling lines in jail. To me it looked like a Ferrari, but bear in mind that I had been in prison a long time and a lot of vehicles looked like Ferraris to me. It was a rear-wheel drive, manual transmission sports car coupe, loaded with all the latest technology. I felt like a boss rolling around in my bright red sports car. I'd never owned anything that nice, and I credited it to the blessings of God.

I tried to stay as close as possible to Doc's treatment centre. I needed that place more than anything, and I could always go there for a meal, a workout, or to give back. I loved the feeling I had when I walked in the door each day. Any time I was struggling, I would go there and talk to someone who would inadvertently remind me of where I had come from, and in the process help them to better themselves, which in turn helped me.

Chapter Fifty-Eight

DIVINE EXCHANGE

One thing I struggled with was being around so many people all the time. It was difficult, because I had gotten so used to being locked in a room by myself. This led to some problems in my relationship with Anna. Although I seemed to be doing well on the outside, I still had some psychological scars—and we didn't pay enough attention to them.

I spent a lot of my nights away from home, out into the early hours of the morning—not because I was doing anything wrong, but because I was uncomfortable at home. It became difficult to deal with someone always needing to talk to me and be around me. The fact is that Anna loved me to pieces and she would have done anything for me, but I was used to only talking to her over the phone two or three times a day.

Our relationship became a strain, and I was trying to create distance. It had always haunted her that I'd been diagnosed as a sociopath, and so she needed constant reassurance that my feelings were real and genuine. But this also drove her to be harsh in trying to evoke emotion in me, almost as if she needed validation of my benevolence. This caused me to shut down emotionally. And when I struggled to show them, she would dig harder to stoke the emotion she was looking for, sometimes in rather unconstructive ways.

The whole thing scared me. Had the doctors been right about my diagnosis? Sociopaths were charismatic master manipulators. Why was it that I had been able to endure being locked up for twenty-three hours a day in a maximum security penitentiary for six straight years and come out with so many social skills? Why was I prospering? Was I such a master manipulator that I convinced myself that I was normal? Was my love life genuine? Was I capable of the sorts of feelings that normal people associated with love? Or was my version of love a warped conception of the real thing? All these questions were detrimental to my spiritual growth.

Anna was emotional, I was trying to deal with psychological trauma, and without either of us noticing our relationship took a turn for the worse. Our fights progressed and I found myself spending more and more time away from the house. No matter how hard I tried, I couldn't seem to fix our relationship's downward trajectory. I loved Anna with everything in me and it hurt me greatly to lose control in this way. Despite all the other positive things happening in my life, despite helping so many kids and speaking at so many treatment centres, I couldn't stop our decline.

She and I broke up about five months after I was released. It was one of the hardest things I'd ever had to do, but I realized that staying in the relationship was toxic and was jeopardizing my recovery. I could have stayed, but what good would I have been if I wasn't sober?

Despite losing my girlfriend, I still gravitated toward God. He was my rock, along with Doc and my family. I continued to go to daily AA meetings and I relied heavily on this fellowship for support.

I didn't let what was happening in my love life impact my climb toward greatness.

Even though Anna and I broke up, we decided to work on things while apart. There was no denying that we loved each other. Our struggle was that we had a hard time reciprocating each other's feelings at the proper moment; when one of us was upset, the other would be happy. We just couldn't seem to connect.

Because we wanted a life together that reflected God, we started going to church. It took us a while to find one we liked. The truth was that I didn't understand religion. I didn't know if I was Catholic or Protestant… I didn't know the difference. All I understood was that there was a heaven and hell, a devil and God. Aside from having attended a couple of midnight masses as a kid, I knew nothing.

I was, however, certain about the God of my own understanding. He existed and was playing a significant role in my life. I lacked in His word, not His will. Truthfully, I didn't know if I believed in Jesus or the Bible. I mostly just went to church for Anna's sake.

As Anna and I walked into one particular church, we were greeted with smiles, hugs, and handshakes. While walking through the crowd, people were saying "Praise God" all the time.

We sat in the front row, close to the action. Prayers and worship filled the morning and smiles beamed from the crowd as everyone praised the Lord. But I didn't understand who I was praising. I praised God but didn't really believe in Jesus. When I prayed, it was to God. I just believed in my higher power.

During the service, an offering plate was passed around. That's when it dawned on me that this was how the church kept its doors open, in much the same tradition as AA. I asked Anna to cradle the offering plate while I pulled out some money. Something happened to me in that moment. Maybe I didn't have a relationship with Jesus, but I was open to one. I placed three hundred-dollar bills in the collection. Anna looked astonished as I passed the plate away.

After a few weeks of dropping hundreds of dollars at a time in the collection plate, I was approached by a church member who pointed out that he couldn't help but notice the amount of money I was placing in the plate. He insisted on giving me a tax receipt. I declined at first, because I hadn't filed taxes in years. Quite honestly, it sounded like a lot of work. But after some convincing from Anna that dealing with taxes was a mandatory aspect of life, I graciously accepted the church's tax receipts.

By October 2013, I had been going to church for more than a month and making large weekly offerings to God. The car industry was struggling in Alberta due to an economic downturn, but somehow I still managed to sell thirty-nine cars that month. It was astonishing, and to this day I don't know how it was possible. By comparison, the other salesmen were selling five to ten. It was like everything I touched turned to gold that month. I hadn't changed much, so the only variable in my life was that I was going to church now and making gracious offerings in the collection plate.

I couldn't help but cock an eyebrow to the sky and wonder about what was going on up there. This was the first time in my life that I truly considered whether Jesus Christ could be real. Maybe it was true that God had walked the Earth two thousand years ago.

Selling thirty-nine cars in a single month, coinciding with my introduction to church, was enough for me to give it some thought-provoking consideration.

Business was crazy. I walked around in a business suit and tie, going around the dealership feeling like a boss. I was more than content with the many blessings that seemed to be bestowed on me daily. I sold more cars than my dealership had ever sold before, and I strived to bring my team up around me. I shared my methods and put others first.

Around this time, Alex really started to struggle. His family life was falling apart and his drinking was getting worse and worse. It became really difficult for me to be around him because of how much it hurt me to see him in pain. He consistently wore a smile, but when he spoke of his son and ex-girlfriend he inevitably shed tears.

Alex spoke regularly of killing himself. This was heart-breaking, because I needed my friend. I made a point to travel to High River as often as possible to be there for my brother. We would play Frisbee or sit in the house and jam out to video games. He was generally in a good mood when I was around.

I knew from personal experience that he needed to share his pain, something he hardly ever did. He kept it bottled inside. But soon he got some roommates, and that made me feel a lot better about the situation. He needed some company to make sure his malignant thoughts didn't consume him.

As the blessings in my life piled up, Doc always reminded me to never forget where I had come from. I shared with him that I was about to receive an award from the city for being one of the top salesmen in Calgary. I had sold two hundred forty cars in my first year with the dealership. Doc was proud of me and kept putting my leadership skills to use with the kids at the treatment centre.

Sometime later, I stood in front of a packed venue and accepted my award with pride. If this was what I could accomplish after only a single year out of prison, I could only imagine what would be possible after five years. I gave thanks to God that day, standing proud as the rookie car salesman of the year. As everyone clapped for me, it occurred to me that it would probably blow some of their minds to know the truth about me—but this wasn't a day to revisit my dark past. This was a day of joyful reckoning, a day to give thanks to my family, Doc, and God for the many blessings that had been bestowed on my wonderful life.

Gratitude overwhelmed me as I shook hands with some of Calgary's bigshots and got pictures taken. I was a star. They didn't know that I was a convicted killer or a recovering alcoholic; they just saw me as one of them. Violence and anger had been replaced with love and peace. Only a true divine intervention could have produced such a radical change.

Cody at age twenty-nine with his Salesman of the Year award.

Chapter Fifty-Nine

HARSH WRONGS

My relationship with Anna was off and on. When we weren't dating, I went out with other girls. This hurt Anna deeply, creating a rift between us. Although she and I weren't together, though, we kept seeing each other.

One day, I woke up in Anna's house to the shock of something hitting me in the face. I shot to my feet just as Anna started screaming at me to get out of her house. I looked down and realized that she had thrown my cell phone at me. While I was sleeping she had gone through all my messages, and now she could barely contain her rage. She didn't care that we hadn't been together when I spoke with those other girls; she was still in love with me and I had wounded her deeply. I did my best to console her, trying all the while to keep my own emotion from bubbling to the surface. Anger was rising inside me and I couldn't let it out. She just kept yelling, getting in my personal space and hurtling the most malicious insults she could think up.

I was trying to leave the room when she stepped in front of me and hit me with her fists. As I pushed her aside, a particularly well-timed jab struck me in the nose. She stopped, knowing she had gone too far. For one brief second, my lip curled up and my inner demons showed themselves. But I caught it, pushing them right back down.

I couldn't let her see me like this. I grabbed Anna by the arm, shoved her out of the room, and slammed the door in her face.

As turned my back on the door, the demon I had briefly forced back down exploded out of me like a bat out of hell. With my teeth clenched, I put all my weight behind quite possibly the most devastating punch I've ever thrown. The door exploded, woodchips flying all around Anna, who still stood on the other side of it.

Our eyes met through the massive hole in the door. I was breathing heavily, my brows were dropped, shoulders hunched forward, and my lip curling up, exposing my clenched teeth. The old Cody had made a special appearance.

The fear in Anna's eyes will forever haunt me. This was the woman who had loved me unconditionally throughout my time in prison and throughout my difficult struggles afterward. Now she was terrified of what I might do to her. It broke my heart.

She ran from me.

I pushed away my feelings of anger or resentment, burying the old Cody as deeply as I could. I then walked out of the room and past the wreckage from my death blow to the door.

"Get away from me!" Anna screamed, recoiling from my touch.

The only thing I could do in that moment, shame and embarrassment consuming me, was turn around and leave. She was ready to call the police.

What had I done?

Walking to my car was one of the most painful trips of my life. Anna and I were done for good, and I had left her in the worst way possible. I felt like a monster.

I had reacted impulsively, in the way I had been conditioned to react from years in prison, and it had scarred her for life. I didn't deserve to be her boyfriend if these demons were still lurking inside me. It was a part of me that scared me to death. The beast had to be controlled.

I went straight from her house to speak with Doc. I broke down as I described the horrific scene that had unfolded. I was honest with him, shedding tears over the fact that I was still sick. He consoled me but also made me confront the harsh wrongs I had committed.

"What are you going to do?" he asked.

I replied that I needed to give Anna space, and in the meantime I need to take care of myself.

He gave me a loving embrace as we parted ways. We both knew that I had the tools to deal with this, and that reaching out to him had been the start of my healing.

It was scary to think about what had transpired at Anna's house. I could pinpoint the exact moment when I'd lost control—it had happened right after I'd realized the damage was already done, after I had known that all was lost and she would never forgive me. When that realization took hold, I had stopped caring.

A change needed to take place. If it didn't, the old Cody would consume the new one.

Chapter Sixty

WHITE, WINDOWLESS ROOM

I missed Anna terribly as the months went on. I tried to fill my time with recovery-based ventures, but it was difficult to sit and share my experience when I was so wounded inside. I didn't understand why I had let that dormant part of myself out to play after having buried it for so long.

I joined some sports and started a floor hockey team in a competitive league. It was good for me to get out and fall into the leadership role of team captain. I relished every minute of it. It was a team built of friends of mine and we generally played twice a week.

When I stepped onto the rink, the beast could come to the surface. I played with a ferocious intensity. My skill level wasn't as high as others, but I gave it everything I had. I fell in love with this team and everyone on it. We even got special team jerseys made that were sponsored by my dealership.

Our team thrived in the league and were a feared opponent because of our size, skill, and vicious defence. The rule was that there wasn't supposed to be any body contact, but animosities developed between rival teams and we broke the rules sometimes. Although fighting wasn't regular, it happened on occasion.

I moved in with a friend from work who was quite literally the funniest guy I had ever met. He also became someone with whom I could share my darker thoughts. We worked together, lived together, and played floor hockey together. I spent a lot of time with him. He didn't drink, which made him a heaven-sent sort of friend to have around. He encouraged me to go out and do things that made me happy, like sports or seeing my family. He was a big reason that I managed to stay sober during this difficult period.

I was so hurt on the inside that I sought outside validation to make myself feel good. This caused me to me stay out later and make questionable decisions. Outside validation, however, is only a temporary fix. The more I needed people to validate me, the further I drifted from my loving God.

Playing poker at the casino into the early hours became a regular thing, and I became obsessed with social media and posting pictures that people would respond to. My selfless actions became few and far between. I still focused on working God's will, but I made compromises. I was slowly drifting back into the pain and sorrow that had once consumed me.

I went to see Alex fairly often, but being around my sad and desperate friend didn't help. Alex had lost his little boy, and now he wanted to die. No matter how much love I pumped into him, he seemed determined to hurt himself and push himself closer to the fateful act of suicide. His roommates told me stories of the pain he was going through and how he would act out. It was very sick. He just wanted to end his suffering.

One night, our floor hockey team was playing a rival and the game took a turn toward violence. We were winning by several points and the other team resorted to taking cheap shots and calling us vulgar names. After the final whistle, one of my younger teammates took a crosscheck to the back of the head by a disgruntled older player. My anger rose as I strutted toward the impending melee. I cut in, standing face to face with the guy who was bullying our player.

"Why don't you pick on someone your own size?" I rasped in a low, aggressive voice.

I fully expecting the situation to taper off, with the two of us walking in separate directions—as it usually did when someone realized they had pissed off the lion. To my dismay and sick pleasure, the man took a step forward. Our noses were almost touching now.

"I am," he said in a threatening tone.

I want you to imagine that you are in a white, windowless room. The walls are bare and the room is empty—no people, no furniture, nothing. Now imagine there's a wolf in front of you on the other side of this room, about nine feet away. The wolf is unrestrained and uncontrolled—and you're alone with it.

What would you do?

If you can't run and you can't hide, I think you would talk to it. "Nice doggy. You're a good boy." Your voice would be trembling with terror as you speak, and the animal would be picking up on it. A low growl comes up from deep inside this beast as he studies you, stalks you as it paces in a circle around the outer edge of the room. That growl feels like it's coming from all directions at once.

You keep your eyes glued to the beast, not wanting to break the connection for fear that it will destroy you if you do. The wolf's hairs stand straight in an aggressive posture. Every fibre of this animal is in battle mode. Its lips snarl as its saliva drips to the floor.

You're going to die, painfully.

Suddenly, something has changed—you are chained to the wolf.

Most people don't know what's it's like to have their limbs shackled. Let me tell you how it feels. The cuffs constrict the movement of your legs. It feels cold against your bare skin and the harsh abrasion of the steel makes it extremely uncomfortable. It gets heavier with each step. At any second, you could be called upon to leap into action, and you won't be able to move.

That's how it feels to be chained to the wolf.

As your gaze falls upon this chain, how does your heart feel? It beats loudly in the silent room. It feels as if the spiritual realm is raining all hell against you.

Look at the animal. It hates you! Its bloodlust will only be quenched by your lifeless corpse being torn to pieces in its unforgiving mouth. Those fangs are about to break your sensitive skin.

Now, realize that I don't believe there is such thing as a blackout rage. What I can tell you is that when I felt this man's hot breath steam roll into my nasal passages, fear and common sense left my body. I lost all control of my thoughts and actions.

His eyes went wide with surprise as I swung at him viciously, as hard as I could and as fast as my body would allow. I growled while propelling lightning-quick strikes to his head, connecting punch after punch. He tried to run, but my grip on the back of his jersey prevented him from getting very far. His teammates tried to get me off him, but they, too, fell victim to my tyranny. Several of them received their own shots to the face as they got too close.

When the referee finally got me off my cowering adversary, I could barely breathe. Not because I was out of gas, but because my adrenaline was through the roof. I stood up, my breath heaving, staring angrily at everyone around me. Even my own teammates were taken aback by the sinister expression on my face.

You might naturally draw the conclusion that I am the wolf in that white, windowless room, and that my enemies are those who are forced to barter with the beast that has no understanding.

Nothing could be further from the truth.

I am not the wolf; I am the trembling soul pleading with the spiritual animal. I beg and plead with this beast daily, praying for a divine intervention to run interference between us. But the animal doesn't negotiate. Its rage is uncontrollable and it is mute.

On the ice that day, I was too great a coward to fight the hellhound off. I let it tear me to shreds.

As the referees escorted me off the rink, I couldn't help but see the damage I had wrought. I wanted to give up so bad, to just let my demons win. But I knew what would happen if I went back to the dark side.

While walking away, I passed the team that had been waiting to play next. They were laughing... were they laughing at me? I couldn't remember exactly what they said, but I yet again lost control of myself. I fought that whole team and found myself kicked out of the league for the rest of the season.

As much as I hated myself for what I was doing, I also felt a rush of bliss. For a brief moment, I had felt good.

Chapter Sixty-One

FALLING INTO PLACE

I stood in the elevator to my condo building one day, heading out for work. Suddenly, the door slid open and a man stepped in. He noticed that I was holding a box of chocolate chip cookies, then smiled and asked me if that was my lunch. I laughed, telling him that was how I separated myself from the rest of the salesmen at work. He introduced himself as the new manager for a major dealership out in Okotoks, a town fifteen minutes south of Calgary. I knew I had made a good impression on this new friend and I could tell he liked me.

The following Monday, I received an email from that man in the elevator. He asked if I'd be willing to have a business meeting with him. I figured I knew what he wanted to talk about, and I was comfortable in my current job. I still remembered the shame of what had happened at the gym that day long ago, and I appreciated the fact that my current employer had been understanding of my charges and believed in second chances.

But I've never been one to turn down a meeting, and I'll always hear an opportunity out.

I met with him at a coffee shop near our condo building. His offer caught me off-guard. He wanted me to launch a new position at his dealership selling subprime car loans. He wanted to mix sales with finance, allowing me to get paid for both roles. The offer would bump my annual pay from around $150,000 to $250,000. It was a no-brainer.

Before the meeting ended, I decided that I needed to disclose my past. I didn't want anything to come in between me and my dream job. I wasn't nervous telling him that I had served time for manslaughter. If God wanted this to be, it would be.

He appeared a little taken aback and then told me what I had heard before: he would speak to the powers that be and do his best to clear the way for my arrival.

I didn't know if I was going to get the job. I was certain that I would accept the proposal if it was still on the table, though. What were the odds of that?

I soon got a call back from my friend in the elevator, who informed me that the way had been paved for me to start working for them. I graciously accepted the offer, figuring that a big change in my life was exactly what I needed.

This was a massive step up for me. I just needed to stay close to my loving God, AA, Doc, my roommate, and my family. It looked as if everything was falling into place.

My new job was out of this world. I was assigned to a managerial role in finance and basically acted as my own boss. My primary role was to help individuals who had struggled with credit in the past. It was the perfect fit for me.

I was making big bucks, too, making more than $21,000 in my first month—and it just went up from there.

I worked my tail off and quickly became a force to be reckoned with. My anger and pain began to subside once again as I proved to everyone what I was capable of. I showed up at the crack of dawn and didn't leave until the sun went down. I hated when I saw the sun start to go down, because it meant the lenders would quite answering their phones.

It's hard to describe the feeling of accomplishment that washes over you after you've convinced an intelligent, educated banker to lend money to someone who's never paid a bill in their life. It made me feel invincible, like I could do anything.

As the months went on, I even started looking at houses on the lake in Okotoks. I couldn't currently afford one, but within a matter of months I got serious about my lake house.

The problem is that I had never been good at saving money, but right now I was making more than I could spend. I didn't drink, and you could only blow so much money on movies and hiking. My bank account just kept growing.

Once again, I returned to my simple routine. I couldn't wait to get out of bed, go the gym, and then head to work in the morning. Halfway through the day I would hit an AA meeting, and after work I usually stopped by Doc's treatment centre for a bite to eat and the opportunity to help a kid. I was becoming me again.

I went out to High River one day to visit Alex, but he wasn't doing well. His roommates had all moved out due to his depressive episodes and he had secluded himself in his house, refusing to see anyone. He made an exception for me. On top of not getting to see his little boy, he had recently lost his license after getting pulled over for drinking and driving. So now he had no way to go to work and was severely behind on mortgage payments. The bank was about to take his house.

As I looked over at him, sitting next to me on the sofa, I couldn't help but think of the spiritual warfare that was taking place in his mind. I could see that he was giving up. He just stared at the floor, squinting as though coming to revelations about what to do next.

Suddenly, it was like he snapped out of his daze, physically twitching from the kick back into reality. His head slowly turned toward me, his eyes filling with tears. Hopelessness shrouded his expression.

"Do you want that picture?" he asked, pointing to a photo on the wall of himself and his boy. Father and son embraced in happier times. "That's a nice picture, Cody. You should take it with you."

When I looked closely at my friend, I could see that he was destroyed—a shell of the exultant personality evidenced in the photograph on the wall.

I was at a loss for words and felt so powerless. I didn't think there was anything I could do to stop him from taking his own life. The police had made so many house calls and he'd taken so many trips to the emergency room that they didn't even take him seriously anymore.

When it was time to leave, he gave me the tightest hug he'd ever given me. I wanted to stay, but he wouldn't let me. He said that he was going to move back in with his mom until things got better. Tears ran down my face as I pleaded with him not to do anything stupid or crazy. I begged him to call me if things got too rough. He promised that he would.

As I made the hour-long drive back to Calgary that night, I prayed that God would send His angels to my best friend, for Alex needed them more than anyone I knew.

Please get him his son back, I prayed. *Please fill his heart with Your love so he has a reason to fight. Please do this for me, God.*

I ended my prayer the way I always did, by telling God that I loved Him.

The next day, Alex was on my mind. His phone had been cut off due to not paying his bill, so I had no way to check on him, but my plan was to head out there as soon as I was done work.

I loved my best friend so much and I wanted to help. I would move him in with me, if that's what the situation called for. I was willing to do anything for him at this point.

As the day came to a close, I heard my phone vibrate on my desk. From the call display, I saw that it was Alex's mom. My heart dropped as a tidal wave of emotion swept over me. I instinctively knew that this was a call I didn't want to answer.

I hesitantly picked up the phone.

"Hello," I said in a low, terrified voice.

When I heard the news, the phone dropped to my desk and my body collapsed from an immense wash of pain. I buried my face in my hands as tears gushed out of me like a faucet.

My childhood brother was in a coma, he likely wasn't going to survive, and it was my fault. I should never have left him.

Chapter Sixty-Two

I CAN'T

Alex's mom hugged me as I walked into the hospital. She didn't blame me for what had happened, but I couldn't imagine being in her shoes. The pain was unbearable enough as his best friend. She updated me on the latest news from the doctors. He had been found unresponsive on the floor of his house. They assumed he had overdosed on insulin, since he was in a hypoglycaemic coma. That was usually fatal for a diabetic such as himself.

Apparently the doctors had yet to write the book on this kind of brain injury, and no one in this hospital had seen it before. As such, we had no way of knowing whether he would wake up, or how much he would change if he did. It was a horrible feeling. Literally the only good news was that he was still breathing, but he was doing so on full life support in the intensive care unit.

His mother and I cried together, leaned on each other for support. We were both crippled with pain. As I looked around the waiting room, I got an eerie feeling from the other people sitting there. We were all there for the same reason. Someone we loved was at death's door, and all of us were waiting for God's coin toss.

When they finally let us in to see Alex, I was shocked at how much he didn't look like himself. Tubes and wires protruded out of every part of his crippled body. His mouth was wide open, his eyes closed, and his head cocked to one side. I assumed the doctors had positioned him that way so the apparatuses going into his mouth would stay clear, but it was disgusting.

He's your best friend, Cody, I thought to myself. *Why did you leave him?*

Once Alex's brother showed up, I reluctantly went home to let the family be together during this tragic time. His brother was one of the toughest guys I knew, and even he had looked lost. I had offered to sleep at the hospital that night, but they'd wanted to be alone, which was understandable. This was not the time to be selfish.

But I did go back and sleep beside Alex's hospital bed several nights. Most aspects of my life took a back seat to staying with my unconscious friend. I found myself engaging in one-way conversations with him, and it was unbearable. I would play poker on my phone, asking my comatose friend whether I should check, raise, or fold. I would study him constantly, hoping for even the slightest sign that he could hear me. Sometimes I even found that I tried to convince myself that he had heard me, jumping up and running down to the nurses only to be told once they examined him that it was likely just a reflex. They tried to convince me to start staying home, even giving his mother and me pagers they could beep in case he woke up.

But I didn't care to leave him. I had done that once already and look what had happened.

Despite what was happening with Alex, I remained the top salesman at work. I had been at the new dealership for almost ninety days and had sold well over twenty rides each month. My personal life wasn't getting in the way of my professional momentum. I was very proud of my accomplishments at work. I sensed longevity, as Okotoks was close to home and away from the stop-and-go traffic of big city life.

One day I left the hospital early in the morning and headed to work. Even though life was hard, I was grateful to still be sober and enjoying such a wonderful career. As I pulled up to the dealership, my thoughts transferred from Alex to work. I walked in, said hello to the manager, and strutted to my office. I sat at my desk and put on my tie. Relief washed over me as the computer came to life and I plunged myself into making deals.

After a few minutes, however, my manager came in and said he needed a word with me.

I followed him outside, feeling worried. A quick mental inventory told me that I hadn't done anything wrong, and something wasn't right. I was their top guy and had just succeeded in getting a whole department off the ground by myself.

The knot in my belly got tighter when I saw tears start to form in his eyes. He struggled to speak as he told me the unthinkable: upon hiring me, he had lied about talking to his superiors about my past.

At first this didn't sound like a big deal to me. Maybe I was just so numb from the pain I had been enduring over the past few months.

"Cody, I'm so sorry. They're making me let you go."

I don't think I can put into words what happened to my soul in that moment. My friend had lied to me, and I was to pay the price. There went my career. There went my future in this beautiful town. There went the last thing that was holding my head above water.

He cried, apologizing over and over again, but I wasn't mad at him. He had made a mistake and hadn't known how fragile a state I was in. That part wasn't his fault.

I left my work for the last time and drove to the hospital, the shock of the news wearing off. I broke down in the car, sobbing uncontrollably.

I can't hurt anymore, I thought. *I can't take this, God. Why? My best friend, and now my dream job. What did I do, God? I just wanted to help people!*

I pulled over to the side of the road, barely able to breathe. I had to stop this hurt somehow. I needed this pain to end.

I didn't want to feel anymore.

Chapter Sixty-Three

THE AWAKENING

I felt the beast stir within me, scared to death by the knowledge of what I was capable of. My pain was overwhelming. As I sat by Alex's hospital bed, I let the creature come up to the surface and direct all its resentment at my so-called loving God.

I placed my elbows on Alex's bed, buried my face in my hands, and traced my eyelids with my fingers. My thoughts were chaotic. What was I fighting for? To be consumed with suffering and despair? Was this the apex of my life walking with God? Everything that mattered to me had been robbed from me. My girlfriend, my job, my best friend. Was this to be my reward? Was this the light He had promised me in my journey through righteousness and redemption?

I closed my eyes even tighter, as if the act itself might make me disappear.

The leafless forest came to life within me, evil assaulting my thoughts. It became like a high, greater than anything I could get from a substance. I felt like the devil was cradling my heart, telling me it was going to okay.

"God has turned His back on you," the devil said. "He doesn't love you. Look at your friend."

The tangible evidence of his words lay before me on the hospital bed.

If God loved me, why had He hurt me so much while walking His path of light? A person didn't do this to someone they loved, right?

I paused for a moment, realizing that I wasn't fighting anymore. The winner was standing victorious.

I opened my eyes, feeling like I hadn't truly opened them in years. Darkness shrouded my gaze as I looked around the hospital room and assessed God's perverse gift to me. My cares and worries vanished as the devil comfortably took up his rightful place in my mind.

I felt almost liberated.

"Without love in your life, you can't be hurt," the devil told me, and I believed him. If I had been in a state of not caring, none of the things that had happened to me recently would have mattered, not even losing my best friend. I thought back to Devon's funeral and how I had felt stroking his cheek while he lay lifeless in his coffin. I'd felt nothing. I had needed to force myself to feel pain that day, turning on a rusty faucet that had taken me almost ten years to turn back off.

I had received a promise from the spiritual realm, one of blissful escape.

My thoughts turned to cocaine, like an eagle spreading its wings, landing in the forefront of my mind, and letting out a war cry. It led me to the path of least resistance.

The road ahead was filled with uncertainty, but I wasn't scared. I was relieved. I didn't need to any longer suffer at the hands of my loving God. I had finally been released from my prison of despair.

I stood and kissed my best friend on the forehead. I stroked his cheek, as I had done at Devon's funeral, and felt nothing. Then I turned my back on my best friend and exited the room.

As I walked by all the other rooms and took in God's peculiar lack of mercy in each bed, my anger rose. Each step I took was more firmly planted than the last. My fists balled up as I left the intensive care unit, swearing all the while. God had turned His back on every person in there. They didn't see that, but I wasn't naïve about it. I called it as I saw it, and I was calling God out. I would not stand by idle any longer.

My destiny was no longer in God's hands. I took it back, promising to destroy anyone who got in my way.

"Cody's dead," I said to God as I walked across the parking lot to my waiting vehicle. I cursed Him under my breath.

Tomorrow was going to be the start of my climb back up the underworld. As I drove away, I turned up my music and let my hate bubble to the surface. I was done with my happy destiny. Instead I chose tyranny.

Chapter Sixty-Four

MEDICATE

At the crack of dawn, I lay in bed with my eyelids shut and assessed how I was feeling. My emotions were very dark, and it was unusually comforting.

I had already laid out in my mind where I wanted the day to go. By the end of it, I wanted to be as high as could be on my long lost love: cocaine, the one thing that had the power to make the hurt disappear.

But before that was to come to pass, I needed to take steps to establish a new empire. Did I want to sell cocaine again? I decided against it. I had learned ten years ago that when I started doing it, I couldn't stop.

I called an old friend of mine, a large-scale marijuana dealer, and asked if I could meet up with him to talk business. I knew he would be interested when I told him that I was getting back into hustling.

I figured it would be best to find another job while I was getting my new trafficking operation off the ground. It seemed intelligent to me to have one foot in the legitimate world and another in the underworld—to throw off police detection. That way, if I ever got charged with trafficking, I would be able to prove to a jury that I had a legal income. Nothing looked worse to a judge than an unemployed individual on the stand wearing a $5,000 suit.

The manager who had tearfully let me go felt badly about what he had done, so he called a friend of his at another dealership in Calgary and spoke with him about possibly giving me a job. This second dealership didn't care that I had a criminal record; all they cared about was that I was a top salesman. They hired me on the spot.

The rest of the day consisted of getting a burner phone under a fake name for my customers to call. Then I headed off to see my friend to negotiate a fair price for a few pounds of weed.

My next stop was a weed shop. I bought one-kilo smell-proof bags. Canadian marijuana is some of the most potent in the world, and if I got pulled over I didn't want the cops to smell the product and give them probable cause to search my vehicle.

I pulled into my friend's house on an acreage outside of town. After some cordial small talk, we got down to the purpose behind my visit. He asked someone on hand to grab something for me from the back room while we talked. When his buddy returned, he was carrying a three-foot smell-proof sleeve of marijuana.

"Think you could work with that?" my friend asked me as he tossed it over.

I examined the massive bag and smiled. "I can handle this."

He looked satisfied and gave me a nod. I left his house that day with my duffle bag full of weed and returned to my place to start networking.

On my home computer, I started reaching out to people on my friends list on social media. I had more than two thousand contacts from several different social circles. I messaged everyone who I knew smoked weed and asked for their phone numbers, saying that I had an important issue to discuss with them. When they sent me their numbers, I called back on my burner phone and hyped the product. It was just like selling a car.

I shied away from saying I would sell small amounts, as that seemed like a waste of time. I wanted to move to large-scale sales as soon as I could.

After my networking session, I got ready to go out for the night. I was still sober in the sense that I hadn't used yet, but I was certainly relapsed in my mind. I had already made my decision. Now I just need to go through with it.

I went to the house of a friend who was having a party, picking up a case of beer on the way there. While I was paying for it, I wondered if this cashier had any idea he was selling beer to someone who'd been sober for four years and hadn't had a beer in almost ten years. Obviously he couldn't have known, but I felt as if everyone in the liquor store could tell I wasn't supposed to be there. Uncomfortably, I purchased my booze and vacated.

I wasn't uncomfortable, however, by the time I got to my friend's house. Everyone was surprised when I informed them that I was going to be partaking that night. They seemed sceptical, but I consoled them by revealing that I was no longer on parole and didn't have any conditions anymore. I made it sound like there'd been some countdown to this day.

When I took my first sip of alcohol, nothing really happened inside me. Alcohol had never been my vice, but as soon as the liquor touched my lips I immediately wanted cocaine. I had known this domino effect would occur. Fortunately, my friends had a cocaine dealer on the way.

When the dealer walked in, I recognized him as one of my old friends. We gave each other a big hug and spent a few minutes catching up before we got down to business. When I said I hadn't done blow in ten years and that I had just gotten off parole, he insisted on doing a big celebratory line of cocaine with me.

As he pulled the bag from a secret pocket in his crotch, a wash of memories swept over me. I missed being that guy—the guy that whole parties were waiting on. I couldn't help but envy my old friend as he poured a pile of cocaine onto the table and began to grind it up.

I felt heart palpitations as he formed two of the biggest lines I had ever seen. He did the whole rail in one breath. There was no turning back now. I took the rolled-up hundred-dollar bill from my friend and breathed deeply, emptying out my lungs. In one gracious swoop, I snorted the entire thing to the back of my head.

My heart slowed down as the initial excitement passed. But as I opened my eyes and plugged the uncontaminated nostril with my hand, I inhaled and the loose cocaine smacked my brain hard, almost physically knocking me back. My whole body exploded with ecstasy. I heaved from the sensational rush.

A huge smile creased my face as my pain, hurts, and worries vanished.

"So that's what cocaine tastes like," I mused, laughing.

Chapter Sixty-Five

BEING PETTY

My marijuana business grew by the number of pounds I was moving, but my stack of cash didn't grow. My new job was taking a hit from the lack of sleep. Cocaine immediately became my go-to solution to everything that was wrong in my life. I hated myself every day at work, and half the time I was in a state of psychosis. I didn't hide the fact that I had relapsed, but I distanced myself from the people who truly cared about me. On the outside it looked to people as if I was fine, but on the inside I was desperate.

I hardly ate anymore, a problem I solved by taking steroids. I bought a couple of cycles for myself and worked out while high. It didn't elude me that this was very unhealthy, but it mattered not to a man who didn't love himself. I polluted my body with anything that made me feel better.

My roommate was knowledgeable of steroids and told me that the cycle I was doing was going to kill me. That didn't faze me. I remember standing in the shower one morning twitching from the steroids, feeling as if I could run through every wall in the house. I had overdone them, as I did with everything I tried.

As I juggled drug-dealing and work, I found myself regularly at the bars making new friends. I introduced myself to everyone I came across, a result of needing constant validation. People were drawn to me and wanted to get to know me. Because I looked so intimidating, though, they were shocked at how friendly I turned out to be. Everyone was fascinated by my story and my love for the fast life. I made doing cocaine look like the most freeing thing in the world. My sales techniques were a perfect fit with my resurgent criminal lifestyle.

I discovered over a short period of time that the type of individuals who were drawn to me were drug users. Selling marijuana was fine, but I was missing out on untapped revenue. Everyone wanted cocaine. The more I socialized at the bar and added people to my clientele, the more irresistible the cocaine business became.

One day I was driving down Calgary's main drag looking for a bite to eat. The day before, I had been pulled over on my way to work and informed that I wasn't supposed to be behind the wheel, since my license was under a thirty-day suspension. I hadn't even been aware of that. The officer was kind about it but gave me a mandated court date for driving while suspended. This meant an automatic loss of my driver's license for a whole year. He was fully in his right to tow my vehicle right then and there and impound it for thirty days, but he believed me when I said that I didn't know about the suspension. So instead he just told me to drive straight home and leave the car parked until my suspension ended in three days' time.

I didn't listen.

The very next day, I pulled an illegal U-turn and invariably found my rear-view mirror filled with the unmistakable red and blue lights of a police cruiser. I swore out loud as yet another officer approached my window. I was already guaranteed to lose my license for a year. Getting caught this second time would mean that I would lose it for two.

I remained calm as I watched the officer shine his flashlight in my side mirror and approach the window. Maybe he would have sympathy for me.

"Mr. Bates, didn't know you were out of prison," he said to me first thing.

It seemed I wasn't going to get off so lucky this time around. I kept my demeanour jovial as I passed him my driver's license along with copies of my registration and insurance. He was polite to me, but I got a bad vibe as he was walking back to his cruiser.

For several minutes I sat waiting for my new officer friend to come and tell me whether he was going to tow away my car. In the meantime, two more police cruisers pulled in with their lights on, undoubtedly because of my violent criminal record. I remained calm. There was no reason to get upset at this point. Losing my temper would only hinder my ability to manoeuvre the situation to a favourable outcome.

The officer once again approached the window and asked me to remove the keys from the ignition. He wasn't going to give me a break, nor did I deserve one. Just the day before, I had gotten a ticket with a warning to leave my vehicle parked until my suspension was over. This was my own doing.

I got out of the car and walked alongside the officer back to the cruiser, where he passed me a seizure form indicating that the vehicle would be impounded for thirty days. Then he flipped over ticket after ticket after ticket, literally fining me for everything he could think of.

My eye twitched as he finished with the pink ticket, yet another summons for a mandatory court appearance for driving while suspended. The second one in two days. This ticket was the worst of the bunch since I would surely lose my driver's license for a couple of years.

Then he caught me off-guard by flipping over a pink form I'd never seen before. Across the top, it read "Notice to seek greater punishment by the Crown." He smiled and asked me to sign it.

This police officer was trying to ruin my life. I kept my face neutral, but inside my emotions were exploding.

"What's this?" I asked without breaking eye contact.

"That's up to the officer's discretion," he replied. His condescending tone struck a dust-covered chord deep inside me, a chord that hadn't sung since my wars with the guards at Calgary Remand. Nothing bothered me more than the abuse of power. "I need you to sign it please."

I made my smile as big and bold as I could. "I'm not signing it."

We stared at each other, neither daring to break the connection and both of us wearing diabolical smiles.

"You're going to sign it," he said.

I laughed, and somehow my smile got even bigger. "I'm not signing it."

More assertively this time: "You're going to sign it."

When I finally broke down and agreed to sign it, he handed me a pen. I bent over the hood of his car to sign the paper while he held it still. After I finished, he picked it up and looked at the signature line.

In place of my John Hancock, I'd written *F*CK YOU.*

"You're hilarious," he said.

"Here's your pen."

When he reached for it, I let the pen slip from my fingertips and clatter to the ground. My brows dropped and my smile turned sinister.

"You dropped your pen," I declared, my scarred lip curling up to expose my teeth.

Just like that, the officer's cocky expression dissolved into anger. "Pick it up!" I shook my head. "Pick up my f*cking pen or I'll charge you with littering."

My smile returned as I realized I had him right where I wanted him. "Because you dropped your pen?"

Even his cop buddies were laughing at him from their positions nearby. Then he yelled at me to get out of there before he decided to arrest me. I didn't know what he could possibly handcuff me for. Perhaps for smiling so much?

A friend of mine showed up to give me a ride, but I refused to get in his car until the tow truck left with my BMW. I wasn't even mad at this point; I was having fun. The cop was walking back and forth between his cruiser, my BMW, and the tow truck. Every time he looked at me, I would smile and call him a b*tch. I could tell it was getting on his nerves so I repeated it over and over again until he turned red with anger.

After being called that about fifty times, and putting up with the laughter of his cop friends, he turned on me and screamed at the top of his lungs. "Is that all you got?"

"No," I retorted. I paused for a moment, letting the suspense build. "You're a fat b*tch."

I howled in laughter. After all, he couldn't arrest me for being a prick. But honestly, I was only matching his own arrogance. If he hadn't played all his cards on the first hand, he might have had a chance of winning this game of wits.

Despite feeling liberated from this tantalizing run-in with the law, I was completely screwed. My car would be in impound for thirty days, and I had court dates with the unavoidable outcome of losing my driver's license for two years. Imagine that, a car salesman and drug-dealer who couldn't drive.

As I lay in bed that night, my phone began to ring. It was a blocked number, and I generally didn't answer those sorts of calls. But shortly after my cell stopped ringing, I heard the unmistakable chime of a voicemail alert.

When I put the phone on speaker, a familiar voice filled my room. It was the police officer from earlier in the evening.

"This is the constable who was dealing with you earlier," he said. "Due to our conversation this evening, I have decided not to seize your vehicle for thirty days. I'm seizing it for sixty now. Have a good night."

His arrogance was boundless. I just laughed.

My life may have already been ruined by his actions, but he couldn't bear the thought of me standing up to him in any way. He had decided to get petty about this.

A police officer needs to uphold the law, despite criminals being morons. My hat goes off to officers who deal with this type of behaviour every day. You're stronger-willed than I would be in that situation. I would have kicked the crap out of myself with a phone book.

But what I wouldn't have done is leave a trail of evidence proving my abuse of power.

When I walked into the courtroom on the assigned date, I played the phone message left by the disgruntled constable. The judge could only shake her head at the clear disregard of my rights. Not only did I have every single fine dropped, and the seizure of my vehicle lifted, but I also got off on driving while suspended.

As I was leaving the courtroom, I noticed the constable sitting nearby. I thrust my hands in my pocket and gave him the biggest smile I could muster.

"Try to keep it a little more professional next time," I said.

The judge lost her mind, banging her gavel and threatening to hold me in contempt. I didn't care. After all, I was aware of my rights.

I looked back over my shoulder and asked the judge, "For telling him to be more professional?"

"Get out of my courtroom," she shrieked.

I strutted out the doors feeling like the man. I hadn't needed to give the officer that last dig, but he would have done the same given the chance.

Chapter Sixty-Six

NO MORE TEARS

I wanted to die, and I think all the steroids I had been doing were affecting my emotions. The only solace I seemed to be able to find was in a bag of cocaine. It was the only thing that made me feel better.

On Super Bowl Sunday, I went to a friend's house to watch the game. Tons of people surrounded me, but I felt like the loneliest guy in the world. My heart was breaking and no amount of drugs or alcohol would make it better.

That day, I got a text from an old friend who invited me to stay with her for a week at her house so she could take care of me. It was out of the province, and I agreed. Perhaps a vacation would fix me. I wanted desperately to be away from here.

My friends told me not to leave, though, since I was clearly wrecked and hadn't slept in many days. I wasn't having it. I needed to feel better. So I said goodbye to my friends and went home to grab some bags. I saddled up quick, got behind the wheel of my BMW, and headed east.

I slammed beer after beer while I drove, also dumping piles of cocaine on my hand to counterbalance the liquor.

As I was driving past Drumheller, the air around me lit up with the unmistakable strobe of police lights. I was being pulled over, likely for speeding.

I don't know what happened to my judgment, but as the cop approached the door I didn't even bother to hide all the booze. He immediately asked me to step out of the vehicle. When I opened my door, he noticed the vial full of cocaine in the door handle. I promptly found myself in handcuffs in the back of his cruiser.

After more units showed up, they searched my vehicle. My heart sank as I considered everything that was in there. Money, drugs, scales, debt lists, brass knuckles, and weed bags. I was done.

When the cop came to the cruiser, he added salt to the wound by saying that he had answered one of my phones and the person on the other end had asked for a half-ounce.

Before long I was detoxing in a holding cell. I hadn't been in one in years, and it looked as though I may as well get used to it. The evidence against me was so incredibly damning. I had done time for a homicide as part of a turf war, and now I was clearly back at it. I was looking at another eight years. Best case scenario, maybe five years.

It was the worst thing that could have happened to me. It only added to the torment I was pushing through.

When the door of the cell clicked open, an officer escorted me to my bail call where I met with a justice of the peace. I was facing a ton of charges and bail was unlikely.

To my surprise, the justice of the peace was in a good mood and set my bail at $500.

Every day I woke up hating that I was still alive. I pushed myself toward suicide day after day, falling short every time. My actions were those of a man with no feelings, but the truth is that my emotions ran very deep. I wanted to shut those emotions off somehow and kept coming up short.

I knew I was going to jail on my new charges. Everything had been done by the book on the police's side of things, so there would be no technicalities to save me this time. I was looking at five to seven years. All of a sudden losing my license for two years didn't seem so daunting.

I had just been released from the Max two and a half years ago. It was too soon to go back. And the worst part about the whole thing was that even though I was facing medium-security charges, I would still go back to Edmonton Max because that's where I had been released from. My security classification wouldn't have changed. I was going back to twenty-three-hour lockdown with no chance in hell of diverting it.

One morning in the middle of the week, I called in to work sick and took the day off. I told them I had the flu, but the truth is that I hadn't slept in a couple of days and was coming down hard off a lot of cocaine. My personal stash had run out and my supplier wasn't answering my calls anymore. I hated myself so much that I could have snapped my own neck.

I pushed myself to get out of bed. The thought of enduring the torturous journey down the stairs was almost enough to cripple me. But this journey had a lot more purpose and meaning than just any old trip to the kitchen.

In my mind, it would be the last trip I took anywhere, ever.

I opened the utensil drawer, reflecting on the peace contained in the collection of knives. I didn't like the idea of slashing my wrists, but this wasn't just a cry for help. This was the real deal.

Next, I examined the poisonous cleaning products under the kitchen sink. I stared at the labels containing the exploding skull and wondered why they used that particular icon to hammer their point home. I had to admit, it suppressed my urge to drink it. If I didn't die, what damage would be left in my suicidal wake? Would I be eating through a tube for the rest of my life? That didn't sit well with me.

What if I used a syringe from my steroid injections and shot bleach into my veins so that it went directly to my heart? That would kill me almost instantly, wouldn't it? Yes, I thought it would.

I grabbed a syringe from my steroid drawer, my heart racing as I ripped apart a cigarette filter to suction the poison into the needle. I filled the needle to the brim and then held it up to my face, tapping it lightly with my finger. I couldn't help laughing to myself. Those taps were to get all the air bubbles out. If I was going to kill myself, wouldn't that be a moot point?

The tattoos on my arm caught my attention. I had gotten them while I was a gang member. What I was about to do wasn't gangster; I felt like a coward. But that didn't dissuade me. In fact, it had the opposite effect, making me want to die even more. I suddenly felt like I didn't deserve my tattoos.

Something dawned on me as I flagged my vein. What if this didn't work? What if this only painfully collapsed all the veins in my arm and I subsequently had to get it amputated? I'd be horribly disfigured for the rest of my life, a living, breathing example of what happens when suicide goes wrong.

I put the needle down on the counter. Back to the drawing board.

Then it hit me like a brick to the face. Exhaust from my truck! All I needed to do was run a hose from my exhaust pipe into the closed window of my truck. I'd die within minutes. I would do it in my parking stall in the back alley where no one would see until it was too late. Worst case scenario, I'd spend the rest of my life on a ventilator. For some reason, that sounded better than losing an arm.

I got in my truck and headed to the hardware store. As I walked down the aisle looking for a short hose, I felt almost at peace. I'd almost accepted that this would be my last day on this earth. It was an eerie feeling.

As I paid for the hose, I couldn't help but reminisce back to the fateful day I had bought liquor for the first time after being four years sober. I remembered looking at the clerk and wondering if they could tell that something was horribly wrong with the situation. I wished they had seen through it, that they had stopped me somehow. Maybe then I wouldn't have been standing here paying for the garden tube I was going to use to extinguish my own life.

I could only imagine how this clerk would feel if he knew that he was going to be the last person I ever saw, that he was giving me the instrument I would use to kill myself. It was difficult for me to experience that type of empathy. If the roles were reversed, would I stop someone who wanted to die? I thought I would, as long as it didn't interfere with me getting high. But it was hard to picture myself caring about someone else that much. I just wanted to get home and get this done. Every minute I spent alive was one of regret.

When I pulled up to my house, I didn't even shut off my truck. I merely got out, unrolled the tube, plugged one end into the exhaust port and the other into the window. Then I closed the door of the truck, shut my eyes, and reclined the seat. The truck filled with smoke almost instantly as I revved the engine.

Google had told me that I should die within twenty minutes. The smoke didn't burn my eyes as I watched the clock on my phone. Fifteen more minutes.

As much as I tried to prevent it, my dad came to mind. His joyful smile, his deep eyes full of life. He was way better off without me around to hurt him. I wasn't capable of loving him. I couldn't see beauty past cocaine. In fact, I needed to do this for him so he could have a normal life.

That thought set me straight—not straight in that I was going to stop, but straight in that I knew I was making the right decision.

Twenty minutes came and went. There were no more tears, only purpose. I accepted that the world would be better off without me in it. The only way I could live was by heavily medicating myself with cocaine. I couldn't go back to Doc or AA, not again. It seemed as though there was only a single path, and I was sorrowfully upon it.

As a whole hour came around with me sitting there, my foot heavy on the gas pedal, I had to wonder: what was taking so long?

A loud noise caught me off-guard. It was the unmistakable sound of the tube being pulled out of the exhaust pipe. Or had it fallen out by itself? I sat for a minute, debating smashing my own face through the driver's window out of frustration, but common sense took hold for once.

I jumped out of the vehicle and saw the hose lying on the ground. I was pissed off because now I would have to start over. I shoved it back in and jumped into the truck—for the last time, with any luck.

As I closed my eyes and put my head back, I once again heard the sound of the hose popping out. I glanced in the rear-view mirror and saw someone darting around the corner of the garage. Someone was trying to stop me.

Frustration exploded out of me as I started kicking the inside of my truck. Why couldn't people just let me die? If only they knew who was in this truck!

But I suspected that the cops were already on their way, and my suicide plan had been completely thwarted.

As expected, the police soon showed up and detained me. They loaded me into an ambulance and sent me to the hospital for an evaluation. To my surprise, everyone there was super kind to me. I didn't feel like I deserved it.

Chapter Sixty-Seven

THE BAD GUY

I hadn't seen David Chow since my manslaughter conviction in 2009, and he was disappointed that I had gotten myself into trouble again. But he was happy to help with my case. He sounded optimistic, but I just credited that to lawyers needing to look on the bright side in order to give themselves a chance. I didn't think I had a hope in hell. The only thing the Crown didn't have was a video of me actually selling drugs. They had cocaine, a debt list, scales, transport bags with residue, and even a phone call from a customer asking for a half-ounce. In the Crown's office, they call that a slam dunk.

I asked David to put off my trial as long as possible, two years if he could. I just wanted to enjoy my time out of prison while it lasted. I gave him a retainer with the promise of more money to come. Then we parted ways.

A week or two later, I received a message from David's assistant. It was an email notifying me that my trial had been set for one month's time. To say I was mad would be a lie. No, I was pissed. I sent an angry email back stating that I wasn't ready to go back to prison yet, as I had yet to wrap up my affairs on the street. I needed the court date put off much longer.

I then notified my lawyer that I would be seeking new council. I felt like it was the only option I had. If I walked into court on the day of the trial without a lawyer, they wouldn't be able to proceed. Then I'd put off finding a new lawyer for three months and hopefully end up with someone who listened to me. Worst case scenario, I would fire that lawyer right before the trial as well. Maybe I could drag this thing on for a few years.

I walked into court that day as arrogant and cocky as ever. I wore baggy shorts and a hoodie with all my jewellery and tattoos on display to make sure everyone knew I wasn't there to proceed with the trial.

While I waited to enter the courtroom, I saw a familiar face headed my way. It was David Chow, and he didn't look very impressed. In fact, he was angry. This kind of confused me, since I thought I had made his job easier by letting him go.

"What are you doing here?" I asked as he closed in. "Didn't I let you go?"

"Don't you read your email?" he snapped. I shook my head. "I got you off all your charges, you idiot. Now come in with me. Sit down, shut up, and only speak if I ask you to!"

I was dumbfounded. I had no idea what was happening.

"How did you do it?" I asked.

"Because I'm good at what I do!" If looks could kill, he would have decimated me.

He wasn't toying around. I hadn't even paid him, and for some reason he was following through. If I were him, I would have let me go to jail for being a tool. It made no sense to me.

But it would have if I had learned how to read emails properly. That letter from David's assistant a month ago had contained an attachment that I'd neglected to look at. It was a drawn-out plea agreement between myself and the Crown prosecutor. It stated that if I agreed to simple possession and fines, I would walk away with no jail time or probation of any kind.

And here I'd thought I had been condemned to another six years.

Before we walked into the courtroom, David looked at me with what could only be described as disgust.

"After this over, never call me again," he said.

David walked to the front and introduced me to the judge. The judge tipped his glasses and looked at me. These guys were about to give me the break of a lifetime and I couldn't even dress for the occasion. I could only awkwardly smile at him from my seat.

The Crown started by notifying the judge that they had reached a joint submission in my case and were dropping the charges to fines for simple possession and possession of a weapon. He then started reading out the agreed statement of facts.

"On February 14, 2015, Mr. Bates was pulled over in his BMW for speeding. Upon the officer approaching the vehicle, it was noticed that Mr. Bates had a twenty-four-case of beer within arm's length with several missing. The officer then asked Bates to step out of his vehicle so he could administer a field sobriety test. When Mr. Bates opened the door to his vehicle, the officer then noticed a vial containing a white powdered substance in the door handle which was assumed to be drugs. Mr. Bates was then detained and placed in the police cruiser. Upon an investigational search of the vehicle, the officer opened the centre console. The contents of that were $4,000 cash, a sunglass case containing ten individual baggies of cocaine, a list containing what appeared to be debts owed, a scale with narcotic residue, and finally a set of brass knuckles. In the cupholders were two phones that were both steadily ringing. When the officer answered one of the calls, the individual on the other end of the line asked for a 'half-ounce.' Bates was then read his rights and subsequently charged. He has an extensive criminal history which includes a homicide from 2006 where a man was killed while Mr. Bates was allegedly protecting his drug turf. Those are the agreed statement of facts, Your Honour."

Everyone in the courtroom had their mouths open in bewilderment. All I could do was twiddle my thumbs and look around at the wall so I didn't have to meet the judge's harsh gaze.

"Mr. Bates, could you stand up please?"

Oh boy. The judge didn't look very pleased. I did as commanded, trying not to make my smile look nervous as I beamed my pearly whites in the judge's direction.

"Let's just say tonight I'm out mowing my lawn, and my neighbour just happened to be mowing his at the same time," the judge said. "Let's just say he asked me how my day was. Not that this would actually happen, but let's say I told him about you and what took place today. He would in return ask me why I have my job. You are a drug trafficker. They should've thrown the key away on you a long time ago. Clearly you think the system is a joke. Now, I have never come in between a Crown and defence joint submission before, and I'm not going to start today, but you better figure out what you want in your life, sir. You're dismissed!"

I couldn't believe what had just happened. David wouldn't even look at me as we left. I remember thinking that it was a shame I had just screwed over the best lawyer in Calgary. All I could do was try to make it back up to him somehow down the road.

I never found out how the hell that came about. David and I didn't speak after that. I always wondered if some sort of divine intervention took place. Or was it just the savvy skills of an incredible lawyer? Maybe because I was starting to move a fair amount of drugs, the cops weren't ready yet to convict me. Maybe they were building a conspiracy case against me so they could put me away for good. To this day, I don't have the answers. I can only speculate.

Getting off scot-free that day paved the way for me to quit working. After all, I had only stayed employed to prove my income to the courts. Now it was time to take my rightful place as a full-time bad guy!

CODY STARTS UP DRUG-DEALING AGAIN.

PART
V

Chapter Sixty-Eight

KING OF THE SOUTH

I was a drug-moving machine. Every night I went out to bars and parties, giving out free blow in exchange for people's numbers. I quickly realized it was useless to give your number out because half the time people would forget they had seen you the previous night. By adding people to the burner phone, though, I had their contact information and could do weekly shoutouts with weekend specials and information on the grade of blow. I also got in the habit of switching phone numbers on a regular basis to throw off police detection, usually about once a month.

My customers loved me even though most didn't know my real name. The handle I gave people was Reckless Rick, a name which grew notoriety in south Calgary rather quickly. When the business hit 120 customers, I hired a couple of shift workers and started a second phone from scratch. This grew the business steadily, and since I rarely slept I was almost always building it, adding several clients per night.

I hit a snag one day when I went to pick up a fresh supply from a guy I had only used a couple of times. After sitting in his house for about an hour, waiting for him to come back from meeting his own supplier outside, I realized he wasn't coming back. This guy had ripped me off.

At first I was going to burn his house down and call it a day. But I remembered a story from prison where a guy had burnt down a house to get even over an unpaid debt and accidentally killed two little kids. Fire wasn't my style, and neither was putting innocents at risk.

After a couple hours of mulling it over, I decided to just leave it be—for the moment. Although I appeared calm and collected on the outside, on the inside I wanted this man's blood. It was the first time someone had messed with my operation. I needed to somehow make sure it was the last. But I couldn't risk going to jail for getting my revenge.

I'd heard a thousand stories like this from my time on the inside, and I knew how to get away with murder. It would just take a lot of patience. If the cops found his dead body the day after he'd ripped me off, it would be obvious. I needed to cast aside my anger and let some time pass. If I detached completely for a few months, I wouldn't be a suspect later on; I needed to appear as though I had cut my losses.

The thought of killing someone didn't bother me. It came with the territory of running a drug empire, something that would eventually happen one way or the other.

One day, I did a drop at a brothel that housed some massage girls. As I stood at the kitchen counter, breaking up lines for myself and the girls, we heard a knock at the door. Two men walked in and immediately looked apprehensive at the sight of me standing there in the kitchen. They must not have been expecting me.

The first guy, heavyset and tattooed, whispered something to the second guy. The smaller one then walked toward me while his friend stayed by the door.

Suddenly, the doorbell rang again and a third man entered. His thousand-yard stare told me this was not a guy I wanted to mess with. Although I didn't know him, I could tell he was a boss the likes of which I hadn't met before.

I ended up walking outside with the smaller guy for a cigarette. His name was Tommy, or at least that was his handle.

"People call me Rick," I said, shaking his hand.

He proceeded to question me, each question seeming to set up another. Without a doubt, an unsatisfactory answer would end the conversation cold.

Tommy was a cool guy, but also on guard. I told him a bit about my background, and in return he opened up to me a little bit. He was a drug-dealer, and not a low-level dealer like me. They had been full-time bad guys a lot longer than I had.

The bigger guy joined us outside at this point and stuck out his hand to introduce himself. Apparently the man with the thousand-yard stare had left as quick as he'd come. Made me wonder.

"Whaz up, bro? I'm Donnie."

That night, we all partied together into the early hours. Donnie and Tommy told me everything they had learned from the dope game. I tried their product and realized I had never done anything that pure before. It was like sniffing a cloud. I had assumed I was well-versed in selling drugs, but these guys made me feel like I knew nothing.

Donnie and I immediately became best friends. He was good-looking, charismatic, asserting, charming, and he had an innate way of drawing me in. I couldn't help but hang onto every word he spoke. It turned out that he was the boss of all bosses, having built a kilo-level operation on his interpersonal skills. He was fascinated by my story and treated me as his equal. He didn't talk down to me, despite knowing so much more than I did.

By the next day, we had made plans to meet and complete some business transactions. I finally had a steady supplier at an unbeatable price, with several different grades to choose from as well as a multitude of almost every drug under the sun.

He was so private that no one knew where he lived, yet he brought me to his house that first night due to our instant connection. I just chalked it up to another case of real recognizing real.

Donnie enabled me to grow my business larger than I could have imagined. One of the things I learned from him was to treat others as equals, something I started to do with every customer on my phones. This had an immediate effect. Soon my customers didn't want to get cocaine from anyone else but me.

I quickly went from a couple of runners to dozens. I assigned different duties to each and they were all paid well. Some did shift work on the phones, taking calls from needy customers. We met regularly at different sushi restaurants around two o'clock every afternoon. For some reason, I liked for my guys to eat sushi. In fact, most high-level gangsters did. Why? Because it meant sharing plates with your brothers.

Over lunch, we would discuss any new clients who had entered the picture and figure out if there was a reason to be concerned about any of them. After a lengthy discussion, I would collect all the money from the past twenty-four hours and reload their supply—thirty bags of cocaine each. If one of the phones was starting to slow down in terms of revenue, we would brainstorm a clever way to boost it back up, such as offering a half-price sale to customers who were willing to refer a friend.

Everything was organized and designed to grow fast. We had Turn-It-Up Tuesdays (one-gram bags of cocaine discounted from $60 to $40 until midnight), Refer-a-Friend Fridays (for every person you referred, you got a free gram of cocaine), and weekend eight-ball specials. We also came up with ways to boost traffic on holidays. We had an option, too, for people to purchase high-heat cocaine, a product of greater purity, for a higher price. We even added vacation giveaways such as flight and hotel packages to Vegas; customers who purchased two or more bags at a time would get their names entered in a draw to win the big prize. Each phone would give away one trip.

We had to be careful about picking up referrals, so I made sure all of my guys asked three follow-up questions about new customers. How long have you known them? Do you know where they live? Do you vouch for them? That last question was the most important of the bunch. We kept track of who referred who, so that if something went wrong we would know who to talk to about it.

Every night I passionately sermonized the drug at bars and parties. I was always the star, blowing thousands and giving out free product. I became so respected that most bars turned a blind eye to my criminal activities, even tipping me off if police were present or asking questions.

On Wednesdays, I would give some of my runners the night off and take shifts myself. I loved getting on the phones and texting customers to let them know the boss was running the phone that night and that I wanted to meet them to give them free blow. My ulterior motive was to create a hierarchy in their heads. When I shook their hand in person, I'd tap it to the bulletproof vest I was wearing, not saying anything. I wanted them to know I was not a man to be toyed with. Then I'd break bread with them and let them see that I was the nicest gangster they'd ever met.

I also created programs to keep wait times to a minimum. I separated the client lists geographically by quadrants and let customers know that if they called and no one picked up the phone, they would get a free bag out of the runner's own pocket. This kept my employees accountable for not allowing business to fall through the cracks. This made sure that my customers didn't go anywhere else but me.

Another idea of mine was to offer liquor after midnight, thus discouraging people from drinking and driving. I wanted everyone to party safe, but it also gave my phones yet another advantage over the competition.

All the while, Donnie's supply kept up with my growing enterprise.

I was making a lot of money and focusing my time on sales with the highest profit margin. This meant I didn't do very much wholesale. If properly dispersed, small sales could net triple the principal investment. With wholesale, the profit margin was a lot smaller, but at least you could unload a lot of product in a single stop.

I moved my employees around a lot, working different phones, running the VIP lines, running the wholesale phone, and networking and building up our clientele. Importantly, I always picked someone different to tag along with me. Everyone would get jealous, because the person who worked with me for the night would get lit up like a Christmas tree.

Within a couple of months, Reckless Rick was the King of the South, with a money train that couldn't be stopped.

As for my own cocaine habit, it increased to about $1,500 a day. I hardly ever slept anymore. I always carried at least a quarter-pound of cocaine on me, and on the weekends it was a lot more. Donnie bought me special underwear that had a secret pocket stitched into the crotch to conceal the narcotics. That way, no one was ever the wiser. Before long, I also made all my runners wear them so there was no chance of them getting caught.

All of my procedures were in place to protect what I had built. For example, my runners were under strict orders to always have an order ready before meeting with a client. That way, they didn't have to pull out big bags of product in front of customers. Also, runners weren't allowed to drink on shift, since checkstops were a common thing in Calgary. I didn't care if they did coke, though.

Everyone got a fake name, chosen by myself. If I heard an employee of mine use their real name, I would tax it off their pay. Even the shift phones had codenames, named after characters from the Ninja Turtles. That way, we could talk about the phones as if they were people: "So how did Leonardo do last night?" This prevented wiretaps from picking up anything damning.

The most gruelling part of the operation was switching phone numbers, a necessary evil to avoid police detection. I would go out and purchase around fifteen phones, then set them all up under fake accounts. We'd send shoutouts to all our clients, which were in the thousands, with instructions to save the new numbers and delete the old ones. Then we'd keep carrying the old phones for a one-week grace period to catch any stragglers who had missed the initial text.

My runners also had a special phone intended only for conversations with me. Because of this, the runners usually had three phones on them at a time—the current phone, the old phone, and my phone. And it meant that I had to carry about five or six at a time. I even had a special phone with encrypted messaging which I'd use to contact Donnie. This phone automatically burned every message two hours after it was sent, whether or not I had gotten around to reading it. Every big gangster had a phone like this—a black phone.

Another rule was that the runners were never allowed to use a shift phone to call another shift phone. That way, the cops couldn't link the numbers and use that information to build a conspiracy case.

I had moved in with a childhood friend who had a cocaine habit himself. He started getting really paranoid after a while, with all my coming and going and pulling in boxes of cash on the weekends.

One particular weekend, he and his girlfriend and a couple of others sat in a room bagging cocaine in an assembly line. Despite working all night long, they still couldn't keep up with the orders. I had been letting them do as much cocaine as they could handle, and maybe that was a mistake on my part.

This childhood friend of mine was a father, but fortunately his kid didn't live there. Regardless, he knew he was in over his head with me. I could only imagine how he would've felt if he'd known about the loaded pistol in my dresser and the AK-47 I had under the deck!

MOST EVENINGS CODY WAS NETWORKING HIS COCAINE BUSINESS AT BARS AND PARTIES.

Chapter Sixty-Nine

EMOTIONAL THINKING

It wasn't out of the ordinary for me to leave town for a few days at a time for a small vacation. I felt that going away was necessary to clear my head. The truth, though, was that I was always super messed-up when I went away, dropping way more money than I would have if I'd stayed in town.

My favourite getaway was to Banff. I liked going there because of the crazy nightlife and also because it was close enough to Calgary that I could get my runners to bring me a steady supply of cocaine and money. It helped that my second-in-command was very capable of running the operation for a couple of days at a time. Truth be told, though, even when I was on vacation I spent most of the time on the phone micromanaging my workers.

The main way in which I kept the police off my radar was by adopting a strict no-violence policy amongst everyone who worked for me. These people hadn't been hired to be gangsters; they'd been hired to be social butterflies. I wanted them to be approachable and easy to talk to. Whenever they didn't have another sale lined up, they were told to go into a bar and buy a customer a beer on my dollar, taking the time to get to know them. I wanted everyone on my lines to feel like they were dealing with good friends, not heartless lunatics.

If a situation ever came up that called for violence, my second-in-command and I would deal with it in the shadows. He and I had both done time for homicide, so we made a frightening team. He was a man who thought with his gun, so I had to be the voice of reason in our talks, and at the end of the day the decisions always landed on my shoulders.

I almost jeopardized everything one weekend when I came home from Banff after blowing $7,000 in four days. I had been vacationing there with an ex who I was still very much in love with despite knowing things would never go back to the way they'd been. My rage and depression had been dormant for a time at this point, and so had my love life. But in my imagination I had thought we would have a romantic weekend in Banff, sleeping together each night. Instead we'd just got wrecked the whole time. She was being considerate of my feelings and didn't want to hook up with me because she knew I still had feelings for her. She treasured our friendship.

So when we finally got home, she went to go catch up on some much-needed sleep while I turned my attention back to my growing business. I couldn't sleep. In fact, the only way I ever went to sleep was by taking copious amounts of narcotics and exhausting myself to the point of falling into a coma. It was a horrifying way to live, but I accepted it as part of my cocaine-fuelled lifestyle.

Out of nowhere, I got a phone call from an old friend from our treatment centre days. He had just relapsed after ten years of sobriety and he wanted to come share a drink with me, and possibly buy some cocaine as well. I thought it was odd for him to reach out, since we had never been all that close. But I was a well-known dealer by this time and it wasn't uncommon for people to approach me for a drug connection. Since expanding my business was at the top of my mind, I invited him over for a drink.

I welcomed him with open arms when he walked in. I casually hooked him up with some cocaine and even prepared some high-grade lines to earn his business. I watched him light up as he tried the high-heat product.

"This is what dreams are made of, my friend," I said to him with a sinister smile.

He nodded in agreement and we started to play some Xbox.

After about an hour, I heard my ex come down the stairs from her nap. As she stepped onto the landing, my breath caught in my throat; she was absolutely stunning and I wanted her back more than anything. She sat down across from my friend and me, and the three of us engaged in some friendly conversation.

Now, I credit my survival in prison with my ability to read people. If you couldn't interpret people's thoughts and actions in there, you were as good as dead. I was the best at it. As the three of us sat around chatting that night, my spider senses began to tingle. My friend and my ex were getting along a little too well.

I suddenly went silent, and my friend became extremely uncomfortable when he noticed. Surely this guy hadn't come to my house, drank my beer, did my cocaine, taking full advantage of my hospitality, only to try stealing away the woman I was in love with and had just dropped $7,000 on. Only someone out of their mind would try that.

He abruptly said that he was too drunk to drive home, and he asked my ex to drive him. My blood began to boil—and then the unthinkable happened.

I lost my marbles, physically tossing him out of the house. My ex ran after him as I restrained myself from grabbing her, too. Once they were both gone, I slammed the door behind me and walked to the kitchen. I screamed at the top of my lungs, making a hateful noise to rival the devil himself. I completely gave up control to the beast inside me.

In my rage, I opened a drawer and pulled out a hammer. I lunged back outside just as his car screeched off into the distance. They had left together.

I ran back inside the house and got my shoes.

"He's going to die tonight," I said to myself. "I may go to jail for the rest of my life, but I don't care."

All I could see was blood, and there was nothing I wouldn't do to get it.

I didn't know where this man lived, so I didn't know what to do other than see if he went to my ex's house. I could never hurt my ex, but she wasn't my target.

As I drove by her house, they weren't there. As expected.

I got on my phone, and within ten minutes I managed to find this guy's address.

There are no words to describe how I felt as I pulled up to his house. I only knew what I had to do to satisfy my inner monster. I was going to hit him in the face with my hammer, at least a hundred times. That was my plan. Maybe then I would be able to feel normal again.

There was no reasoning with me. He needed to die, and she needed to see what she had done to me.

As I stepped into the shadows of his backyard, my heart beat fast. I peered into his detached garage and saw his car. I pictured in my head what he was doing right that moment to the woman I loved, what she might be doing to him. I hunkered down in the bushes and started to dry-heave from the adrenaline rush. My blood was pumping so fast, I felt like I might faint.

The only thing that stopped me from kicking his door in was the fact that he had roommates, and they were sober graduates from Doc's treatment centre. They didn't need to pay for his indiscretion.

But he did.

Minutes turned into hours. Although I was only wearing a T-shirt, my body burned like a furnace. I fantasized over and over about bashing his skull in until it no longer resembled a skull, just a pile of grey matter sitting atop a neck stump. I pictured myself standing over his dead body, covered in the blood of my enemy, watching my ex cry as she finally understood. I could only imagine the euphoric rush I would feel when it happened in real life, any minute now.

As the time dragged on, I got up a couple times to leave, promising myself that I'd be back first thing in the morning. But I couldn't leave. I was immobilized by the thought of what might be happening in that house. I needed vengeance, and it couldn't wait until tomorrow.

After a few hours, I reluctantly accepted that he wasn't going to come outside. But I couldn't leave without sending a message. Even something small would suffice, at least until I had the pleasure of watching the life vanish from his eyes.

I walked out to the railway across the street and found the biggest rock there. It was about half the size of my torso and I had to dig it up out of the ground using the hammer. It took me almost an hour to excavate it. Then, dirty and bleeding, I carried the heavy rock into his backyard.

I looked through the garage window at his beautiful sports car. Ironically, I had sold it to him when we'd both been sober.

With all my might, I hurled the stone through the window and right onto the car. The deafening sound reminded me of an explosion—music to my ears.

Almost as fast as my rage had come on, it disappeared, my bloodlust quenched by the destruction of his vehicle. I knew for certain that he had heard it, so I stood under the light in the backyard for a couple of minutes, hoping that he would see me. That way he'd know that if he had stepped out of his house that night for a cigarette, he would have died.

By the time I arrived home, my rage had returned. I was still determined to leave bright and early in the morning and wait at his house until he came outside.

I've never been an emotional thinker. One of my greatest attributes is my ability to step back from a situation and play the tape. But that night with my ex, I lost control. For the next couple of days, I staked out the guy's house.

When my second-in-command found out about this, he was pissed. Just as I had the ability to talk sense to him, he now had the same effect on me.

"Why throw away everything?" he wanted to know. "And if you're going to do this, why not at least try and hide it?"

We had this conversation at a crowded football stadium, and my first reaction was to decapitate the guy closest to me right there in front of all those screaming fans. That's when I knew my anger needed to be reeled in. I had an empire to run. I had worked too hard to throw everything away.

Gradually, my rage receded.

CODY'S HEAVY STEROID USE CREATED EXTREME EMOTIONAL INSTABILITY.

Chapter Seventy

THE DEVIL'S
PLAYGROUND

Donnie and I grew close over the following months as he taught me more about counter-surveillance. Helicopter surveillance was also key. The only problem with this was I was high out of my mind all the time and had the consistent ring of police sirens and helicopter propellers in my ears. Half the time I couldn't tell if they were real or imaginary, so I just blocked them out.

Donnie lost it every time I walked up to his house with my jewellery not tucked in. No one was supposed to know where he lived and he didn't want that kind of attention in the neighbourhood. He demanded that anytime I went to his house, I looped around the adjacent neighbourhood to see if I had any tails.

Once I flew through some basic manoeuvres around the neighbourhood, I would park a few blocks away and approach Donnie's house from the alley. Walking up to his place was always a daunting feeling, since I had so much cash on me. And when I'd leave I would have a ridiculous amount of cocaine. These trips to and from his house always made me want to poop myself, half-expecting someone to give me a baseball bat to the teeth.

But inside his house was a different story. He would open his back door, wearing nothing but a housecoat, sunglasses, and a big smile. Inside he played loud music, dimmed the lights low, and had gorgeous naked women running around everywhere. There was a cocaine buffet to boot.

We would eventually vacate to the basement where we did business while the devil's pleasures kept the girls busy. He had a money counter for counting stacks, a frequency jammer to shut down cell phones and wireless networks, a bug detector, and every drug under the sun along with tools to cut, press, seal, weigh, and mix them. While we cut the cocaine, music would be bumping all around us. I would laugh as his legs went spread-eagle in his boxers from trying to get enough leverage to use the press. Afterward, we'd count the money and sample the product.

After cutting the coke, it was usually necessary to put it in the oven overnight at a low temperature to turn it back into rock, but Donnie had a unique trick. With a couple dabs of scentless hairspray, it would solidify in a half-hour. Then I'd break up all the rock on dinner plates and point a blow-dryer at it for twenty minutes. I did this all in my underwear to prevent powder from getting on my expensive clothes. Then we bagged all cocaine into quarter-pound and one-ounce bags.

Next, we went upstairs, turned on the gas-burning stove, and prepped a mason jar. Donnie had been taught how to cook crack by some L.A. gangsters in the early 90s. I had never seen it done the way he did it. I watched him confidently dump thousands of dollars of high-grade cocaine into the jar and place it in a pot of boiling water on the stove. The girls would gather around as he added hot water to the cocaine with a turkey baster. As he spun the jar to the music, the girls would sing and shake their lady parts.

"Wait for it to drop," he would then say, stopping everybody. "Wait for it, wait for it…"

We'd be sitting in suspense, waiting for the cocaine to sink to the bottom of the jar. When it did, he shoved an ice cube into the jar and slammed the mixture upside-down onto a paper towel. Sure enough, when he lifted the jar again, we'd have a perfect baseball-size piece of crack. There wouldn't even be any stuck in the jar.

Then we'd cheer, turn up the music, and start the process all over again.

Once the business part of the night came to an end, the pleasure part would begin. Strobe lights lit the Jacuzzi room, bubbles rising to the ceiling. You would have to navigate around by blowing paths through those bubbles. The music pounded loud and all kinds of drugs were at our fingertips as we mixed ketamine (horse tranquilizer), ecstasy, GHB (gamma-hydroxybutyrate, the date rape drug), and of course cocaine. I would get lost in Neverland while soaking in the tub with gorgeous naked women all around me.

It was like this every time I went to Donnie's. This was our way of life. My depression completely disappeared while I was working for him. I became content once more as the pleasures of the world took hold of me.

Chapter Seventy-One

JUDGMENT DAY

For months, I had been planning my revenge against that cocaine supplier who had ripped me off in his house, but only for the past thirty days had I worked out the details of a specific plan. He didn't know it, but I woke one morning and knew that judgment day had arrived. That man would never see another sunrise ever again.

I had finally found his social media profile after scouring the internet for weeks. Once I confirmed that I had the right guy, I purchased a burner phone to set up a fake profile on the same network he was on. I then used a public venue IP address for anything that had to do with that fake profile, to throw off any later police investigation. I even went so far as to add several of his acquaintances to my profile so that he would be more likely to accept my friend request. Once he did so, I messaged him and requested his phone number. He excitedly sent it to the black-haired beauty I was portraying. Phase one was complete. I then deleted my fake profile and threw the burner phone in the trash.

Phase two was a little bit more complicated. The one thing I needed at this point was a hot young girl to help me out. After a process of elimination, I found a girl who suited my plan perfectly. She was a customer of mine whom I hadn't known long. When I reached out to her, I proposed that she meet this guy a few different times in specified locations and flirt with him. The premise of the meeting would be to buy crack cocaine.

I gave her a phone I had bought that same day, with his number being the only one in the contacts list. I also gave her very strict instructions not to use the phone for anything else. Using that phone, we texted him together.

Hi, this is Brittney, I texted, with her sitting next to me. *I can't remember where I know you from but I have your number saved in my phone under party favours, my friend and I are looking for hard (crack).*

He responded within minutes.

She was kept in the dark completely over what this was about. I had just told her I needed intel on this guy so I could figure out who he worked for. I told her she was going to meet him a couple of times a week for the next month. Each meeting would involve flirting a bit, purchasing the crack, and then leaving right away.

It was imperative that she only communicate with him over text, because I needed him to trust text messages from her number.

When the brown-haired bombshell jumped into his car, he instantly dropped his guard. As planned, she met him several times over the weeks. She had no idea I had just set up a murder through her.

Now for phase three. My enemy came to completely trust the phone now in my possession, thinking it belonged to a frisky twenty-year-old hottie. My plan was to now make him an offer he couldn't refuse.

I had a stolen car prepped and ready. As I jumped into the hot ride, I double-checked my kill kit to make sure I wasn't forgetting anything. I had a full outfit of throwaway clothes—hat, gloves, shoes, mask, and bulletproof vest. All but the vest were to be tossed in a river once the execution was done.

As I parked my car in the predetermined alley, I tried not to second-guess myself. But hesitation set in as I pulled out the burner phone to send the text that would lure him in. My thoughts were chaotic. I didn't enjoy hurting people, and I didn't particularly want to do this, but I felt that he had forced my hand. Why had he robbed me? Well, because he was a drug addict of course. He was just like me.

Would I have done the same thing, though? Probably not. I would have had the brain capacity to see the long-term gain of staying on my good side. His drug-addled mind hadn't been able to foresee the long-term consequences of his actions. Maybe, like me, he just didn't care whether he lived or died.

I wasn't going to let him get away with what he'd done.

I typed the text: *Hey cutie, so my friends parents are out of town tonight and they have a special room designed for a good time, a swing and many more toys. We were wondering if you wanted to bring some party favours and have a good time with us?*

Looking down at the screen, I pressed send. From the other conversations he'd had with this girl, I knew he would respond within minutes.

I sat in that pitch-black alley, consumed by darkness. It felt like it was where I belonged. I opened the chamber of my pistol-grip shotgun and pushed in shell after shell until it was fully loaded. It crossed my mind that all I needed was the one shot, since he wouldn't see it coming, but it was better to be safe than sorry.

The click of the chamber closing spiked my adrenaline levels.

My grip tightened around the handle. As I squeezed it, it squeaked from my rubber glove. The noise made me feel powerful. It was the sound of death.

Suddenly, I realized that a lot of time had passed. Where was this guy?

I dumped a pile of cocaine on an open CD case and began to crush it in preparation of the impending rush. As I stared at the fine powder, a thought crossed my mind: how many people had died or lost everything because of this stuff? The number had to be incalculable, and I was about to add to it. Two lives were on the line tonight, his and mine. Was this really worth it, over cash that had been stolen more than five months ago? In that time, I'd built a money train that couldn't be stopped. I wondered if this crackhead was really worth it.

But it wasn't about the money for me; it was about the principle. No would ever find out about it.

As I sniffed back a massive line of cocaine, I looked down at the phone. Fifteen minutes had now passed. I had offered the guy a threesome in a sex room. Why wasn't he all over it?

I started to get impatient, because my conscience was kicking in. Somewhere deep inside me, I could sense goodness.

What are you trying to prove, Cody? Or Reckless Rick, whatever your name is? Everyone already thinks you're a killer. Why would you vanquish a man you're never going to see again otherwise? Just to show yourself that you're a monster?

It was almost as if I was trying to convince myself that I was something I wasn't. I loved selling cocaine because of all the fake friends that came along with the territory. Everyone kissed my rear when I was the one with the drugs. Being high all the time and always having people pumping my tires for free blow was the only thing keeping me from killing myself. How would I feel at the end of the day if I was sitting in a cell charged with the murder of a crackhead?

After thirty minutes, I finally gave up. He wasn't answering and it wouldn't look good if I was seen in this alley with a shotgun and a kill kit.

I learned something about myself that night. I had almost made myself do something I didn't want to do just to show that I was a monster. Maybe I wasn't a creature from hell after all.

Chapter Seventy-Two

EMPTY FACES
OF THE NIGHT

The time between 2:30 and 5:30 a.m. is called the witching hour, and this when it became most difficult to rationalize or ignore the wreckage I was inflicting on people. The only people out on the road at that time are taxi drivers, police officers, and drug-dealers. The creatures and ghouls of the night come out to play.

When someone gets in my vehicle during those hours, it's not because the party needs to stay fun, it's because they are in excruciating pain. Cocaine doesn't let you sleep. It's relentless in its psychological assault.

I knew that the drug I was selling people would make them hurt worse by the time morning came. They thought it would fix their problem, but that's not the way it works. When you get high, you only add to the pain. I made my money by inflicting devastation and loneliness. At least I had an unlimited supply of blow to cover my suffering, but my customers would run out eventually and then they would have to make a decision: get clean or blow their heads off.

When I met people during the witching hour, the pain in their faces reflected my own. I'd be over the top nice to them, but I'm sure they could see right through it. They could probably see that I was trying to sustain my own addiction. When we looked at each other, it was almost as if we were silently telling each other that it was going to be okay, both of us knowing it was a bald-faced lie.

Who was truly winning in this situation? It wasn't them, but it wasn't me either. There was no true winner.

I couldn't remember the last time I'd slept. By then I was regularly going five days at a time without sleep. I had never made it to day six before—until today. As I hunkered down at my house, I could tell something wasn't right. My roommate and his girlfriend were speaking to me, and I could hear them and understand them, but it was like someone else was talking to me. Someone I couldn't see.

Suddenly, the girlfriend was snapping her fingers in front of my face, trying to get me to look at her. I found it difficult because I kept hearing noises somewhere nearby. I understood that they were worried about me, and every time I managed to give them my attention I could see that they didn't know what to do.

Something inside me tried to speak, but I stopped myself from letting it out because I'd already scared my friends enough.

"Do you want to step in the shower?" my roommate asked me.

I reluctantly agreed.

As I closed the bathroom door and faced the tub, I talked to myself. I checked behind the shower curtain, where I thought I could hear faint voices screaming at me.

It's all in your head, Cody. Take a shower.

The sound of the falling water was loud in my ears, drowning out the screams. If I expected the water to provide relief, it didn't.

"Am I going crazy?" I realized that I'd said it out loud, my voice trembling with fear from confusion.

Maybe I *was* going crazy.

"You're not going crazy, Cody. You're just a f*cking junkie. Look at yourself. You can't even control your bowels, you f*cking crackhead."

I stood in the shower, perfectly still, taken aback by the words that had just fallen out of my mouth. It was the scariest thing I'd ever heard. It had been calm, cold, calloused. I'd never heard myself sound like that.

"You're hilarious. Shaking like a f*cking little b*tch in the shower. What's wrong, boy? Can't find words? You forget how to talk?"

And then I laughed, and the sound will haunt me for the rest of my life.

I couldn't control what was coming out of me. I tried to keep my mouth shut, to prevent myself from speaking, but I was powerless over it.

I tried to reason with myself. I spoke in a low, terrified voice.

It just interrupted me with its dark laughter.

"What do you want?" I finally managed to say, in a completely different tone of voice.

"Take one God damn guess."

I lost my breath as the sheer magnitude of the evil inside me surfaced with that statement. It was hateful beyond measure. I shook violently, my mind racked with confusion.

I wanted to run, but how could I run from myself?

Scared to come out, I stayed in the shower for about an hour. I didn't want my friends to hear what was coming out of me.

When I turned the faucet off, my ears filled with screams and sirens. It sounded like the cops were raiding the house, but of course they weren't. My body had lost all control of itself. I worried that I would accidentally defecate all over the floor if I tried to walk out of the bathroom.

The bangs and screams in my head got louder. They were deafening.

I stayed away from the door, because my senses told me that the police were about to kick it down. My eyes darted from one side of the bathroom to the other. The sirens were so loud!

As I reached for the door handle, it felt as if every horrible sound crashed against my eardrums, my head physically bobbing from the assault.

I jerked open the door as fast as I could.

A cold blast of air washed over my face as the steam from the shower caked the ceiling in a wave. The house fell completely silent. I stepped out, half-expecting to be hit with a bat or baton, or to find my friend and his girlfriend dead.

But all I heard was eerie silence. The door was still on its hinges. The tables hadn't been flipped over. The windows were still intact. There weren't any dead bodies or police officers.

I had never experienced a true psychotic break before. As I sat on the couch, I picked up my roommate's iPad and tried to distract myself from the chaos in my mind. The cruel and sinister voice was gone, leaving behind only a trembling boy. I sat on the couch taking pictures of myself with the iPad. What was happening to me? I never wanted to hear that voice again, but I worried that this would mean not taking drugs anymore. I couldn't do that, I couldn't stop. It was the only way I could make it from day to day.

That night, my runners ran the operation. The only reason I stopped doing lines that night was because I became so paranoid from the noises I was hearing. What if I put my head down to the table to snort the cocaine and someone grabbed my head and pushed it right through the table before I had time to react?

The next day, my friend begged me to get help. He had listened to the dark conversation I had with myself in the shower, and it had scared them. I replied by saying that it had never happened before and if it kept happening I would go get help.

Well, it did keep happening. From that day on, that voice came out every time I got to day six of my sleepless cycle.

It wasn't the wolf from the white, windowless room. It was something within me that could understand me and talk back. And it hated me.

I never knew exactly what would trigger it. All I knew was that it was going to happen, no matter what. Maybe it would start because of something someone said. I didn't know. It could have been a thought that induced it. But my mind would split right in half and the evil voice would assault me, telling it would rape me, kill me, tell me to kill others… and it paid special attention to the fact that I was a junkie son whom no one loved. I would be bawling my eyes out by the end of it, trembling with fear.

Whenever I woke up again, I knew it would be back in six days. No amount of booze or drugs could interrupt the cycle.

Chapter Seventy-Three

RECKLESS

Things didn't get easier after that. Getting high relieved me of the pain, but it was also the cause of my psychosis. Only complete abstinence could save me, and that wasn't an option. The thought of living in my hurt was more than I could bear. I concluded that I would rather take my chances with this demon that was haunting me.

I continued to hustle as hard as I could. Weekends became insane for me. The amount of money I was pulling in each time I stopped the car couldn't even fit in my pockets. It seemed like every hour I was meeting up with a runner to collect a bursting envelope full of cash.

This forced me to adopt a few different counter-surveillance measures. Donnie and I both felt that I was getting too big too fast, and since I was so involved on the front lines of my operation I imagined that the cops must be on to me. So I hired a friend to let me keep a safe full of drugs and guns at his house. I also paid him to do all the bagging for me; my runners and I were way too busy for that. I bought him a phone with strict instructions only to use it with me.

I filled the safe with cocaine and made a code for it that only the two of us knew. When I needed a resupply, I would text him asking for football or hockey tickets. I'd say something like "Whaz up brother, just wondering if I could pick up tickets for the game tomorrow." Instead of the section, row, and seat numbers I'd plug in the grade of cocaine, how many sacks of eight-balls, and how many one-gram bags. I had a key to his house, so I could get in unimpeached if he wasn't there. When I cracked the safe, I would collect the premade sacks of cocaine, put them in my secret underwear pocket, and leave payment. He was paid a buck per bag.

I had to adopt another counter-surveillance measure. The foot traffic at my house was getting too much attention, not to mention my roommate was getting uncomfortable with all the activity, so I had to stay in different hotels on the weekend. I never disclosed to customers where I lived, so it was primarily my runners coming and going, but the frequency became overwhelming.

On Friday, I would pack a bag and head out to a rented room for the night. I'd switch hotels the very next day to avoid detection. I always kept with me a change of clothes as well as a supply of alcohol, drugs, scales, and bags. It was a very concentrated operation. The hotel room served a single purpose: to warehouse the narcotics and cash while I caught up on the bagging that couldn't be done by the friend whose job that was. I was moving the product so fast that he couldn't keep up with the demand.

One morning, I spotted a police cruiser park behind my convertible sports car in the hotel parking lot. My heart began to race as I contemplated what was happening. It couldn't be because the staff at the hotel had reported me. If that had been the case, the officer would have come straight to my door. Instead he had parked by my car. Because it was registered in my name, it suggested that he was looking for me personally. But since I always rented hotels under aliases, he would have no idea what room I was in.

I was on the third or fourth day of my sleepless cycle, way too high for this. I turned away from the window and gauged the prison sentence I would earn for everything I had with me. I had $25,000 worth of cocaine in the room, along with bags, scales, and phones. I also had cash. It was enough evidence to put me away for years.

I also had two runners with me in the room!

After taking some time to gather my thoughts, I dumped a massive pile of cocaine onto the counter and crushed it with the speed and efficiency of someone who had done this hundreds of times before—and I had. Instead of using a snorting utensil, I just dropped my face on it and heaved with both nostrils. The coke hit the back of my head like a brick to the face.

Now I could focus on the task at hand. As I rubbed my fingers over my upper lip, cocaine lifted into a cloud in front of my face. My eyes dilated as I returned to the window. I would wait this cop out all day if I had to.

Fortunately, I didn't need to wait all day. My patience paid off as I watched him pull away. I wasn't out of the woods yet, though. He was probably heading to the front desk now to try finding out what room I was in. I needed to vacate, and quick.

My runners offered to take the drugs, but I told them if anyone was going to jail it would be me. Neither of them had been to prison before, and I didn't want them to go down for my transgressions. I was a leader who led from the front, not the back.

I dumped out another enormous pile of blow on the desk and crushed it all. I didn't know how long it would be till I could get another dose, so I needed to make this count. I inhaled as hard as I could again through both nostrils, feeling the euphoric rush. I then swept what was left onto the floor—probably $200 worth—and grabbed the rest of the supplies, dumping it into a bag. My only hope was to stash it in the trunk of my car and keep the actual cocaine in my waistband; it was too big a package to fit in my underwear.

I walked swiftly from my hotel room to the car, put my bag in the trunk, and then hopped into the driver's seat. I had a feeling the cops could see me, so I tried not to show that I was stuffing another bag under my seat. However, there wasn't enough room under the seat. I calmed myself and just let the bag roll out of my hand and onto the floor, trying not to look suspicious.

As I pulled onto the road and picked up speed, my heart felt like it was about to burst out of my chest. I had done too much cocaine and was going to throw up. I grabbed my chest as my heart pounded. But I couldn't puke in my car, because the cops would be coming after me. While driving down the road at sixty kilometres per hour, I nonchalantly opened the door and puked out onto the road. For what it's worth, it's not the easiest task to dry-heave while holding open a car door, steering, and operating a manual transmission.

When I was done, I closed the door and glanced back into the rear-view mirror. I was a total wreck. My face was beat red, my teary eyes were bloodshot, and my pupils were the size of pennies. Was I having a heart attack? It wouldn't have surprised me. The amount of blow I'd taken should have been enough kill a few people.

I pulled into another hotel parking lot, wiped away all the cocaine from my face, and walked inside to get another room. Unfortunately, there weren't any rooms available. I walked back into the scorching sun and to my car.

As I began to pull out of the lot, police cars swooped in from every angle with their sirens on. Before I could blink, they jumped out of their cars with guns drawn and screamed at me to get out of the car. I could barely grasp the scene unfolding in front of me as I put the car in park and opened my door. A police officer was right there to greet me.

They pulled me out and slammed me onto the hood face-first.

"What's this for?" I yelled. Not that it mattered. The question was almost redundant.

"Traffic stuff," an officer screamed back.

They emptied out my pockets and put the contents on the hood of the car. Three cell phones and $2,400 in cash. It wasn't nearly as damning as the contents of the bag on the floor—drugs, bags, scales, and cash—just waiting to be spotted.

"If it's traffic, don't I have the option of paying it on the spot?" I said in the direction of one of the arresting officers.

"We don't want your drug money," one replied.

I shut up, my thoughts drawn to all the cocaine on me. They put me in the back of the cruiser with the windows up and the AC off. It was a furnace. No doubt they'd turned it off on purpose.

I was sweating profusely as I watched all the police convene outside my car. They weren't even looking inside it. They didn't even need to, the blow was right there on the floor with nothing to obstruct their view. Unbelievably, not a single one of them checked the bag.

I watched them slap a tow tag on the car as we left to go to Calgary Remand. What was going on? I was way too high for this.

I hadn't been to Calgary Remand in years. As soon as I walked into Admission/ Discharge, several corrections officers started laughing. They had gotten word of my arrival. They put me in a holding tank and told me that they would use my money to pay the traffic fines, then cut me loose. That sounded like a great plan to me.

The officers got a roar out of counting all my small bills. To add to the hilarity, they placed all three of my phones on the counter, each of which was ringing off the hook. They humorously called out the names of who was calling. Everyone in the room knew they were drug phones and drug money.

I sat in Remand for two hours before they sent me on my way. They gave me back what was left of my money, minus the $1,400 for the fines, as well as my ringing phones.

I had one of my runners pick me up and we went straight to the impound lot to get my car. As I approached the car, I wondered whether anyone had discovered the stash. But no, there the bag sat, exactly where I had left it.

Someone or something was obviously watching over me.

I had already made a few thousand dollars during those two hours in Remand, and I happily collected this cash from my runners. Then I went on with my night, business as usual.

As I walked up the steps to a house party, I heard loud music coming from inside. My face took on an expression of purpose and focus. I stepped into the house with my jewellery out, my tattoos on display, and my sunglasses hiding the deep bags under my eyes.

The whole party stood still upon my entrance. Although the music pounded, everyone was silent as they stared at me. I smiled as I gazed at all the potential clients. I wasn't here to make money… no, I was here to expand my empire. After all, it costs money to make money.

I approached the kitchen counter and pulled a half-pound of cocaine out of my crotch.

"How many people here have tried high-heat cocaine before?" I asked.

I dished out free line after free line. Anyone who decided to partake just needed to give me their number so I could add them to the phones. In my deep raspy voice, I educated people on the drug I was so incredibly passionate about.

"Is that actually his voice?" I heard a young man say behind me. He thought I sounded like Batman. "So cool!"

No doubt that voice was a gift from the spiritual realm.

Despite my confident sales pitch, I couldn't forget that I had just forty-eight hours or so left before I hit day six in my cycle. Then that sinister voice would be back to torment me into blowing my head off.

If these people knew what was happening to me, they would have run screaming out of the house at my generous offer of free blow.

Chapter Seventy-Four

FOLLOW THE LEADER

My heart beat loudly in my ears as I sniffed line after line of cocaine. It had almost become as innate as breathing. I could feel my pulse in my eyeballs, and the dark black bags under them provided evidence of the intense workout they put me through daily.

I'd lost my voice almost completely and it didn't sound like it was going to come back anytime soon. I can't tell you where it went. But the deep rasp that replaced it sounded of hopelessness and death.

Anyone who had the pleasure of being around me could feel my presence when I walked in a room; I had a dark, sinister energy. People had to step back when they looked at me, as if they had been struck. But I'd learned how to draw people close to that blackness. I was almost forced to share it so I wouldn't feel so alone.

I'd also lost my senses of smell and taste. This obviously wasn't as noticeable to the people around me, but it really bothered me. I once read some research that claimed there's a direct correlation between a poor sense of smell and sociopathic traits. Apparently the same part of the frontal lobe that controls a person's sense of smell also has jurisdiction over their emotions.

On the one hand, the doctors must have been right about my diagnosis. On the other, they must have been wrong, considering everything I'd achieved while I was sober. Not that it mattered at this point. My actions currently reflected those of a man without a conscience. But it wasn't because I couldn't feel; it was because I hated myself.

I was still interested in expanding my empire. One of my runners approached me one night with a couple of compelling ideas. He wanted to branch out within the ranks of my business, so he proposed the idea of establishing a dial-a-dope operation in the small towns south of the city. His idea struck a chord in me for two reasons. First, I wanted to see this young man grow. Second, these were the same small towns

I had grown up in. I already had a network of loaders out that way, but there was an untapped market in the area of small sales.

It was worth looking into, especially considering the recent run-in with the cops fresh in my mind. They said they hadn't wanted my drug money, and that meant they were investigating me. Maybe moving out of town and letting someone else man my operation in the city would be a good idea.

Since the cops had taken me down outside the hotel, I'd changed all my phone numbers and vehicles. Now the police didn't know what I was driving, so they couldn't impound my vehicle in order to place a bug in it. The fact that they'd taken me down easily told me they had probably done exactly that. I'd have been stupid to keep driving it.

I sat down with my crew one day and devised a plan to set up shop outside of town. I picked four guys, each with a different set of skills, and placed them in the biggest town. I got them a large place to live, with the intention of having them be home cases for the next month. I set them up with a few burner phones and supplied them with enough product to spread the word with free samples in exchange for phone numbers.

It was brought to my attention that there were several dealers already set up in these towns, though, and my boys wanted to make a statement with violence. The problem with this was that the towns were controlled by the RCMP as opposed to a city police force. These guys were smart and didn't mess around. I'd rarely heard stories that ended well for people who were caught selling in their jurisdiction.

So I commanded my men to fly under the radar and avoid violence at all costs. We didn't want to bring unwanted attention to ourselves. If anything needed to be dealt with, I would do it in the darkness of night by myself.

I also sent my second-in-command to oversee operations, and he carried my word and my will. It was time for these men to graduate and take on more responsibility, and I hoped they could handle it. But my procedures needed to be followed to the letter, or all of us could go down.

What could possibly go wrong?

The next morning, while counting the cash brought in from a Friday night, I got a call from the boys out of town. I smiled, counting dollar signs as I picked up the phone. I was met with an excitement to match my own. As my runner gave me the rundown of the night, however, my feelings of benevolence slipped away, replaced by confusion and anger. After the bar had closed, my boys had gotten drunk and high and thought they would surprise their boss with a gift of unspeakable value. They went to speak with all the dealers in town, kicking in their doors between three and five in the morning. They'd tied up everyone in those houses and proceeded to inflict various forms of torture on them, such as burning them with cigarettes. Then they'd robbed the homes of anything of value, including drugs. To put a cherry on top of their sundae of disobedience, they'd informed all these dealers that they were now working for Cody Bates.

I couldn't believe what I'd just heard. It was almost unfathomable. Not only had my men lost any chance of doing business in that town, but I now had a bunch of enemies I hadn't even met. I liked knowing who my enemies were; it made me feel in control. In this situation, I had zero control.

I ordered everybody to come back to Calgary. I had to come up with a quick plan to enact some damage control. And hopefully no one called the cops.

I sat by myself, brainstorming what to do. One thing was obvious: I'd have to let all these men go. They had disobeyed a direct order and defied my will. I didn't have time in my day to protect people from themselves. I couldn't risk my entire operation for kids who couldn't even follow instructions. The problem was they all wanted to be gangsters, the kind of violent people the cops tended to pluck off the street before more people got hurt. I didn't need gangsters! I needed social butterflies who heeded instruction.

I came up with a plan that could very well cover everything. But it was a longshot.

I had just picked up a new Pitbull a few days prior, so I loaded her into my car and headed out of town. Her name was Molly and there wasn't an aggressive bone in her body. She immediately stole my heart, along with everyone else's who met her. Indeed, my friendly dog wasn't meant for intimidation but for a higher, more manipulative purpose. She was to be an example of how nice of a guy I was. I treated my dog as I did all my friends, with uncompromising love and respect.

My plan was to head out of town and break bread with potential disciples, not to make a scene with an already traumatized group of people. I was going to recruit them.

When I got to the first house, I walked up the steps of the porch and glanced in the windows. They were heavily covered, so I knocked on the door with my dog beside me.

A young woman answered, looking nervous. I may have been a nice guy, but when you look at a hooded man covered in tattoos who sounds like Batman and wears sunglasses, I think anyone would be nervous. I told her who I was and that I wanted to talk to her boyfriend. She glanced in the direction of the living room, almost too afraid to speak as she told her man who was there.

"Well, let him in," I heard from the living room.

I stepped into the house and quickly took in the scene. There were several individuals sitting around the sofas in the living room. One of them had a crossbow, although he wasn't being threatening with it; I just noticed it was there.

As expected, Molly excitedly introduced herself to everyone. They all let their guard down a bit. The tension dropped as I told them about my lovely dog and how much she meant to me.

With the introductions out of the way, Molly having executed her duty with pinpoint precision, it was time to talk business. I apologized to them for what had happened. I explained that my men had gone against my orders and that it wasn't right for them to be forced to work for someone they didn't know. I informed them that they were relieved of that responsibility. Indeed, I had brought all their drugs, money, and stolen belongings back. It would never happen again.

After that, it was time to separate myself from every other drug-dealer out there. I pulled a quarter-pound of product out of my crotch and asked for a scale. I then weighed out some of the high-grade cocaine.

"You ever tried high-heat?" I asked, smiling at them.

They shook their heads as I prepared lines for them. I then asked if they liked crack or if they had a market for it. I passed them a big rock the size of a popcorn and told them to try it. They all sat around, lit up like Christmas trees, as they tried my cocaine in its various forms.

After they were all good and high, I told them that the cocaine was theirs to keep for the transgressions levelled at them the previous night.

At last, I made them an offer they couldn't refuse. I told them they could have the high-grade stuff for only a tad more than what they were currently paying for the crap they were already selling. I asked them to join my team, and in doing so become my partners.

"The men that rolled on you the other night did so without my direction," I said again. "It won't happen again, and if someone messes with you out here it'll be me who comes to correct the mistake, along with individuals who would die for me." That statement must have sounded scary enough. "Do you know what the difference is between a leader and a boss? A boss will direct his expendable followers and thrive by himself. A leader will die for his followers."

As they nodded in agreement, I could tell that my point had hit home. I was a leader, and if they agreed to follow me they would have my protection and everything that came with it. They quickly realized who they were dealing with. They wanted a guy like me backing their moves.

The other stops in town went down the exact same way. Everyone accepted my offer without hesitation. I had a big name and everyone was happy to come under my flag.

I had started the morning under the threat of federal police heat and potential new enemies, not to mention anarchy in my ranks. By the time I drove home, I had three new loaders and had sent a message to everyone left working for me that I wasn't going to tolerate any nonsense.

Importantly, I also had a brand-new out-of-town money train that would get me away from the heat of the city. It seemed like every time I was put to the test, I somehow came out on top.

CODY WITH HIS LUXURY VEHICLES.

Chapter Seventy-Five

LIFE'S TERMS

I loved the idea that everything happened as it was supposed to, and I was but a pawn being moved on God's chessboard. It was such a simple way to live when all I had to do was be a good person and let God's plan of destiny unfold. One thing I knew about myself is that I was my own worst critic. Living on life's terms, to me, meant allowing thing to unfold naturally.

When I finally accepted Donnie's offer to try pure crack cocaine, it felt like fate. Something that was meant to be. It felt so natural to hold the crack pipe in my hand.

I had never pictured myself picking up a crack pipe again. Crack was for junkies, and it was antithetical that a gangster could smoke it. But Donnie was an anomaly, and it was hard for me to say he was wrong while he was pulling in over $30,000 per day.

But I knew I was a junkie, and that I had been in survival mode for a long time. There was no point holding on to righteous validations about my drug use by convincing myself that at least I didn't have it as bad as some other guy. So, I reasoned, all I was doing was holding out on myself when it came to potential outlets to make myself feel better.

Donnie gave me instructions about how to breathe as he lit the crack rock on the pipe he held up to my mouth. Just as cooking the crack was a science to him, so was smoking it. His guidance enabled me to take complete advantage of everything going into my lungs. This was far more intense than snorting it.

I lay my head back on the couch as a wave of blissful heat washed over my body. My breathing became erratic. I couldn't hear anything. I looked over at Tommy and Donnie on the other couch and saw their mouths moving, not making a sound. They were talking to me.

I rolled my head back up and studied the ceiling. My whole body was lit by a fire of uncompromised passion. Who cared if they were talking to me? I felt perfect, completely sublime. This is what I'd been looking for. This was what it was all about. It was the pinnacle of my drug-using career, what I'd been chasing since I was twelve.

For once in my life, I felt okay in my own skin. I wanted to be me in this moment.

Contentment was such a beautiful emotion. Why had I put this off for so long? I melted into the couch and let the high take over.

As I lay reclined on the couch, my hearing slowly came back. The guys were talking, and gradually the volume increased until my head was twitching. All my goodwill drained out of me, leaving me cold, naked, and confused. The blissful silence was replaced by a noisy assault. The torment became relentless as I was filled with hopelessness, despair, and paranoia.

I went completely silent as I visited the leafless forest in my mind. I could hear people whispering everywhere, the sounds coming from all directions. Were they setting me up? Would my best friends really do that to me? I was so confused. I couldn't tell what was real and what wasn't. The only thing that I knew for certain is that I wanted to disappear.

Donnie offered me another hoot. As he asked, I looked over his shoulder, thinking about an impending attack that would no doubt take place any second. My heart constricted in pain as I closed my eyes and told myself it was all in my head.

They wouldn't do that do you, I told myself. *Your mind is fractured from another psychotic break. You're hallucinating, Cody.*

My eyes slammed open as if I had been struck.

I took in sporadic gulps of air as I struggled to control my reflexes. There was someone around the corner, I was certain. I could hear him. Or maybe there was a person behind the couch, as another sound caught my attention. I tried to convince myself not to trust my own senses. It's a terrifying feeling not to be able to believe what your mind is telling you.

I trembled in fear, struggling to steady my shaky lips as Donnie put the pipe to my mouth again. He directed my breathing just as he had before and once again I took full advantage of the thick smoke entering my body. I instantly felt better as I let it settle inside. Relief set in. Thank God.

I again dropped my head back and melted into the couch as I blew a milky cloud of smoke up at the ceiling. All my senses left me again. I couldn't see, couldn't hear, and most importantly couldn't feel.

But this time the bliss didn't drown everyone out, as it had before. After a few seconds, I could hear their muffled voices. I could tell that this high wasn't going to be anywhere near the as good as the first. I start to panic as the daunting realization set in that I wouldn't climax with this hit. Desperation slammed into me like a cement blanket.

It wasn't enough. I needed more.

I came crashing down as if falling from space. I immediately went back into my psychosis, only this time it was worse. My ears felt like they were about to burst from the malevolent sounds crashing against them. My skin felt as if it hated me and was trying to crawl away. I was in so much pain. My throat tightened as if in a vice grip. I let out a cry of dismay and confusion.

Every single time I took a blast, I felt better for a second. But it was always followed by the most excruciating pain imaginable. The reality is that, for a junkie, the potential for relief, the desperate need to chase that first high, becomes more important than anything this world has to offer. You need to make the pain stop, even if only for a few seconds. It's worth more than life, more than family.

When you're in a state of emotional and physical affliction, your mind switches into survival mode to protect itself from the brutality being levelled against it. Being in survival mode inhibits you from seeing what's right in front of you. If you're in pain, you don't consider long-term consequences; you only focus on escaping the moment. There are no other levels of thought. No empathy or compassion. No articulation or logistic dictation. You become animalistic and primal.

Welcome to the life of a junkie in survival mode.

The next few minutes didn't matter to me. My only companions in life were pain and suffering, so every thought in my head was focused on finding relief.

This type of behaviour is exactly why I was diagnosed as a sociopath.

The only thing that kept me from reflecting on what I had become, a bottom-of-the-barrel junkie, was the fact that I was making money whether I decided to get up and tackle the day or not. My empire was almost running itself at this point. So why not chase euphoric bliss? Wasn't that the reason I had started down this road?

EVEN THOUGH CODY WAS RARELY SOBER, HE WAS RUNNING ONE OF THE LARGEST DRUG DISTRIBUTION NETWORKS THE CITY HAD EVER SEEN.

Chapter Seventy-Six

DO NOT DETAIN

I used to think that a Do Not Detain order was a fairy tale made up by people with inferiority complexes. It didn't seem logical or realistic that the police would put a flag next to a person's name indicating that they weren't allowed to be arrested, yet I couldn't help but consider the possibility. I wondered if the police were building a conspiracy case against me and thus didn't want me to be arrested and charged with petty charges that could kill all their hard work. It seemed to me that such an order would only be given to the highest level gangsters, if such orders were ever given at all. It seemed unlikely.

Even if I did have such label attached to my name, I wouldn't divulge it to anyone. It sounded so pretentious. I'd occasionally heard people brag that they were the subject of such an order, and it always made me want to puke. I hated fake gangsters. True gangsters didn't need to brag about stuff like that; their presence alone would command respect.

But as I dealt with the police more and more, I started to drift toward the idea that such an order might very well exist.

One night while I was at a nightclub carrying on with my usual socializing and networking, I met a guy who claimed to have stature in the nightclub industry, whatever that meant. He and his friend wanted to try whatever it was that had me feeling so high. So I took them to a bathroom stall and pulled out the cocaine I regularly kept in my crouch pocket. I graciously poured out a pile of the drug and put the remaining sack in my front pocket.

As I was cutting lines, my new friends and I heard an authoritative call to us from outside the stall: "Put everything down and come out of there now."

I disobediently snorted the evidence just as one of the guys with me opened the stall door. I turned to face the club's bouncer, powder cocaine undoubtedly falling from my face from the enormous pile I'd just snorted.

The disgruntled bouncer stared at me with a look of dismay. I supposed it was a good thing this idiot wasn't allowed to search me, and then my gaze turned toward the bathroom exit and I saw a couple of officers from the police gang unit.

"He was selling drugs in the bathroom stall," the bouncer informed the police while pointing at me.

My heart practically stopped. Being too high to come up with an intelligent retort, I just put my hands up and said the first thing that came to my mind.

"I wasn't selling drugs," I said. "I was just doing them."

Brilliant, Bates, I thought to myself. *Maybe the truth shall set you free. God only knows how you've stayed out of prison this long.*

I felt the cuffs close over my wrists. Although they didn't search me immediately, they took me out to a waiting cruiser. One cop hopped into the car to run my name through the system while the other held the back of my cuffs with a death grip. I started to wonder if there might not be grounds for an arrest despite having been accused of selling cocaine in the bathroom.

"Did you know you have a warrant for your arrest, Mr. Bates?" the officer in the car said in my direction.

I didn't know how many times a man's heart could come close to stopping in one night, but I knew I was pushing my luck. If they had a warrant for my arrest, that meant they had reasonable grounds to search me. It looked like I would be going to jail for a while.

The cop holding me looked over-the-moon happy. When our gazes connected, I could tell he hated me. I was scum to him.

My high was wearing off as I thought more about what was in my pocket: about an ounce and a half of high-grade cocaine, half of it individually wrapped for small sale, the other half devoted to my personal stash.

Suddenly, something happened that I didn't expect. The cop who had been searching my name jumped out of the cruiser and called his partner over for a private conversation. The man sat me roughly down on the curb and walked over to his comrade. They whispered together for the next few minutes, looking in my direction periodically to make sure I hadn't gone running off with my hands cuffed behind my back.

When they returned, they seemed livid and I seriously considered that they might kick me in the head. But just as I was bracing myself for the cheap shot, one of the cops helped me up and uncuffed me. His partner slouched in the passenger seat of the cruiser, sulking like a toddler and refusing to look me in the eyes.

"Despite having a warrant, we are going to let you go. It's almost the end of our shift and we don't want the paperwork."

I was dumbfounded. I almost asked out loud why they didn't at least check my pockets, considering the accusation that I'd been selling drugs only a few minutes ago.

As my wrists were released, I rubbed the spot where the steel had cut into my skin.

"Run," the cop said in my direction as he turned and walked back to the cruiser.

I wasn't stupid. I hadn't gotten a break. Something had stopped them from searching me despite the fact that they'd had full authority to do so. These guys had been forced to let me go.

After a few condescending remarks between me and the cops, they drove away and walked across the parking lot to my car. What the hell had just happened? It seemed so impossible.

Over the next couple of weeks, I often thought back to what had happened at the nightclub. I had heard of Do Not Detain orders, but I hadn't thought they would apply to me. I was just a street-level cocaine cowboy, not a high-ranking member of the mafia. I just couldn't picture myself being large enough to draw that kind of attention.

So I cast the thought aside and carried on with business as usual.

The only time I ever carried large amounts of dope on me was when I was leaving Donnie's house. I'd take it from there to my safehouse, where everything was bagged and stored by my secret accomplice.

One day, I popped out of Donnie's alley and hurried to my waiting car. My recent loads had gotten rather large because of my new out-of-town pipeline. That day I was carrying cocaine cut in many different grades along ketamine, molly (the pure form of ecstasy), and GHB. It was my largest shipment to date. I jumped in my car, manoeuvred my bulging crotch to a comfortable position, and started my way down the road.

About five minutes into my journey, I passed a police cruiser. All my phones were lighting up, as they always were when I was leaving Donnie's with a reload. I tried not to look suspicious as the cop pulled in behind me. I calmed myself down by reassuring myself that I had done nothing wrong, but I couldn't forget what that cop at the nightclub had said about having a warrant for my arrest.

I pulled my ball cap low over my eyes and focused on the road ahead. It was always important in these sorts of moments to drive as though I had nothing to hide. Unfortunately, my attempt to look like a father driving home from work somehow backfired. The sirens turned on and I knew I had trouble.

As I turned on my hazard lights and pulled onto the shoulder, I took the three phones from my cupholders and placed them behind my driver's seat. There was no hiding the massive bulge in my crotch, though. If the cop asked me to get out of the vehicle, I would be done for.

I took some deep breaths as the cop approached my car. It didn't help that I was high.

I rolled down my window and smiled at the officer as he reciprocated with a smile of his own. I asked him if I had been doing something wrong.

"No, you didn't do anything wrong at all, Mr. Bates," he replied. "But when I ran your plate, I recognized your name and thought I would say hi." How nice of him. "I was one of the responding officers in the southwest for that homicide you were involved in. I guess it tweaked my interest when I saw your name. What you been up to these days?"

It was friendly chit-chat. That was it. He was super nice and didn't seem to have any intention of giving me a hard time. After a couple of lies about how I was a finance manager now and doing really well, he said the words that knocked all the air out of my lungs.

"Did you know you have a warrant for your arrest?"

My shoulders slumped and my eyes went wide with surprise. The cop from the nightclub hadn't been lying. As soon as he asked me to step out of the car, I would be busted. I turned my eyes forward, as it was getting harder and harder to act normal— not that I looked normal anyway; my tattoos and jewellery were hanging out and I must have looked really high. To make things worse, all three of my phones suddenly started to ring loudly at the exact same time.

As I looked the police officer in the eyes, I could tell we were both thinking the same thing. He was looking at a drug trafficker.

Then, as if the skies opened up and God Himself bent down to give me a kiss, the cop informed me that he didn't deal with peace officer warrants. Too much paper-work. I stared blankly, confusion taking over.

I could tell he was lying about the paperwork, but I wasn't about to call him out on it. I awkwardly thanked him and asked if it was okay to leave. He wished me all the best and let me drive off, slumping onto the steering wheel in a moment of complete exhaustion.

It had finally become obvious what was happening. Somewhere in a police office there was a picture of me on a wall with a web of attachments connecting me to other people's pictures. And under my name? A "Do Not Detain" label, likely attached to the Reckless Rick alias. I had no doubt now that they were building a substantial case against me and didn't want me brought in on a petty charge.

But it didn't make sense, and I found it hard to believe the cops would care about me. I was Mickey Mouse compared to the much larger fish out there. The only difference between them and me was that I had a larger distribution network, selling small quantities to thousands of people at a time.

I dodged a bullet that day that could have otherwise seen me sent to prison for ten years or more.

What did they have on me? Counter-surveillance was my way of life at this point. It would have been impossible to track the countless phones numbers and vehicles that had been recycled through my operation.

But they had to have something. The words "Do Not Detain" rang loudly in my years as I contemplated my next move. I needed to focus—and for that, I needed more cocaine.

CODY LOSING WEIGHT RAPIDLY FROM HEAVY COCAINE USE.

Chapter Seventy-Seven

FEMALE VERSION OF ME

Every time I woke up after a psychotic break, relief filled me and I felt grateful that I was one hundred forty-four hours away from the next appearance of that sinister evil. Before I even opened my eyes, I would do a quick assessment of my sleep quality. I could usually tell how long I'd been down for. Anything over five hours would reset the cycle, allowing me to get up and tackle the day without any pesky psychological interferences.

Day one of the cycle was always hit or miss. At first I needed alcohol to counterbalance the effects of the cocaine. But if I let that balance slide, I would inevitably slip into another psychotic break. The key was liquor.

Day two was always a write off-for me. I would go on a twelve-hour trip, and it happened no matter what I did. This day was usually spent sitting on my couch sketching out over my surveillance cameras; I always assumed that intruders would be smashing me with a bat at any second. It was awful, but I had grown accustomed to it over the years.

Day three was my jam. I couldn't say why, but when I finally snapped out of my day two trip, I would snap back with a vengeance. On this day I had no fear and incredible focus. I was also able to start eating again despite the copious amounts of drugs I was consuming. Every day three, I tackled a long to-do list, but I always got every single thing done. It was a common joke in my social circle that my empire was built on day three. That's when I felt determined and got all my best ideas.

Day four was generally a diluted version of day three. By this time, the drugs and alcohol I'd consumed would be wearing on my psyche. This resulted in frustration toward myself and my psychological misfires. It always ended up in me venting my frustrations through sex and violence. Debt-collecting, payback, fighting, and drug-fuelled sex parties were common day four activities.

Day five was always terrible because I knew that day six was next. I was always trying desperately to put myself to sleep by overwhelming my brain with insane amounts of narcotics and alcohol. But it never worked, not even a single time. Heavy depression would set in and I'd want to die rather than face my day six horrors. By the end of the day, I'd be contemplating various methods of suicide. Insanity would slowly creep in as I scrambled for a way out of what always came next.

My life completely revolved around this six-day countdown. I could never decipher exactly what time the psychotic break would happen, but it always did. Suddenly, my mind would split in half and the dark voice would calmly tell me everything it wanted me to know about myself. It was so calm and commanding, reminding me of everything it was going to do to me. It wanted to make me suffer forever in the most horrific ways imaginable. It would even tell me what other people thought of me, how much they thought I was scum and a worthless piece of crap.

I believed everything it said, because I couldn't control it. It was honest, unforgiving, and uncompromising in its torment. Anyone who had the pleasure of hearing one of my day six breaks would think there were two people in the room; one voice was mine, and the other was something completely different. The conversation would last for hours, and I'd be bullied to the point of tears.

I can only assume that these breaks ended when my mind eventually just shut down in defence against the brutality being levelled against it. Then I'd wake up five or six hours later, relieved that I was six days away from it happening again.

As I walked up the alley to Donnie's house, I watched over my shoulders and attempted to decipher every sound I heard through my drug-addled ears. Everything screamed that an impending attack was on the way, but I knew it was mostly in my head.

I hurriedly knocked on the back door, getting super impatient as I stood waiting. This back porch was the perfect spot for an ambush. He kept his lights off so the neighbours couldn't see me coming or going. It also meant I couldn't see anything.

As the back door swung open, I was met with a surprise. The gorgeous Asian girl on the other side gave me a smile as she walked back to her cooking in the kitchen. She was wearing tight black shorts and a crop top. Her stunning hair hung down to her butt. She must have been around twenty years old and I was mesmerized by her beauty.

I confidently walked up behind her and held my hand out for an introduction. "Hi. My name's Rick."

She turned to face me, her beautiful hair flowing out of the way of her eyes. Our gazes connected and I stared into those eyes, feeling weak. It had been a long time since I'd felt this way, and certainly never to this magnitude on a meet-and-greet. I smiled and wondered what her voice would sound like. Probably like an angel.

"My hands are dirty," she finally said, basically telling me to take a hike. But it was still the most beautiful thing I had ever heard.

I laughed as I walked downstairs to see Donnie sitting on the couch, already cutting all the cocaine I was to be picking up.

"Who's that?" I asked about the woman upstairs.

"Oh. That's Jewel. You like her?"

"She's the most beautiful girl I've ever seen."

I didn't know it at the time, but this girl was the beginning of the end for me. My relationship with Jewel would end up turning into the sickest and most toxic in my life. We fell in love with the devil inside each other. She was just a female version of me, and we propelled one another into an unfathomable darkness the likes of which we hadn't imagined possible.

Looking back now, I can't say I'm surprised that I was attracted to her so instantaneously. She was a hustler like myself, stunningly beautiful, and had a passion for cocaine that rivalled my own.

I decided in that moment that I would do anything to have her. I believed in my cold dark heart that she could make me happy—but it was a recipe for disaster.

Chapter Seventy-Eight

OLD FRIENDS

It was incredible how far I'd drifted from the person I had been when I got out of prison. Only a shell of Cody Bates existed anymore. There was no life in my life, just the pleasures of the flesh. I had lost all hope of ever being me again. I'd accepted that this was the way I'd die, and hopefully it would happen soon.

Because of my new operations out of town, I didn't have nearly enough people working for me to keep up with client demand. To fill the gaps, I vetted new people who I thought would be a good fit for the business. I didn't want gangster wannabes; I wanted young men who could listen, take orders, and be capable of thinking for themselves when the situation called for it. These young kids would hang on to every single word I spoke. I hired farm kids and dapper teens; the more unorthodox they looked, the better.

I knew I wasn't the person I had once been, and sometimes the childhood friends of mine who worked for me found this out the hard way. One day, an old friend was short money from working one of my phones. He claimed it was because the guy he'd hired to help him had ripped him off.

I believed him, but a message still needed to be sent.

He sat across from me, looking nervous in his chair. He wasn't short a large amount of money, but he was nonetheless short. In my dark dungeon of an office, I looked at him over my sunglasses even though the only light in the room came from the TV and surveillance monitors. Gangster rap played in the background to keep my mind reeled in from not sleeping for days on end, the cocaine keeping me numb from the world.

I had to make sure this type of delinquency didn't become a habit.

I busted up a line of high-grade cocaine for him, making sure it was bigger than anything he'd ever done before. I knew that if I got him high out of his mind, paranoia would shortly follow. For now, I acted as though I was content with his efforts.

Pushing the cocaine toward him across the desk sent the message that all was forgotten, my true motive evading him completely. I made idle chitchat and made sure he saw my lip snarl periodically to help propel his paranoia.

After about twenty-five minutes, the cocaine had settled nicely into his already hopped-up system. That's when I passed him another huge line and told him to snort it. He nodded in approval and did it. I could tell the blow hit him right in the sweet spot.

We had been staring at each other for over a minute now without saying anything, and he knew something was wrong. But the cocaine prevented him from piecing it together. This created an abundance of fear in my old friend. He was confused and didn't know what to do.

I pulled out the bottom drawer of the dresser beside me, placed it on the ground, and reached into the cavity, pulling out my shotgun. His eyes went wide with terror as I held it firmly in my lap, not breaking his gaze. He started to apologize, but I immediately cut him off.

"Do you know what I usually do to people who owe me money?" I asked in my usual raspy voice. I could tell that it scared him.

He nodded reluctantly, the high he was experiencing turning out to be his worst enemy. I knew his mind would be cycling through unforgiving torment right now.

I asked him if he was ever going to be short again, and his answer was filled with sincerity: "No, of course not." I smiled at the man's conviction. I needed him to feel it.

I then tossed him a couple bags of cocaine and excused him.

After he left, I sat alone in my dark room and thought replayed the scene that had just unfolded. I'd known this guy since I was sixteen and he'd been one of my best friends. But even my best friends didn't know who I was anymore. No one had any idea what I was going to do from one day to the next.

My friend never came up short ever again.

Although I thought I was better at reading people than anyone, one thing I hadn't factored in was the possibility that he could be permanently scarred from having a shotgun pulled on him by his so-called brother. Our friendship was never the same again. For him, that was one of the scariest moments of his life. For me, it was Thursday.

My daily routine at this time mostly consisted of working the out-of-town pipeline myself while my runners worked the city. I spent most days alone driving around in a truck. I relaxed on the highway, doing cocaine until I couldn't feel my fingers. It got lonely sometimes and I often found myself going through my contacts to look up old friends to keep my company.

One day I got in touch with one of my oldest friends from Turner Valley. I was elated when he accepted my offer to take him for some road beers and a few lines in the country.

As he climbed into my massive truck, I greeted him with a hug. We booted out of town and cruised back roads, reminiscing about growing up together.

I was likely too high to understand that there was an underlying meaning to his conversation. While driving down a back road, he suddenly turned to me and asked if I was going to kill him, swearing that he would promptly pay back the money he owed me. I had totally forgotten he even owed me anything; I had just wanted to see an old friend.

We had known each other twenty-three years, but when I saw the fear in his eyes it hit me that he was being serious. He truly didn't know if he was going to be coming back from our road trip. In that moment of realization, pain overwhelmed me. I tried to assure him that I could never do that to him, but I could tell he didn't believe me.

This wasn't what I wanted. I didn't want all my friends wondering if I would one day orphan their children.

I forgave his debt and gave him a quarter-ounce of free blow, along with some extra cash to help him with his bills and put some food in his family's fridge.

As I drove out of town alone that day, I hoped he would spread the word about my good deed. The rest of my friends probably all looked at me the same way he did.

No wonder I was so lonely.

Chapter Seventy-Nine

COMES WITH THE TERRITORY

My roommate approached me one afternoon and asked if I could start looking for somewhere else to live. He was so paranoid having me around that he slept with his pants on so he could escape out the window in one fluid motion should the police ever show up. He didn't feel safe with me in the house and dreaded coming across more evidence of my lawlessness. One day he opened the freezer for a pizza pop and found a kilogram of drugs taking up most of the space. In truth, he didn't know about half the stuff I had stashed in his house.

He also felt really uncomfortable about having firearms in the house, so without him knowing I graciously transferred my cache of guns to the deck outside—but I kept my shotgun inside, of course. I needed that for protection.

I found a place even further south, next to the highway on the edge of town. This proved to be a big advantage, since it meant I could get around better under the cloak of night. The house was large, alarmed, and dog-friendly so I could bring Molly along. It also had a hot tub in the backyard. It couldn't have been more perfect.

I think my neighbours got a little wary of me as the weeks passed. For the most part, I was a veteran at hiding my coked-up condition, but the closer I got to day six the worse I got. It must have raised a red flag when I started shovelling snow off my neighbours' walkways at four o'clock in the morning in an attempt to dispel energy. I thought I was just being a gracious neighbour, but to them it was proof that I rarely slept.

I was living with a couple, and one weekend the girlfriend left town for a few days because of hardships she was experiencing with her boyfriend. I jumped all over the opportunity to bond with the boyfriend when he asked me if I had cocaine. I couldn't wait to give him the best blow he'd ever tried in his life. He and I became brothers in a few short hours of getting wrecked together. I couldn't believe someone this cool now lived under the same roof as me.

When his girlfriend was about to get back, we were high and hadn't slept in four days, so we bailed, not wanting her to put a damper on our fun. We drove aimlessly around country roads loaded with alcohol, cocaine, and crack. He told me he had never been awake that long. I was honoured to be a part of that experience with him.

As we rounded a bend, we came to a little dirt path that led up a hill into a forest. I figured my one-ton diesel would have no problem trekking this, so I gunned the engine. We ploughed through dirt and trees until something caught my attention—his head was jerking from side to side. The cocaine was turning on him.

I tried to calm him down with a soft low voice, but he couldn't even hear me. To make matters worse, we broke through a line of trees and came to a sudden dead end. As I turned the truck around, he started freaking out. He wholeheartedly thought I was going to kill him. I sped back down the hill, hoping he would calm down when he saw the main road again.

He did seem to calm down a bit and I breathed a huge sigh of relief. It looked as though my quick thinking had saved the day.

"I love you, brother," I said.

As soon as the words fell from my mouth, he whipped his head around like a striking cobra. "What did you say?"

I will never forget the look in his eyes. Before I had time to react, he planted his feet on the centre console and propelled himself as hard as he could out the passenger window. As he flew out of the moving truck, he didn't break eye contact. He was gone in a flash, plunging ten feet to the road.

I slammed on the breaks and jumped out of the truck, half-expecting to find a dead body waiting for me. At first I couldn't locate him. He wasn't under the truck or in the bush along the side of the road. As I looked around, though, I spotted him running across someone's front yard about a kilometre away, screaming in terror. I tried desperately to call him back, but he wasn't hearing me.

He ran in through someone's front door and I could hear people shriek inside. He then came out of the house and ran to the adjacent home, flying through that front door next. He literally invaded every home on the block.

And I thought my psychosis was bad!

I was in shock as I climbed back up into my truck. I felt bad driving away, knowing full well that this was just the beginning for him, but I had no other choice. I had thousands of dollars in cash and drugs in the truck, not to mention the fact that I was drunk and hadn't slept in four days. The cops were undoubtedly on their way, and I didn't know what he would tell them about me.

Not knowing what to do, I drove to Bragg Creek, far enough away that no police would come looking for me there. I hid away a pound of cocaine at an outdoor hockey rink and then made my way to a pub where I ordered a steak sandwich. I imagined all the cops coming down on my house right that moment, but I didn't think I had anything to worry about. We had no drugs or guns there.

After lunch, I got a call from the girlfriend. I didn't know what to say when she accused me of trying to kill him. Depressed, I hung up the phone.

So my new friend was in the hospital now, ranting and raving from a drug-induced psychosis. Fortunately for him, that would wear off after a few hours.

The girlfriend called me back a short while later and clarified that she wasn't kicking me out, but I had to stay away for a couple of days. She felt bad for not having told me earlier that he was an addict, which had been the reason for her leaving in the first place. She told me that he was finally willing to get help at a treatment centre in British Columbia. She wanted me to stay away until then. I happily agreed.

I don't know what had been going through the boyfriend's mind when he had jumped out of my truck. I've always wondered what he saw and heard that day, but I never had the chance to ask. The pure terror he'd worn on his face hadn't been anything new to me, though. People who hung out with me regularly ended up in the hospital, jail, detox, rehab, the drunk tank, or the psych ward. It just came with the territory.

––––––––––––

With police and haters always trying to take me down, it was imperative I always stay a few steps ahead of everyone. It almost became a blessing that I only slept every six days. But every once in a while the police would catch me off-guard, and that's when I was thankful for my ability to think proactively under pressure.

One of my runners, Toolman, called me in a panic one day. He had just gotten in a high-speed chase with the police and he was currently facedown in a field, hiding. Apparently the neighbourhood was filled with police. He'd had the presence of mind to ditch all the phones, dope, and money in a hiding place.

I left the movie I was watching, jumped in my car, and sped off to his rescue. It didn't take long before I glanced upward and saw a police helicopter circling above my vehicle. After some basic manoeuvres through a few nearby neighbourhoods, I figured out they were on to me.

Toolman texted to say he had somehow escaped the cops' grasp and made it home. All the goods, though, were sitting in the wheel well of an SUV a few blocks from his house. I was happy he was safe, but my concern now lay with my empire. The three phones he'd had on him contained damning evidence, enough to shut down my operation. I couldn't let the cops get them.

Unfortunately, the helicopter wouldn't be easy to shake. My thoughts racing, I pulled into a gas station and proceeded into the store as though I were a normal customer. I could still hear the chopper overhead as I racked my brain, all the while pretending to look at candy in one of the aisles. When I glanced outside the store to see if cruisers were sweeping down on me, I saw that the parking lot was still clear. I walked outside again under the protection of the gas pump overhang, pondering my next move, and came up short to discover one of my best clients filling up with gas at one of the pumps.

"What's up, Rick?" the guy said when he saw me.

"Dean, I'm glad to see you. I need your help."

He agreed to sneak me out of there, so I hopped into the back seat of his truck and got down low as we exited the parking lot. The helicopter was right above the store, but it didn't follow us.

I asked him to drive through the neighbourhood so we could scoop out the scene and try to get back the damning evidence. I stayed low, since the cops were everywhere. As we pulled up onto the street where Toolman lived, I saw the SUV where he'd stowed the goods. I glanced around everywhere, trying to figure out the best window of opportunity to jump out and grab it, but police cars kept cruising by. I was going to get caught.

Just as I was about to jump out and try my luck, Dean offered to do it for me. I was taken aback by the guts on this farm kid. I told him what type of sentence he would be looking at if he were to get caught, and he argued that it made more sense for him to do it. After all, the cops were looking for me, not some cowboy like him.

He jumped out and walked up to the SUV just as a cop passed by. It didn't slow down. Dean coolly reached up under the wheel well, pulled out a massive clear plastic bag, and tucked it under his shirt. This kid was gold.

As we drove away, I immediately started pulling all the batteries and SIM cards out of the phones, including the ones I was carrying. In total, I ripped apart seven phones... then it hit me that this didn't make sense. Toolman had been carrying three phones, and I had been carrying another three...

Dean and I burst out laughing when we realized I had accidently torn apart his phone. At least he thought it was hilarious.

We drove out of town and met a friend of mine who agreed to take everything and hide it for a few days.

When Dean dropped me off at home, I gave him an eight-ball and some cash for his bravery. He was exactly what I wanted for my organization, and I asked if he would be willing to work for me. He excitedly said yes, and he even had another friend who was interested, a guy named Lenny.

The whole thing felt like a divine appointment.

Chapter Eighty

PRECIOUS GIFT

I've often heard people describe the gift of life, saying that it's precious. I couldn't see it in that light, no matter how hard I thought about it. Life for me was a curse. Every time I came down from a high, I was filled with pain and anger that I couldn't achieve that beautiful mountaintop of euphoric bliss I was always trying to achieve. No matter what drugs I took, I could never reach it. I was just doing the same things over and over again.

I needed to change things up. It had been twelve years since I'd done needles, so I decided it was time to try them again. After stopping at a drugstore for syringes, I returned home and went into my room. I only had five bags of cocaine on me right now, which was as close as I'd come to running out in a long time.

I had an idea what I was doing as I dumped cocaine onto the spoon on my nightstand. I stirred in a touch of water and attached a ripped cigarette filter to the needle to soak the product into my apparatus. I tapped the syringe and got all the air bubbles out of it. After all, I wouldn't want the dirty air getting into my veins.

As I pushed the cocaine into me, my pupils dilated. I stood up so I could feel everything that was happening to me. I could taste the cocaine in my mouth, a sign that I had hit the right spot. My ears rang loudly from the blood rush. I sat back down; in case I passed out, I didn't want to hit my face. I closed my eyes and let the cocaine take over. I would be happy to die like this.

But the high went away as quickly as it had come, and as with crack I came down hard. I felt cold and exposed, imaginary voices constricting my heart with terror. I needed to feel better, so I promptly jammed another needle in my arm. I poked myself with needle after needle, my suffering becoming almost unbearable. But the highs were each so relieving that I couldn't stop chasing them. I hammered through all five bags in no time, slamming the entire fifth bag in one shot in a desperate attempt to reach that mountaintop.

It didn't work.

I went into my closet and started checking my pockets. I rarely ran out of cocaine, but when I did I could always find lots in my dirty laundry, bags I either hadn't sold or left in my pocket. I found six bags of pressed blow, and one very special bag of Christmas cocaine which I'd forgotten about. Donnie had given it to me as a present and said it was the purest cocaine he had ever tried. For him to say that, I knew it must be good.

By the time I sat down and began dumping it into the spoon, my suffering was all-consuming. I would rather have had my fingernails ripped out than spend another second hurting this bad. My hands shook as I watched the syringe fill, not sure how much to put in. I needed to be careful, because I'd never done this before.

As I watched the milky fluid hit the halfway point of the syringe, the fear of it not working began to outweigh my concern for my own life. I decided to rather risk death than not get the high I needed. I filled the syringe all the way to the top, a full gram of the purest cocaine I had ever tried.

This will do it, I told myself. *This will relieve me from the unbearable anguish that's destroying me right now. I need the pain to go away. I'll do anything, even if it kills me.*

A blast of pleasure washed over me before the drug even entered my system.

This is it. Finally you're going to feel better.

As I pushed down on the syringe, injecting until there was a quarter left. I hesitated for a second before continuing, waiting to see if I felt anything. Yes, there it was; something was beginning to happen. I pulled out the needle and stood up, as I always did. I looked at the ceiling, waiting for the heat blast of pleasure.

It felt suddenly as if someone violently slammed a brick of cocaine into my mouth. I fell backward, knocked onto the bed, and began to choke as it cut off my airway. My eyes went wide with fear. I instantly realized that I'd taken way too much.

I lost all control as I dropped lifeless to the mattress. I couldn't move a muscle, but my mind felt as if it was about to explode with thought.

Too much, too much, too much...

My body convulsed with seizures as I lost all control of my movements. My speeding heart felt as if it was about to blow my eardrums out of my head. I knew I was going to die. I could tell by the rate of my heartbeat that no human on the planet could withstand this much cocaine. How could I have been so stupid?

I begin thinking about my life. I could see my dog freaking out. My poor puppy. I was going to miss her. My dad came to mind, too. I hadn't seen him in longer than

I could remember. I hoped he knew I loved him. If he knew how much pain I'd been in, maybe he would understand.

Everything went completely silent as my body stopped moving, but I could still see. I couldn't move my eyes, but I could see my hand in front of my face and my dog licking me, trying to bring me back to life.

And then my heart stopped. I couldn't hear it anymore. My vision began to fade.

This is it, Cody. It's over. Is this what you really wanted?

Suddenly, I willed myself to move. Screaming in my head, I kicked my left leg, just a little. Slow at first, but then harder.

Kick... please kick...

I shrieked inside, desperate to bring myself back to life. Both legs moved, but I still couldn't feel my heart beating. The thought crossed my mind that this made no sense at all.

My heart exploded back into a rhythm and I seized, every muscle flailing. But as quick as I lost control, I just as suddenly got it back. I got to my hands and knees as my vision came back into focus. I struggled to breathe, and I couldn't see anything except flashes of light.

In my peripheral vision, something caught my attention. I tried to turn my head, to get a look at it, but something was preventing my head from moving. If only I could straighten my eyes...

Realization set in. I wasn't alone in the room.

I took a blow to the face. Someone hit me! I couldn't feel the pain of it, but the force knocked me right across the room and through my standing mirror. I tried to focus, but not before another strike sent me through the television screen. I couldn't see who was hitting me, couldn't stop my eyeballs from rolling around in their sockets.

As my head absorbed blow after blow, it dawned on me that I was being hit from multiple angles. It was more than one person, and they were using baseball bats. I could do nothing to stop it—nothing except scream. The sound that came out of my mouth didn't even sound human.

I tried to scramble away, and somehow I made it to the door. I escaped to the stairway, but before I could crawl down my assailant smashed me in the back of the head and I fell head over heels down the steps. I tumbled headfirst into the wall.

My vision and hearing still distorted, I clambered across the kitchen to the sliding glass door at the back of my house. Hearing the perpetrators closing in behind me, I head-butted the glass, smashing my face into it over and over again with all the force I could muster. Somehow, the broomstick propped in the door as a stopper popped out and I felt a blast of cold night air.

Realizing that I had a chance of escape, I careened off the deck and ran to the fence, leaping over it—but I missed, and soon I was being hit over the back of the head again. I collapsed to the ground and attempted to crawl away from my attackers. Malignant blow after malignant blow rained down.

I struggled to maintain consciousness as my vision began to go black. Unable to protect myself, I lay in the mud, being beaten to death. My attackers looked like translucent shadows, moving too fast for my brain to track.

The lights were going out. I was going to die. I had narrowly escaped an overdose only to meet an even crueller fate. Death clearly wanted me this night.

At least I couldn't feel anything.

As everything was finally goes black, I forced myself to crack an eyelid. My vision was filled with red and blue lights, and for the first time in my life I was happy to see them. Voices yelled in the distance as the police officers poured into the yard, guns drawn.

A cop rolled me over, and to my surprise I was able to crawl to my hands and knees. I had assumed all my limbs were broken. Maybe they were and I was still too high to feel anything.

"What the... boys, wait till you see this guy's record," the cop said. He proceeded to ask me how much drugs I'd taken. Why did that matter? Why weren't they worried whether I was going to live?

I answered my own question as I looked down at my body and saw that it was covered in mud and dirt, but there was very little blood—and no bruises. I brought my hands to my face, expecting to find it mangled from the assault. It was completely intact. What the heck?

I had hallucinated the entire thing. There had never been anyone in the house, but how could I explain the blows I had taken during the assault? I heard a cop say that it looked like there had been a struggle in my room. Several needles were found as well amongst all the broken glass.

They strapped me to a stretcher and put me in an ambulance. The fog in my mind was clearing with each passing second. I came back to reality, in complete and total shock. Perhaps I had hallucinated the attack, but I hadn't imagined my heart stopping. Someone or something had restarted my heart by grabbing my legs and swinging them, causing my heart to start pumping blood. That had been too close for comfort.

I was given a precious gift that night: the knowledge that injecting pure cocaine would kill me. Obviously I'd never do that much again, but I would look for a happy medium that would deliver me to the pinnacle.

For now I just needed to rest.

But my heart was already racing at the prospect of finding that perfect high. I had almost died, but the reward was priceless.

Chapter Eighty-One

GOING DOWN
IN CHINATOWN

Did I care about myself so little that I would risk going through that awful experience all over again? The answer terrified me.

As I lay in bed at Toolman's house, I contemplated my end game. My addiction was out of control. I had allowed myself to believe I could quit anytime, that I just hadn't wanted to stop. But now I knew the truth: I couldn't stop.

So what was the solution? The only answer was to accept that I wasn't going to live very long. If I could just manage to stay high until the end, I'd call that a win.

I liked to lie to myself and convince myself I was a good person, but the truth was that I barely had any humanity left in me. My only reason to be kind to people was to build my empire. Anyone who stepped in front of me got destroyed. It was clear to people that Reckless Rick had no fear of death.

A couple of days passed as I recuperated from my traumatic experience. Toolman let me stay with him as long as I needed. He truly cared about my well-being, a rarity for those like me. He brought me food and kept me posted on what was going on with the business. My top runners were controlling everything while I sat on the sidelines. It turned out I made a lot more money when I wasn't out there snorting all the profit. Who would have guessed?

Well, Donnie had. As I strung together a couple sober days, I noticed shifts within the ranks of my crew. Donnie was acting weird, and so was my top runner. The more I pondered it, the more I convinced myself that these guys were planning to make a move on me.

After just three days in Toolman's room trying to straighten out my head, the weasels and vultures had already come out of the woodwork to try and steal what I had created.

Donnie wasn't a gangster; he was a drug-dealer. He wasn't prepared to kill for anyone or die for anything. When things got real and he needed backup, he called me, because he wasn't willing to get his hands dirty. He was smarter than me, I'd give him that. But when I sent him a text message saying that I had a bad feeling about his intentions, that I would kill to protect what I had built, it gave him second thoughts. He replied by saying that I just needed to relax my drug use, hinting that I was too blasted to know what was happening. But we both knew I had caught him with his hand in the cookie jar. Up to that point I would have done anything for Donnie, but this showed me that I didn't matter to him. The only thing that mattered to him was the money I brought in.

Donnie wasn't expendable, but my top runner was—and he was going to be taught a lesson he would never forget.

The next day, I asked the runner in question to come to my house to bring me up to speed on everything that had happened while I'd been out of commission. My plan was simple, and it would be set in motion easily given that today happened to be the man's birthday. He walked into the house and embraced me as a brother. I wished him happy birthday and excitedly told him that I had the best present he was to ever receive—but there was one catch: he had to do it all at once. I pulled out an eight-ball and crushed it to a fine powder on the counter.

He hummed and hawed at first, citing dinner plans with his family, but he finally conformed to my will. He snorted the whole thing in one heave.

After five minutes, with my runner as high as a kite, I deployed the next part of my plan. I did a rail the same size and then pulled out another eight-ball, busting it into fine powder. He looked at me, bewildered. I could tell his mind was already playing tricks on him.

He shook his head as the revelation of what I was going to do set in. I lowered my sunglasses to the bridge of my nose and gave him an opportunity to look into my soulless eyes.

"You're going to do the line," I said. It wasn't a request; the jig was up.

He looked horrified as my sinister smile contorted my face. He was so high, he could barely speak. Every time he tried to say something, I cut him off and reminded him that I had given him an order to snort the other eight-ball. I wanted to see him break.

His hands shook as he reluctantly sniffed half the line. Then he looked up at me, as if pleading with me to let him stop at half. I just shook my head. He was going to do the whole line, for no other reason than that I said so.

After he did the rest, I ordered him to sit on the couch. I'd never seen such a big guy look so small. He was easily two hundred fifty pounds, but he resembled a mouse now as he cowered on my couch. The expression I gave him was the look I reserved for my gravest enemies.

"I have some very simple questions, and I'd like some very simple answers," I said through my crooked smile. I snapped my wrist and a police-issue retractable baton extended out from my hand toward the ground.

The cocaine had completely turned on my petrified friend. Now it was playtime.

About an hour later, I went to Donnie's house, where I shed light on the transgressions of my top runner and his punishment. I didn't blink as I watched his reaction. I was making him extremely uncomfortable, and I relished every second of it. Donnie was evil, but he was no killer. I didn't tell him everything my runner had told me. I decided to hold some of it back, my ace in the hole. Anyway, it was way more fun to watch Donnie squirm.

The truth was that I needed Donnie more than he needed me, but I wasn't about to lose this game of psychological warfare. From that day forward, I knew he wasn't really my friend.

My relationship with Jewel progressed when she moved in with me on Christmas Day. It didn't escape me that she only moved in because of my steady supply of narcotics. I could relate to that. I didn't love her or have any sincere feelings for her, but I called her my girlfriend. She was simply a means to an end. When people saw her with me, it took some light off the tragedy that was my life.

Night after night, Jewel watched me kill myself slowly, and she did absolutely nothing to stop it. We lied to each other constantly about where we were and what we were doing. We told one another we loved each other even though we were incapable of such an emotion. But she held me while I suffered, and in return she got to stay high. If it hadn't been for the cocaine, we wouldn't have been together at all.

It often crossed my mind to wonder what she thought when she looked at me. No doubt she was disgusted with herself. But she always lied to make me feel better, telling me I was sexy even though I could barely control my bowels. I was a wreck. Nobody could have been in love with me.

Jewel couldn't have picked a better time to leave Donnie's. A week later, right after pulling in a massive New Year's weekend, I got a call that completely changed my life. Tommy phoned me and said the words that I'd prayed I would never hear: "Sh*t has gone down in Chinatown!"

It was code. The police were raiding his house.

As soon as I hung up, I tore through my house, grabbing anything that had to do with my illicit activities. Cell phones, SIM cards, debt books, surveillance footage, bug detectors, cocaine books, bags, scales, pipes, smell-proof bags, weapons, ammunition, guns, bulletproof vests, cash, police radios, pictures, car keys, walkie-talkies, licence plates, and anything else that could possibly incriminate me.

I'd be lying if I said I wasn't a jittering wreck as I walked out of the house carrying everything in a bag. It was enough damning evidence to put me away for ten years. Up until now, I hadn't even realized how much I had.

I drove everything to a friend's empty house and stashed it away in the basement ducts. Not even he knew it was there. At least this would keep it safe. I then proceeded to go with Jewel to Tommy's house downtown.

As we pulled into the neighbourhood, I noticed the police helicopter hovering above us. Jewel didn't want to go near the house, but I insisted we check it out. I figured we would just look like civilian observers.

There were police cruisers stationed at every entrance to the neighbourhood. When we pulled onto Tommy's street, we came up to a massive tactical vehicle. It resembled a tank. I could see from where we'd parked that the cops were lined up beside his place in SWAT gear, getting ready to kick in the door.

It wouldn't have been a good idea to go back to my house, so I called an old friend of mine and asked if Jewel and I could stay with him for a couple of days until things calmed down. He was happy to oblige.

As I lay in bed holding my girlfriend, emotionally exhausted, I couldn't help but think of the ramifications. Donnie was my supplier, and I was his biggest runner by a long shot. I thought about the cops going through his things. I knew exactly what they would find: a drug superstore, with guns and ammo for a cherry on top. He didn't have a safehouse like me.

The most damning thing they'd find pertaining to me was his debt book, which included the name Reckless Rick. If cops hadn't had a reason to take me down before, they would have a million reasons now.

Although I was worried for my friends, my paramount concern was how I was going to satisfy my drug addiction. I needed to shut everything down, or almost certainly go to jail. I would have to get more resourceful. I just needed to do some cocaine to help me devise a new strategy.

Chapter Eighty-Two

DIVERSE CRIMINALITY

I waited approximately one week before going back to my house. My roommate was rather confused by my absence, but I reassured her by explaining that I just needed to go out of town. There was no sense in telling her the truth and getting her upset for no reason.

When Jewel and I returned, the house was intact and the cops hadn't raided. So far I was in the clear.

As for maintaining my addiction, I got lucky. I had a really good connection with a chop shop, so I focused my attention on how I could fill it up with vehicles. They agreed to pay me on delivery, so it was well worth putting in my greatest effort.

Cody Bates didn't do anything halfway.

I worked with a buddy to clear out compounds full of vehicles in a single night. We spent hours grinding our way through razor wire fences and covering our heads with blankets to prevent the grinder's sparks from drawing attention to ourselves. We moved gigantic cinder blocks out of the way, clearing the path to unload a long line of stolen trucks. I picked out all the vehicles I wanted, putting on U.S. license plates and then tracking down their keys. I chose the ones that didn't have trackers and would pull in the biggest profit.

We usually took ten vehicles at a time, driving them to parking lots throughout the south side of the city and leaving them there for a few days. The reason? In case any of them had trackers, I wanted the cops to pick them up quickly instead of risking the chop shop itself due to our own impatience. After three days of waiting, we'd go back and get them, taking them to a ranch outside the city where they'd be re-sold. Then we'd get anywhere from $10,000 to $25,000 per unit. Not bad for a single night's work.

I also had a hell of a time on buy-and-sell websites. Most sellers would include their address on their ads, so I could find them on Google Earth and creep the scene from the comfort of my office to see if there was a potential payday. We scoped out a lot of crotch-rocket motorcycles in older neighbourhoods where the garages were most likely to have separate entrances. We would force open the doors with crowbars, jump on the bikes, and be gone in ten seconds. I stole an abundance of bikes because of how simple it was.

But our prime targets were speedboats and motorhomes. My buddy and I would find something we liked on the internet, then find an old diesel truck in an adjacent neighbourhood that could be easily hotwired. First we'd get the truck, which usually took less than thirty seconds, especially if it was older than 2008.

Next we called the seller of the boat or motorhome—from a burner phone, of course—and asked what kind of hitch we needed. They'd tell us, we'd find a truck with the appropriate hitch, and then head over.

The first time I tried to steal a boat, it was a disaster. My partner knocked away the blocks holding it in place, thinking we would be able to control the heavy boat. We couldn't. It started rolling down the street at three in the morning. At the last possible second, I managed to prop myself against a curb and stop it. I blew my back out and could barely stand up as I guided the boat onto the hitch of the truck. When it was finally attached, I dove into the back seat in more physical pain than I'd ever been in. We drove straight out of town, heading for the British Columbia border. It was imperative that we got out of Alberta before the sun rose because that's when the boat would be reported stolen.

A stolen boat paid out about $10,000 per unit. It was just about the easiest ten grand you could ever make. We got paid on delivery, then went out for a night on the town.

Money came and went so easily that we regularly got on a plane home the next day broke. Drugs and strippers were always to blame. We threw the money away because we knew we could just as easily get up the next day and do the same thing all over again.

Anything I wanted, I took. At one point, my partner and I even planned on stealing two helicopters, with a buyer lined up overseas who was willing to pay $300,000 apiece. But the more research we did, the more unlikely it looked that we could get away with it. Despite our countless hours learning to fly helicopters through YouTube videos, the idea of actually taking flight didn't seem realistic. The greatest problem with stealing helicopters was that every single component was serialized, including insignificant parts such as cables. After about a month of planning and researching, we gave up.

For the most part, I just woke up every day and decided how much money I wanted to make. I had no concerns, cares, or worries. Everything I did was deceptive, manipulative, and illegal.

But it sustained my addiction.

Chapter Eighty-Three

BROKEN EXPRESSIONS

With Donnie in prison, my partying took a new direction. Although I kept using an abundance of cocaine, I also heavily consumed other drugs such as molly, ketamine, crystal meth, and most of all GHB.

I loved GHB because of the uncompromising pleasure blasts it delivered. It would bring you right to the edge, then reel you back in for another rush of bliss. The only problem with GHB stemmed from the product's variable quality. Good G would get a person high as a kite with a single bottle cap full. Two bottle caps was too much. It would be too easy to kill yourself if the quality varied. Also, sometimes it took a while to kick in, so if you were impatient you might think you needed more. Big mistake. If only I could moderate it, I could have the greatest time ever. I regularly did the drug with people I didn't know from a hole in the ground, becoming best buds by the end of a night.

The other incentive was that it was so incredibly cheap for me. Because I bought it in bulk, a one-litre bottle only cost me $200. One cap would make your night incredible, and a full litre easily produced 150 caps, so I would pump them out for free to everyone all day long.

One day, while partying with some friends at my place, two friends and I got into the hot tub and bumped up the stereo. After taking GHB, we started getting rowdy, dancing and wrestling to the beat of the music as we let the date rape drug take us away. The last thing I remembered that night was laughing uncontrollably.

Suddenly, I felt cold. Why was I so cold? As I opened my eyes, the realization set in that I wasn't where I was supposed to be. I was looking at the ceiling in my living room, suffering a splitting headache. As I looked around, I noticed that my two friends were sitting at my kitchen table in silence, staring at the floor. An eerie feeling had fallen over the house. I stood up, walked to the table, and asked them what had happened. When they both looked at me, I could tell something was seriously wrong.

All three of us had passed out in the hot tub. I laughed at the thought that we could have all drowned, but fortunately our heads had stayed above water somehow.

Finally, one of my friends did go under; he took three or four gulps of water before waking up and pulling me and my other friend out of the tub. He dragged us into the house without either of us regaining consciousness. Apparently one of the reasons my head hurt so bad was that he'd dropped me at one point, my head smacking against the corner of the tub.

I could tell that my friends felt awkward when I excitedly told people about our close encounter with death. I can honestly say not a single person thought this story was as funny as I did. But death didn't scare me. I embraced the idea of ending my existence. There wasn't a drug I wouldn't try or a crime I wouldn't commit. I was the quintessential junkie.

This fact became even more obvious when I woke up one morning after a day six psychotic break and decided this was the day I was going to try heroin. I figured anything had to be cheaper than my cocaine habit, and I honestly didn't know how much more of these psychotic breaks I could take. Maybe heroin would provide the relief I so desperately desired. I found myself scratching my head that I hadn't tried it sooner.

I was already using needles daily, so this wasn't a dramatic step up—or down, however you want to look at it.

I remember telling Jewel that I was going out. She seemed confused since it wasn't like me to wake up after a day six terror with so much pep in my step. She looked almost worried as I kissed her goodbye. She later disclosed to me that she'd had a strange feeling she was never going to see me again.

When my dealer met me at my car, she pulled out the one-gram bag and dropped it into my hand. I passed her some cash in return. It had been a while since I had been on the other end of a drug deal. I stared at the bag intently, examining it. She asked if I had done heroin before.

"Nope," I replied. "I'm going to try it right now."

She seemed shocked. I expected that she would try convincing me to only do a tiny bit my first time. But I wasn't about to listen to some hogwash about how dangerous heroin could be.

It's heroin, I thought. *I get it.*

I strolled nonchalantly into the gas station where we were parked and politely asked the attendant where the washroom was. Once inside with the door closed, I pulled out the bag and looked at it closely. It was dark brown, very glossy, and in the form of a solid rock. I had seen it in prison many times, but this stuff looked different. It looked better.

I dropped about half of it onto the spoon and hesitated for a second. My thoughts rang loud and clear as I dumped the rest of the bag into the spoon. My tolerance for narcotics was unreal. I then added some water and quickly discovered the difference between shooting cocaine and heroin. Heroin didn't dissolve in water; you needed to cook it. So I lit my lighter and watched the brown rocks quickly dissolve into the liquid.

My heart was racing, but I wasn't nervous. Excitement gripped me as I watched the syringe fill to the top.

I sat on the toilet and cut off the circulation in my arm. The needle felt good, and I hit the vein on the first try. I took a deep breath, slowly emptying the whole thing into my arm.

I stood up, hoping to feel the heat blast all at once.

Something was happening, but it was nothing crazy. I relaxed and looked in the mirror, watching my pupils dilate. I gathered myself, put the empty spoon and syringe in my pocket, popped the door open, and walked out. As soon as I exited, I noticed a woman giving me a weird look. What was her problem?

That's the last thing I remember.

I've read a lot about different people's experiences with near-death, coupled with my own. Sometimes people see a bright light. Others see fire or total darkness. Me, I didn't see anything. It didn't feel as if I was in a dream, and I didn't sense any time lapse. One second I was falling to the floor, the next my eyes snapped open. It was ten minutes later and I was in an ambulance.

"He's back," I heard a paramedic scream.

I looked down and all my clothes had been cut off me. I knew I had overdosed again. I could hear sirens and all sorts of people in uniforms were plugging tubes into me and hooking me up to machines. The first thing that crossed my mind was that I might be going to jail for something. I almost lost my breath at the thought of not being able to get high while in prison; for a moment, I lost sight of the fact that I had just flatlined. Thoughts of escape swarmed in my mind; it was as if I'd kicked a beehive loose and now its denizens were wreaking mayhem. I couldn't go to jail! I had to get out of there.

In a moment, I was on my feet, dragging and ripping the machines off me. I screamed and swung wildly as the stunned paramedics scrambled to stop me from hurting them or the expensive equipment I was attached to. They quickly subdued me, baffled as they explained that they were trying to save my life. My eyes were wide with fear and incomprehension.

"What are you doing?" an EMS yelled in my ear. "We're trying to help you, Cody!"

Tears streamed down my face as the struggle left me. I felt so empty. Why had they needed to bring me back to life? I didn't want this.

If it was possible to will yourself to death, I would have done so in a moment. I just wanted to escape, to end this somehow.

As they strapped me into the gurney, I lay my head back and sobbed uncontrollably. I closed my eyes and tried to feel the heroin in my veins, desperate for even the smallest pittance of bliss.

I couldn't feel it. It wasn't there.

Anguish washed over me. Whatever they'd given me to bring me back to life had robbed me of my escape. I felt sorrow at the prospect that I wasn't going to get high that evening. When would my suffering end?

The paramedics asked the police not to charge me with assault from my attempted escape. I think everyone in that ambulance knew that they were looking at a very lost and damaged young man. It reminded me of the day when I had given my stool presentation alongside Aaron, back at the treatment centre when I was sixteen. The people in that room had looked at me the same way. I was once again that devastated child who didn't know what to do or where to go.

These paramedics hurt for me, felt sorry for me. But that's how everyone looked at me these days. Even the people who came to see me in the coming days, old runners bringing by enough cocaine to sustain me, looked at me with broken expressions.

Shortly after that, I spoke to a friend who had much more experience with heroin. When I told him how much I had taken, his jaw hit the floor. He explained to me that I had taken fifty times more heroin than he'd taken the last time he'd been hospitalized from an overdose.

It didn't make sense to anyone how I was still alive.

Chapter Eighty-Four

COCAINE COWBOYS

There was an itch inside me that hadn't been satisfied in a while. Stealing millions of dollars' worth of property had been fun, but it wasn't me. I'd been wearing a mask that didn't quite fit. I needed to get back to being me.

I held a meeting at my house with some select individuals who I'd hand-picked to help start up my new empire. Much as Doc used to do, I spoke to them without saying a word for the first little bit, my head bobbing to the rhythm coming out of stereo, gauging them through my dark sunglasses. I nodded and smiled, grinned and winced. I'd learned how to silently tell people different things at the same time with simple motions and expressions.

Feeling like I was back in my element, I had everyone seated on fine leather couches, surrounded by big-screen TVs and surveillance monitors. Cocaine covered the glass table in the middle of the room, along with guns, ammunition, and counter-surveillance equipment. I also had a laptop computer set up in front of every seat, solely to give these people the illusion of importance. I made every single person in that room feel like a boss. When they looked around, they saw opportunity.

Everything about this setup was designed to coerce. I watched everyone partake of my cocaine buffet and knew that it was working.

I had invited eight people, including Jewel, and everyone was bonding as expected. They would all serve a different purpose to me. Some were drivers, others were builders, and one was meant to run everything for me so I could keep my hands clean.

I asked a girl to kill the music so we could move the meeting along. A drawing board was nailed to the wall with the layout of the intended operation. With marker in hand, I began my pitch. I anticipated a simple client list of about 1,500 customers, all individuals I knew personally. This customer base would receive mass texts letting them know they had been handpicked to be part of a specially organized party favour program. The phones would be split into two of the city's four quadrants—southeast and southwest. People would call the phone designated to the quadrant they were currently partying in. All the clients would receive regular shoutout specials to keep the business going.

I explained that I would personally run both phones every Wednesday so that I had the chance to break bread with all the new clients and show my face to long-standing customers.

I then went over the shifts and how the hours and pay would work. I decided not to go with the same payment plan I had created the year prior. I had now developed a much more team-friendly structure that encouraged growth and unity. They would still be paid based on sales, but instead of being cashed out nightly as individuals, they would be paid every Sunday afternoon from an accumulated pot according to their percentage. Everyone would be paid based on what they brought to the table.

On top of the weekly pot, I created a bonus program for my runners that allowed me to quantify their individual efforts. The program would see them making piles of extra cash by surpassing targets for adding clients to the phones. The bonuses would include cocaine, money, and if they impressed me I would buy them a brand-name tracksuit.

I also had another bonus in place. If certain sales targets were broken by the last Sunday of the month, I would shut the operation down and take everyone to Banff for the night, all expenses paid. If there was one thing I'd learned from the car industry, it was that the most successful operations were built on incentives.

My friend Dean would be part of this, along with his friend Lenny. They were a couple of country boys with zero fear. What they lacked in the hustling department they sure made up for in sheer guts. They also worked full-time legit jobs on the side, so I had to customize shifts to their needs in order to have them on my team. They listened and were the most teachable workers I had. And if the cops saw them drive by, no one ever looked twice. They looked like they belonged on the farm, chucking hay bales.

As I wrapped up the meeting, I gave everyone their aliases. This was always my favourite part when it came to new hires. As I went around the room assigning handles, my disciples all nodded with excitement, in part due to the stupid amount of cocaine they were doing.

After that, I informed them that we were going to be working for an organization. It had been a long time since I'd been part of a gang, but my new supplier was a member of a notorious biker gang—and this meant we would be, too.

As the meeting drew to a conclusion, I shed the sweater I was wearing to reveal to my new runners the fresh-pressed T-shirt with the signature gang colours and skull. The seams of my bulletproof vest could be seen protruding through the shirt, and my various lengthy chains dangled in front. Everyone in the room nodded in discernment.

Donnie had been arrested two months ago. Since then, my life had been nothing but chaos. This was what I needed to finally ground myself again, although working with a biker gang hadn't been my first choice. Bikers were generally bullies who liked to think everything was theirs. They didn't have a large presence in the Alberta prison system because they worked smart and stayed under the radar.

Also, they frowned on heavy drug use. It wasn't like Donnie at all. I did the math and discovered that if I wasn't snorting $9,000 worth of drugs every six days, I would be making $30,000 in profit during that timeframe. Because I was a cocaine user, I was to be an outsider in my new gang. I didn't want to be part of a criminal organization, but it was a means to an end.

I wrapped up my meeting by introducing myself by my new name. Reckless Rick had to be retired now that Donnie was out of the picture. According to the text I sent out to all my old clients, Reckless Rick had left the country and become a family man; his brother Kane was now taking over the empire. I got back hundreds of texts with sad faces and farewells for Reckless Rick. Apparently he had made quite the splash. People were genuinely upset at the prospect of never seeing him again.

I find it amusing that each name I've carried went on to become infamous in the Calgary underworld. Cody Bates, Reckless Rick, and Big Kane were all prominent figures in the city's drug scene.

Cody Bates gained notoriety over the years as a killer, gangster, sociopath, maximum security inmate, and large-scale cocaine trafficker. He had entered the scene at a young age and became infamous.

Reckless Rick burst into the southside narcotics trade out of nowhere, completely taking over in order to become the boss of a sophisticated operation with some of the highest-level small-sale distribution networks the city had ever seen. He was charming, charismatic, and excellent at networking.

Big Kane came last and was to be one of the scariest individuals a person could ever meet. His eyes were the sort of thing nightmares were made of—if you happened to be around when he dropped his sunglasses off the bridge of his nose. He was Jewel's unfaithful boyfriend and had no regard for life. His voice had been almost extinguished from the copious amounts of cocaine he'd consumed.

All three men were cocaine cowboys. While most people in the underworld have heard all three names, hardly anyone figured out that all three were one and the same.

Chapter Eighty-Five

SLOW DEATH

As I heard a light knock at my back door, an unpleasant feeling washed over me, comparable to the emotions you feel when your alarm clock buzzes bright and early after a long night of partying. Who the hell was at my door at this ungodly hour?

I dropped my feet over the edge of the bed and they landed on a loaded Ruger on the carpet. Fortunately the safety was on! While staring at the weapon, I heard a second authoritative knock. I knew a cop knock when I heard one. Instead of answering, I counted the hollow-point shells through the transparent extended clip.

I pulled a towel over the gun, put some sweatpants on, then walked over to my private bathroom. On the floor were countless pinched cigarette filters, remnants of my night of shooting cocaine. How did Jewel put up with me? I looked at myself in the mirror, registering the fact that I hadn't slept in days.

After a third knock—more of a "wake up now" bang at this point—I put some sunglasses on and walked downstairs to see what the police wanted. As my feet landed on the kitchen's hardwood floor, I glanced at the clock: 7:00 a.m. Several of my runners were in the house, too, pretending to sleep to avoid having to answer the door—just like my girlfriend upstairs. They were no doubt high out of their minds from the night before, on my dollar. I laughed to myself as I was reminded why I was the boss.

As I approached the back door, my assumption was proved correct: a uniformed police officer stood there. I opened the door, plastering a smile across my empty face.

"How you doing this morning, Cody?" he asked in a surprisingly friendly tone.

I intuitively knew they weren't here to make an arrest. "The birds are chirping and it's beautiful outside. How could this morning get any better?"

The last thing I wanted to do was talk to the police right now.

"Don't suppose you know anything about this stolen truck we found in your backyard?"

I glanced over and looked at the truck he was referring to. A couple of other officers were standing beside it, one of them in plainclothes. The brand-new half-ton truck had been draped with a cover, so they must have come into the yard and uncovered it to get the vehicle identification number. It was worth about $60,000.

"I was wondering where that came from," I said. "I was going to take a look at it today. Thought maybe a friend parked it there."

"Well, it's been reported stolen so we have to take it."

This officer was being awfully nice about the situation. I walked off the back deck with him and approached the truck, nodding at the other officers. The one in plainclothes explained that he was their district supervisor. I could tell he was lying. He was obviously a detective, and detectives didn't get called in to clean up recovered stolen property. But when he said his name, I memory-banked it so I could find out who the guy was later.

I caught the detective off-guard when I asked him for a business card so I could call him if any other suspicious vehicles showed up on my property. He fake-patted his pockets for a card, then politely asked one of the other uniformed cops to give me theirs, which was promptly handed to me. I thanked them for keeping the community safe, then walked back into my house, swearing silently to myself.

I hated having to deal with cops first thing in the morning, but it had been an interesting interaction—one I would have to ponder after I sniffed a couple piles to get my day going.

As I walk into Walmart later that day, it didn't escape my notice that the greeter was greatly taken aback by my question about where I could find the arts and crafts section.

I lowered my sunglasses, flashing my teeth. "What? Don't I look like a guy that enjoys arts and crafts?"

She almost reluctantly pointed me in the right direction. I quickly acquired the items I needed and paid for them at the front. I then skipped over to the coffee shop and bought ten coffees, twenty sausage English muffins, and twenty hashbrowns. I wanted to get back home fully prepared.

On the way back, I watched carefully for a police tail.

At home again, I dropped the box with everyone's breakfast on the counter, walked over to the stereo in the living room, and blasted tunes at full volume. I smiled, a small sense of pleasure washing over me as everyone struggled to open their eyes. I then went around to all the rooms, waking everyone up and telling them to congregate at the kitchen table.

Once everyone was seated, I laughed and wished everyone a happy Easter.

"The reason you guys are up so early is that this weekend is Easter," I said. "So I want to do a Sunday special for $200 Easter balls. As you will find, there are several plastic eggs in which to insert cocaine, and I want you to decorate all the eggs with the crafts I purchased."

Everyone was laughing. Here was glue, glitter, crazy eyeballs, streamers, and about $50 worth of decorations they could use to dress up the eggs.

"I'll get a shoutout ready," I continued. "When it's done, I want Lenny to send it out to all the customers."

Once I was finished my charismatic sales pitch, I had Lenny take the phones to send out the shoutout. I then used an encrypted smartphone to email my supplier and arrange a meet. I was going to be short money again, a happening that was taking place more often than not lately. My monster addiction was partly to blame. The rest of the fault lay in how bad the product was. Half the time I debated whether there was any cocaine in it. This was a fry cry from Donnie's supply. But I was on credit and my new supplier didn't take too kindly to criticism of his awful product. That's just the way these bikers were; they figured everyone was stupid and didn't know they were pushing garbage.

My customers, however, were used to the best blow money could buy, and I'd lost most of them after their first purchase. I had rebuilt by adding new people who didn't have the old product to compare it to, who didn't know the new product was so inferior.

My business had dropped down to about ten percent of what it had been with Donnie and I was falling into more and more debt with people who didn't care about anything. They were regularly threatening me with violence and various forms of body-part-collecting if the debt wasn't paid soon. Because I felt it was my own fault, I just took the abuse. I was ashamed that I couldn't pay my debts.

As I jumped into the big guy's vehicle, I noticed the blood spatter on the passenger window. It was a ploy. He was doing exactly what I did; planting thoughts in people's heads was a way of life for him. I passed him an envelope that was light on cash, the second in two days. The exchange was followed by the usual lecture and threats I'd become accustomed to. Trying to convince this man that I wasn't a drug addict was becoming a full-time job in itself. He started referring to what I'd built as "ours" and said that I belonged to "the Club." It was disgusting. But that's what you have to expect when you deal with bikers.

I just assumed it was all a bluff, since I knew these guys never got any kind of police attention. If they were actually cutting fingers off and hurting people, the cops would have taken them out a long time ago. I bobbed my head, the abuse coming in waves. Then we said goodbye—at least until the next time I was forced to jump into his truck short money, which we both knew would happen.

I was excited to get home and I retreat into my office to be by myself. Jewel and the others knew how bad my addiction was, but I tried to keep it out of their sight. After all, the phones were bumping and everyone was out making money to help fuel my slow death.

I locked myself in the office and proceeded to the locked desk drawer which contained my crack pipe, spoons, baking soda, syringes, and some water. I cooked some cocaine into crack, as I'd done a thousand times before, then prepared a spoon to fill up a needle. This was followed by busting up powder cocaine into lines to freely use as I went through the rest of the process. My pain was overwhelming and my heart felt as if it would burst out of my chest.

Blowing out a massive breath, I leaned down to inhale again. I took back an inhuman amount of cocaine, and relief came almost instantly. But just as quick as it arrived, it disappeared. As always. The blissful escape from sniffing powder had gotten shorter and less intense over the years. Then again, maybe the high just disappeared because I knew I had a crack hoot and a full syringe waiting for me.

I grabbed the pipe and melted the crack into the ash. As I fluttered the choke and sucked as hard as I could, my ears filled with the beautiful ring I desired so much—the ring that snorting didn't provide. I blew it out and achieved victory as I lay my head back and let the crack sing to me. Its harmonic melody only lasted a few short minutes, but for those minutes the world stood still and Cody Bates was no more.

Then my skin came to life and the harsh cold of coming down consumed me like fire consumes gasoline. But I was prepared. Next, I slammed a needle into my arm and emptied the cocaine-fused water directly into my bloodstream. The taste hit my mouth, which was followed by an even louder ring than the crack provided.

This was the way I was forced to use cocaine now. I filled my nose, lungs, and veins to the brim day after day, never stopping until I hit my day six coma. My nose hardly worked anymore, and it was getting harder and harder to find an adequate vein.

My leafless forest screamed to life as I retreated deep into the woods of my psychosis.

Chapter Eighty-Six

DEAR DAD

As I drove through the familiar countryside, I took in the passing trees. It was the first time in a very long stretch that my mind hadn't been clouded by the consuming fog of cocaine. I'd been sober for twenty-four hours now and the emotional affliction, the torment, was overwhelming. The physical pain was intense, too, but it was but a small droplet of water in an ocean of grief, sorrow, and despair.

My will had been dissipating with each passing day, and my operation was suffering. The low-quality cocaine I'd been getting lately had all but ruined it. The new stuff was so low-grade it couldn't even be cooked. The bikers assumed that by cutting the product with numbing agents they got from a dental office, people would mistake it for a better high. What they hadn't considered was that although people got numb, they didn't get the same release of dopamine that cocaine bestowed on the brain; in fact, it was almost completely absent. It was quite literally the worst cocaine I'd ever tried in my life.

Unfortunately, that hadn't stopped me from craving it. Because the quality was lower now, I found myself selling less and doing a lot more. I desperately pounded as much as I could into my veins and up my nose, chasing the faint rush it gave me.

You were almost there, Cody, a voice seemed to whisper to me. *Just a little bit more next time.*

There may have only been a tiny amount of the drug in the mix, but it still led me to my day six psychotic break—a testament that the drug was definitely there. Psychosis was my constant companion. The sounds, voices, and faces I heard and saw had gradually grown to become a daily fixture in my existence.

I brought my attention back to the passing trees. They looked so peaceful, their leaves dancing in the wind. I would have given anything to be a tree... then again, I would have gladly traded lives with anyone or anything. I just hated being me.

I let my held tilt back against the headrest, my gaze falling on the road through my dark sunglasses. My head seemed almost too heavy to even hold up. As I extended my right arm toward the steering wheel, I felt the pulse on the inside of my arm. My sleeve covered up the damage I'd inflicted on myself with the constant needles. The previous morning, my day six demon had convinced me to inject a syringe full of bleach to try and quell my pain. He was reminding me of the life I had given up and his words always seemed to have the ring of truth.

"Aren't you sick of your pain, you worthless junkie?" the demon had demanded. "Do the world a favour. Is this the man you want your dad to call son? There is only one way out. Do it for your father."

I replayed these words as I drove, each word driving excruciating pain into my arm. I wondered if I might lose it. It seemed within the realm of possibility.

But the physical pain was of little concern to me.

Protruding out the sleeve of my shirt was an accessory I'd grown accustomed to over the past several months: a hospital wristband. I'd suffered yet another heart attack a few days prior and left the hospital without rest. My skin was yellow from my liver giving out and I was constantly defecating blood from stomach ulcers and pancreatitis. The heart attacks had become regular, too.

A blue ball of puss and bleach leaked from my arm, but I was more bothered by the condition of my hands. I stared at them with disgust. They were filthy, caked with dirt and grime, a permanent fixture along with my many track marks. These symptoms were all there to remind me that my day six devil wasn't lying: I was a junkie of the highest order, unable to stay sober even to save my own life. The awful things he told me made perfect sense, and that was the worst part. I couldn't take care of myself. I didn't brush my teeth or take showers. None of that mattered to me. I didn't care about family, friends, money, respect, food, the weather… nothing. Cocaine was everything.

I listened to music, barely paying attention to my girlfriend, who rode next to me in silence. I felt bad for her, but I knew why she stayed with me. She certainly wasn't with me for my dashing good looks; she just needed my unlimited supply of cocaine.

She had recently left me for a few days, having gone to stay with a friend of mine. She thought I didn't know where she'd gone, but I did. If I had been in the same state of mind I'd been in a year ago, they both would have been dead for their transgressions. But the truth was that I hated being alone. Her presence comforted me, so I'd led her to believe that I was naive enough to buy her stupid story of sleeping in her car for three days, crying about our deteriorating romance.

I understood why she had done it. She was trying to convince herself that she deserved better than me. We had a very toxic and painful relationship. Without her, I would be alone—and I couldn't stand to be alone with my own thoughts and demons.

The mountains grew bigger upon my approach to Turner Valley. I was infamous in this town, a tragic story of the rise and fall of someone with great potential. At one point I had been a beacon of hope, speaking at AA meetings and helping kids find light in a world of hopelessness. Now I was nothing but a cancer to everyone I came in contact with. I had destroyed every relationship in my life.

To me, the town itself was a reminder of my wreckage and destruction. My whole family lived here, most of whom I hadn't seen in years.

Fifteen minutes later, I pulled into my dad's property. My grief swelled as I contemplated my nefarious purpose. The plan I'd concocted made me want to beat my own teeth out of my head. I'd done an abundance of cocaine over the last week without selling anything, and now I'd dug a huge debt with my supplier. If I didn't pay up today, I was going to feel the repercussions.

The chop shop I'd been working with had recently been taken down in a police raid, so that cash faucet had run dry, and none of my other ventures could produce enough money quick enough. My phones could have made the money back in a matter of hours, but the bikers wouldn't reload me without cash in exchange.

So I needed to go back to my dad, to manipulate him to my own advantage.

If only the bleach I'd injected up my arm had killed me. Re-victimizing my father was only going to make me hate myself more.

I saw my dad by the barn, staring in question at the unfamiliar vehicle coming down his driveway. As I pulled up, I saw recognition flash across his face. His smile was quickly replaced by the realization that I likely wasn't here on a social call.

I sat still for a second, not moving. What I was about to do was going to hurt him beyond measure. I wanted to drive away, but I couldn't. I felt overwhelming despair as I stepped out of the truck and walked toward him, my eyes black, my cheeks sunken. I resembled a corpse.

Sorrow washed over him as he took in what was left of his only child. Tears came to his face as he stepped forward and wrapped his arms around me, squeezing me tight. I looked down, unable to bear it. I closed my eyes, feeling his hot tears against my own. I couldn't remember the last time someone had hugged me like this. For a second, I felt safe. My pain rose to the surface for the first time in years as I sobbed uncontrollably, my face pressed into my dad's chest.

Time stood still for a few seconds. In that moment, I wasn't a junkie. I wasn't a gangster or a killer or a sociopath or a drug-dealer. I wasn't Reckless Rick, Big Kane,

Hollywood, or anyone else. I wasn't Jewel's unfaithful boyfriend or my mother's abused son. With my dad's heartbeat ringing loudly in my ear, I became the only thing I was capable of being in that moment: daddy's little boy.

That afternoon, I told my dad everything. I didn't need to lie or embellish to get the desired reaction from him.

He was horrified, as intended, but I hadn't yet convinced him to give me the money I needed. He didn't think it would help.

Now I did tell a lie, implying what would happen to me if I fell short of the substantial payment due that evening to my supplier. I led my father to believe I was going to die, and Jewel backed this up.

Still, my efforts fell short. He still wouldn't give me the money. But I knew I was close, so I went for my trump card, my ace in the hole, the one thing I knew would crush my dad into obedience.

I rolled up my sleeves, showing him the damage I'd done to my arms.

I'll never forget my dad's expression as his gaze landed on my track marks. He turned away from me and cried. I had deployed upon him the worst of pain, the sort of pain no father would ever want to see on their only child.

My dad sobbed quietly in the silence. I had crushed him, holding the proverbial gun to his head. The unspoken message was this: *If you don't give me the money, you'll be sitting at my funeral by the end of the week, thinking you might have been able to save me.*

He finally gave in, went to the bank, and withdrew the full amount of what I needed. I told him a second lie to rationalize what I was doing. I told him I would try to get sober, but I knew there was no chance of that. I was as hopeless a drug addict as could be.

When my dad gave me the envelope, I thanked him and turned away. I could feel his tearful eyes plead silently with me as I walked away and sat in the vehicle with Jewel. As we drove away, I saw my dad standing in the road behind us. He looked so defeated. We were both thinking the same thing—that we were never going to see each other again.

On the ride home, I tried to convince Jewel that the tears were all a show. I even laughed about what had happened. But the truth was that I had never been more devastated in my entire life. I wanted to die for what I'd done to my father. If he hadn't given me the money that day, I likely would have gotten my butt kicked, but that punishment would've paled in comparison to spending another night sober.

I wanted this to be over.

But I'd worry about that later. For now, I could get more cocaine and quell my addiction for a little while longer. With any luck, I'd never come down again.

Chapter Eighty-Seven

MOVING DAY

"Cody Bates, we need you to wake up and come downstairs."

I didn't sleep often, but the authoritative voice that filled my bedroom at 6:00 a.m. told me I had picked the wrong day. I assumed that I'd find police officers standing in my doorway, and this was immediately confirmed when I opened my eyes: my house had been raided.

I had in the house about $20,000 worth of cocaine, an office full of evidence that would prove the existence of my drug trafficking ring, cash, and two loaded guns in the closet with body armour and a kill kit right beside it. Oddly, I didn't have a gun in arm's reach, as I usually did.

I sat up in bed, groggily assessing my room while the impatient police officers stared intently in my direction. To my left, about a hundred empty bags of cocaine sat atop my dresser, a common decoration in my house. They piled up faster than I could dispose of them. The officers looked at the mess in disbelief. They must have thought I never cleaned up, but little did they know that these bags were the result of just a couple of days of personal use.

I reluctantly put some clothes on and proceeded to the door. The waiting officers followed me out. In the hallway, I passed an officer standing in the entry to my office, no doubt protecting the mountain of evidence inside. The police would find so much evidence in there: surveillance equipment, countless phones, copious empty bags with the corners cut, frequency jammers, bug detectors, scales, and debt books. It was enough to take my breath away.

Even more officers adorned the doors to my bathroom and spare bedroom. Obviously they had taken up strategic positions, funnelling me downstairs to the living room.

As I approached the bottom of the stairs, I noticed eight of my runners sitting quietly on the couches. Most appeared to still be high from a night of partying. Every single one of them stared at their laps.

There were about twenty officers in the house, all watching me intently. Outside, the street was littered with police and other emergency vehicles. It crossed my mind that it was odd an ambulance had attended the raid, too.

The officers directed us toward the back of the house.

"Hey Rick," one of the officers said to me, no doubt trying to get a reaction out of me. I didn't even bat an eye.

Once my runners and I had been filtered into the back lounge, the men were placed in handcuffs and women were lowered to the floor.

"What's going on?" I asked the police officer cuffing me.

His response took a second to sink in. "One of your friends overdosed. An emergency medical call was placed."

It turned out the police had only attended the call because they knew I lived here. My chest began to heave as I glared angrily at my runners. One of them had brought this down on me, and no one had even considered waking me up. I was furious.

Then it occurred to me that the police had no grounds to search my house, because it technically wasn't a raid. The police could look at all this damning evidence, but they couldn't touch it. Even a half-decent lawyer would be able to save me from any illegal search and seizure today. That gave me a boost of confidence.

My runner was going to be okay, too. The paramedics had arrived in time to save him and prevent any major damage from taking hold.

But I still had a warrant for my arrest, as did all the other men in my house, which explained the cuffs.

The police escorted me out the front door where red and blue lights polluted the morning sky. They clearly weren't taking any risks. They put each of us in a different police cruiser to await the trip downtown to be processed.

It had been a while since I'd sat in a police car. As I tried to make myself comfortable, I took solace in knowing that my warrant would be the only thing holding me rather than a plethora of new charges. I watched through the windows as the cops walked around inside my house. Likely they were planting bugs or other types of surveillance. No doubt they would capitalize on this medical call. But I had counter-surveillance equipment to deal with that. I'd worry about it later.

My mind raced, fighting off the fog of narcotics from the previous night. It dawned on me that I might not be released from holding. For a split second, relief swept over me. Maybe this would all come to an end. With me behind bars, I could get sober for the first time in years.

As quickly as the relief came, it dissipated, replaced by consuming anxiety at the thought of coming down. I couldn't be sober. That wasn't an option for me. Sweat pooled in my palms at the thought.

An officer knocked on the window to signal the officer processing me to come out and have a private conversation with him. They stepped about ten feet from the car and whispered to themselves. It felt like déjà vu.

When the officers returned, they opened my door and asked me to step out and turn around. They unlocked my cuffs and told me they were just going to issue me a notice, with a promise to appear at a court date. Just like that, I was cut loose. I asked about my friends, but apparently my warrant was the only one minor enough to sanction such mercy.

Three words rang loud and clear as I walked back into my house: Do Not Detain.

After all the police had left, I went to my office, pulled a mound of cocaine out of my safe, and proceeded to quell my anxiety. I did a few lines, then sat on the couch and looked around the office. No doubt they had put bugs in here.

As always, I had an escape plan. I had recently rented a second-floor condo and could move into it in a single day with the help of all the people I had working for me. There wasn't any point in staying here any longer with this kind of heat.

I immediately got on the phone and arranged trucks to move all my things.

The rest of the day was spent packing up the house with the help of ten people. I got everybody nice and high so they would work hard to get the job done. Somehow I managed to pull a rabbit out of my hat and by the evening I was sitting in my new condo watching my new surroundings through a fifty-two-inch surveillance monitor.

My new place was perfect. It was a corner unit on the back side of the building facing the road. The entrance was at ground level and could be easily barricaded. Because it was a corner unit, my balcony provided the perfect unobstructed view of the area. I had one of my runners, an electrician, set up the surveillance cameras so I could see everything from my couch. A loaded gun sat on the ottoman in front of me. I also had six phones nearby, connecting me to counter-surveillance measures and my money train. Cocaine was littered about, easily accessible for my thirsty nostrils.

This house was going to work just fine.

While my people set up the furniture, electronics, and décor, my eyes remained glued to the cameras. My paranoia made me feel like the cops would come kicking down the door the second I looked away.

As I stared intently at the monitors, one thing was top of mind: one day soon this was all going to come crashing down, and the odds of me living through it were almost non-existent. But I was okay with that. I needed peace and just couldn't keep living like this.

Chapter Eighty-Eight

TWO-TIMING

Jewel was my small shimmer of light in a world surrounded by darkness. We didn't leave the house much, but the loneliness inside me would be temporarily stabilized when I held her. I hated being alone; there was nothing more horrifying for me. I practically lived in a state of psychosis, so it gave me comfort to look at her while hearing all the awful screams and whispers and recognize that she couldn't hear them. When I was alone, I couldn't tell if they were real or not.

Business was steady and I watched my surveillance cameras from the moment I woke up until six days later when I passed out. Countless times per day, I unbarricaded the door so my runners could give me all the money my phones were bringing in, do a quick account, reload them with product, then send them on their way again.

Jewel and I mostly did cocaine together and watched TV. I would turn my head toward the TV, but my eyes never left the surveillance monitors. I may have had my arm around her, but I wasn't present. It was an awful way to live.

One night, while watching a movie on the couch with Jewel, my phone rang. It was my supplier. I answered in a jovial yet condescending tone; I got a small neurological release when I pissed him off.

Anyway, this wasn't a social call. The conversation started with him asking why I would hit a woman if I was such a tough guy. I had no idea where he was going with this since I had never laid a finger on a girl. As I dug deeper, he made accusations that made zero sense. This quite literally was coming out of nowhere.

Finally, he confessed that my girlfriend was texting him to say that I was abusing her. Two things were odd about this. First, how had she even gotten my supplier's number? Second, I'd been sitting with her on the couch all night watching movies, and had been laughing with her just two minutes prior. So why would she say such a thing?

He asked me to prove it by putting her on the phone. I passed her the phone with an angry expression on my face. I stood overtop her, listening as she nervously took the phone. After a couple of yeses and nos, she passed the phone back and I asked my supplier if he was satisfied.

Subsequently he apologized for his accusations, but that didn't put my suspicions to rest.

After hanging up, I found Jewel in the bedroom hurriedly packing her bags. When I asked what she was doing, she replied that she was leaving me. I was shocked. How had we gone from laughing on the couch to her packing her bags without saying a word? Obviously she was leaving because of something my supplier had said to her. I suspected they had eyes for each other, but I tried to convince myself it was just my paranoia and that she wouldn't do that to me.

As I pleaded with her not to leave, I was taken back by how cold she was. She hated me; that's the only way I could describe it. Her warm touch was gone, replaced by cruel intentions.

I couldn't blame her—in fact, I was surprised she had hung on this long—but I knew exactly where she was going. She couldn't wait to get out of my house.

It was sick and demented, but she was all I had. She was probably the only reason I was still alive. Without her, I would be alone with my demons. The thought was terrifying and she knew it. She even coldly pointed this out to me on her way out the door.

She kept saying I was a master manipulator. The things she was saying didn't make sense, and I suspected she was just stalling until her mom could get there to pick her up.

She called me out on my fake tears and kept saying that she deserved better. Well, she was right. I didn't love her.

Jewel left me that day without even saying goodbye. It hurt, but the truth was there were lots of girls out there who would lay around and do drugs with me, but that meant I would have to leave my house to find them.

No big deal, I told myself. *Since being with her, my operation has suffered. Now I can focus on being present and making money.*

Losing Jewel also came with an unexpected gift. When she moved out to be with my supplier, it removed my loyalty to him. I could finally break off and go my own way again, finding better-quality blow that my customers would actually appreciate. I had hated working for that guy, but I'd stuck around because I always paid my debts. Jewel gave me the perfect excuse to leave.

It hurt a bit, but I took solace in knowing that I didn't need to pay back my remaining debt, which was substantial. No way would I pay a guy who was sleeping with my girlfriend!

Chapter Eighty-Nine

NOT TODAY

The music and lights were low, and I wasn't comfortable or stable. I was used to living in psychosis, but without Jewel around to gauge her reactions to the sounds I heard I was terrified, not knowing what was real and what wasn't.

Down the hall, I had an unobstructed view of a dresser with a stereo on top of it—and between the wall and the stereo was a face. I took my sunglasses off so I could see if that would make it go away. It didn't. It had hideous glowing eyes, pearly white teeth, a fiery complexion, and a demonic smile. And it was taunting me.

I tried to convince myself it was all in my head. Whispers filled the air around me, making it hard to focus on the surveillance monitors. Was this some kind of ploy to get me to leave the condo and go into the hallway?

In every camera around the house, I saw orbs floating in the screens. I'd heard such orbs were spiritual in nature, and I couldn't help but believe it. I looked into the surveillance monitor of the couch, where I was sitting, and saw the orbs floating all around me. But when I turned my head toward them, I saw nothing there. I would rather have faced a police raid than face this. I needed to get out of there.

I strapped on my bulletproof vest and covered it with a T-shirt. I had decided that my supplier's transgressions with Jewel were unforgivable. And there was a very real chance that the bikers would retaliate against me for walking out on my massive debt. I was risking violence every time I left my house. But I had to leave.

I grabbed my phones so my runners could get in touch with me, as well as some cash. I stuffed it into my satchel and slung it over my shoulder. I also stuffed a few thousand dollars' worth of bagged cocaine in my crotch, for when my runners needed a reload. Next, I took a small bottle of GHB to counterbalance the blow. I filled my necklace vial with about $1,000 of high-grade cocaine for myself, so I could do quick bumps off my hand.

Finally, I snatched my motorcycle keys and helmet and headed out the door.

The unfamiliar sun pounded off my face as I exited the condo. I hated the light. I had become a creature of darkness, so the sun was offensive to my pasty yellow skin. At least there was no one waiting outside as I headed to my crotch-rocket. If that gang was ever going to come to exact revenge, it wouldn't be today.

One advantage I had over them was that they didn't like attention, and they cared whether they ended up in jail or dead. I, on the other hand, didn't care. If they came after me, they would need to kill me. If not, I would retaliate by wrapping every one of their houses' in police tape. When I left, I'd taken a lot of money off their table, but I was a wild card and they wouldn't want to risk an assassination attempt or home invasion.

My psychosis kept me prepared at all times, prepared for anything, and it was next to impossible to catch me sleeping or not staring into my cameras. In fact, I was almost completely insane by this point.

As I rode my stolen crotch-rocket down the road, I felt relieved—not because I felt untouchable, but because driving through residential neighbourhoods, taking corners at a hundred fifty kilometres per hour, brought me out of psychosis and back into reality. Something about putting my life in peril, about almost skimming vehicles and blowing lights and stop signs, clicked my mind out of the spiritual realm. Since this was my only remedy, I found myself regularly speeding up to death's door.

There was actually one other thing that helped snap me back to the living: GHB, which I often took while bombing around on my motorcycle.

While heading down the Deerfoot Trail, Calgary's fastest and busiest thorough-fare, I started barking like a dog, trying to fight off the impending blackout. I lifted the visor on my helmet and let the wind beat off my face in a feeble attempt to sober myself up. It didn't work, and I soon found myself laying my head down, incapable of looking up at the road because of the speed I was going. The last thing I remember was a little boy around the age of seven looking at me questioningly through the back passenger window of a vehicle in the lane next to me. Then the lights went out.

When I opened my eyes, my head felt like it was splitting in half. The sun was beating down on my face, so I quickly shut my eyes again. My whole body felt crushed, the unmistakable effect of a GHB overdose. I had no idea how I'd gotten here. I wasn't on the Deerfoot Trail anymore; I was on the gas station lawn down the street from Doc's treatment centre. The busy roadway was bustling with afternoon traffic while my stolen bike lay on the ground beside me, still running.

I'd never been so confused in my life.

I struggled to get to my feet. How long had I been here? A quick glance at my phones told me that a lot of time had passed. I'd missed thirty text messages and twenty-four missed calls over four hours. I'd spent four hours on a gas station lawn with thousands of dollars of drugs, cash, a bulletproof vest, and a stolen bike. And I didn't have so much as a scratch on me.

It didn't seem possible. Neither death nor jail seemed to want me.

I turned off my bike and headed into the gas station bathroom. Locking the door behind me, I turned and looked at myself in the mirror. My eyes were as deep as caves. I looked awful and I couldn't stop heaving. My face was beat red and my eyes were more bloodshot than I'd ever seen them. I resembled a demon.

I gathered my thoughts by dumping massive heaps of cocaine onto my hand and snorting it in an attempt to bring me back to life. Before I left the bathroom, I added one more pollutant to my body: another cap of GHB. Clearly I wasn't supposed to die. If death wouldn't take me, no way was I going to come down. One day I'd give the spiritual realm no other option than to take me, but I guess it wouldn't be today.

Chapter Ninety

LOOMING TRAGEDY

Over the years, I'd become accustomed to seizing opportunities to further build my empire because my lifestyle was grossly expensive, teetering on unaffordable. My runners also had their own cocaine addictions that needed to be satisfied; if they weren't, these people would surely steal from me. However, I wasn't upset about their habits. Quite the opposite. I knew that their addictions were at least partially my fault. I couldn't stop, so I couldn't hold it against them either. As long as we were all working to keep business thriving, there was no quarrel.

I had long since lost any passion for making money, but I capitalized on business opportunities as they came up, such as the Calgary Stampede, music festivals, and my personal favourite: May long weekend open-site camping at Mclean Creek. This long weekend was a breeding ground for new customers. I'd leave half my runners in the city to run the phones and bring the other half with me to Mclean, where tens of thousands of outdoor enthusiasts were congregating. There were raves, campfires, four-by-fouring, and partying in the bush—and most everyone was from Calgary.

I assigned my runners to patrol the campsites in pairs, loaded with bags for sale and free samples. One runner would hold the dope for sale and the cash while the other networked with free samples. In cases where people wanted to buy, my runners would make the transaction from the bags on hand. He would never have more than a couple bags at a time; that way, if anything happened with the police he would only get slapped with a simple possession charge. Meanwhile, the other runner would hold all the cocaine and money and stay in the shadows. The second runner also carried a CB radio since there was no cell service out there. With the radio, they could contact me for reloads and cash drops.

However, there were many undercover police officers around. When my guys approached potential customers, they had to start by asking the group if they knew where to find cocaine and gauge their response. It was too dangerous to ask point-blank if a person wanted to buy cocaine, because some people would find that very offensive and maybe even call the cops. By starting out with this question, the offended person wouldn't know you were selling drugs; their response would tell you everything you needed to know. To weed out any undercovers who slipped through the cracks, all potential customers had to then try the free sample, witnessed by my runner. Cops couldn't actually do the cocaine.

I created a lucrative pay plan for my workers on these special occasions. For every ten customers they added, they could choose from a $200 cash bonus or two grams of high-grade cocaine. The program practically ran itself.

This year I even had a runner do all the reloading for me, so all I had to do was accept cash. I needed a backpack to hold it all. As my runners built my empire this particular long weekend, I socialized and networked to everyone I talked to. I was generous in giving out lines and did as much as my heart desired.

At some point in the weekend, though, I disappeared. I was doing lines of cocaine, ketamine, and molly all mixed together. I was also drinking like a fish, smoking weed and honey oil, doing acid and mushrooms, and taking a new drug I'd never even heard of before.

I completely lost my mind. I remember walking through the bush with my backpack of money and drugs, feeling higher than I'd ever been in my life. Each time my foot touched the ground, a sensation of heat washed up my body to the top of my head. I had never felt this way in my life, climaxing with each step I took. I never wanted to leave this place.

On the last day, my runners somehow found me lost in the woods. I resembled an animal, filthy from head to toe and barking like a dog. I didn't seem to have any control over my body, so I flailed in every direction as they led me to a waiting vehicle. I tried to communicate, but the only sounds I could make were barks.

As we drove away, I was scared we were going to hit a police checkstop, something that was quite likely since this was the end of May long weekend and it seemed as though at least a quarter of the city was coming back from camping and partying. I told my people that if we got pulled over, they should throw a blanket over me—not that it would have helped, since I couldn't stay still. I honestly don't know if a cop would have wanted to arrest me, thereby taking responsibility for me. All I could do was hope for the best.

When we got to my house, I couldn't stay still. I became more disconnected by the minute and my friends were at a loss. They finally resorted to the one thing that would put me out, guaranteed: GHB. I took more than enough that day to put me under, and after about twenty minutes I began to resemble a human being again. They put me in my bed and left the room.

Something wasn't right. I couldn't move. I could see, but I couldn't talk. My heart was beating loudly in my ears, but the beats were becoming further and further apart. My vision went completely black as my heart slowed to a stop, then somehow sped up again.

I was dying. I tried to call out for help, but it was useless; only faint gasps fell from my mouth. The downer effect of the GHB was interacting with four days' worth of stimulants, literally stopping my heart.

An indeterminate amount of time passed and many blackouts followed, my heart suddenly stimulating after each. Throughout this, I began to consciously accept that this was the end.

I couldn't move, but my mind kept working as if nothing was wrong. I thought about my dad. I had only seen him periodically through my tyranny. Tears streamed down my face as I thought his warm embrace. He deserved better than me. I hated myself for who I'd become—a monster at the best of times. For some reason, my psychosis had left me and I found clarity. My tears weren't a sign of regret; they affirmed my gratitude that my suffering was finally coming to an end.

But I couldn't explain why my heart kept starting again.

My runners came into the room after a while, all wearing expressions of sadness as they sat around my bed and checked my vitals. They had strict instructions from times past that they weren't supposed to call the cops if I died. There was too much damning evidence in the house—guns, drugs, stolen goods, surveillance footage, and drug trafficking paraphernalia. They were to clear the house before calling for help.

As they watched me with tears in their eyes, every person in the room rightfully assumed this was the end.

But it never came.

After a couple of hours, I came out of my paralysis and began to speak and walk around again. I immediately smoked crack and snorted more cocaine to alleviate my sadness. How had the devil not taken me yet? It didn't make sense.

I sat on the couch and went through the phones from the camping trip. Hundreds of new customers had been added. Then I counted all the money from the weekend. Despite the obvious hiccups, the event had been more than profitable.

Although this hadn't been the end, I knew in my heart that this couldn't last much longer. With any luck I'd die before the day six demon came back again—in two days.

Chapter Ninety-One

DIRTY BROKEN TOYS

When I came back from another GHB blackout, I heard low music playing in the background. This confirmed that I was still in my house.

Something metal was poking me in the face.

As I sat up and tried to shake off the fogginess, a scary realization set in. I was cuddling one of my own guns! I glanced around and saw a few of my runners sleeping on the adjacent couches. I thought it was strange that no one had thought to take the gun out of my hands. Ammunition was scattered about the floor, and I found the clip sitting amidst a pile of hollow-point bullets.

I examined the gun in my lap, my attention grabbed by the switched-off safety. When I opened the chamber, I almost lost my breath. Inside was a single bullet. I shook my head at how reckless I'd been. I was going to get someone killed if I didn't die soon.

That firearm had a hair-trigger, so I didn't know how it had failed to go off. Someone in my house should have died, most likely me.

I clicked the safety back on and placed the rifle on the ottoman. I began picking up all the bullets and plugging them back into the clip. Once again the gun was loaded and ready to use. Peace of mind always accompanied the sight of it within arm's reach.

Getting up, I walked toward my bedroom. When I opened the door, I found Jewel sitting on my bed doing lines and listening to music.

"Hey baby," she greeted me cheerfully.

Recently she had come back to me, having lied about leaving me for my old supplier. I knew she was being deceitful, as she had done before, but I accepted it because I hated being by myself.

I had seen a documentary that helped explain my feelings for Jewel. It was about a mission into the heart of Africa. The missionaries would go into an area and build houses for the poverty-stricken population, giving the people hope, love, and faith. While building the homes, the missionaries unearthed broken toys from generations past. They would put the toys in the garbage, because they were practically unusable after being buried for so many years, but the kids would retrieve the toys from the garbage and cradle them as though they were their most prized possessions.

It was very unsettling. My heart broke to see these children take the dirty, broken toys, fearful that someone was going to steal them. These toys were the only things the kids had—and that's what Jewel and I had become to each other. Dirty, broken toys. To anyone on the outside looking in, we were hopelessly lost. But in our world of tragedy, addiction, and chaos, we were all we had left. Letting go wasn't an option.

All of sudden, my doorbell started to ring. Ding ding ding ding ding ding ding ding ding. My first thought was that the police had come. As I strutted into the living room and glanced at the cameras, my blood ran cold. Facing the camera at the front door was my old supplier, filling the early morning air with screams and death threats.

Funny how the first time he showed up was right after my girlfriend came back to me.

Any lingering effects of psychosis left me as my adrenaline skyrocketed.

Jewel let out a gasp as she entered the room and saw the image on the monitor. Fear paralyzed her. My runners woke up, too, to the barrage of doorbell rings, looking intimidated. My old supplier was dressed in his gang colours and he was trying to get into the house by jiggling the doorknob.

Methodically, I walked to the cupboard in my living room that contained the guns and the safe. I put weapons in each of my runners' hands and directed them to take Jewel to the spare bedroom. I also gave instructions that they were only to use the guns if absolutely necessary, in the case I couldn't kill all the gang members before they reached the bedroom. After all, it wasn't likely this guy had come by himself. As they disappeared down the hallway, I sprang into action.

It didn't escape me that this was the time of day when home invasions and police raids were most likely to take place, to catch everyone off-guard; people more often than not could be caught in their beds sleeping. This guy had chosen this time because people wouldn't be up to witness him break into my place.

I slammed open the hallway closet and pulled out a stack of bath towels, then proceeded back to the kitchen counter. My dark purpose completely took over as I callously pondered where to place the towels. My plan was to hide in the living room cupboard. When they came up the stairs, they'd clear the living room and head to the bedrooms. As soon as they turned into the hallway, I would come out and shoot them all in the back of the heads, then grab the towel to catch the blood before it dripped through the floor into my neighbours' units. I would then get the bodies into the tub as quick as possible to drain them and figure out what to do next.

I took a look at the monitor and noticed that my old supplier was gone. Possibly he'd gone out to the car and would soon return with a whole bunch of guys. I grabbed my gun with the extended clip and crawled into the cupboard; it was rather large, so I could sit comfortably on my safe. I brought one of the surveillance monitors in with me so I could follow what was going on outside. On the screen I had views of each side of the house, the front door, the stairs coming up to my living room, and a clear shot of the living room and hallway. I would literally be able to see all their movements from the moment they approached the house until I put a bullet in the back of their heads.

Tremors shook my body as I struggled to control my rage. If they came into my house, where my girlfriend and friends were supposed to feel safe, where I was supposed to feel safe, I would kill every single one of them.

I watched the cameras intently with the gun gripped in my hand. I knew I was capable of the unthinkable. I didn't care about my life at all, so I may as well die protecting the people I loved.

I sat in that cupboard for hours waiting for the invasion to begin. From the piles of blow I was snorting, I got paranoid.

Finally, I stepped out and consoled my shaky girlfriend. She kept telling me that we couldn't keep living like this, that we needed to get clean. But I just couldn't bring myself to entertain that thought. How in the world could I get clean? It seemed impossible. I knew that my reign of tyranny was coming to an end, but none of the conceivable outcomes were going to be pretty. Tragedy loomed. Dark, uncompromising tragedy.

Jewel and I needed to get away from the house, though, so we headed out in my favourite vehicle—a re-plated, jacked-up diesel one-ton. I drew a lot of attention as I drove around in it, massive clouds of smoke bellowing behind me. I loved it. It was the closest thing I could get to driving a tank down the streets of Calgary. In it, I could outrun or outpower any police vehicle short of a helicopter.

The two of us fought about our lifestyle as I drove. She wanted to leave town, but I wanted stay and try exercising some self-control. Ironically, I said this while snorting bumps off my hand.

We pulled into a mall parking lot and continued bickering until I finally just told her to stay in the vehicle while I went and got myself a pair of shoes. I just needed a few minutes of space. Before I left, I pulled out a massive pile of blow and sniffed it all to the back of my head. Doing cocaine while I was angry was always a terrible idea, like somehow I was teaching Jewel a lesson by pushing myself to the brink of death. That would show her.

As I walked into the mall, I was high but feeling okay. My heartrate was up, but I thought anger was to blame. What a terrible day. I didn't think it could get any worse.

But while standing in a store looking at a pair of shoes, my eyes went wide in surprise from a sharp pain in my chest. Something was very wrong. I began to panic as I exited the store and tried to find a safe place to sit down.

I woke up with people gathered all around me. I could barely breathe. My heart was giving out again and everyone was upset, trying to get me to stay down. I attempted to get to my feet anyway. I had cocaine, cash, and a bulletproof vest on. I needed to get out of there.

But I went back under before I could get to my feet.

My distorted vision rang into focus the second time I came to. An even larger crowd had congregated around me this time. My breathing was erratic and I could feel my heart exploding out of my chest. My vest felt as if it was suffocating me. I glanced around helplessly at everyone's stares, feeling the need to get up. But I couldn't move. The last thing I remembered was one more feeble attempt to get up. That just induced another blackout.

When I come back to consciousness, I was on a gurney, again—in an ambulance, again. Police and paramedics were present. There were all kinds of tubes and IVs in me and my clothes had been cut off. The police had been called when the paramedics discovered that I'd been wearing a bulletproof vest, which I knew perfectly well was illegal.

I lay my head back and decided not to struggle. With the sirens blaring, all I could think about was how familiar this was. I was becoming accustomed to waking up in ambulances. I didn't need to look to know that I was cuffed to the stretcher. It was the second time I'd been in handcuffed in recent weeks. The last time had been for running into a drugstore at two in the morning to steal some needles. The police had witnessed my speeding vehicle and followed me in, subsequently arresting me for driving a stolen car with a stolen license plate. I spent a few hours in holding, passing the time by snorting the blow I'd had hidden in my crotch. They had released me on my own recognizance as soon as the sun came up. I couldn't help by wonder if my Do Not Detain order was still in effect.

With all these hospital trips, I wondered if the cops were questioning the information they were getting about me. A junkie of this calibre couldn't possibly be a cocaine kingpin, right? The new bulletproof vest charge wasn't about to help their perception of me.

To no surprise at all, I was released the next day on $1,000 bail, which I had on me in cash. So no problem there. When I walked into my house, Jewel greeted me. She had been sitting in my truck for hours, wondering what had happened to me, worried out of her mind.

This only validated her position in our argument. We needed to get out of town.

Chapter Ninety-Two

FATAL PROGNOSIS

Despite the cost to sustain my addiction, money came in steadily. Week after week, stacks of cash filled my table and safe. My runners did all the deliveries and worked the shift phones. I was almost exclusively attached to my couch, watching the cameras. The only time I got up was to get cash from my runners through the barricaded door, do a quick count, and then reload them.

The shoutouts I sent to my thousands of customers were always mixed with personal sales pitches. For the most part, everyone loved them. But the purpose behind the shoutouts was to keep my product relevant in everyone's minds. The stuff I was acquiring now was absolutely amazing. It was more expensive, but that also meant it was more profitable and easier to market.

Still, my operation wasn't what it used to be, because of my absence. My runners were good at following instructions, but they weren't hustlers like myself. They thrived when you put a ringing phone in their hands and directed them go from one stop to the next. On the rare occasion when I did go out, I networked and partied with everyone I met. I could add thirty people in a single night. Left to their own devices, my runners generally returned each evening having added two or three.

One night, I was out with Jewel working the phones. She was always blown away when watching me work, and my customers loved it when I was on the lines. I was always generous, so people loved introducing their friends to me. Lots of customers would only buy if I was on, so I'd do a shoutout on the phones to let everyone know that the boss was on the prowl. The phones would light up steady all night long.

Since I never slept, sometimes I'd work them for days. I knew how to keep people using into the late hours, watching throughout the night as they emptied their bank accounts into my pockets. "Just one more time," they would tell themselves. But for most people, that was a bald-faced lie, told to make themselves feel better. Generally people could only stop using because their drug-dealer quit answering the phone—when the sun was coming up. Not me. I was the man who never slept.

One Friday night, the lines were bustling with impatient customers. I had been working one of the shift phones since the evening before, and I had no intention of slowing down. When I caught that kind of momentum, I became a drug-dealing machine, procuring profits at an astonishing rate. I had Jewel returning the countless texts pouring in from the south side of the city while I induced my workers to deliver with the shortest wait times possible. These poor suffering customers needed cocaine.

As I pulled up in one of the deep south neighbourhoods that night, my foot suddenly began to tingle. At first it was more annoying than painful, possibly due to how much cocaine I had coursing through my body, but as I stepped out of the vehicle I realized that something was very wrong. I quickly trotted into my customer's house and rolled up my pants. My entire leg was swelling below the knee.

I didn't think much of it. After all, it was Friday night and there was money to be made.

By the time I walked back to my vehicle three minutes later, I was almost screaming in pain. I couldn't put any weight on the leg. Jewel had to help me into the passenger seat of the truck. I had several stops lined up near a hospital, so I decided to head in that direction in case I needed to visit the emergency room.

I had never felt pain like this before. I was writhing in it.

At the next stop, I had my customers help me into the house so I could assess the problem more thoroughly. I was almost in tears as my friends dropped me on the couch. One of the girls there turned out to be a nurse. She removed my shoe and sock and rolled up my pant leg, only to look up at me with a horrified expression. My leg and foot had swelled to three times the normal size. It was splitting, pussing, and bleeding now.

I slammed as much cocaine as I could, but it didn't work. I lay back on the couch, staring at the ceiling, and screamed in agony.

The other leg began to swell as well. What the hell was wrong with me? The nurse was almost in tears when I told her that I didn't want to go to the hospital. Her professional reaction—of dread—caused me to think twice. She said I might be dying, that without proper medical attention I might lose any chance of survival. The problem, as she explained, was that my heart wasn't pumping blood to my furthest extremities, and that could mean my heart was failing. When I informed her of all the heart problems I'd been having, she lost her mind and even threatened to call the police herself.

Her intense state of panic incited me to take her professional advice. I asked Jewel to call a couple of my workers and get them to meet us at the hospital. That way, we could pass them our work phones and the product I had on me. After all, the show must go on.

By the time we got to the hospital, I was in excruciating torment. I couldn't believe that a little lack of blood to the legs could hurt so badly. I had to be wheeled into the emergency room.

As soon as I got in to be treated, the doctors gave me morphine, soon followed by more morphine. I mentioned that my tolerance might be a little high.

They parked me on a hospital bed behind a closed curtain with Jewel. As I sat there, dumping cocaine on my hand from my necklace vial, she lowered her face into her hands and shook her head.

"I can't keep doing this," she said.

Wiping the cocaine from my face, I stared intently at her. I could tell she was being truthful. She had tears in her eyes, and for the first time I thought maybe, just maybe, she actually did care about me.

But I didn't know how to bring this whole nightmare to an end.

When the doctor came back, I decided to be honest with him. I told him the truth about my usage, only leaving out the fact that I'd been doing blow right up until he'd walked in. When I finished going through this quick rendition of my life, he was beside himself. He said it was a complete miracle that I hadn't already died, but that it would be an even greater miracle if I lived another thirty days.

Some of my symptoms were reflective of congestive heart failure, thus proving that my nurse friend had known exactly what she was talking about. My heart wasn't strong enough to pump blood to my legs.

He asked me to wait patiently so they could run some tests on my heart to find out for sure. Before he left the room, though, he turned and looked directly at me.

"Whatever's wrong with your heart, Cody, the only thing that will save you is complete abstinence, and even that might not be enough at this point."

When he left the room, I saw him look into the room next to us, whisper something, and point at me. I knew from when we had entered that there were cops in that room with a prisoner. Whatever the good doctor said to the cops, I concluded that it wasn't in my favour. I told Jewel that I would sneak out the first chance I got. She didn't like this plan and begged me to stay for the tests; all I could think about was getting arrested and being forced to come down.

"They said I don't have long to live," I said. "That's all I needed to know."

Despite her protests, I casually walked into the bathroom across the hall. I didn't even look in the cops' direction, knowing that would draw unwanted attention. After a short minute in the restroom, I came out and nonchalantly walked away.

When I got outside, though, Jewel wasn't at the truck. I was in a panic to get out of there—after all, the cops could be coming for me at any minute—but she was taking her time. When she finally exited the hospital, I noticed something odd about her demeanour; she was walking very slowly, her head down. She seemed almost defeated. I wanted to rush her, but I couldn't, perhaps sensing that this was one time I needed to keep my mouth shut. I could tell she didn't want to be around me. My presence reeked of death and I didn't blame her.

As we got into the truck, I could see her asking herself why she was going along with it. Perhaps in a sick way Jewel did love me. It hurt to see her so upset with me.

On the way home, Jewel cried like I'd never heard her cry before. She pleaded with me to find help and started asking me about my dad, something we had never discussed in the past because she knew how much I hated myself for what I'd done to him.

Something clicked inside me on that ride home. Maybe it was time to give sobriety one last wholehearted try. I was suddenly stirred with a passion to save my own life, something which hadn't happened in years.

I may not make it, but let me make my stand, I thought.

I couldn't bear the thought of fighting for myself, but I concurred with Jewel's message. I would do it for my family.

My heart began to beat fast, and not from an oncoming heart attack; it was beating fast because I knew this was my one and only opportunity. If I failed, death was surly in the cards.

The next day, I got on the phone and started calling treatment centres. I was dead serious about getting sober. I wanted to do it for myself and my family. There was no time to waste, either, so I needed to find somewhere fast.

As I got in touch with different places, though, I became more and more disheartened. Nowhere would take me—half of them because of my manslaughter conviction, not to mention my recent bulletproof vest charge, and the other half because of my medical condition. The likelihood of me dying during detox was very high.

However, I discovered that private treatment centres were more lenient, and some of them would accept me despite the medical risks associated with admitting me.

When I called one of the least expensive private treatment programs in the country, to my relief they said they could do an intake after I had detoxed for five days. They needed me to be past the first stages of a no doubt painful comedown. I didn't mind. I had never felt so urgent about anything in my life. It was literally do or die time.

One obstacle was still in my way, though: I needed money for treatment. I thought about going to my dad, but after our visit on the farm I had promised myself I would never ask him for money ever again. There was only one person who could save my life at this point, and I hadn't seen her in years: my mom.

As they say, desperate times call for desperate measures. I would need to tell her what the doctor had told me, and surely she would be willing to save her desperate son's life given the luxurious lifestyle she was leading now.

I was finally ready to get clean. It was time to call in the big guns.

CODY DESPERATE FOR HELP.

PART
VI

Chapter Ninety-Three

BLACK AND WHITE

My decision to talk to my mom was a testament to how desperate I was. Deep in my memory bank were all those times when she'd sent me money and visited me in prison. She had showed up when I needed her most, and I thought she would show up for me now, especially if she saw me. One look at me and anyone would draw the correct conclusion that I was at death's door.

The last time I'd spoken with her it hadn't gone so well. She had messaged me on social media seven months prior to ask for advice with my sister. My little sister was struggling with addiction, and my mom had believed my sister was going to die that particular evening. My mom always did have a flare for the dramatic. I knew she was just being manipulative. My response to her had been simple, not to mention connected to my own upbringing: "Don't abandon her when she's struggling. Don't turn everyone she loves against her. Try being her mom and showing her what unconditional love feels like instead of resorting to what you did with me and always placing conditions on it." I had felt so unbelievably abandoned by my mother since I was little that it was hard to hold back when my little sister's life might be on the line.

The conversation ended with me telling her that if she resorted to her tough love philosophies, my sister might not make it. She just replied that my sister and I were drinking the same Kool-Aid. She still didn't think she had done a single thing wrong in raising me. This had left me furious.

So reaching out to her meant I was desperate. No one was capable of hurting me more than she was. Making myself vulnerable to her could be a recipe for catastrophe. But I had nowhere else to turn. I could only put my life in her hands and hope she didn't kill me.

The second I heard my mom's voice, I broke down into tears. It was the hardest phone call I'd ever had to make. I begged her to help me, informing her that I was dying and didn't have long to live. She consoled me as I told her everything and plead-ed with her to take the wheel. I assured her that I was willing to do anything. I would go into private treatment, the only facilities that would take me, but I needed her help footing the bill. It was my only chance for survival. She made more money in a single day running her successful business than I would need to pay for treatment.

She agreed to help me, for which I was grateful. I thanked her over and over again, telling her that she wouldn't be sorry, that this was going to save my life. When she asked if I'd be willing to go to detox in a few days, I agreed but told her I didn't have long. In fact, it needed to be tomorrow. After all, I was currently on day four of my sleepless cycle and the thought of facing my day six devil was more than I could bear.

I sent her my address and promised to be ready to go first thing in the morning, knowing full well that I still wouldn't have slept.

At six o'clock, my mother rang my doorbell. I was completely out of my mind from psychosis. I just watched her on my cameras, repeating to myself, "I can't believe my mom's here." She had never seen me like this, and I had a good feeling how she was going to react.

I got to the bottom of the stairs and unbarricaded the door. When I cracked it, I stuck out my crazy face and told her I would be two minutes. She looked mortified, but after a nod of agreement she closed the door.

I shook my head in confusion as I ran back up the stairs. My heart was beating out of my chest and my eyes were wide with panic. But I knew this was the only chance I would get to solicit my mom's help. This was it. I needed to make my stand.

I didn't even say goodbye to Jewel when I left. I was too high and out of my mind to have a conversation with anyone. I was literally thinking that I needed to get to my mom's car before my thoughts and feelings convinced me otherwise.

As I opened the door and looked at my mom, I almost backed out. She stared at me with disgust, and I could tell she was regretting coming to my aid. I couldn't blame her. I looked nothing like me. I was one hundred thirty pounds, dirty, eyes sunken, and acting out of my mind. I wouldn't have wanted to be around me either.

Before we got to the detox centre, I told my mom that we needed to stop at a gas station so I could get high before I went in. If I got really high, it would be enough to get me through the doors and into the hands of the professionals on the other side. If I wasn't high, I didn't think I could go through with it; the torment of coming down would be too much.

She wasn't having it. Nonetheless, the cold hard fact remained: I wasn't going into that detox centre unless I was high. After I told her to bring me back home, she reluctantly gave in.

I ran into the gas station bathroom and pulled some cocaine out of my crotch. I had brought a single eight-ball. My mind went crazy and my heart fluttered with cravings as I crushed it on the toilet paper dispenser.

This was the last time I would ever do cocaine. The thought was horrifying. But as I sniffed the entire ball in two breaths and my cravings subsided, I found myself ready for the change.

This was it. This needed to be it.

When my mother and I walked into detox, I was taken aback by how many people were there. About twenty-five individuals sat in the waiting room trying to get a bed that day. Unfortunately, not everyone would get in. The staff explained that there were only three beds available. As I looked around the room, the realization set in that I probably wouldn't be admitted today. The room was full of people detoxing from heroin, fentanyl, and alcohol. Some of them were literally twitching on the floor. With opioid drugs or alcohol, you can die from coming off it without medical attention; I was just detoxing from cocaine.

I kept the daunting reality to myself so as not to dishearten my mother. But the whole time we sat waiting, she gave off the coldest vibe. It was hard to believe she loved me at all.

I tried to convince myself that this was all in my head.

She must love me, I thought. *She's my mom.*

My mother sat in silence as I proceeded to socialize with the entire group. I could tell it was making her sick to her stomach. I was over-the-top friendly and the people clearly liked me, even though I was out of my mind. I could see her wincing every time I opened my mouth.

Finally, a nurse came into the room and announced the three people who had been accepted that day. I was the first one.

I couldn't believe it. The nurse looked me dead in the eyes as she read out the names, and I nodded in her direction to say a silent thank you. I was finally going to get the help I needed.

My mom gave me a hug and rushed out. She couldn't wait to get away from me. I hated the way she made me feel, but I was grateful for her.

Despite my relief at being admitted, I watched in sadness as all the other people—people I'd just made friends with—were forced to pick up their stuff and leave. I knew that some of them might never make it back. Most of them were accompanied by hopeful family members who were there to lend support, and it occurred to me that any one of those support people would have shown more gratitude than my mother had; every single one of them looked crushed not to have been selected. They looked at their loved ones and told them it was going to be okay, all the while not knowing if they would make it another day. It was a heart-breaking scene.

I had no idea why I was so lucky, but I picked up my bag and stared for a second at the door being held open for me by the nurse. This was it.

Do it for your family, I repeated to myself.

The nurse sat me down at the intake desk and asked me how I was feeling. My mind was going crazy. When I asked the nurse why they had picked me, she looked at me with an expression I'll never forget.

"We took you because we know that you're the one person in that room that isn't going to make it back," she said.

The gravity of that statement hit me hard. That room had been filled with the lowest level addicts and junkies I had ever seen, and she was telling me that I was the worst one. I was delusional. I had looked around and thought everyone needed help more than I did, but it was obvious to anyone with eyes to see that I was at the end of my rope.

I begged the nurse to put me to sleep, because I was on day five and I was terrified to make it to day six. I don't think she really understood why I was so terrified, but she kept reassuring me that I would be fine.

As the minutes wore on, I felt my high begin to leave me. Waves of pain struck and I squeezed myself, almost as if I was trying to console myself. This hurt so much. I kept pleading with the nurse to put me down, but the best she could offer was to pump me full of Valium and put me in a bed. I lay the blankets over my head and shook uncontrollably.

After about an hour, the Valium took hold and put me to sleep.

———

I slowly came back to consciousness, not opening my eyes. But I knew where I was. I was in detox, and I could never do cocaine again. Hurt washed over my entire body at the thought. I squeezed my hands tight under the blanket, as if exerting energy in this way would take away some of my anguish. I closed my eyes as tight as I could, wanting to disappear.

The nurse gave me more meds and finally the hurt went away.

It had been years since I'd been sober for forty-eight hours at a time. As the all-consuming fog of cocaine left me, the wreckage it had inflicted on my brain became apparent. I couldn't sit still. I shook so hard that I almost fell out of bed.

My mind had been destroyed. I cried in agony as wild emotions washed over me. The psychological torment I was living in felt like more than I could bear. Under the blankets, my eyes darted from side to side. It was hard to breathe or exert control over my twitching body.

I soon got called into an office to be interviewed by a caseworker. She greeted me with a warm smile when I walked in, although I was so uncomfortable that my skin felt as if it was trying to detach itself from my body. I listened as she spoke about applying for entry into every treatment centre. She told me to stay hopeful and to make sure my parents were ready to help pay for private care

On the third day of detox, I was in really rough shape. I was lethargic and struggled to muster any energy. My physical ailments were awful enough, but that was nothing compared to what was being levelled against me psychologically. I kept thinking about my old life.

You can do this, I reminded myself.

When the caseworker called me back into her office, I struggled to get down the hallway. My mind felt as if it was caving in and I could barely stop myself from crying. Upon sitting down, I saw the sadness on her face as she gave me the bad news: no government-funded treatment centre would take me.

It was a loss, but I didn't let it get me down. We had expected this. Besides, my mom had said she would back me up, so I wasn't worried. I just needed to focus on this painful detox and let my mother take the reins.

I went to the phone and called my mother. As the phone rang and I waited for her to pick up, I still wasn't worried. She had deployed some brutal tactics over the years, but this was a life and death situation. She knew that. I was her firstborn; surely she wouldn't let me die when she was more than capable of helping me—especially since I was showing her how hard I was willing to fight. The past three days had been torture.

When she answered the phone, I recognized immediately that something was wrong. I told her what the caseworker had said about the government-funded treatment centres.

"I've decided not to help you, Cody," she said when I finished. "I've never seen a good return on my investment with you, so I'm out."

She added that my dad felt the same way.

I can't express what that did to me, but it was catastrophic. It destroyed everything that was left of my soul. In that moment, I was the loneliest person in the world. My situation was hopeless. No one loved me. No one cared if I died. My mother had objectified me, referring to me as nothing more than an investment.

I dropped the phone, walked to my room, and packed my bags. There was no chance for me, no point in continuing the painful detox. I figured that I may as well go use until I finally died. It wouldn't be long now.

I walked out the doors and hurried into a cab. I needed to get high.

The hurt was so unbearable. My family didn't love me. No one loved me.

When I got home, I took to social media, writing a long post about how I was dying and not even my rich mom would help me. I wrote about my childhood, telling story after story about my mother's abuse. As I did it, I started to see the totality of what she had done to me. I was finally looking at my life in black and white. For the first time in my life, the blinders were lifted to my mother's abuse.

I posted my writings and watched the comments pour in. I kept my eyes on the screen as person after person told me that they had my back. If I died now, at least everyone would know the truth.

Then I started to think about what would happen after I passed. I didn't want this to be my last message to the world. I didn't want to be remembered like this. All I was doing was stooping to my mom's level, and I was a better person than that.

It was hard, but after ten minutes I deleted the post. If I was going to die, I wanted to at least have a small piece of dignity.

So that was it. It was time to die.

I buried my head in the cocaine and tried to forget about my mom's actions. She had known what it meant to deliver that final message. Perhaps seeing me in person had convinced her that I was better off dead.

Well, she had gotten the better of me yet again, only now I could see her for what she really was. She didn't love me. Her love had always been conditional.

Not that I can really talk. Look at me. I'm garbage. I don't deserve to be loved. I didn't deserve it when I was young, and I certainly don't deserve it now.

Chapter Ninety-Four

LOST BOY

I couldn't tell what was more tragic, the fact that my family was gone or the realization that I'd never had one. It had never occurred to me until now that my mother could be at fault for what I had turned into. She certainly wasn't responsible for what I had done, but the more I thought about it the more I came to realize that I never stood a chance. Right from my toddler years, she had abused and manipulated me. Perhaps she had been angry that I'd come into her life at such a young age, and perhaps she still blamed me for holding her back.

The fact that I was killing hundreds of animals before I ever did drugs is a testament to how messed up my childhood was. Not that it matters now, but I stopped killing animals the day I realized I was hurting them. Somehow, despite my mother's abuse, I managed to develop a kind heart. I knew I was a good person even though my selfish actions didn't reflect that. I'd always put others ahead of myself when it didn't interfere with my need for escape. In fact, my favourite part about being a drug-dealer was uprooting the assumptions people had about the profession; people couldn't believe how nice I was.

But it didn't matter anymore. I was going to die, and my mother would sit at my funeral playing at being the victim of the monster she had created. No one would ever know, and I would fade away as nothing but a tragic memory.

Would people look at my fall as a process that unfolded quickly? Objectively, it took three years. But for me, having only slept a few hours every six days, it seemed to have taken a lifetime. It seemed so long ago that I had been a pillar of strength in the community, sponsoring kids, selling cars, and making the world a better place one small piece at a time.

I found myself in a unique situation. The big book of Alcoholics Anonymous tells of the jumping-off place. When a man has reached his breaking point, there are only three ways for his addiction-focused rampage to end: death, prison, or institutions.

I had knocked on death's door countless times, yet death had refused to have me.

At first I'd found my Do Not Detain order to be my friend, but I came to the point of realizing I would give anything to be put away, forced to detox, and given a length of time off drugs. But no matter what I seemed to do or what laws I got caught breaking, the police refused to detain me.

Finally, there were institutions, but due to my laundry list of health concerns and long criminal record, no public treatment centre would touch me, and all the private options went out the window when my mom refused to help.

So I now found myself at a jumping-off place—with nowhere to jump. I would have taken any one of those options without thinking twice. I was truly cursed with a loneliness few people could understand. The doctors hadn't given me long to live, but I'd proven to be a tough specimen to kill. Honestly, I had my doubts that I would die. Part of me was scared I would be stuck like this forever.

As I sat on my couch, Molly whined with her head in my lap as if she could sense how much pain I was in. I stared deeply into her soulful eyes, so full of nonverbal vocabulary. This animal loved me unconditionally. I massaged her head with my fingers, didn't break eye contact, and kissed her on the forehead.

Something came over me as I whispered in her ear how much I loved her. She was the only companion I had left in the world. She deserved so much better than me.

I pulled out a laptop and began typing as if possessed with purpose. If I was going to die, I wanted her to be happy. She deserved that. I wrote a testimony about how much I loved her and what she had meant to me in my life. After a half-hour, I reread what I had written. It was perfect. I then went to a popular selling site on the internet and posted the ad to rehome my dog. My heart broke as I stared contently at the words on the screen. I wanted so bad to be the one who gave her a good life. She had been so good to me. The thought of her ending up in Jewel's hands, or at the dog pound, was more than I could handle. I needed to get my act together long enough to find her a good home.

Molly was the only family I had left. When I posted on social media the notice that I was going to die, condolences came pouring in from countless people. I appreciated every word they said, but something was still missing. It was a cry for help to my family, and they didn't answer. The Bates side of the family had about thirty members and only my brother, one of my sisters, and my auntie reached out to say they loved me. I felt utterly abandoned. Why fight any longer?

Suddenly, my stepfather Gary reached out and told me that I was his son, and that he loved me very much. My heart swelled with gratitude. Then, slowly, I received messages from every single member of his family, whom I hadn't seen for the past eighteen years since Gary and my mom had divorced. They all expressed their love for me and asked me to come for dinners and coffee. They were all praying and pleaded with me to keep fighting. What they expressed to me was what I desperately wanted from my own family. It was overwhelming, but also crushing to realize that my own people were okay with the fact that I was slated for death, yet this family I barely knew anymore was willing to be there for me in my time of need. The only thing I could do was keep consuming narcotics, to quell the agony.

A couple of days went by and I turned down many offers for Molly. I wanted to make sure she ended up in the perfect home. One afternoon, I received the email that would dramatically change both her life and mine. The email contained a passionate and powerful message from a woman who was in love with Pitbulls. She was very moved by what I had written about Molly and could relate to my story. She empathized with my heartbreak, and I agreed to bring Molly over for a meet-and-greet that night.

When Molly and I arrived at her place, I was taken aback by the beautiful property. The woman came out to greet me and brought her dog Peter out as well. As we walked around to the back of the house, I saw the small lake her house backed out on. Molly freaked out as she ran to the dock with her new boyfriend Peter in tow. She looked so happy. I knew in that moment that I had found her the right home.

The woman and I then went into the house and chatted about Pitbulls for hours. She adored them and had become an advocate for the breed. She had special food, a strict exercise regimen, and everything she did came second to her love for her dog. I was infatuated.

After a few hours, I was finally saying goodbye to my girl. The transition went as smoothly as I could have asked for. Molly loved it there. But as I was leaving, she stared at me with confusion. She didn't want me to leave her. She who had been the most loyal companion, even at the worst of times, could sense that this was goodbye.

I hadn't told the woman that I didn't have long to live; I'd just told her that my house was too small. On the ad, I'd asked for $1,500 for Molly, but I happily took $200 because of how grateful I was to have found such an amazing home for her. I hugged her tight, gave her lots of kisses, and said goodbye to my last friend in the whole world.

I knew in my heart that I would have died by now if it hadn't been for her love.

On the drive back home, I sobbed so hard that I had to pull over. Heaving and hiccupping, I couldn't believe that I had just let my beautiful Molly go. Now I was truly alone, with no one left to console or comfort me. I knew it was the right thing to do for her. Perhaps it was my least selfish act in years. But I was in so much pain! Raindrops falling on the window caught my attention and made me look up into the sky.

Heavy clouds had gathered, reflecting my mood. As it began to downpour, I needed to get home. I didn't want to be out and about this night. I felt so lost.

I walked into my house soaking wet. I didn't care. I was used to being kicked when I was down.

Relief washed over me as I reached the living room and saw that Jewel wasn't there. I didn't want to be around her. She knew how much I had loved Molly and yet she hadn't even offered to come with me to drop her off. She was as cold as ice to me.

I sat down and let my head rest against the back of the couch, tears welling in my eyes as I pondered how utterly alone I felt. I then leaned forward again and pounded line after line of cocaine up my nose. When that plugged up, I started cooking and smoking it. Nothing seemed to quell the pain I was in. I cried as the drugs finally stopped working. There was no more escape. Only pain, sorrow, despair, and grief. I just wanted my heart to finally quit.

Sitting on that couch, I looked at a table full of money and cocaine—everything I had been fighting for. It made me feel utterly alone. I had been promised by the devil that this was how I would find freedom, but looking at it now made me want to puke. This is why I had destroyed every relationship in my life? There was no freedom in this, only suffering.

The truth finally came into focus. Too little too late.

I looked at my iPad and noticed some more comments from people offering condolences and prayers. My heart skipped a beat when I saw that my uncle from my mom's side had written a comment. I really needed to hear some kind words from a blood relative right then.

But when I opened it up, I was horrified. His comment was making fun of my post about Molly and calling her a "p*ssy a** pit." I was used to being kicked when I was down, but that comment crushed me. All I could do was consume more cocaine and try to stop the waves of anguish debilitating me.

Suddenly, I had an idea. Recently a friend of mine had shown me some pictures that were divine in nature—masterpieces worth millions of dollars a pop and which had been painted by a seven-year-old girl who claimed that Jesus Christ had taught her to paint. When I looked at these portraits, I believed her. They were incredible works of art, beyond the capabilities of anyone her age. One portrait in particular had received countless hours of my undivided attention. It was a painting of Jesus Christ called "Prince of Peace." As I stared into the eyes of this man, for some reason it brought calm to my heart, even when I was suffering from a psychotic break.

I put on some music and pulled up the picture on my iPad, experiencing a small sense of relief in being able to look at Him again. With the iPad in my lap, I rocked my body back and forth, unable to sit still. I didn't peel my eyes from it, as if breaking the connection would destroy the divine calm I'd been feeling. I'd never believed in Jesus Christ, but I couldn't deny that this girl wouldn't have been capable of painting such a masterpiece without Him.

For the first time in my life, I believed that this man I was staring at was God, and that this was exactly what He looked like. Jesus's eyes were so beautiful. Staring at the painting, it was like they spoke to me. I closed my eyes and tried to see Him, but I couldn't. There was a pair of eyes staring at me from inches away; I could see them clear as day, the pearly whites enclosing pupils of pure evil. I knew they belonged to the devil, just as I knew I belonged to him.

I opened my eyes again and was greeted with Jesus's face. Tears streamed down my cheeks as I realized I was scared to blink; every time I did, I saw the devil's pupil.

Wave after wave of pain and shame washed over me. I was so incredibly lost, too far gone. What could Jesus do for me? The devil was real and I'd been tricked. He'd convinced me to believe his lies, and now I was scared and alone, lost and broken.

I stood up, barely finding the strength to get to my feet. Heaving from my sobs, I made it to the door leading to my deck. The cool night air hit me and I stepped out into the rain, letting it beat off my face. I spread my arms wide, refusing to close my eyes even though the raindrops were hitting them. I raised myself onto my toes as if just those extra couple of inches would propel me into flight.

"Please help me!" I cried out to the sky. "Please, Jesus! Show me something, please. I'm going to hell! Please help me!"

Lightning filled the sky, followed closely by rolling thunder. The cold rain on my body didn't feel right, like my body didn't even belong to me. It felt dark and demonic, and I inched myself further up, trying to separate myself from it. I sobbed uncontrollably, pain bursting out of me as I pleaded with the heavens. I cried out, my face as high as I could hold it. My hot tears felt as though they were the only part of me that was real anymore—the only part of me that still belonged to me.

I focused on the tears and separated myself from everything that belonged to the devil. For a brief moment, as I cried out to God, I felt faint. Maybe my tears were the only part of Cody Bates still left, but at least it was me.

CODY SAYING GOODBYE TO MOLLY.

Chapter Ninety-Five

THE IMPOSSIBLE

January 4, 2017

I knew I was going to die that day before I even opened my eyes. The late morning sunshine filled my room, stirring my first conscious thoughts. As always, they were malicious in nature. My self-hate literally took up every second of every day now. I'd finally had enough. I couldn't go through the pain of waking up anymore.

With my eyes still closed, it felt like all the treachery from my life sat heavily on my chest. It had been five months since the doctors had said I was going to die. Recently one physician had told me that the sheer amount of cocaine I was doing was the only thing keeping my heart beating; he had predicted that when I finally came down, I would die. Wasn't it just my luck? The same thing that was killing me was also keeping me alive.

I had reduced my usage dramatically. Cocaine hadn't gone up my nose in weeks; I'd only cooked it. Crack was my only way to feel bliss now. The pipe had become my only friend.

After the night I gave Molly up, I cut most of my clients off my phones, only keeping the customers who bought $200 or more at a time. I didn't want to work anymore. I also cut loose everyone who'd been working for me. I just wanted to seclude myself until the devil finally came to bring me home.

I hadn't heard from my day six demon in months since I didn't have enough cocaine in my system anymore to carry me to the sixth day. I thought voiding him from my life would provide a sense of relief, but in exchange I was coming down much more often, which was painful beyond measure. I'd rather have put up with the devil's torture than be sober in my own skin.

And yet all that pain had brought me to this day, the day after which I would never have to come down again. Today I would claim my place in hell, whether death wanted to take me or not. I wouldn't give him the option.

Jewel had finally had enough. She had left me and found her ways into the arms of my so-called best friend. She was such a creature of habit. I had been crushed to learn where she was living now and who she was with, but it didn't surprise me. That friend of mine had always been a grease ball and she was just doing what she always did.

At first I thought I'd be better off without her, so I didn't understand why I started to hurt so much over someone I hadn't really cared for. Perhaps I was just confusing the rest of the pain in my life and associating some of it with her. Either way, she was gone. In a weird way, she deserved some credit for keeping me alive until now. Left on my own, it had only taken me a couple of weeks to hit rock bottom.

I finally opened my eyes and began the painful process of sitting up. It took an enormous amount of energy, and I had to attempt it several times before I actually made it. All of my drive was gone.

Before I pulled myself to my feet, I envisioned the journey I'd have to take to the kitchen, taking into consideration that I would then have to drag myself back up the stairs after I'd gotten what I needed. The thought occurred to me that I could just kill myself tomorrow, give myself one more day.

No, that wasn't an option anymore. It had to be today. It had to be right now. The thought of living in my own skin another hour was unthinkable. I couldn't live another day. My energy may have left me, but I at least had the determination to make this happen.

It hurt to move. When I finally planted my feet and stood up straight, I kept my eyes focused on the floor to catch my breath. The state of my room was disgusting. Charcoal and ash stains caked the carpet and crack paraphernalia lay everywhere, including crack pipes that I'd cut in half to scrape for resin, evidence of my desperation.

My hands, too, were covered in ash and grime—from the tips of my fingers to my elbows. I hadn't showered in days. Consumed by my cravings, I had lost the ability to take care of myself.

I'd lived in this new place for about three months, renting the room from a friend. When I had vacated my last house, I'd left in a hurry and left most of my things behind. Once upon a time I'd had a three-level home filled with decor and furniture, products of my hard work ethic. Now all I had was one crooked poster on the wall. I hated that poster so much; it reminded me that I was hopeless junkie. But I left it up because I couldn't pull myself away from the crack long enough to fix it, even something like this that caused me constant anguish.

Walking to the kitchen felt like embarking on a gruelling trip to the store without a winter jacket. When I finally stood on the tile floor, I glanced around the room in silence. The quiet almost seemed loud to me, as if my mind was picking up sounds that my eardrums couldn't.

I pulled out the drawer containing the kitchen knives and ran my thumb down the edge of each blade. My judgment led me to the largest and most daunting knife in the drawer—a butcher knife. As I walked back up the stairs to my bedroom, I couldn't help but notice that the tip of the blade extended past my knee as I walked. I felt comforted by the fact that I had the proper tool for the job.

I entered my room and closed the door behind me, collapsing on the floor with my back against the wall, completely exhausted from my expedition to the kitchen. As I gained control of my war torn body, a single thought paraded through my mind: *This is going to be the last time I ever sit down!*

I propped my feet on the mattress and leaned my head against the wall. How had it come to this? How had I gone from having everything I ever wanted to sitting on the floor in this ravaged bedroom with a butcher knife, ready to die? I slowly dragged the blade across my wrist and let the blood wash away the ash that covered my hand. The blood brought comfort. I watched it flow from my wrist with clear eyes. But the cut wasn't deep enough; the next one would be better. The next one would find the vein that released me from this unbearable anguish.

As I stared at the bloody butcher knife, for some reason my tattoos grabbed my attention. Embedded throughout them were scars from the many battles my life had taken me through. Lately I'd even started branding my own skin with hot knifes. When I felt the flaming red blade sear through my skin like butter, it relieved me of my psychological torment. The physical pain was excruciating, but it was bliss compared to the anguish in my heart. I inhaled the smoke from my burnt skin, blowing out clouds in honour of the pain.

People who witnessed this were taken aback by my darkness. I knew I was possessed. The devil lived in me and had total control over my mind. Even my acquaintances were at the point where they couldn't deny that a spiritual entity had taken over. I had long since lost my voice and sense of smell. When I spoke, I sounded of death. Nobody would hang out with me anymore, not even for free cocaine, because the energy around me was so incredibly dark. To them, Cody Bates had long since disappeared. What was left was a monster that didn't belong in this world.

I was losing control of the situation. I needed to regain my strength and finish what I had started—and I knew how to do it. I crawled onto my bed, leaving blood and ash stains behind. I needed to get high. On my hands and knees, I brought my face over the edge of the mattress and scoured the carpet. After a few minutes, I found what I was looking for: a dropped piece of crack.

I filled a pipe with ash and dropped the crack on top of it. I tried to steady my shaking lips as I melted the crack into the ash with my lighter, working the flame in a spiral toward the middle of the bowl. Then I brought it home, fluttering the choke of the pipe as I sucked back with all the determination of a marathon runner. I wasn't going to let this one get away.

I held the smoke in as long as I could. As expected, I didn't feel even an ounce of bliss. I blew out the cloud of smoke as I once again took in my disgusting surroundings.

Cody Bates, everybody! Here he is.

My leafless forest screamed to life as my mind opened up to the familiar realm I didn't belong in. The eerie silence of the room was replaced with the screams, sirens, and whispers I'd become accustomed to when I was on cocaine.

*You're f*cking garbage, Cody. Look at yourself. Do it for your family, you coward. Nobody loves you.*

I grabbed the knife and punched it through the skin on my wrist. It went deep— deep enough, I could tell, to get the job done. I sat still for a second. When I pulled the knife up my wrist, it would finally be over. My tears stopped as I stared into hell.

Let this be your stand. Let this be the one good thing you do for this world—the one good thing you do for yourself. There are no more tears, only purpose. It's time to die. It's time to claim your place in hell. Say goodbye to Cody Bates.

With all hell raining down against me, though, something stopped me in my tracks. The screams and sirens vanished. As I lifted my head, a wave of grief and despair crashed against my heart in the most profound way—and in a moment it was replaced with overwhelming joy and peace... and grace. Tears gushed out of me as my mouth opened wide at the experience of these unfamiliar emotions that were filling me to the brim, about to burst out of me like a volcano.

What was happening? Glancing from side to side, a voice filled my thoughts, louder than any thought I'd ever had. In a beautiful and compassionate tone, it said to me, *It's over. It's over, Cody. Your suffering has come to an end.*

It wasn't my own thought. I knew this because I wasn't capable of thinking it. As the voice consoled my broken heart with a love unlike anything I'd thought possible, I knew unequivocally that a King was speaking to me, His grace overwhelming me with wave after wave of unconditional love. I knew beyond a shadow of a doubt that Jesus Christ was in that room telling me that my suffering was over.

My shame, it was gone. My guilt, it was gone.

Everything that had made me *me* for the last thirty-one years fell off my shoulders. The chains broke through absolutely no effort of my own. I was a killer, a gangster, a sociopath, a drug trafficker, and an addict. I had done nothing in my life to deserve this, but I knew in that moment that if I died, I belonged to Jesus. He had found me.

He told me to call my dad. He assured me that my dad would help me, that my family would help me.

I picked up the phone and dialled his number. When the call went to voicemail, I hung up and called my sister.

"Please help me," I said, the words barely audible through my cries.

"I'll be there in ten minutes."

I put my head back against the wall and let the emotions take over.

"It's yours," I said to Him. "My life is Yours. Please take control. I can't do this."

My phone rang, and when I looked down I saw that it was my dad. When I answered the call, his loving voice filled my ear. All the pain I'd been carrying poured out of me. Through my intense sobs and hiccups, I could only get out four words: "Please Dad, please help."

He said he was coming for me.

As the weight of the world fell off my shoulders, I was left with a feeling I had never felt before: freedom. Jesus was speaking to me. He told me that He loved me, and to follow His instruction. The first thing He directed me to do was to take all my jewellery off. I peeled thousands of dollars of bling off my neck and hands without hesitation. His next instruction was to drop all my phones into a bucket of water. I had about thirty of them in my closet, all filled with customer phone numbers. That clientele list was easily worth $100,000. But it wasn't worth anything to me. To me, it was a pile of dirt. A death sentence.

My sister burst into my room as the Lord spoke to me. She crawled onto my bed and wrapped me in her arms. She pulled the bloody knife from my grasp and threw it away. Balling uncontrollably, I kept saying the same thing over and over again: "I don't want this anymore. I just want my family."

I summoned all my energy as we went downstairs, grabbed a bucket, and filled it with water. Without skipping a beat, I dumped the phones into the water, all the while smiling through my tears and repeating what Jesus was saying to me.

"My suffering has come to an end."

I believed Him. She was confused as to why I was laughing, but she knew I was telling her the truth. She asked if I wanted to grab any of my things, but in my heart the Spirit of God told me to leave it all behind.

I walked out into the brightest sunshine I'd ever seen. The darkness inside me was completely gone, and all that was left was me. Jesus had done for me what I couldn't do for myself. He had done the impossible.

Cody Bates died on the floor that afternoon and what arose from the ashes walked out the front door of that house a new creation.

As my sister and I drove away, the Holy Spirit said one more thing to me: "Don't look back."

Chapter Ninety-Six

BORN AGAIN

In a split moment, my life changed forever. Still reeling from what had happened in my bedroom, I felt safe for the first time in years. My dad and my stepmom graciously took me in at their acreage—without hesitation or a plan. But I think they realized rather quickly that they were in over their heads.

I couldn't leave my room for days. Shaking, shivering, sweating, and crying under my sheets, I went into a painful detox the likes of which I had never experienced. My parents would come into my room several times a day to wrap their arms around me and tell me I was safe, something I needed to hear constantly.

As the days passed, the fog cleared and the true wreckage of what I had done to myself became apparent. I was far from the charismatic extrovert I'd once been. My eyes were wide with fear as emotions hit me in unforgiving waves. Everything felt so extreme. One minute I'd be the most grateful man in the world, and the next I'd be wanting to die for all the treachery I'd wrought. When I looked in the mirror, I hated the man I saw looking back. All I could see were the horrendous things I'd done. How could I forgive myself? How could God forgive me?

As I white-knuckled my way through the torment, though, I realized that I no longer craved cocaine. I cried out to God countless times a day, begging Him to talk to me again, to tell me what to do. But no matter how hard I pleaded, His voice didn't return.

The problem I had was that I knew Jesus had saved me, but what about all the different doctrines and teachings? I didn't know if I was Catholic or Protestant, Baptist, Anglican, or any of the others. I didn't know the first thing about the Bible. Where should I go for help? I knew I needed to go to church, but what did Christ want me to be?

There was only one person I could trust in this moment: the seven-year-old girl who Jesus had taught to paint. In hindsight, I don't think it was by accident that I came across her "Prince of Peace" portrait. I knew in my heart that her painting was Jesus, so I decided to trust anything that little girl said. If Jesus had taught her to paint, then surely her theology was on point.

I watched documentaries and YouTube videos of her, listening intently for instruction. I discovered that she called herself a Christian, which meant that I was a Christian. It was a platform to stand on and a foundation to build upon. I knew I was on the right track.

One of the conditions of staying at my dad's acreage was that I needed to actively look for a treatment centre. Since I was confined to my bed, that wasn't a problem. I compiled a long list of treatment centres from my hiding place under the bedsheet. But call after call, I was rejected on the same premise I'd been warned about before: they either weren't medically staffed to handle my complications or couldn't take me because of my violent criminal record.

Deep down, I was terrified that my family would soon bail on me, give up on me as I had come to expect. I felt like a creature in the basement, writhing in pain and emotional torment. I was waiting for them to come to their senses and realize that they were in over their heads with me, but that day never came. They tirelessly comforted and cared for me when I thought I didn't deserve it. Something was different about me, and they could feel it.

After four days, I started waking up at 4:00 a.m.—religiously, without fail. Four o'clock on the dot. I found an old broken laptop that had no battery and was missing an R key. It was also void of any programming. But something inside me was on fire. I needed to write. I had zero typing skills, so as soon as I began to finger-peck away I realized that my thoughts were coming out too fast for me to keep up with them. My mind was in utter chaos.

However, as I wrote the words, I started to understand why the desire had been laid so heavily on my heart to write. The story was beautiful. I was confused, because the words going onto the page didn't sound like they were coming from me. I had never written or read anything in my life, but I was producing one page of poetry after another.

I wrote from bed, rocking back and forth while I typed. On the outside it must have seemed impossible for a single cohesive thought to come out of me, but for some reason I found myself able to write clearly.

Four days sober, I began writing the book about my journey.

Chapter Ninety-Seven

REVELATIONS

I hadn't seen my family doctor in years. I was seven days clean and looked as if I belonged in a mental institution, but I ran into the doctor's office and semi-patiently waited for my name to be called. When he was finally able to see me, he took an abundance of time hearing out my story and heavily considered all the complications I was facing in my detox.

From looking at me, it was pretty obvious that I had some glaring mental health problems, but his priority lay in addressing the physical ones.

He looked at my laundry list of health issues on his computer screen and subsequently asked me to go for organ and blood testing at the local hospital so we could anticipate the complications no doubt soon to follow. I agreed and went to the hospital under his direction, scheduling another appointment with him a couple of days later.

The last five-minute stretch of every trip back to the acreage was the hardest for me. My mental state always deteriorated on our approach. By the time we pulled into the driveway, I would be practically jumping out of the moving vehicle to run as fast as I could for my bed. It was the only place I felt safe. My trips to town were usually followed by me not leaving my room for twenty-four hours. I was a complete wreck.

A couple of days later, I found myself back at the doctor's office awaiting the test results. When he walked into the room, he immediately asked if I was okay because I was nearly falling off the chair from rocking back and forth so hard.

When he sat down he locked eyes with me, assessing the trauma I was going through. He then smiled wide, earning my full attention.

"Cody, you belong in a medical journal, my friend," he said. "Your test results came back. It's like your body has never touched a drug in its life." I was in total shock. He turned on the computer screen and showed me the test results. "Look, the only line that's in the red is your protein levels. You're a medical miracle. Praise God."

He was a man of faith.

"Praise God," I replied with a smile and a laugh. I liked the sound of it.

My dad was in the room with me that day. He wasn't a Christian, so he looked absolutely astonished.

"But how could this be, Doctor?" my dad wondered. "Look at him!"

We all laughed, because anyone with half a brain would have thought I was on the verge of death. I weighed one hundred thirty pounds and was shaking violently from withdrawal pains.

The doctor just reiterated that he couldn't explain it. He had never seen anything like it in his thirty-year medical career.

My dad hugged me when we left the office. He told me how much he loved me and that he wasn't going to give up on me. I believed him, because Jesus had told me to call him, and now I had a complete bill of health just seven days into my recovery. The miracles and blessings were piling up.

However, the doctor did suggest one thing that day: serious therapy to help me gain control over my mental health issues. Many conditions can fall under the umbrella of posttraumatic stress, including bipolar disorder, depression, addictive personality, anti-social personality, and superimposed anxiety. Much of this originated from the abuse I'd suffered at my mother's hands. Getting diagnosed would be a relief. No one had ever asked the underlying question of why I had succumbed to my addiction. Now people were finally listening to me, and for the first time in my life I saw my addiction as a symptom to a larger problem. I was finally getting the help I needed.

Days turned into weeks as I clawed from one minute to the next. My mental health issues only seemed to get worse as time unfolded, but I prayed constantly for strength and guidance. I knew Jesus had me and He wasn't letting go.

I felt so unsafe when I left the house for AA meetings, therapy, and short walks up the driveway and back. But as time went on, my walks extended farther. My dad even got me a dog. I named her Princess Aya and she played an integral role in helping bring me back to life. She was identical to Molly in terms of temperament. She loved me unconditionally and taught me that I was capable of loving her back despite all the wretchedness of my past. We became inseparable.

Every day started out the same, with me thinking I wouldn't be able to make it to nightfall. I was in so much mental duress that it seemed impossible to even get through the next hour. I spent an abundance of time in prayer and looking at that seven-year-old's paintings. They brought peace and calm to my elated heart.

My dad informed me one day that one of my uncles on his side was also a Christian. He even helped run an orphanage in Africa that focused on spreading the gospel to kids there. My dad said that when he was in town, he always attended a specific church in Black Diamond. I decided that I could trust this advice, so the next Sunday my stepmom and I went to church. I felt comforted that she was willing to do that for me. She loved me very much.

When we walked into the church, I ran down the aisle to the front pew and sat down front and centre, gripping my midsection and rocking back and forth. I made eye contact with the pastor and could tell he was intrigued by me. I don't think he was used to seeing someone like me sitting there, and no doubt my shaking was very distracting to everyone. But he smiled at me and made me feel as though everything was going to be okay. He made me feel safe.

As soon as the service was over, I bounced up and hightailed it out of there before people had a chance to get up. The pastor caught up with me, though, and asked if we could have a word.

We stepped into his office and I found myself sharing the story of what had happened on the floor of my bedroom on January 4. He nodded and listened. I don't think he'd ever heard so much cursing in his entire life, but he didn't interrupt. I was instantly attracted to his presence and knew in my heart that this was where Jesus wanted me to be.

At the end of the meeting, he gave me a Bible. When he put it in my hands, I squeezed it to my chest and looked at him as if he had just handed me a cheque for a million dollars. Since Jesus was the one who had saved me, and He had brought me to this church, I knew that everything in that book was truly the inspired Word of God. To me, it was a treasure.

The pastor also gave me his phone number and politely asked me to call him with any questions I had about the gospel. Before I left, he asked how much I knew about Jesus and the Bible.

"Let's just say I'm on level zero," I told him.

He laughed as I ran out to my stepmom's car.

The hardest thing was finding a way to love myself. I had hated myself for so long that I still wasn't convinced there was anything in me to love. I struggled day after day to look in the mirror, repeating to myself, "I can't do this."

My dad had to get me my own vehicle, because after a while he couldn't handle driving with me anymore. I would regularly break down into a tornado of emotions I didn't understand, crying and trying to jump from the moving vehicle. I greatly doubted whether I would ever be able to live normally again.

One day, while driving on a back road and listening to country music, singing at the top of my lungs, the overwhelming presence of God consumed me just as fully as it had on that fateful day in my bedroom. I immediately pulled over, heaving from the abundance of emotion gushing out of me.

As the car stopped, the road disappeared and I had a vision. I was in an old house, looking down on myself lying in a bed. I could tell that I was dying and trying to call out for help, but no one could hear me. I remembered this. It was the May long weekend when my runners had given me GHB to bring me down off all the drugs I had taken. As I looked down on myself, though, I saw a new detail: someone was holding me, cradling me. As his face came into focus, I realized it was Jesus. I hadn't known at the time He was there. Every time my heart stopped, He started it again.

The vision left as fast as it had come. I sat there in the car, my shirt and pants covered in my own tears. I had never felt love like that before. Jesus hadn't just come into my life at the moment when I decided to kill myself; He had been there the whole time.

He didn't need to show me other visions, but now I understood why I hadn't died all those other times when the doctors hadn't been able to explain why I was still breathing. Jesus was the reason, the only reason, I was still alive.

Everything started to make sense.

Jesus then told me something else. He had me now and was never going to let me go. Whenever I thought I was all alone, He was there. Even though I still couldn't see Him, I knew He was with me.

I was right to think I couldn't do this. But He could.

Chapter Ninety-Eight

FORGIVENESS

Slowly, the weeks turned into months, the emotional and psychological trauma continuing to wreak havoc on me. At the best of times, I couldn't even say I felt normal.

But life did get better. My comfort zone expanded from my room to the rest of the house, and my dog and my family showered me with love. I needed them to love me when I was incapable of loving myself. It gave me something to fight for.

It was also difficult for me to feel safe. I didn't feel that I was in physical danger, but the spiritual attacks were overwhelming. The enemy was working overtime in my state of weakness. I found solace and comfort in my Bible. Desperate to feel better, I also went daily to AA meetings, talking with a sponsor and calling the pastors from the church. I even went to weekly therapy sessions to try and work on myself.

I constantly needed to be reassured by God that He hadn't left me. I was terrified that one day I would wake up and everything would disappear and I'd be back to living the life of that hopeless junkie. It was difficult to turn everything over to God and give up the control I was accustomed to. God was always on my thoughts. I cried out to Him day after day to show me signs that I was on the right path.

One such day, He showed me this in the most incredible way. I was in the back seat of my dad's vehicle, watching the clouds pass by. My dad and stepmom were in the front seat, watching me through the rear-view mirror as I scurried around the back seat. They knew I was looking for faces in the clouds; I wanted God to show me he was there.

At one point, I panicked and told my parents to pull over. For a moment, I thought I had found what I was looking for. They were caught by surprise when I screamed at them for not pulling over fast enough.

When I finally got out of the vehicle, I broke down in tears when I realized that the thing I'd seen wasn't there anymore. I apologized and got back in the car. My parents assured me everything was going to be okay as we pulled away.

When we got home that day, my dad unexpectedly asked me to step out onto the back porch with him. Then he told me something that had occurred to him on the drive, relating to my frantic desire to find faces in the clouds. Our house was located in the beautiful foothills on the edge of the Rocky Mountains, and as we stared at God's majesty my father pointed at a specific mountain. He told me to look at it, and when I did I instantly saw what he was pointing at: a giant face carved into the rock, clear as day. My mouth dropped in awe as my heart swelled with God's love. My dad said that he had seen the face in that mountain ever since he'd bought the property. In fact, every time he looked in that direction it was always the first thing he saw: the eyes, the mouth, the nose, the hairline... and a paw. The face on the mountain looked like a lion.

As I silently thanked God for this image, my dad said there was one more thing he needed to show me. He pointed at the mountain directly beside the one we'd been staring at. This, he explained, was called Holy Cross Mountain. The reason it was called that was because a perfectly symmetrical snowy cross appeared on it during the summertime.

These were the two mountains closest to my house, and they displayed the Lion of Judah and the Lamb of God side by side, watching over me. I almost dropped to the ground from how weak my knees suddenly felt. God had been trying to get me to see this for days. That's why I had been desperately searching for faces in the clouds. My prayers had been answered: God was telling me that this was where I was meant to get sober.

I instantly felt safe, a feeling that had been eluding me since my arrival. God had told me in the biggest way imaginable that He was there, and that this was where I was supposed to be.

I sat in my basement and finger-pecked my way to victory while writing the book God had placed on my heart. Every once in a while I would look up and see the lion's face staring down at me through the bay windows. God was persistently reminding me that He was with me.

The chapters were more difficult to write than I could have imagined. With each one, I had to put myself back into the situation, focusing on what I had felt, heard, smelled, tasted, and touched, to intelligently articulate what God wanted me to write. It was emotionally draining. I often rocked back and forth, writhing in pain from the hurt and sorrow I was forced to relive.

One day while typing, a message popped up on my screen from one of my social media accounts. My heart almost stopped as I saw that it was from my mother. I felt conflicted about my relationship with her, especially since writing the opening chapters of this book had brought on an abundance of understanding of how my life had gone sideways. I'd also learned recently that she hadn't told my dad about the time when she'd taken me to detox—or rather, she had told him, but she had lied, telling him that I had been trying to get into a luxury treatment resort. I saw the error of my ways and realized I should have called him myself instead of leaving it to her.

Well, I'd been over a month sober by this point. Perhaps she was writing to show her support. As much as she had hurt me, she was still my mom, and I loved her.

I opened the message and began reading, my heart breaking. She wrote that there was a public outrage that I had returned to the community. According to her, the people of the town thought I was a paedophile.

My mom knew exactly what she was doing when she sent that message; she was trying to get me to leave. By telling me the community didn't want me here, she hoped I might be pushed over the edge. But I knew she was lying. She had obviously heard through the grapevine that I was writing a book and she had some dirty laundry she didn't want aired. Her reputation was everything to her.

I was done being manipulated by my mother. I responded with objective words rather than letting my feelings consume me. I told her that if the community thought I was a paedophile, then I knew very well where that rumour had spread from. Her sabotage had missed its mark this time. The last thing I said to her was that I had no choice but to believe she had chosen not to help me because she'd wanted me to die.

She responded with a thumbs-up emoji.

After that conversation, I spent some time praying. I stared at the mountains with comfort, knowing that something extraordinary was in my future. The miracles He was showing me were so big that I couldn't believe He was going to drop me on my face.

The only thing I could do for my mom was pray for her. Clearly she couldn't be a part of my recovery. One day she would sit at the throne of judgment, guilty of many sins, and God would be just. If God can forgive a wretch like me, who am I to hold back forgiveness for others? I surrendered her to my Father in heaven that day and forgave her in my heart for everything.

Chapter Ninety-Nine

THE PATH FORWARD

A s the weeks progressed, God granted me another huge blessing. After only two months sober, I managed to get off my antipsychotic medication. I was completely clean. It was a difficult transition, but I was desperate to never need a substance to feel better ever again.

Through prayer and scripture, I powered my way through the emotional turmoil that followed. Every day I would wake up thinking I wasn't going to last, and every night I thanked God for the growth that had come with it. My mind was finally being returned to me.

One day I woke up from a nap with a thought heavy on my heart: *I can't eat meat anymore.* I found this very odd, but I had learned to see it as a spiritual mandate to trust my intuition. The Holy Spirit was trying to tell me something.

This wasn't going to be easy. I had hardly eaten anything in years, and my dad had a successful restaurant and a cattle ranch. Meat was life at my house. But God didn't make it a struggle; I nonchalantly texted my stepmom and told her that I had decided to become a vegetarian. By this time she was used to my kooky impulses, so she just laughed and went out to get a vegetarian cookbook.

I started working in the car industry again, at four months sober. It felt good to wear a suit and financially support myself. My dad had been paying for me to this point, so it was time for me to take responsibility.

I no longer looked as if I was about to kill someone, and I was excited to be selling cars on the floor again. There was just one problem: I had lost all my passion for money, and it showed in my sales. I had once been a shark in the world of car sales, but now I walked around loving everyone out loud and losing the dealership money.

After a few months, I quit. I didn't really have a plan, I just knew that making money wasn't important to me. In fact, I hated it. I always emptied my pockets at church and AA meetings, which drove my parents nuts, as it meant they would have to support me until my next paycheque. But I just didn't want anything to do with money. I wanted to give everything away to help make the world a better place. God had placed on my heart an urgency to put others first.

The more I stuck to simplicity and structure, the easier it was to make it through the days. I stuck to my routine so I could be proud of myself when I looked in the mirror, no matter how bad my emotions had beat me down all day. To my surprise, I started to love myself again. The more wins I got under my belt, the bigger my smile got. But I wasn't smiling because of money or power, but rather as a testament to God's grace and glory in my life. The day I quit calculating my value by dollars and cents, and began quantifying it by how many people I helped in a day, my existence shifted onto a new plain.

I stopped by the church in Black Diamond to visit the pastors, Matt and Bryce, something that had become part of my spiritual routine. Sitting with my brothers in Christ, Bryce caught me off-guard when he asked me a question I hadn't considered. What did I want to do with my life? Did I have a plan? I pondered this for a little while before answering, "I love God, hate money, desire to be like Christ, and want to spend every waking minute telling people the good news about Jesus."

What could I possibly do that matched all the items on my wish list? Bryce asked me if I'd ever thought about going to Bible college. Before he was even done saying it, I nodded in affirmation. It had never occurred to me that I could become a pastor, for obvious reasons, but in that moment the Holy Spirit gave me a surge of energy that confirmed this new path for my life.

Bryce and Matt went on to tell me that they were both graduates of Millar College of the Bible. God had brought me to this church and put these two men in my life, so I could be confident that they spoke His true word. The fact that Matt was a member of Millar's board, and the fact that they were both graduates with strong ties there, was enough for me. It was like God parting the Red Sea, making my path obvious. He was in control. I was merely on His roller-coaster, enjoying the ride with my hands in the air.

I asked my brothers about getting baptized, as a rite of passage to publicly declare my love for Jesus. They scheduled my baptism for August 13. I took an application for Millar College and made my way home.

When I told my family that I wanted to go to school to be a pastor, they were beside themselves. We cried together as we spoke about the unbelievable miracles that were taking place in my journey.

One night, while my father and I were sitting on the deck watching the sunset over the mountains, he turned to me, with tears in his eyes, and professed how proud he was of me. He told me that he was sorry for my childhood.

My dad loved me more than any human being on this planet. He had never hesitated to help me in any way he could. We had both made many mistakes, but his compassion for me in that moment was as genuine and sincere as the Lord's love for me.

I readily accepted his apology and reciprocated with my own for the wreckage I had caused in his life. He forgave me, as any loving father would. I shared with him that my dream was for him to share my love for the Lord. Although he was unsaved, he always prayed with me, knowing how much it meant to me.

BY GRACE ALONE

As I drove along the beautiful country road, I took in the passing mountains, trees, fields, and houses. The sun was high in the east and I let it beat off my face through the passenger window of my dad's car. It felt good.

A smile creased my face as I closed my eyes and angled my face to catch the magnificent sunlight coming through the window. What an honour it was to be alive. God was great, and today I got to profess His glory in front of the congregation of my church in Black Diamond. After that I would be taken to the Sheep River for my baptism ceremony.

I opened my eyes and once again found comfort in the beauty God had bestowed on me. Tears filled my eyes. Everything looked so beautiful. The greatest gift God had given me was a new perception of beauty. I was becoming accustomed to tearing up over beautiful sunsets and watching God's majesty unfold all around me. Seven months ago I hadn't been able to see the beauty in anything beyond the cocaine I was doing. Now I had a hard time reining in my emotions. Everything was just so precious to me now. My heart was singing a new tune, one of hope, freedom, and surrender.

My proud father asked me if I was ready. I laughed and told him I was as ready as I'd ever be.

Matt and Bryce greeted me at the entrance to the church, just as excited as I was to share my story for the first time. The audience was comprised of small-town folk who lived a rather sheltered existence in contrast to my nutty journey to Christ. This was going to be fun for all of us.

I think I surprised everyone when I walked up without cue cards or a speech and instead asked everyone to bow their heads in prayer. The prayer went like this: "Dear heavenly Father, I just want to thank You so much for bringing me up onto this podium today and giving me the strength to glorify You through my testimony. I ask that

You please open my brothers' and sisters' hearts today as I shine a light on something very much outside the realm of conventional thought, I assume, for most of these people. Let me glorify You and show how sovereign Your love can truly be as I share the greatest gift and blessing You have bestowed on my life. Amen."

My reserved brothers and sisters all sat in compassionate silence as I shared how I had gotten to their quaint little church. By the time I was done, most had tears in their eyes from my gut-wrenching tale of pain, triumph, and glory. It was obvious to everyone in that room that being here hadn't been my own doing. It was all God.

I wrapped it up by announcing that I had been accepted to Millar College of the Bible and would be starting classes the following month. I received a loud cheer from everyone, a cheer that melted my heart and filled me with joy. I was very proud of myself.

After Pastor Matt brought the service to a close, a couple approached me. I'll never forget the desperation in their eyes.

"This isn't our church, but God brought us here to hear you today," the man said.

They went on to explain that their son's addiction had all but destroyed their family. They had been living a complete nightmare for the past four years. Their boy's name was Bobby and he was a crystal meth addict. When they elaborated on his condition, it was easy for me to see that he was just as hopeless as I had been, lost in psychosis most days and unable to string together a couple of days of sobriety to save his life. They asked me if I'd be willing to meet with him. I replied by saying that this was exactly why God had saved me.

When I met Bobby for the first time, I could see the hopelessness in his eyes from a mile away. I recognized the familiar darkness in his gaze. My throat constricted from the memories of it. I was standing in front of a dead man walking. Lost and broken, he didn't think it was in the realm of possibility to find the freedom I had, but he agreed to join me for a ride to a nearby coffee shop.

Bobby had heard my name before, although none of what he'd heard was good. So when his parents had asked him if he would be willing to go for coffee with Cody Bates, he had originally thought they were joking. He knew I was a drug trafficker and cocaine cowboy. In his drug-addled thinking, he thought his parents had hired me to kill him. By agreeing to come, he had submitted to his own execution. He was ready to die.

I asked God to guide me in what to say. Becoming one with God's will had become a fixture in my life. I always tried to remove myself and let the Big Guy do the work. It didn't escape me that I was helpless to save someone so lost; without God, Bobby didn't stand a chance.

I talked to him about psychosis. When I brought up the sirens and whispers that accompany this horrible mental state, his eyes went wide with surprise. I had his attention. I then went deeper into how I had felt going day to day without any hope of coming out the other side. He nodded in agreement with everything God had put on my heart to talk about.

Bobby began to open up to me about his own darkness. When I asked if he was willing to let his parents' marriage be sacrificed for his addiction, a wave of emotion hit him. The last thing this man wanted to do was to hurt anybody. He was but a lost and broken soul with the curse of drug addiction.

Out of intuition from the calling of the Holy Spirit, I made him an offer that could save his life. I had two and a half weeks until I started school, and I suggested that he come stay at my house until then. I would support him through detox. Worst-case scenario, he would just go back to where he was right now. Best case, he would surrender to Christ and the Father would close the demonic door of addiction he'd been constructing for so many years.

My faith was strong. His, not so much. But Bobby knew this could be his only shot. He reluctantly agreed.

I spent a fair amount of time giving back to this struggling drug addict. But when I picked him up to come to my house, the totality of the task became apparent. He was as low of a drug addict as they came. Most people would never waste their time on someone so far gone. But I had done over a million dollars of cocaine in two years. If Christ could save me, He could do it for anyone.

Bobby and I said a prayer with his family before we took off. He was beside himself that he was praying with Cody Bates, one of the most notorious bad boys to ever come out of our small town. The notoriety was an advantage in this case, because I was attractive to someone like Bobby. If he hadn't heard my name and the many stories associated with it, he might never have agreed to this.

My family was nervous about having a flailing meth addict come to stay at the acreage, but they had met Bobby's parents at church and could relate to their story. The Holy Spirit gave them the conviction to trust my judgment.

I knew there was hope for Bobby. As long as he invited the good Lord into his heart, he would survive this. The other fundamental component to this lofty rescue was love. Bobby had been treated like garbage, just as I had been, and I wanted to show him what it was like to experience genuine care from someone without expecting anything in return. I refused his parents' offer to pay me for my time, because that would make Bobby question my motives. I didn't want the money anyway.

Bobby struggled over the following days. He constantly talked about meth and how being sober just didn't seem possible. It was taxing for me, too, since I could relate to him so strongly. In order to identify with my struggling cohort, I needed to relive all the pain and torment I'd gone through in getting to the point where I finally broke enough for Christ to save me. It was hard to convince my friend that he was even worth saving. He had been brutalized and beat down by his addiction and didn't feel like he was worth my time and effort.

Because he had only been sleeping every few days, he had a lot of sleep to catch up on. He rarely came out of the room the first few days and it was difficult to even wake him up for food. The drugs were leaving his body, but his leafless forest was still very much alive. I knew he was experiencing torment without any relief. On the rare times he was awake, all he talked about was how badly he needed meth.

We consulted a doctor and he was given some sleep medication to help him through the first week. This was necessary because his demon was very much alive inside him, whispering lies mixed with truth: *You can't do this, Bobby. You know you're going to give up. Why even bother trying if you know the outcome?* The devil was working overtime against the will of God. It seemed as if every time we experienced a breakthrough, the dark entities in his mind launched an assault.

I pleaded with Bobby to invite God in, but he just couldn't seem to grasp the importance of it, and on the sixth day everything came to a head.

While Bobby and I were returning from an AA meeting in the city, he ranted about crystal meth and how he didn't think he could do this. He even asked if I would meet his drug-dealer. He couldn't picture life with or without the drug. It was disheartening, because I could see where this was going. He was letting the demons win.

I knew from personal experience how impossible it could be to come back after you'd already given up in your own mind, and Bobby seemed to have done just that. Once you make that decision to relapse, there's almost no talking someone back from it.

I was frustrated and didn't know what to do. Had God given me more than I could handle?

When we pulled into my house, we both felt defeated. Out of my frustration, I decided to give him the cold hard truth. I told him that maybe he just needed to go die, to destroy his family. Maybe he needed to look them in the eyes and see the anguish written over their faces as they helplessly watched him kill himself.

Soon he was in tears, for the first time since coming to stay at the acreage. My frustration was replaced with compassion. I told him that I loved him and that so far he was doing well, but he was missing the single most important thing—Jesus. Bobby still hadn't prayed or read the Bible. Therapy had helped me, AA had helped me, church had helped me, and the love of my family had helped me. But Jesus Christ had saved me. Without Him, he and I never would have met.

Bobby wanted to be alone. He went downstairs while I walked into the kitchen where my parents were chatting. I sat down and lowered my face into my arms on the counter. What could I do to help this man? I didn't stand a chance. Perhaps I'd gotten overzealous in my passion to help the lost.

The chances of him having a divine revelation at this point seemed unlikely. It was going to take a lot of hard work to turn him around, and I just couldn't see him putting in that kind of effort when he felt so defeated.

Out of nowhere, something inside me clicked. All my muscles tightened as I grinded my teeth with the ferociousness of a lion. Suddenly I was seeing Bobby the way Jesus did. My heart swelled for him.

"You know what?" I said, standing up. I slammed my fists on the counter and looked my parents dead in the eyes. "We're not giving up this kid. No way. He needs us to fight for him right now." My voice rose in volume. "Let's get down there and show him he's not alone."

My parents were in agreement. As we all bustled downstairs to the spare bedroom, we found him lying on his back, with hands and arms covering his face. The lights were off, but we could tell he was really upset.

We circled around him and sat on the bed, all of us holding him, and then each told him how proud we were of him and how much he meant to our family. We weren't going anywhere. We showered him with the love he deserved. Even though we barely knew him, we were fighting for his life and loving him even when he couldn't love himself.

After about fifteen minutes, my parents went back upstairs to bed and Bobby and I went outside for some air. I prayed for God to give me the right words.

"Bobby, I don't know if you're going to make it, brother," I began. "But I want you to be able to look back at this moment, right now. Whether you succeed or not, I want you to be able to tell yourself that this is where you made your stand. Put everything you got into this opportunity and utilize everything I'm teaching you. The one thing you're missing right now is the one thing that matters most—God. If you don't pray, you're going to die."

We sat in silence for a few seconds, staring at the mountains as the sun disappeared behind them. Then Bobby turned his head and said the words that would set him free: "I just was!"

When I turned my head, I realized he was smiling. His eyes were full of light, a stark contrast to the darkness that had enveloped them only a few minutes ago. He explained that while I'd been upstairs, he had said his very first prayer in years, and meant it from the bottom of his heart. He had asked Jesus to come into his heart and show him what His love felt like. At that very moment, my parents and I had walked into the room and showed him the love he had prayed for.

I looked into his eyes and called for my parents to come outside. They came running and I told them to look him into Bobby's eyes. As they examined him, they both broke out in laughter and gathered him in their arms. We were all hugging in the backyard, praising God for the good work He had begun in my friend.

Bobby was a new creation, and it had happened the exact same way Christ had done it for me. Bobby said that this was the first time in his life he knew he would go to heaven. And he wanted to go to treatment, to get away from this town where all his damage had been inflicted.

I couldn't stop praising God. The significance of what I saw that night was more than I could wrap my head around. I had thought I might be special for some reason, that other people might have a different experience coming to Christ, but God showed me right then and there that He would do for anyone what He had done for me. Bobby was only the beginning. The Holy Spirit was filling me with knowledge and discernment.

Anyone who surrenders to Christ can have the same freedom I do. No matter how far we fall, Jesus Christ is the bread and the life. Only He can close our minds to the demonic realm and open the heavens for us. The gift of instant healing is available to anyone who believes in their heart and professes with their mouth that Jesus is Lord.

That night, everyone went inside except me. I couldn't believe the things God was showing me. I didn't understand it. Why was He using me? I loved Him so much, but why did He have faith in a wretch like me?

As I asked these questions into the clear night sky, my stepmom joined me outside to tell me she was proud of me. She agreed that we had just seen a miracle. As I nodded in agreement, though, something insane happened: a sheet of light flashed across the sky. We both stopped dead and looked around, trying to figure out where it had come from. When we discovered no explanation for it, the realization hit us both at the same time. We both grabbed each other's arms and jumped up and down in excitement.

"That was God!" we said in unison. "That was God!"

We were beside ourselves. The flash had covered the whole sky like sheet lightning, without a cloud to be seen.

I ran into the house, calling for Bobby so I could tell him about the majesty my stepmom and I had just witnessed. He smiled and laughed as all three of us went back outside and stared into the starry sky.

"That's God, bro," I said, giving Bobby a light punch to the arm.

As the words fell from my mouth, another flash draped the sky for a half-second. The three of us roared in laughter as the magnitude of what had happened sank in.

Bobby hasn't craved crystal meth a single time since that incredible day. God closed that door of addiction, just as He did for me.

That night, God gave me strict instructions about what I was to do with my life: tell people about what had happened to Bobby and me. I had been confused when I'd only been armed with my own testimony, but now Jesus showed me that He was ready to do the same for anyone who asked it of Him.

I dropped Bobby off at a treatment centre in Kelowna on my way to my new Bible school. Before he went through the front doors, he said the one thing I wanted to hear: "Praise God for this." He also thanked me. I accepted his gratitude, despite how I felt about taking credit for the Lord's work through me.

I'm not deserving of praise. I am but a vessel for Jesus Christ.

Bobby inadvertently blessed me with a gift of unspeakable value. That fateful evening, I saw the most beautiful thing I'd ever witnessed: a hardened heart soften to Christ. It was the best night of my life.

My parents met me at the college to help me get settled. The campus was full of young adults fresh out of high school, so I stood out like a sore thumb. Most of these kids had been home-schooled and hadn't seen a lot of… this. My entire body was scarred and tattooed, and I definitely didn't have the average Bible school look. But as we went through orientation, I quickly made friends.

What I liked most about Millar was that everyone loved God out loud. People cared more about their spiritual growth than anything. I knew I was in the right place.

My dad teared up as he hugged me goodbye. Nine months ago, he had expected to receive the news any parent dreads—the news that their child has died. Now he was dropping me off at Bible college to start my journey to be a pastor!

As my parents drove away, I walked out to the lake right next to the campus. I gazed across the water, taking in the splendour of the mountains on all sides. I felt safe. Although I couldn't see God's angels all around, I knew they were there, filling the valley.

This was where I was meant to be. These were my people.

But Millar was only my training ground. As Jesus said, *"It is not the healthy who need a doctor, but the sick. I have not come to call the righteous, but sinners"* (Mark 2:17). My life belonged to Christ. He hadn't saved me to sit comfortably with the righteous. My life had been spared so I could call the sinners.

So that's where you'll find me: on the front lines of addiction.

Cody's baptism in the Sheep River in Turner Valley on August 13, 2017.

CONCLUSION

Only God can bring a dead man back to life. When I look back through the lens of time, I can see the influence of God and the influence of the devil—God had blessed me with some amazing gifts, but the devil manipulated them for his demonic kingdom.

But God took what the devil thought was a sure win and turned it into a testimony of His glory. He calls the weak to lead the strong. I am not a strong man when it comes to the temptation of sin, for without the Holy Spirit I don't stand a chance against it.

One thing I need to make clear is that God did not save me to make me big; He saved me to make *Himself* big. He is the reason I'm ten months sober today. I tapped out, many times over, but He was there all along, carrying me through.

When I consider the many divine forks in the road I've come to, I can see how making different decisions at critical points could have greatly altered my life story. For me to be where I am today, I feel as though I flipped a coin and came up heads a thousand times in a row. In other words, I shouldn't be here. I gave up completely, but that was what He needed from me. He needed me to break in order to be fixed. I needed to kill the person I used to be for Him to breathe life into me.

My ten months living in His love hasn't been void of lapses. I still fall short of the holiness of God, and always will. But one thing helps me to move forward: discernment that God will not judge us by our accomplishments when we stand at the throne of judgment, but by what He sees in our hearts.

I am not perfect, but when God looks at me He sees His Son Jesus living in my heart. When Jesus died on the cross, He bridged the gap between us and the Father. Anyone who professes that Jesus is Lord will be seen as perfect in the eyes of God. My advice to new believers is to not be hard on yourself when you fall short, but rejoice in knowing that God is building your character into the person you're meant to be. He always forgives, no matter what you've done.

But when the Spirit dwells in you, it will always push you toward holiness. I didn't get struck by a bolt of lightning and become perfect in a day. Over time the Spirit of God continued to push the sin out of my life.

So don't be hard on yourself. Continue through your setbacks and keep inviting Jesus into your life. We will continue to be works in progress until the day we go home to be with the Father.

For everyone out there who feels that addiction is a choice, not a disease, I pray that your closedmindedness doesn't kill someone you love. I am a recovering addict, and yes, I chose to use drugs, but the predisposition for my addiction was forged many years prior to me picking them up. Using drugs is a symptom of a much deeper underlying mental health issue, and it transforms into a spiritual malady the day we open the door to the demonic realm by taking narcotics. I got sober through Jesus, therapy, and many other positive outlets, such as the love of my family. Without that love, I would surely be dead right now. I needed them to love me when I couldn't love myself.

For those who believe in "tough love" ideologies, realize that you're taking away any chance for your friend or family member to beat this debilitating disease. True happiness is derived from us building meaningful connections with others, and I only got sober because I was loved—not because I was isolated and kept on the outside looking in, as advocates of tough love sometimes preach. For people who feel this way, I wonder if you will change your mind after you're forced to bury someone close to you, someone you turned your back on. I read about that worst-case scenario all too often on social media and in the news.

Ignorance will not fix this problem. We will only beat it by addressing the issue together and caring for others. We need to love our suffering brethren! I'm not saying you should open your wallets or doors to those who are still suffering, but I challenge you to pick up the phone and call that person you've been thinking about. Tell them you love them and are waiting for them to come back to you. You have no idea what that could mean to someone who's surrounded by demons whispering lies in their ears day and night.

Love and faith will change the world. Planting the seed of love and faith by telling someone who's suffering that they have something to fight for. That's the way to save lives.

I used to hate it when people told me to get clean for my own sake. When I looked in the mirror, all I could see was garbage. I didn't feel that I deserved to be saved, and being told that didn't stir any conviction in me. I only saw my own worth when other people showed it to me. That's when the momentum started to shift.

I believe that we will watch thousands rise from the ashes, and they will in turn lead thousands more out of darkness. That's the cycle we need to begin, the cycle that will break this devil. So let's begin!

Some may argue that the Bible refers to addiction as a spiritual malady. To this, I refer my readers to Galatians 5:20, which describes sorcery as one of the practices that inhibits us from inheriting the kingdom of God. The direct translation for the word sorcery in Greek is *pharmakeia*, which refers to administering drugs. This tells us that we have constructed a doorway into our thoughts for the demonic dominion. When we take narcotics, we give the devil and his demons an open door policy into our minds.

So when my mind was fractured by psychotic breaks, it was wide open to a realm I didn't belong in. The sirens, whispers, screams, and faces that manifested for me every sixth day weren't my imagination; they were a peek into a terrifying dimension no human being should ever witness. That's what we're up against in dealing with addicts. To say they're lost is a huge understatement; they are possessed.

The good news is that they can be saved. If a wretch like me can be pulled from darkness, nobody is too far gone. God saved me to show people the way. He is the word and the truth, the bread and the life.

I want to leave one final message for the devil. Twenty-five years ago, you started a work in me. You coerced my young soul away from God so you could use me for your treachery. You lied to me and led me to break every commandment by the age of twenty-one, including "Thou shalt not murder." After that, you were able to take your throne in my mind. But God is bigger than you. God's sovereign grace set me free from your grasp and I stand here today as a child of Jesus Christ. I vow in front of man and God that I will spend the rest of my life flipping over tables to tell people the truth and expose your lies. I no longer belong to you. Get behind me, Satan. My life sentence is served!

The Devil whispered in my ear,
"You're not strong enough to withstand the storm."

Today I whispered in the Devil's ear,
"I am the storm!"

FINAL WORD

I want to thank you so much for taking the time to read my story and share my journey. It truly is a miracle that I'm typing this today, so full of joy, peace, and love. I lived in darkness for so long that it seemed impossible to escape. I can't stress enough that Jesus did everything I couldn't do.

Perhaps this has stirred something inside you. Maybe the Lord is knocking on your heart. If so, it means you were meant to read this book. You were meant to receive this message. Maybe He's been knocking on your heart for a long time. Maybe you've felt empty for years and never considered that He is the thing that's missing in your life. Maybe you still don't know what to believe.

Well, I'm going to invite you to ask God to show you. The Bible says that we are saved by faith alone, which means that no amount of works can equal the power of the name of Jesus. He loves you and His plan for you is working perfectly. You just have to say yes. I realize some of you will not know how to do that, so I encourage you to please say these words out loud and receive the free gift of eternal life:

> Father, I don't know You yet, but reading Cody's testimony has caused something deep inside me to shift. It's like You are speaking to my heart, like You are right here with me, like You knew I would be reading it. I don't know yet what Your plan is for me, Jesus, but I believe from this point on that You and Your love are the only ways to fill the void of darkness in my heart. I am ready to move on, but not in a way I ever considered until now. I want You to fill this void, Lord. Holy Spirit, I need You in my life and to turn this darkness into light.
>
> Father God, I believe You sent Jesus to die for all my sin, shame, and every lie that has tormented me. I believe in my heart that You raised Him

back to life and because of that I can now be free and know the truth of Your promises and eternal life! Jesus, I invite You to be the Lord of my life and want Your Holy Spirit to fill my heart. Amen.

DECEMBER 2017, CODY LAUNCHES THE CHRISTMAS ON HASTINGS PROJECT.
THIS IS A TEN DAY BLITZ OF GOOD WILL IN CANADA'S POOREST POSTAL CODE.
CODY IS INTENDING ON RUNNING THE PROJECT ANNUALLY.